The Integrity Gap

Edited by Eugene Lee and Anthony Perl

The Integrity Gap:
Canada's Environmental Policy
and Institutions

UBCPress · Vancouver · Toronto

09 08 07 06 05 04 03   5 4 3 2 1

Printed in Canada on acid-free paper that is 100% post-consumer recycled,
processed chlorine-free, and printed with vegetable-based, low-VOC inks.

National Library of Canada Cataloguing in Publication

Main entry under title:
The integrity gap : Canada's environmental policy and institutions /
edited by Eugene Lee and Anthony Perl.

   Includes bibliographical references and index.
   ISBN 0-7748-0985-X (bound)

   1. Environmental policy–Canada. I. Lee, Eugene, 1960- II. Perl, Anthony, 1962-
GE190.C3I57 2003   363.7'00971   C2003-910151-7

Canadä

UBC Press gratefully acknowledges the financial support for our publishing
program of the Government of Canada through the Book Publishing Industry
Development Program (BPIDP), and of the Canada Council for the Arts, and
the British Columbia Arts Council.

This book has been published with the help of a grant from the Canadian
Federation of the Humanities and Social Sciences, using funds provided by the
Social Sciences and Humanities Research Council of Canada.

UBC Press
The University of British Columbia
2029 West Mall
Vancouver, BC V6T 1Z2
604-822-5959 / Fax: 604-822-6083
www.ubcpress.ca

To Michael Donnelly
— Eugene Lee

To Andrea Banks
— Anthony Perl

Contents

Figures and Tables

Tables

Acknowledgments

The origin of this book goes back to the summer of 1998, when the idea of having a conference in Seoul on Canadian environmental policy was first mooted. Anthony Perl was a long-time observer of Canadian transportation policy, where negative environmental impacts were increasingly noticeable during the 1990s. Eugene Lee was the director of the Centre for Canadian Studies at Sookmyung Women's University. After months of preparation, the conference was held in February 1999 in Seoul, hosted by the Sookmyung Centre for Canadian Studies.

As in any book-length project, many people and organizations have aided our work.

We are indebted to the Sookmyung Centre for Canadian Studies for all the support that made it possible for the contributors to gather and present their papers and exchange ideas. The Korean Ministry of Environment and the Canadian Embassy in Seoul provided us with generous support. Perl's work on editing the manuscript was supported through the Social Sciences and Humanities Research Council of Canada's Research Grant #410-99-0800 and the Research Unit for Public Policy Studies at the University of Calgary.

Most of all, we would like to express our appreciation to the contributors, who not only provided us with the substance of this book but also exhibited considerable patience during its completion. We are thankful for their detailed and valuable feedback throughout the process of editing the manuscript. We also would like to acknowledge the discussants of the initial papers. They made a great contribution to developing the manuscript with their insightful comments and questions.

We also wish to thank our research assistants, Donald White and Iftekhar Ul Haque, who, along with Miryo Lee, provided diligent and dedicated support. Ella Wensel and Carol Murray contributed excellent secretarial support during the production of the manuscript.

The Integrity Gap

1

Introduction: Institutions and the Integrity Gap in Canadian Environmental Policy

Eugene Lee and Anthony Perl

In trying to understand Canada's environmental policy making, the relationship between what is said and what gets done merits more systematic attention than it has received to date. From global climate change to local air quality,
it is worth comparing the ways in which Canada identifies environmental
challenges with the means that are adopted to deal with them. The resulting contrast yields a range of dissonance between policy aims and outcomes
that demands explanation.

By and large, all levels of Canadian government exhibit a willingness to
identify environmental challenges rather than deny their existence or minimize their importance. Once problems are recognized, however, Canadian
policies often fail to deliver solutions or even launch efforts to attain those
solutions. Trying to explain why Canadian environmental policy regularly
falls short of acting on identified problems has led us to consider the concept of integrity in Canada's environmental policy and seek evidence of
where and when the gap between objectives and efforts exists, as well as
what difference it makes to Canada's governance.

Analyzing that integrity gap yields insights into the role that Canada's
politico-economic institutions play in enabling certain kinds of environmental policy initiatives while frustrating other policy efforts. In the chapters that follow, the distinctive configuration of Canada's politico-economic
institutions will be explored by fourteen authors who document and assess
its influence on the integrity of environmental policy performance. They
will consider different degrees of constraint and opportunity that Canada's
institutional arrangements can place upon achieving declared environmental
policy goals, thereby yielding different degrees of a gap between the rhetoric and the reality of Canada's environmental performance during the 1990s.

Canada's international reputation as a country with so much unspoiled
nature and seemingly strong environmental concerns among the public
gives the impression that environmental policy performs well and yields
efforts that are aligned with defined problems. Contrary to such a popular

image, Canada's environment is fraught with challenges and threats to sustainability where policy and reality are often quite divergent (Boyd 2001). At the heart of most of these challenges, one finds institutionalized constraints on government's ability to deliver upon stated environmental policy goals. Before turning to the institutional variables that influence this integrity gap in environmental policy, we need to fully define this concept and operationalize it as an analytical variable.

Integrity as a Dependent Variable in Environmental Policy Making

We begin by defining the key variable in this study. Environmental policy integrity is the degree to which Canadian policy makers can align environmental problem definitions, objectives for dealing with those problems, and the measures that are implemented to attain those objectives. The level of integrity behind Canada's environmental policy initiatives will be seen to vary considerably across different sectors and at different points in time. Thus, the dependent variable that we will be assessing throughout the coming chapters is environmental policy integrity. The challenge of explaining such variation falls to a typology of environmental policy integrity that Figure 1.1 presents in schematic form.

To simplify as well as clarify the range of integrity in Canadian environmental policy, we defined the integrity level as a dichotomous variable. In cases that exhibit a high level of environmental integrity, one finds policy instruments being implemented in line with the problems and challenges that have been identified. In cases with a low level of environmental integrity, one finds a divergence between rhetoric and reality. Here, policy fails to live up to its commitment to resolve an environmental problem in one way or another, yielding an integrity gap. Our understanding of environmental policy integrity presumes a good-faith effort to recognize environmental challenges and make commitments to solve such problems.

Figure 1.1

Institutional influences on environmental policy integrity

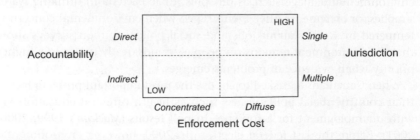

The findings presented in this book suggest that the level of environmental integrity in a given policy domain very much depends upon the configuration of politico-economic institutions influencing that domain. We have grouped these independent variables into three clusters that can be summarized as jurisdiction, accountability, and enforcement cost. Let us briefly consider how each of these clusters can influence the level of environmental policy integrity.

Political jurisdictions are a ubiquitous feature of Canadian environmental policy, influencing virtually all policy domains because of the federal division of powers. While Ottawa can commit to international environmental initiatives, such as the Framework Convention on Climate Change, and set environmental standards, such as the minimum levels for adequate ambient air quality, it is largely up to the provinces to implement and enforce these policies. The relationship between federal and provincial jurisdictions, as well as among multiple provincial jurisdictions and municipal governments (which assume responsibility for policies with significant environmental influence, such as public health and urban transit, that are delegated by provincial governments), thus becomes an important influence on aligning environmental policy performance with goals.

Our research has found that jurisdictional cooperation is associated with a high level of integrity, whereas competition among jurisdictions is generally found in instances of low environmental integrity. Others have documented this correlation between low effectiveness of environmental policy and jurisdictional competition, as captured in Harrison's phrase (1996) of "passing the buck" in environmental policy. What our research highlights is that such jurisdictional buck passing does less to inhibit the formulation of environmental policy goals than to impede the implementation and attainment of such goals, thus yielding an integrity gap in environmental policy.

The accountability that government officials face, or are perceived to face, for both the state of the environment and their stewardship of it forms a second institutional cluster that influences the level of integrity in environmental policy. Public support for the environment has been uneven over the years (Brooks 1998), with peaks correlating with publicized incidents of environmental damage such as oil spills, toxic bacteria in drinking water supplies, or extreme weather events. Even when environmental concern is tempered by worries about jobs and social policy, opinion surveys show that the environment remains on people's minds, ready to rise to a higher priority when evidence of problems emerges.

When Canadians are asked to choose the most important problem facing their country, social policy issues such as health care and education vie with unemployment for a top spot in poll results (*Maclean's* 1999, 2000, 2001). Before the last federal election, in 2000, however, environmental issues ranked ahead of much-discussed topics such as corporate and personal income tax cuts as policy priorities among eligible voters. A pollster at Environics International stated that their pre-election polling signalled "a re-emergence of trends that were at work in the late 80s when the environment became the most important top-of-mind issue [among Canadians]" (Greenelection.org 2000).

This uneven nature of public support makes environmental policy a tricky domain for public officials. Decisions about how to address environmental impacts and problems often have to be made amid both scientific uncertainty and shifting public priorities. No official wants to get caught out on a limb with environmental issues, but predicting which decisions could trigger public reproach is not an easy matter. Officials with clear and direct public accountability will be quite careful to see that environmental policy commitments are carried out, or at least seen to be carried out. Conversely, officials who are insulated from public accountability will feel less pressure to ensure that policy outputs are closely aligned with previous commitments.

Wilson (1973, 1983) and Stanbury (1986), among others, have explored how the distribution of economic costs and benefits will influence different political mobilization and engagement in the policy process. When costs are concentrated, affected interests have considerable incentive to mobilize in opposition to a particular policy. When the costs of policy initiatives can be diffused, however, political mobilization around a policy process is less likely. The contrast between air quality management efforts in the Greater Toronto Area versus the Vancouver region, explored by Anthony Perl in Chapter 7, illustrates how a concentrated distribution of costs can constrain environmental integrity, as Ontario's automotive interests strongly resisted the adoption of more effective policy options. Vancouver's policy options were far less constrained because of the ability to diffuse the economic costs of auto pollution abatement efforts across the region.

The influences generated by these domestic political and economic institutions each have their counterpart in Canada's relationships with the global political economy. Ranging from multilateral environmental policy initiatives like the Framework Convention on Climate Change to the trade and security arrangements with the United States, these international relationships can either magnify or offset the domestic institutional forces influencing environmental integrity. For example, Canada's commitment to the Kyoto protocol has given Ottawa a greater jurisdictional weight in environmental policy deliberations where some provinces see matters very differently. Steven Bernstein's chapter in this volume (Chapter 4) thus suggests that a multinational normative framework could help Canada overcome the effect of domestic institutional constraints.

On the other hand, the development of a continental free trade zone creates pressure on natural resource industries to extract more output at lower cost, thereby increasing their opposition to environmental regulation or impact mitigation. Michael Howlett's analysis of Canada's transition from a "staples" to a "post-staples" political economy (Chapter 3) sheds light on the link between continental economic integration and environmental policy making. Thus, the international dimension of institutional influence upon environmental policy integrity can often help explain instances where domestic institutional influences appear to be magnified or mitigated.

**Neo-Institutionalism as a Window on Integrity
in Canadian Environmental Policy**
This section lays out how a neo-institutionalist analytical framework will orient assessment of Canada's environmental policy integrity. Although the new institutionalism has several analytical variants, one common feature is that they all seek to examine the influence of existing rules and norms on policy making. This approach assumes that both formal and informal institutions shape the preferences of policy actors and their capacity to achieve desired policy outcomes.

We explain the differences in environmental policy integrity in various sectors by pointing out how institutional legacy in the cases assessed by the contributors to this volume creates a policy inheritance that facilitates deliberating about environmental policy options while at the same time placing significant limits on environmental policy implementation. Organizationally, certain interests and groups become privileged by these institutional arrangements (e.g., those that benefit from and/or prefer environmental policy making that favours "talk" over "action"), while others are disadvantaged. In terms of the cognitive framework that orients policy actors, certain values and ideas will appear to be legitimized by these precedents and ongoing practices, while other beliefs come to be cast as unorthodox, or even "un-Canadian," as a result of institutionalized norms. Taken together, the organizational and cognitive dimensions of Canada's institutional inheritance tend to hold back the achievement of declared environmental policy goals. A key question arising from our analysis will be how durable the institutional legacy behind Canada's environmental policy inheritance may turn out to be in the face of domestic and international pressures for enhanced policy performance.[1] At home, the Canadian electorate appears open minded about post-industrial environmental values, while abroad Canada's trading partners and competitors are making significant international commitments to environmental protection. Institutional structures, however, remain "hard-wired" in legal, and in some cases constitutional, arrangements that regularly serve as barriers to acting upon Canadian environmental initiatives.

An early theoretical elaboration of the new institutionalism in contemporary political science and public policy was offered by March and Olsen

(1984). They highlighted the neo-institutional focus on the relative autonomy of political institutions, legal precedents as applied by the judiciary, and administrative structures as offering valuable insights into public policy. Institutions structure political reality and define the terms and nature of political discourse, and therefore influence the outcome of policy decisions. "Political life in general, and the preferences of political actors in particular, are likely to be heavily influenced by institutional experience," according to Atkinson and Coleman (1989, 5). Neo-institutionalists thus seek to understand policy process in terms of the structure and configuration of institutions. Atkinson (1993, 6-7) defined institutions as "configurations or networks of organizational capabilities ... that are deployed according to rules and norms that structure individual participation, govern appropriate behaviour, and limit the range of acceptable outcomes." The concept can include rules of behaviour, norms, roles, routines, established processes, inventory of formal and informal procedures, and physical arrangements.

Institutions are neither neutral reflections of exogenous environmental forces nor neutral arenas for the performance of individuals driven by exogenous preferences and expectations (March and Olsen 1984, 742). Institutions reflect the power relations among actors in the polity. That is, institutions have historically embedded relations among various interests in the political economy, often designed to protect certain groups or disadvantage others (Cowhey and McCubbins 1995, 10). As such, they have a certain level of continuity and durability so far as the power relations exist, and "reforms to existing policies are often not possible without basic changes in institutional arrangements" (Atkinson and Coleman 1989, 6). Institutions can also learn, however. "Institutions accumulate historical experience through learning. The results and inferences of past experience are stored in standard operating procedures, professional rules, and the elementary rules of thumb of a practical person." Institutions learn by modifying the strategy, the competence (skills), and the aspirations (expectations) of actors working within their guidance (March and Olsen 1984, 745-46).

Although all neo-institutionalists base their work on the assumption that institutions matter, answers to the question of how and to what extent they matter vary among different approaches, which include rational choice institutionalism, sociological institutionalism, and historical institutionalism (Koelble 1995; Kato 1996; Hall and Taylor 1996). Historical institutionalists emphasize policy outcomes as the product of institutional context where policy actors interact. Institutions guide the actions of individual policy makers. For them, social causation is path-dependent. Policy outcome is "a function of institutional capabilities that were put in place at some earlier period" (Krasner 1988, 67). Situational factors, policy legacies from the past, and state capacities each work to structure, condition, and influence the future path of policy (Koelble 1995, 232; Hall and Taylor 1996, 941). Institutions also shape policy outcomes in the sense that they are not neutral. They "structure conflicts so as to privilege some interests while demobilizing others." "Institutions give some groups or interests disproportionate access to the decision-making process" (Hall and Taylor 1996, 937, 941).

Earlier works by historical institutionalists paid attention primarily to the state (Katzenstein 1978; Krasner 1978; Skocpol 1979; Nordlinger 1981; Evans et al. 1985; Hall 1986). They also extended the scope of their interest to other institutions in the political economy, such as labour and capital, and to state-society relations (Schmitter and Lehmbruch 1982; Zysman 1983; Hall 1986; Steinmo et al. 1992). There are also meso-level analyses that differentiate the influence of institutions on policy actors according to categories known as policy communities and policy networks. The fullness of such meso-level institutional influences on policy making is best interpreted using the analytical framework that Atkinson, Coleman, and Skogstad have developed in their analyses of policy communities and policy networks in Canada's various public policy areas (Atkinson and Coleman 1989; Coleman and Skogstad 1990). More recently, Coleman and Perl refined these concepts to take explicit account of international interactions. The policy network concept seeks to identify participants in the governance structure and the patterns of their relationships. The idea of a policy network aims to pinpoint differences in the manner by which public power is shared among policy makers and other interested parties (Coleman and Perl 1999, 694-95).

Sociological institutionalism holds that individual decisions are influenced by a broader social and cultural frame of reference. Here, individuals are dependent variables and culture and society generate the key independent variables. Institutions, which are socially constructed and propagate culturally specific practices, function as an intervening variable (Powell and DiMaggio 1991; Koelble 1995). For sociological institutionalists, the definition of institutions itself is very broad, including "formal rules, procedures, norms, symbol systems, cognitive scripts, moral templates that provide the frames of meaning guiding human action," and is indistinguishable from culture. As such, institutions influence behaviour by forming individual preferences and by providing the individual with self-image and identity in a given cultural context (Hall and Taylor 1996, 946-48).

Sociological institutionalists theorize that institutions are created because they enhance social legitimacy (Hall and Taylor 1996, 949-50). For instance, professional communities with cultural authority set up institutions to press certain standards upon their members. Institutions may emerge from an interactive process of discussion among actors in a given network. This can also happen in the international arena, where the actors are nation-states. We see the emergence of international norms or authority, developed among leading nations and subsequently accepted by others (Meyer and Scott 1994).

Rational choice institutionalism argues that policy decisions can be explained by utility-maximizing individuals' strategic calculations made within the parameters set by institutions (North 1990; Rosenbluth 1993). Here, institutions are also considered as an intervening variable, but one that operates in a world where preferences regarding instrumental values (e.g., efficiency, individual gain, and corporate profit) are virtually homogeneous. Under such congruent motivation, "political institutions create incentives for individual behavior by raising the costs of some actions ... and facilitating or rewarding individuals for choosing other actions" (Cowhey and McCubbins 1995, 10). Rational choice institutionalism suggests that individuals create institutions to pursue their interests, to lower transaction costs, and to induce cooperative behaviour (Koelble 1995, 232, 239). Institutions are formed to avoid collective-action problems. Thus, institutional change comes about when the individuals who created the institutions see new means to attain their ends.

All three institutionalisms are useful to better understand certain attributes of policy making, and the contributors to this volume implicitly or explicitly draw upon various aspects of these institutionalist perspectives in their analyses of Canadian environmental policies. Before moving to discussions of specific sectors presented by our authors, we now provide a brief description of the macro-institutional context within which Canadian environmental policies are formulated and implemented.

Institutions reflect the way Canadian political power is defined and distributed, and in turn structure political and policy-making process and the relationship among various state and societal actors. Some relevant institutional features of the Canadian system would include the constitutional order, rules and regulations, the electoral system, the party system, policy communities, and policy networks. International norms and formal regimes also influence the behaviour of actors. Even other background factors such as public opinion and ideology have institutionalized aspects that influence policy actors in a patterned way.

We may first consider some of the macro-institutional factors that set the broad parameters of Canada's environmental governance. Among Canada's political institutions, the most basic is the constitutional order. As a former British colony, Canada inherited the Westminster model of the parliamentary system. Its principle of parliamentary sovereignty stipulates the supremacy of the parliament as the sole law-making body of the land. In practice, political power rests in the majority party, and ultimately in the cabinet and the prime minister who controls it. Thus, Canadian federal politics and policy process display a strong form of executive leadership typical of the Westminster model, with fusion of power as opposed to a presidential system with division of power. However, Canada's constitutional order is significantly modified by federalism: the division of powers between the federal and provincial governments.

The British North America (BNA) Act determined the legal, organizational, and political setting for policy making. The BNA Act thus structured relations among various actors in the federal and provincial governments, and set parameters for conventions and practices of decision making. At the inception of the Canadian confederation, however, "environment was not perceived as a coherent subject for the legislators' attention" (Hessing and Howlett 1997, 54). Although the constitution delineated governments' jurisdictions concerning areas that bear on environmental management, it did not define the jurisdiction of an environmental mandate per se. In principle, the federal government makes national environmental policy, sets guidelines for provincial regulatory standards, conducts scientific research, and deals with international or interprovincial matters. Implementation of federal policies and administration of regulations is mainly the responsibility of the provinces. The reality is not nearly so straightforward.

In accordance with the division of powers laid out in the constitution, both the federal and provincial governments can and do claim their jurisdiction over environmental matters. Provincial governments get involved through their control over public lands, management of resources owned by the provinces, and all matters relating to municipal government. The federal government acts on the environment through its jurisdiction over federal lands, taxation and spending, international trade and commerce, shipping, fisheries, and treaty powers, to name a few (Doern and Conway 1994, 84). Thus, the responsibility for Canada's environment is divided, and "this situation has led to a patchwork response to environmental concerns by both levels of government in Canada. Different aspects of environmental problems are dealt with by different levels of government in accordance with resource ownership and jurisdiction as initially laid out in 1867 and modified in 1982" (Hessing and Howlett 1997, 57). Such jurisdictional overlap is both a cause for policy fragmentation and a potential source of federal/provincial conflict (Doern and Conway 1994, Chapter 4).

Moreover, this tendency towards fragmentation and jurisdictional conflict is exacerbated by an important feature of Canadian political economy. That is, many Canadian provinces have resource-based and politically influential industries such as forestry in British Columbia and energy in Alberta. This structural perspective has inspired the line of argument that because Canada's provincial governments have been dominated by resource extractive industries, they are therefore less protective of the environment than larger and/or more diverse jurisdictions, where policy making cannot be easily dominated by resource interests (Paehlke 2000, 161). A similar argument can be made about Ontario's transportation policies (which have significant environmental effects) and the influence of the auto industry. To the extent that this argument is valid, Canada's national environmental governance is limited by provincial policy capture.

Ottawa sometimes makes attempts to influence provincial policies, by utilizing its spending power or jurisdiction over interprovincial trade, but provincial governments are extremely sensitive about federal intervention on environmental matters when it challenges their region's dominant economic interests. In recent years, the already fragmented and decentralized environmental administration in Canada has moved towards further fragmentation and decentralization. Decentralization has been carried out in the name of reducing duplication and increasing efficiency in the age of fiscal retrenchment and global competition. It is also the result of persistent centrifugal pulls from decentralizing forces in Quebec and other provinces throughout recent constitutional wrangles (Howlett et al. 1999, 197-99; Paehlke 2000, 172-74).

As a corollary to the British-style parliamentary system, Canada's electoral system adopts a single-member district with plurality, or first-past-the-post, decision for federal and all provincial elections. This has a bias towards a middle-of-the-road two-party system, with a serious disadvantage for smaller parties or parties with support from single-issue groups. Groups espousing environmental causes would better translate their votes into seats through an electoral system with proportional representation, as Green parties in several European countries and the European Parliament have demonstrated. In addition, representation in Canada is based on geographically specific electoral districts, which encourages regionalism in electoral politics, exaggerates regional cleavages, and tends to reward the geographic, as opposed to ideological, concentration of voter support. It has been amply demonstrated in recent years by the emergence of regional parties such as the Reform Party/Canadian Alliance and the Bloc Québécois. Thus, parties with a diffuse base of support are penalized, leading to under-representation of groups focusing on issues such as women, the poor, and Aboriginals (Howlett et al. 1999, 189). This electoral deficit also affects environmentally oriented groups. Such an electoral and party system is one of the reasons the environmental concerns of the Canadian public are not translated into campaign themes during electoral contests. Voting in Canadian elections is determined primarily by economic issues, national unity, and regional concerns (Paehlke 2000, 163).

Another major feature of the Canadian political system derived from the parliamentary model has to do with public administration. In a parliamentary system of government, the cabinet controls the policy-making process through its dominance of the parliament, and the bureaucracy has great influence in the policy process through its advisory capacity to ministers. Not all bureaucratic agencies are equal in power, however. There are powerful central agencies such as the Privy Council Office and the Prime Minister's Office, which perform control and coordination functions over the bureaucracy (Campbell and Szablowski 1979). And in an era of globalized finance where capital outflows can quickly "punish" governments with nonconforming policies, departments with financial responsibilities are among the most influential: the Treasury Board Secretariat and the Department of Finance are Canada's budgetary and financial watchdogs. Their influence increased during the 1980s, when governments around the world sought to curb deficit spending. During such fiscal retrenchment, environmental agencies became among the weakest bureaucracies in most countries, including Canada. When the Finance Department implemented massive budget cuts in the 1990s, Environment Canada was an easy target.

In Canada systematic state intervention in environmental management started in the postwar years, as both the federal and provincial governments began to introduce regulations against pollution. In the earlier period, rather than face the complications of creating a completely new administrative structure with an environmental mandate, governments often added environmental responsibilities to existing resource mandates. "This approach contributed to the division of administrative resources and environmental functions, both vertically between different levels of government and horizontally between different agencies and departments with overlapping jurisdictions" (Hessing and Howlett 1997, 51). To deal with the inadequacies of such an approach, environmental ministries were later established at both federal and provincial levels. In 1971 the Trudeau cabinet created the federal Department of Environment (DOE), which integrated various existing functions of environmental protection and resource management. The department was launched with ambition, was supported by political leadership, and exhibited early policy innovation. It grew rapidly as an important organizational and legal framework for environmental regulation and assessment was established. Canada wielded considerable influence as a number of DOE experts took on leadership roles in the international environmental policy community (Doern and Conway 1994, 12-15).

The DOE's influence declined progressively during the 1980s, however, due to structural shortcomings, a series of budget cuts, limited political support, and loss of leadership. From its inception, the DOE faced problems stemming from structural fragmentation and legal deficiency. Environment Canada suffered from serious internal division as it "was put together ... from a complex mix of 'organizational orphans' drawn from throughout the federal government, and was then basically left to sort itself out and bring some coherence and direction to its activities" (Doern and Conway 1994, 16). Moreover, provincial governments soon established their own environmental ministries, and the DOE's capacity was undermined by the realities of divided environmental jurisdiction between the two levels of government (Doern and Conway 1994, 99). The DOE also had weak statutory capacity to regulate the environment, and the department was supposed to achieve its policy mandate by coordinating the activities of other departments (Hessing and Howlett 1997, 52), which is difficult under the best of circumstances.

Ultimately, the DOE suffered the fate of a politically weak department with responsibility beyond its capacity. Frequent ministerial turnovers were a sign of weakness typical of such a department, with the average ministerial term lasting just over a year. The department was always on the defensive, while its mandate required assertive leadership. Such leadership was hard to come by partly because most of the environment ministers were of junior status within the cabinet. Attempts by ministers and higher officials of the DOE to develop coherent and comprehensive policies largely failed, with certain exceptions such as the 1990 Green Plan (Doern and Conway 1994, 38-39).

Over the years, the institutions of Canadian environmental administration were also affected by the shifting tides of the Canadian political economy. In the mid-1970s and early 1990s, Canada's political economy experienced sharp recessions. And from the 1980s onward, Canada witnessed the growth of neoconservatism and was transformed by economic globalization. Each of these influences had a profound impact on Canadian environmental policy institutions. Particularly in the early 1990s, the government was faced with a prolonged and painful recession and ballooning public debt. In order to resuscitate the economy and avoid pressures towards higher tax and interest rates, the federal government carried out drastic financial retrenchment measures and decentralization of public administration. After sweeping spending cuts for a number of years, the Liberal government in Ottawa balanced its budget in 1997, for the first time in twenty-eight years. Environmental spending suffered severe reductions.

Among the consequences of federal budget cuts were the off-loading of environmental protection functions to the provincial level, the weakening of federal coordination over provincial governments, and the further decentralization of an already decentralized system. Simultaneously, provincial governments were also going through their own process of far-reaching budget cuts, including cuts to environmental expenditures. Right-wing governments in Alberta and Ontario have been particularly enthusiastic in their cutbacks. In Ontario, for instance, the environmental budget was cut by two-thirds from a high of over $700 million in 1992 to around $200 million at the end of the decade. Staff cuts in the province's environmental ministry were equally dramatic, leaving 41 percent fewer employees in 2000 than in the mid-1990s. When only full-time staff are considered, the head count has shrunk by 58 percent. Such drastic cuts in environmental spending did not cause any serious backlash to the governments in power. Canadians were experiencing hard times, environmental protection was not a priority that translated into votes, and environmental budget cuts were not particularly noticeable when they were combined with massive cuts in social expenditures (Paehlke 2000, 165-71).

So far, we have considered how Canada's domestic institutional features affect its environmental governance. Canada, however, is part of the international community, whose institutions can also have an impact on national environmental policy making. This is particularly so as Canada has a very open economy, whose growth is greatly dependent on trade. International institutions set the external parameter for Canada's environmental policy, and can be a double-edged sword that acts as both constraint and facilitator for Canada's efforts to deal with environmental issues.

International regimes that govern Canada's trade relations, such as the North American Free Trade Agreement (NAFTA) or the World Trade Organization (WTO), have both direct and indirect impacts on Canada. Canada has been increasingly exposed to the forces of global economic competition and the dominant neoliberal "global standard." The WTO represents the ultimate regulator of accelerating global economic integration, which significantly affects Canadian environmental policy making. For instance, Canada as a trading nation highly oriented towards resource extraction may find it difficult to be too protective of the environment at the expense of its capacity to compete in the global market, and globalization tends to create pressures against strict domestic environmental regulations. "Moreover, to the extent that environmental policy is a provincial, rather than federal, responsibility, the reality of competitive pressure looms even larger. The economies of some Canadian provinces are dominated by only a few industries, making those industries very powerful indeed within that limited political context" (Paehlke 2000, 174). The environment, or certain aspects of it, may be a low priority in those regions.

In the 1970s, however, Canada was known for its environmental internationalism in the multilateral arena. Along the lines of the Pearsonian foreign policy tradition, Canada played a prominent leadership role in shaping international environmental regimes through efforts such as the 1972 UN conference on environment in Stockholm and the Brundtland Commission, and in building the momentum for subsequent achievements, culminating in the 1992 Rio Summit and Agenda 21. In those years, Canada was instrumental in fostering international environmental policy paradigms based on the concept of sustainable development (Doern and Conway 1994, 124-25). Such international successes did not necessarily facilitate stronger domestic environmental leadership, however, and Canada in the 1990s turned from a leader to a follower (see Chapter 4).

Canada currently participates in various bilateral and multilateral treaties, international organizations, agreements, protocols, and other international regimes that govern global environmental norms and regulations. For instance, Canada is a signatory of the North American Commission on Environmental Cooperation, the United Nations Environment Programme, the United Nations Framework Convention on Climate Change, and other UN agencies and programs such as the Kyoto Protocol, to name a few (Hessing and Howlett 1997, 67-68). To the extent that Canada is committed to these international regimes, there is pressure on Canada to comply with their norms. "Perhaps the best current prospects for returning Canada to positive sustainability initiative ... may come from a federal government emboldened by international environmental pressures," according to Paehlke (2000, 174).

Organization of This Book

The impact of the macro- and meso-level institutional influences identified above fosters the patterns that we have sketched out in Figure 1.1, which influence the integrity level of environmental policy. Each chapter in this book will apply the neo-institutional framework that has been outlined above to illuminate the relationship between aims and efforts in specific episodes and examples of Canadian environmental policy making. They cover a representative, if not exhaustive, range of the environmental challenges facing Canada, including global climate change (Steven Bernstein, Chapter 4), nuclear power and the issue of energy mixes (Michael D. Mehta, Chapter 5), forest resource management (Fikret Berkes and colleagues, Chapter 6), urban air quality improvement (Anthony Perl, Chapter 7), planning for sustainable cities (Richard Gilbert, Chapter 8; David Gurin, Chapter 9), and the environmental implications of macroeconomic change (Michael Howlett, Chapter 3). The contributors cover different levels of environmental governance, from systemic (William Leiss, Chapter 2), to international (Bernstein), to national (Howlett, Mehta), to provincial (Berkes and colleagues, Perl), to local (Gilbert, Gurin).

Leiss characterizes environmental problems as a latecomer to Canada's public policy agenda and identifies the structure of the government and federal/provincial conflict as the main culprits behind the integrity gap. Consequently, Canadian governing institutions require politically difficult restructuring to effectively address environmental problems. He also finds that high uncertainty regarding the causal connections underlying environmental problems promotes government indecision and industry obstruction. Leiss emphasizes effective risk issue management, risk communication, and public engagement as means of enhancing environmental policy capacity.

Howlett's chapter sets the stage for understanding why the integrity of Canada's environmental policy often suffers by situating this policy domain within a political economy framework. The general relationships between natural resource and environmental policy making in Canada are explored, and the environmental policy implications of the natural resource sector's gradual decline as a source of investment and employment in the Canadian economy are discussed. Using the notion of a transition from a "staples" political economy to a "post-staples" political economy, the chapter compares the general features of a staples political economy with the less resource-intensive and more urban attributes of Canada's emergent post-staples economy.

Howlett notes the short-term increase in political polarization regarding the environment, and the consequent policy stalemate evidenced by a simultaneous increase in diffuse public support for environmental protection coupled with opposition to specific sustainability measures on the part of traditional resource interests and constituencies. To the extent that the transition to a post-staples political economy is uneven across regions, the possibility of an integrity gap in Canada's environmental policy remains real. In terms of accountability, diffuse public support for environmental protection in urban areas would put less direct pressure on the government, given the nature of Canada's electoral system, compared with resource-dependent regions, which would have more focused and direct electoral pressure to resist protection measures that might undermine the source of their wealth and employment. The costs of enforcing such protection would also be felt unevenly, with the resource-dependent regions bearing the brunt. This would intensify their resistance to policies that respond to environmental concerns. Howlett predicts that post-staples economic restructuring would shift the focus of Canadian environmental policy away from debates over wilderness protection and sustainable resource management, which would eventually accommodate preservation, and towards issues affecting urban health and quality of life, such as smog, green space, and water quality. The author does qualify this forecasted convergence between Canadian and European environmental policy, noting that it could be constrained by any limits that arise in Canada's transition to a post-staples political economy.

Employing a sociological institutionalist perspective, the chapter by Bernstein argues that the climate change regime evolved internationally to fit with liberal environmentalism, which has become the normative structure of the day. The Kyoto Protocol establishes an international institutional structure for domestic responses to climate change, and establishes a normative framework for countries to respond to climate change. This chapter probes how Canada, one of the largest emitters of greenhouse gases per capita, has promoted commitments and mechanisms on climate change consistent with its own domestic institutional constraints. Bernstein observes a gap between the greenhouse gas reduction targets that Canada committed to in a multilateral negotiation process and the likely inaction that would be the case if the typical domestic constraints on environmental policy remain unchecked.

This low level of integrity can be attributed to the institutional features outlined in our typology. One of the main institutional constraints on Canada's environmental policy is the existence of multiple and competitive jurisdictions. Within the federal cabinet, Environment Canada and Natural Resources Canada often have divergent interests on matters related to climate change. The existence of different levels of government claiming jurisdiction also complicates domestic policy implementation. Enforcement cost of abatement measures is another constraint. The cost of meeting the Kyoto commitment would probably be concentrated in certain sectors and regions, which could be the major source of resistance to the Kyoto agreement. In addition, because of the vagueness of accountability due to competing jurisdictions and the long-term horizon of climate change debate beyond the electoral cycles of political competition, policy makers may not be under direct pressure to act. The challenge facing Canada in meeting this commitment will not be easy; it could, however, be made easier by the weight of international norms and of Canada's international reputation as they begin to enter the institutional context of environmental policy regarding climate change, and this is where Bernstein sees some sign of hope.

The chapter by Mehta presents Canada's nuclear energy sector as a cautionary tale for those concerned about environmental integrity. Certain resource-poor countries chose nuclear energy as their future energy mainstay. To a lesser extent, Canada's province of Ontario followed a similar path. The public credibility of Canada's nuclear industry has been undermined by safety issues and evidence about the costly life-cycle economics of nuclear development, but the insulated nature of discourse and deliberation regarding nuclear power in Canada continues to promote the technology and resists broader public engagement on alternative energy sources. Manufacturers, suppliers, and regulators form an insular policy community that is both resistant and hostile to citizen participation. Here, the level of environmental policy integrity is low and an integrity gap arises from the insensitivity of policy participants to the environmental risks being generated.

Because of its insular and inaccessible nature, Canada's nuclear policy network lacks accountability. It has not faced much direct pressure from the public. For instance, the Atomic Energy Control Board (AECB), the federal regulator, is not required to hold hearings at any stage of its regulatory activities. Environmental assessment of nuclear projects is conducted by the AECB, and unless it finds a serious problem or significant public concern, no further review is done. In addition, despite the increasing awareness that nuclear energy is risky and uneconomical, the cost of reducing dependence on nuclear energy will be enormously high and will be borne mainly by the few utilities and ultimately by federal budget allocations. Mehta argues that a country's energy mix should reflect an awareness of the associated environmental, economic, social, and human health implications, and that Canada's current reliance on nuclear power fails this test. He also suggests that developed countries, including Canada, should break the barriers to innovation erected by nuclear power policy communities, which would enable more effective pursuit of renewable energy development.

Berkes and his colleagues explore the sustainability of natural resource extraction at the local and regional levels by emphasizing the Canadian experience with participatory processes and the use of local environmental information. The chapter relates participatory resource management to six areas of Agenda 21 (forests, mountains, biodiversity, oceans, indigenous peoples, and nongovernmental organizations, or NGOs). His case study of a project in southeastern British Columbia's forested mountain environment shows how a variety of environmental and resource databases can be used to assist with sustainability planning in a multiple-use area. The incorporation of local values, priorities, and knowledge into environmental decision making, along with the use of ecosystem-based management, has the potential for improving sustainability by breaking with institutional arrangements that constrain integrity and by institutionalizing new ideas and modes of considering information. The local and regional approach may be more conducive to overcoming obstacles associated with jurisdictional contention and lack of direct accountability.

Perl's chapter compares air pollution control efforts in Canada's two largest anglophone urban areas to highlight the constraint that conflicting policy communities can impose on environmental policy implementation. Perl demonstrates how different policy network configurations resulted in different approaches to dealing with analogous air pollution problems. In southern Ontario's "Drive Clean" program, multiple policy communities based in both different political jurisdictions (urban and provincial rivalry in the Greater Toronto Area) as well as different economic interests (the automotive sector versus environmental and community groups) have placed considerable limits on the direction and pace of limiting the emissions from motor vehicles. Here, the clash between three policy communities representing environmental professionals, the auto industry, and local governments yielded a policy bias in favour of the industry. By contrast, British Columbia's "AirCare" program has met with considerably more success under the guidance of a single policy community that embraces multiple political jurisdictions and most organized social and economic interests concerned about urban air quality. In the Canadian context, the results of Toronto's and Vancouver's policy experience suggest that institutional initiatives intended to improve urban air quality must cross both jurisdictional boundaries and the organizational structure of firms and governments in order to close integrity gaps.

The chapters by Gilbert and Gurin focus on city planning and sustainability. Gilbert's chapter is about long-term city planning by the new City of Toronto, which was formed by the 1998 amalgamation of six municipalities. The author reveals an integrity gap in land-use and transportation planning in Toronto, as he describes and evaluates the city's planning from the perspective of social, economic, and environmental sustainability. Establishing four regional governments surrounding Metro Toronto created difficulties in overall planning of the city as a whole. According to his assessment, amalgamation of the municipalities into a "megacity" did not change the situation. Gilbert observes that almost all the Greater Toronto Area's (GTA) growth in population occurs around the city in areas of low-density development, characterized by high per capita levels of energy use in buildings and for transportation and resulting high levels of emissions of pollutants into air, water, and land. He considers this urban sprawl grossly unsustainable and a prime contributor to the growing integrity gap in urban sustainability.

Gilbert argues that achieving sustainability in the GTA will require the absorption of a greater proportion of the region's population growth within the City of Toronto. Such a shift in population cannot be achieved without effective regional planning, but there is in effect no such process, only various forums for discussion of relevant issues. The city thus faces quite a challenge in planning how to grow its own population in order to secure a more sustainable region. The dimensions of this challenge are discussed, highlighting the evident dysfunction of institutional arrangements in the GTA that must be overcome to enable progress towards overall sustainability. The current integrity gap here is between the laudable objectives of the city plans – which occasionally yield advances towards sustainability in parts of the GTA – and the unsustainable growth patterns and trends of the GTA as a whole.

Gurin's chapter brings the issue of cities and sustainability to life with a historical example. Toronto's Exhibition Place originated in the nineteenth century as a venue for Ontario's agricultural fair, the Canadian National Exhibition (CNE). Compared with the rest of Toronto's waterfront, however, it has experienced little physical change during the past century. There have, however, been significant changes in public attitude towards the use of Exhibition Place. Attendance at the annual Canadian National Exhibition has declined and the grounds are empty much of the year. Exhibition Place no longer has an important place in Torontonians' consciousness. It has languished partly because of the institutional structure that governs its management. The stagnation of the CNE site can be traced to its governing body's conflicting and unattainable mandate. The site is a public property owned by the City of Toronto. It is a park by official designation, but a park that is expected to generate revenue. This is a contradiction that prevents Exhibition Place from being either commercially successful or a satisfying park. Once again, institutional arrangements are shown to limit the environmental integrity of this significant waterfront space in Toronto. Gurin seeks principles that can guide city planners towards transforming Exhibition Place into a sustainable Toronto neighbourhood. The chapter deals with the possibilities and the political constraints of making this vast site a model of environmental integrity.

The concluding chapter by Perl and Lee considers what the integrity gap attributes revealed in preceding chapters tell us about institutions and environmental policy in Canada.

1 The integrity gap is often a clear symptom of a lack of fit between the environmental problems that challenge Canada and the policy capacity to deal with them. Federal/provincial power sharing often inhibits the capacity to act on environmental goals.
2 Canadian environmental policy capacity is heavily influenced by powerful natural resource development interests. Integrity in policy often depends upon politicians finding the will to impose some costs from environmental goals on powerful resource industries. When such resolve flags, the integrity gap widens, but political leadership can also narrow it by standing up to regional resource interests.
3 Canada's environmental policy capacity is constrained by the tension between the liberal multilateral environmentalism on the one hand and the policy priority of competitiveness and growth in the North American economy on the other.
4 There is insularity among technocratic public sector elites with regard to assessing and communicating environmental risks, as highlighted in the chapter on nuclear energy by Mehta. Insulation from democratic accountability acts as an institutional damper to achieving environmental policy goals.
5 The multiplicity of jurisdictions needed to implement most environmental policies leads to escalating conflict over objectives and the means to achieve them. The chapters by Berkes and colleagues, Perl, and Gilbert demonstrate this point.

Moving Canada's political economy closer to environmental sustainability would require closing the integrity gap at least in part through institutional change. How, then, could such changes come about? Our conclusion assesses some potential changes in Canadian institutions and presents three scenarios that could yield some major enhancement of environmental policy capacity. The first scenario explores what an explicit initiative to renew environmental institutions from within Canada could look like. It envisages change resulting from feedback from existing environmental policy arrangements, precipitated by significant policy failure or crisis. Such change could be launched by an electoral realignment of national or provincial governments in which environmental concerns figure prominently. New political priorities on the environment could lead to the launch of new policy institutions, the shape of which would likely seek to correct the perceived limitations of contemporary institutions.

In the second scenario, environmental institutions gain new effectiveness as a result of far-reaching domestic political reforms that address governance challenges not specifically connected to the environment. Such reforms could range from a constitutional amendment of the relationship between Ottawa and the provinces, to judicial review of governing arrangements that entrench individual rights, to fiscal and administrative renewal of both federal and provincial governments' policy responsibilities. In this case, new governance practices grounded in wider Canadian domestic politics, such as the balance of power between Ottawa and the provinces or the place of Quebec in Canada, would have the collateral effect of renewing the effectiveness of environmental policy making.

In the third scenario, international political and economic engagements become the catalysts for institutional change within Canada. The Kyoto Protocol and NAFTA are but two commitments that have introduced foreign inputs into Canadian environmental policy. Environmental policy initiatives of the United States, in particular, could compel institutional redesign in Canada.

The integrity gap in Canadian environmental policy documented in the following chapters merits greater attention than it has received to date. The 1990s were a time when both international economic influences and domestic political dynamics pressed Canada's leaders to "solve" budget deficits and shore up national unity (through, among other initiatives, significant reorganization of federal/provincial fiscal institutions). But while Canada's public accounts showed an impressive surplus and the threat of "deconfederation" has been kept at bay, the deficit in environmental sustainability persisted, and has likely grown. This environmental deficit cannot be ignored indefinitely, and is likely to be a more important policy priority for Canada's governments during the twenty-first century's first decade.

During its heyday of budget surpluses in the late 1990s, Canada enjoyed international distinction as a nation with the highest level of human development in the world. Although the much-cited human development index from the UN Development Program does not include measures of environmental well-being per se, environmental well-being is often assumed to correlate with human well-being. In 2001 Canada lost its top spot in the United Nations ranking, a sign that policy issues other than balanced budgets may require attention if Canada is to remain such an enviable place in which to live.

Canada's pristine nature and vast landmass appear far removed from the environmental risks that face other nations. If this image has any truth at all, however, it is largely by accident and not from any conscious efforts on the part of Canadians. Despite Canada's international reputation and the rhetoric in its environmental policy goals, evidence abounds that Canada faces numerous environmental shortcomings and even some outright disasters. The chapters in this volume show where the integrity gap lies and suggest how it might be closed. Canada's established institutions are increasingly ineffective in meeting environmental challenges, and they will sooner or later require adjustment. It takes political effort to build institutions, and it may take even more effort to reform them. The contributors to this book are not pessimistic, however. Disasters such as those in Walkerton, Ontario, or Sydney, Nova Scotia, strong domestic leadership, and international pressures and obligations may each contribute to raising the level of Canada's environmental policy, despite today's institutionalized constraints.

Note
1 Perl (1991) provides an overview of the concept of institutional durability.

References
Atkinson, M., ed. 1993. *Governing Canada: Institutions and Public Policy*. Toronto: Harcourt Brace and Company Canada.
Atkinson, M., and W. Coleman. 1989. *The State, Business, and Industrial Change in Canada*. Toronto: University of Toronto Press.
Boyd, D.R. 2001. *Canada vs. the OECD: An Environmental Comparison*. Victoria, BC: University of Victoria, Eco-Chair of Environmental Law and Policy. <http://www.environmentalindicators.com> (13 December 2003).
Brooks, S. 1998. *Public Policy in Canada: An Introduction*. 3rd ed. Toronto: Oxford University Press Canada.
Campbell, C., and G.J. Szablowski. 1979. *The Superbureaucrats: Structure and Behaviour in Central Agencies*. Toronto: Macmillan of Canada.
Coleman, W., and A. Perl. 1999. Internationalized Policy Environments and Policy Network Analysis. *Political Studies* 47(4): 691-709.
Coleman, W., and G. Skogstad. 1990. *Policy Communities and Public Policy in Canada*. Toronto: Copp Clark Pitman.
Cowhey, P.F., and M.D. McCubbins. 1995. Introduction. In *Structure and Policy in Japan and the United States,* edited by P.F. Cowhey and M.D. McCubbins. New York: Cambridge University Press.
Doern, G.B., and T. Conway. 1994. *The Greening of Canada: Federal Institutions and Decisions*. Toronto: University of Toronto Press.
Evans, P., D. Rueschemeyer, and T. Skocpol. 1985. *Bringing the State Back In*. New York: Cambridge University Press.
Greenelection.org. 2000. *New Environics Poll: Environment as a Major Election Issue among Voters*. <http://www.caps.20m.com/poll.htm> (13 December 2002).
Hall, P.A. 1986. *Governing the Economy: The Politics of State Intervention in Britain and France*. New York: Oxford University Press.
Hall, P.A., and R.C.R. Taylor. 1996. Political Science and the Three New Institutionalisms. *Political Studies* 44: 936-57.
Harrison, K. 1996. *Passing the Buck: Federalism and Canadian Environmental Policy*. Vancouver: UBC Press.
Hessing, M., and M. Howlett. 1997. *Canadian Natural Resource and Environmental Policy*. Vancouver: UBC Press.
Howlett, M., A. Netherton, and M. Ramesh. 1999. *The Political Economy of Canada*. Toronto: Oxford University Press.

Kato, J. 1996. Review Article: Institutions and Rationality in Politics – Three Varieties of Neo-Institutionalists. *British Journal of Political Science* 26: 553-82.

Katzenstein, P., ed. 1978. *Between Power and Plenty.* Madison: University of Wisconsin Press.

Koelble, T.A. 1995. Review Article: The New Institutionalism in Political Science and Sociology. *Comparative Politics* 27(2): 231-43.

Krasner, S. 1978. *Defending the National Interest.* Princeton, NJ: Princeton University Press.

–. 1988. Sovereignty: An Institutional Perspective. *Comparative Political Studies* 21(1): 66-94.

Maclean's. 1999. Maclean's/CBC Poll: Peering Inward and Outward. 20 December, 48-50.

Maclean's. 2000. Maclean's/Global Poll: Politics, Social Attitudes and Sex. 25 December, 52-54.

Maclean's. 2001. Maclean's Year-End Poll: Since Sept. 11. 31 December, 38-40.

March, J.G., and J.P. Olsen. 1984. The New Institutionalism: Organizational Factors in Political Life. *American Political Science Review* 78(3): 734-49.

Meyer, J.W., and W.R. Scott. 1994. *Institutional Environments and Organizations: Structural Complexity and Individualism.* Thousand Oaks, CA: Sage Publications.

Nordlinger, E. 1981. *On the Autonomy of the Democratic State.* Cambridge, MA: Harvard University Press.

North, D. 1990. *Institutions, Institutional Change, and Economic Performance.* New York: Cambridge University Press.

Paehlke, R. 2000. Environmentalism in One Country: Canadian Environmental Policy in an Era of Globalization. *Policy Studies Journal* 28(1): 160-75.

Perl, A. 1991. Financing Transport Infrastructure: The Effects of Institutional Durability in French and American Policymaking. *Governance: An International Journal of Policy and Administration* 4(October): 365-402.

Powell, W.W., and P.J. DiMaggio, eds. 1991. *The New Institutionalism in Organizational Analysis.* Chicago: University of Chicago Press.

Rosenbluth, F.M. 1993. *Financial Politics in Contemporary Japan.* Ithaca, NY: Cornell University Press.

Schmitter, P., and G. Lehmbruch, eds. 1982. *Patterns of Corporatist Policy-Making.* Beverly Hills, CA: Sage Publications.

Skocpol, T. 1979. *States and Social Revolutions.* Cambridge: Cambridge University Press.

Stanbury, W. 1986. *Business-Government Relations in Canada: Grappling with Leviathan.* Toronto: Methuen.

Steinmo, S., K. Thelen, and F. Longstreth, eds. 1992. *Structuring Politics: Historical Institutionalism in Comparative Analysis.* New York: Cambridge University Press.

Wilson, James Q. 1973. *Political Organizations.* New York: Basic Books.

–. 1983. *American Government: Institutions and Politics.* Lexington, MA: Heath.

Zysman, J. 1983. *Governments, Markets and Growth.* Berkeley: University of California Press.

2
How Canada's Stumbles with Environmental Risk Management Reflect an Integrity Gap

William Leiss

We in Canada have shown ourselves, so far, to be better at talking about and studying contentious issues where environmental risks are involved than in managing these risks. This leads us to emphasize talk over action in environmental policy making. We do well at formulating policy frameworks for interpreting our environmental problems, crafting agendas for acting on them, and deliberating over goal and vision statements for what we would like to see accomplished. But the outcomes of these considerable environmental policy efforts remain disappointing, for the most part. This chapter will identify some shortcomings in Canada's attempt to manage environmental risks and link them to institutional constraints that lay behind our integrity gap in environmental policy during the late 1990s.[1]

It is quite possible that the challenges in managing risk documented here and elsewhere in this book will become a thing of the past, for we may be ambushed soon by an issue – namely, global climate change – that will compel a narrowing of the environmental integrity gap between intention and action. At stake is whether there are human-induced effects on climate, caused by increases in the amounts of greenhouse gases (GHGs, especially carbon dioxide) that we emit into the atmosphere, that might have major, perhaps catastrophic, adverse impacts on agriculture, forests, rainfall patterns, violent storms, insect populations, disease vectors, and other domains in our lives. The stakes in *this* game of chance will not permit us to take refuge in uncertainties as an excuse for either indifference or inaction: for although the relevant uncertainties are indeed huge – including whether the ultimate outcome of global warming may be a new Ice Age! – so too are the possible consequences. Where stakes are relatively modest, say, a day's pay, many of us might roll the dice and take our chances. But where the stakes involve some possibility of truly catastrophic dislocations in the course of civilization, are most of us prepared to roll them and see? Actually, when the stakes start getting that high, most of us are too risk-averse for the game anyway, and we would (if we could) refuse to play. Alas, *we cannot opt out of the climate change game,* because GHGs are rising steadily and will continue to do so for the foreseeable future, perhaps even at an escalating pace.

Of course, maybe it isn't so. Certainly, we will conduct more scientific assessments to try to get a better idea of what is likely to happen to our climate as greenhouse gas concentrations in the atmosphere continue to rise, and to be more precise about what types of actions would be required on our part if we wished to stabilize them at some level. So couldn't we just wait and see? Yes, perhaps. There is some probability that only good things will happen, because plants love carbon and we could all end up living happily ever after in a botanical paradise. There is also some probability that nothing very bad will happen as GHG concentrations rise, because offsetting changes in the atmosphere will occur naturally, and everything will stay just about the way it is now. And there are the other possibilities, namely, the advent of either minor, major, or catastrophic dislocations in our established ways of life from human-induced climate change. The awkward problem is that if we wait for "convincing scientific proof" one way or the other that, first, climate change is or is not significantly related to anthropogenic GHG emissions and, second, that the net results look either all right or, alternatively, quite bleak to us, *it may be too late to do anything at all about the prospect if it does look bleak,* for all practical purposes, because we may not be able to reverse the course of events, despite our technological prowess, should the natural systems thus set in motion turn out to be resistant to further influence from us.

Thus, no matter how any of us calculates the risks associated with climate change itself, or the risks associated with our responses to this issue, what none of us can avoid is a confrontation with the unpleasant business of decision making under uncertainty, where the stakes – including the economic costs and benefits – are very, very large. We will have to manage disagreements among our own citizens over whether or not to take actions that impose real costs to us, and if so, which ones, a process that will provide the first real test of the "precautionary principle." We will have to participate in international disagreements over who is responsible for what part of this problem, and who should pay to fix it, and whether developing countries should pay anything at all. (For example, there will be monumental fights over what actions by various countries will count in the way of garnering credits for sequestering carbon.) In the meantime, we will all be hoping that science will come up with definitive conclusions one way or another, so that we can all agree on what we must do, however expensive it proves to be – an expectation that is, unless I miss my guess, almost certain to be frustrated for some considerable time to come.

In short, the climate change conundrum will demand that we do much better at risk issue management than we have in the past, better, that is, at handling large uncertainties about health and environmental impacts where perceived economic stakes are high. And since those are the characteristics of risk issues generally, the baptism of fire we must sooner or later undergo in dealing with climate change should be beneficial to us in more ways than one.

Environmental Policy and Risk Management

Environmental policy and its stepchild, environmental risk management, wander Canada's political landscape in permanent disarray, hounded by coteries of special interests awaiting the next swing of the public mood in their favour. There are two very different reasons for the disarray. One has to do with the irreducible uncertainties in environmental risk assessments, which for the most part prevent clear attributions of blame for harm done and, often, even a clear sense of just how serious the hazard itself might be. (Was it seals or birds that ripped out the stomachs of the Atlantic cod strewn on the ocean floor that were captured in the videotape once shown by Newfoundland's minister of environment?) The other is simply a reflection of the public's deep and abiding ambivalence about the need for environmental protection measures at all, when economic advantage beckons or remediation cost looms: Let's just get the gold out of the mine near Yellowknife, and worry later, if at all, about how to deal with the huge repository of arsenic waste left behind when it closes or who should pay to clean it up (Robinson 1999). Moreover, do grizzlies and cougars really need that much territory to call their own, if the land in question happens to include the site of a mine or golf course that could bring even more prosperity to Alberta?

For whereas the public is well aware these days that adequate health protection is expensive, the environment traditionally has been perceived as a "free good," there for the taking, which needs little regard from us and will always adjust somehow to the demands we place on its resources. Nature is nice to have, but we really don't see why we should have to pay to use it.

Judging from the way we ordinarily behave in such matters, it appears that to many of us the need for assiduous environmental management is rather dubious, and the reasons why we should care all that much about human impact on nature not very clear or compelling at all. Then why was the renewal of what is actually a rather inconsequential piece of federal legislation, the Canadian Environmental Protection Act (CEPA), so bitterly contested for six years, among the phalanx of federal departments; in the social arena, particularly between environmental groups and industry; and, rarest of sights, even publicly among politicians within the governing party? Since so little turns on the outcome – a reflection of the minor role in environmental management assigned to the federal power by the Canadian constitution – what explains the passion? And was it really a passion play at all, or rather just a political soap opera, since the roles of the actors seemed so conventionally scripted and the story line took so painfully long to unfold?[2]

The answer is, what we observed in the battle over the CEPA was a symbolic contest, and this is the type of contest about which an essentially peaceful people, such as Canadians are, can get very excited. (Other examples that spring to mind are the protection of Canadian culture and the definition of an authentic Quebecker.) The essence of symbolic contests is the disparity between the scale of portentous rhetoric and the lack of any perceptible changes in the prevailing state of affairs after each episode is finished. After six years of agony, the new CEPA turned out to be pretty much like the old CEPA, with a few new bells and whistles added.

In everyday life, Canadians appear to be highly ambivalent about environmental issues. On the one hand, in recent times these issues dropped far down the citizens' list of political and social priorities for action by governments, seemingly overwhelmed by concerns over employment security, health care, balanced budgets, and national unity.[3] Yet the public polling experts who track the shifting sentiments of our citizens insist that those same issues remain "top of mind," matters of deep and abiding concern, ready to be transformed at any time into broadly based demands for resolute actions to "clean up" the environment. The president of the polling firm Environics told a meeting of the National Round Table on Environment and the Economy in spring 1998 that 73 percent of those surveyed said they would choose environmental protection over economic growth if the two conflicted, and he predicted that the next "great green wave" would hit the political system early in the new century.[4] We shall see.

On the other hand, and at the same time, the stakes in some controversies over environmental quality, both domestically and throughout the world, have been raised. In the global arena, the matter of climate change has already been mentioned; in addition, there is the relentless increase in human population and industrial development and their impacts on arable land, potable water, breathable air, and wildlife habitat. On the domestic front, the always-testy exchanges over toxic chemicals management (especially dioxins and endocrine disruptors) have now spread across the most feared domains of human health impacts, namely, breast cancer and an entire range of hormone, endocrine, immune, and reproductive system effects.

Viewed from the standpoint of national politics and the federal policymaking capacity, the public management of environmental issues goes beyond mere ambivalence and approaches a state of acute schizophrenic disorder. As noted in the *1999 Report of the Commissioner of the Environment and Sustainable Development* to the House of Commons, "federal departments are deeply divided on many key issues. They do not share a common vision of how toxic substances should be managed. They disagree strongly on such issues as the degree of risk posed by some industrial chemicals, the interpretation of federal policy and the need to take action on it, the relative merits of voluntary and regulatory controls, and their own respective roles and accountabilities."

Although surely we cannot be unaware of how prominent environmental issues are or can become in these times, in Canada we appear to wander into their orbit half-consciously, as if sleepwalking. Think of the implausible federal/provincial "agreement" on climate change thrown together just before Canada sent its negotiators off to Kyoto, which had begun to unravel before their flight landed; or the half-hearted regulatory oversight of Ontario Hydro's nuclear plants; or the regrettable decision to exempt the sale of Candu reactors to China from an appropriate risk assessment; or just nonsensical little things, such as the abortive attempts to ban the export of PCB wastes or the import of the gasoline additive MMT. These episodes in the twentieth century's closing decade turn out to be symptomatic of more general underlying weaknesses in Canada's policy-making competence in environmental matters. The capacity limitations that are noted in the section below have plagued us for some time, and can partly explain the growing gap between Canadian rhetoric and results in environmental risk management.[5]

Politically Induced Organizational Chaos at Environment Canada
Environment Canada, already among the smallest government agencies in the federal system, suffered severe personnel and budgetary reductions under "program review" during the first Liberal mandate of the 1990s. These cuts exacerbated the long-standing structural woes of Environment Canada as a department – the adding and subtracting of bits and pieces from other departments, the revolving door of ministers, and, above all, the endless turf battles with other departments (Brown 1992; Doern and Conway 1994). These bureaucratic troubles began with the creation of the department in 1971 and have persisted down to the present. They were politically induced in the sense that the core leadership of various prime ministers and their most powerful ministers, in both governing parties, never bestowed full legitimacy on Environment Canada's mandate, never gave it clear originating legislative authority, and never put it on a firm organizational footing.

During this past decade, the seemingly endless review of the Canadian Environmental Protection Act was marked by some furious backstage bureaucratic manoeuvring between Environment Canada and the "resource management" departments (Natural Resources, Industry, and Agriculture), in particular over authority for the regulation of biotechnology products.[6] And although from an issue management standpoint Environment Canada should be the authoritative lead agency for global climate change policy, so far it has been forced to share this mandate awkwardly with Natural Resources Canada, which has quite different interests in this matter, producing the embarrassing spectacle of then-environment minister Christine Stewart literally sitting speechless during Question Period in Parliament as this policy was being debated. Finally, Environment Canada "carried the can" on behalf of the entire federal system for one of the most humiliating political losses in recent memory, the withdrawal of legislation banning MMT. The fragmentation of authority reaches into the departmental organization itself, where protracted turf warfare over the internal ownership of issues (such as pulp mill effluent) among Environment Canada headquarters and regional units is not uncommon.[7]

Federal/Provincial Jurisdictional Squabbles
The historical record in this matter is interesting, especially against the backdrop of the attempt to harmonize federal and provincial initiatives on environmental matters during the last few years. There is some reason to think that if the so-called harmonization initiative succeeds, the status quo ante in federal/provincial interjurisdictional relations in this domain would be restored. Before the period of endemic conflict between the two (starting in the latter half of the 1980s), which was marked by an assertion of a larger federal presence, the provinces had the leadership role in environmental regulation, with the federal government playing a backup role, especially in providing scientific research capabilities.[8] If we should witness such a restoration, it may not bode well for Environment Canada's situation in the context of program review cuts. Doern and Conway (1994) have described in detail how the department tried to wrap itself in the mantle of science before 1985, and how this strategy continually fell victim to the budget cutters.

Environmental Assessment Games
The long-overdue Canadian Environmental Assessment Act (CEAA) was finally proclaimed, after many delays, at the beginning of 1995 – yet it arrived, after a truly agonizing birth, over the strong objections of all provinces and the open defiance of Quebec in particular! Can we ever hope to get anything right in this area (Vanderzwaag and Duncan 1992)?

The question is necessary because, simply stated, Canada has an embarrassing and consistent record of failure in credible environmental assessment for high-profile, large development projects, which include, in just the past few years alone, the "Windy Craggy" site and Alcan's "Kemano Completion Project," both in British Columbia, both of which have cost that provincial government a considerable sum in the way of monetary settlements and political capital. And there is the long-running Cheviot Mine saga in Alberta, in whose latest episode a federal court agreed with the claim by the Sierra Club of Canada that a combined federal/provincial assessment panel did not carry out the act's requirements for a cumulative impact assessment.[9] Passage of the CEAA followed the farcical episodes of the Rafferty-Alameda Dam in Saskatchewan and the Oldman River Dam in Alberta, where courts ordered environmental assessments to be done on major projects already underway, thus discrediting the assessment process itself, and where, in the first-mentioned case, "Canadians witnessed the spectacle of federal and provincial ministers challenging each other's version of a backroom deal in Court" (Harrison 1994; Doern and Conway 1994). Since the act has not yet been fully tested, it is too early to tell whether we can ever hope to get anything right in this area. The determined opposition of the provinces does not auger well for success, however.[10]

The Mysterious Fate of Economic Instruments
Despite a steady stream of reports and studies, with overwhelmingly positive findings suggesting clear benefits from implementing this approach, Canada does not seem able to take even the most tentative steps in the direction of using market-based instruments (such as tax regimes or emissions trading) for environmental regulation. Why not?

The concepts on which such instruments are based have been around for at least twenty-five years.[11] In 1992 Environment Canada issued a comprehensive discussion paper, entitled "Economic Instruments for Environmental Protection." In November 1994, the Department of Finance and Environment Canada issued "Economic Instruments and Disincentives to Sound Environmental Practices," the output of a multisectoral task force. In all of these sources can be found strong reasons for utilizing market-based instruments. In June 1995, the House of Commons Standing Committee on Environment and Sustainable Development said: "The Committee strongly urges the federal government to continue the important work begun by the Task Force to ensure that barriers are eliminated and appropriate economic instruments are implemented."[12]

Despite all this, for all practical purposes, *nothing has been done*. How many more reports will be commissioned, laboured over, submitted, and praised, only to be shelved by policy makers?[13] Canada's ill-prepared state in this respect is now much more serious than in the past, since emissions trading regimes will be a crucial part of global action to reduce greenhouse gas emissions. The promise to utilize economic instruments has been reiterated once again in the new Canadian Environmental Protection Act; does this mean that we shall actually see some of them in operation before, say, the onset of the fourth millennium?

The Tension between Science and Policy in Environmental Risk Management

It is reasonable to think that environmental policy should be science-driven, in the sense that "good policies" ought to be rooted in "good science." Or, in other words, "ecosystem management" – which means regulating human impacts on the biosphere in such a way as to assure a sustained basis for the satisfaction of human needs – should be based on ecosystem science, that is, a detailed understanding of how ecosystem interactions among species and their habitats actually happen.

Now, it is certainly true in general that if we wish to do intelligent ecosystem management, we must have a continuous growth in our scientific understanding of ecosystem dynamics. This is not the same thing, however, as saying that ecosystem science can or ought to be the *primary "driver" of* – as opposed to being a *primary component of* – environmental policy making. The reasons are fairly straightforward, and among them are the following.

First, policy requires yes/no decisions, whereas science is often continually evolving from one level of uncertainty to another (in many cases, the more we learn, the more questions we have). Second, and even more important, environmental policy making is often driven in a political context by just those issues for which we have at that time the most imperfect scientific understanding. (The anthropogenic contribution to global climate change and the possible health effects of what are called "endocrine disruptors" are two current cases in point.) As a general rule, the cause-and-effect pathways in broad ecosystem impacts are difficult enough to isolate scientifically, and to this are added the further requirements of a level of "proof" that will satisfy evidentiary standards for legal and regulatory purposes that have been adapted from quite different realms.

Third, environmental issues usually lack immediacy in that they are based on long-term trends, whereas, in the total context of government policy making, economic, jurisdictional, political, legal, and other factors have a stark immediacy that simply cannot be overlooked by politicians. In this context, policies driven primarily by long-term ecosystem trends framed within inevitable scientific uncertainties are doomed to disappointment or crippling compromise. None of this means that science is irrelevant to the environmental policy-making process, but these factors do point to the tendency for science to become entangled within the nets of institutional inertia and interest-group conflict. These nets become "policy traps" that can lead to protracted policy warfare.

This entanglement in policy traps has had, and continues to have, a telling impact on the organizational structure of government departments of the environment everywhere, but perhaps on none more than Environment Canada. As Doern and Conway (1994) have shown, "the DOE from the outset ... saw its scientific and technical capacity as a central pillar of its hoped-for influence." It filled its professional staff slots with scientists, sought to align many of its program delivery functions in terms of the scientific description of reality, and sent forth these highly trained legions into policy battles – but it was unable to translate scientific competence into policy competence, as perceived by many others within the federal bureaucracy: "[To] the rest of the Ottawa system, the [DOE policy] ideas seemed too quixotic and intermittent, too frequently unrelated to economic realities, and too uninformed by a coherent view of where the DOE ought to be going" (Doern and Conway 1994).

To the extent to which the scientific personnel drop their primary focus on actually doing scientific research and get drawn into protracted policy warfare, they are asked to perform functions for which they have had no decent training or experiential background whatsoever, becoming easy prey for the professional policy specialists in the system, especially those who haunt the central agencies of government. And to the extent that their primary focus is on remaining practitioners of ongoing scientific practice, they are often ill-equipped to safely negotiate the quicksands of policy development.[14] The lesson for Environment Canada is that scientific competence alone is not a sufficient basis for policy influence. Indeed, policy competence, which means being able to find ways to defeat institutional barriers to needed changes in our ways of doing business, is probably independent of scientific competence, even in environmental management.

We find a clue to the supposition that something important is going on here in the low credibility that governments today generally have in the eyes of citizens. Governments (and those working for them, including scientists) are not perceived to be "neutral" in matters such as environmental management, or to be positioned "above the fray" in relation to conflicts among interest groups in society. Instead, government scientists share a relatively low credibility ranking with their compatriots in industry, while environmental groups and academics occupy the upper end of the spectrum, apparently because both are perceived to be disinterested parties.[15] The institutional weakness reflected in this credibility gap reappears at a higher level of significance in what I have called the "issue-response gap." This issue-response gap is a contributing factor to the integrity gap in Canadian environmental policy.

From Risk Management to Risk Issue Management
The issue-response gap is rooted in long-standing deficiencies in the organizational structures and personnel complements among agencies charged with health and environmental risk management. These deficiencies stem from a failure to understand the essential difference between *risk management* and *risk issue management*. My colleagues and I have explored this

difference in an extensive series of case studies in previously published books.[16] Here I will give an explanation of the concept in general.

Industrial societies have come a long way along the path to the better management of health and environmental risks since the 1970s, when the new approach to such risk management began to take shape. There is still, however, a terribly long hike ahead before its real benefits can be glimpsed, much less reaped. For Canada, the following list will give some indication of our latest wanderings:

- Our flagship environmental protection federal legislation, administered by Environment Canada, still perversely confuses hazard and risk (Leiss 2001).
- Our premier federal risk management agency, the Health Protection Branch of Health Canada, has been desperately trying to renew itself for most of this decade, so far unsuccessfully.
- Neither Health Canada nor Environment Canada has made much progress towards implementing a publicly credible priority-setting approach for relative risk, which is needed so that investments in risk reduction can achieve the highest possible pay-offs and ad hoc decisions based on short-term perceived political expediency can be avoided.

The phrase "risk issue" refers to any of the following types of risk management challenges:

- *stakeholder confrontation,* or the existence of some controversy – about the scope or existence of a risk and how it should be managed – among interested parties, such as between environmental non-governmental organizations (ENGOs) and government or industry (dioxins, genetically modified food crops, and so on)
- *intractable behaviour,* or the persistent inability of risk managers to change risk-taking behaviour to some desired degree (drinking/driving by young males, tobacco use, and so on)
- *high uncertainty,* or the public expressions of concern over risk factors that are poorly characterized from a scientific standpoint, or where uncertainties in risk assessments are quite large despite the fact that technologies giving rise to them are already in use or in active development (cellular telephones, cloning, GHG emissions and climate change, and so on).

Public sector risk management agencies get caught up in such issues daily. Indeed, for public sector risk managers, this is the stuff of everyday life: a good deal of ongoing scientific review is mixed with some low-level issue management, but the organization never seems to know when something is going to erupt into a high-profile controversy. This is because such agencies are not organized or staffed explicitly to deal with risk issue management.

Risk management relies on scientific risk assessment to estimate the probable harm to persons and environments resulting from specific types of substances or activities. As such, even when risk managers seek to honestly take into account varying perceptions of the risk in question among different sectors of the public, they are necessarily and properly constrained by the scope and limitations of their scientific assessment in recommending specific courses of action. This is an inescapable part of their duty to protect public health to the best of their ability, taking into account the uncertainties that are always a factor in risk estimates. Mistakes can and will be made in this regard for a whole host of reasons; the public has a right to expect only that the risk management protocols will be sufficiently self-critical and iterative so that serious mistakes are discovered and corrected in the shortest possible time frame.

Risk issue management is fundamentally different from risk management. The most important difference is that risk issues, as they play out in society at large, are not primarily driven by the state of scientific risk assessments. Rather, such assessments are just one of a series of contested domains within the issue. Risk issues are configured by the competing attempts of various stakeholder interests to define or control the course of social action with respect to health and environmental hazards. Issue management refers to the relationship between an organization and its larger social environment, where reigning public policy provides the basic rules of the game; and it is inherently governed by *strategic* considerations as developed by an organization or even a loose collection of individuals (see Table 2.1). All those who wish to become skilled intervenors in risk controversies, such as ENGOs,

Table 2.1

Risk management versus risk issue management

	Risk domain	Risk controversy
Type of responsibility	Risk management	Risk issue management
Type of expertise required	Risk/benefit assessment	Risk communication
Key activities	Hazard characterization	Science explanations
	Exposure assessment	Science/public interface
	Benefits assessment	Science/policy interface
	Uncertainty analysis	Explaining uncertainties
	Options/decision analysis	Stakeholder relations
Orientation of activities	Substantive	Strategic
Principal "language"	Technical/probabilistic	Non-technical/graphics

Source: Leiss 2001: 12.

as well as those who will inevitably be caught up in them, namely, industry and governments, become issue managers (by choice or by default). To do so entails understanding the internal dynamics of risk controversies and seeking to influence them towards some final resolution; in most cases, this will be called the "public interest," although inevitably there will be diverse definitions of what this means in practice. These resolutions may include, for example, introducing a new substance or activity or banning an existing one; changing laws or the regulatory environment; adopting new principles, such as the precautionary approach; introducing changes in business practices; approving a new economic development project or creating wilderness preservation zones; and so on.

To put the main point a bit differently: Whereas risk management seeks to assess and control a *risk domain,* risk issue management responds to a *risk controversy.* A risk domain is a collection of risk factors associated with a specific activity or technology, such as smoking, biotechnology, or radio frequency fields; the risk factors as assessed or perceived by various parties over time, quantitatively and qualitatively, become the subject of risk management decision making, which may lead to risk reduction strategies or other action options. A risk controversy, on the other hand, is a risk domain that becomes the subject of a protracted battle among stakeholder interest groups, the outcome of which may or may not be consistent with any set of decision options preferred by the risk managers (in government or industry) who have official responsibility for the file in question.

The evolution of a risk controversy is determined primarily by the competing strategies of whatever groups or organizations choose to, or are compelled to, enter into it; as mentioned earlier, the objective of these strategies is to steer the outcome of the controversy towards some preferred risk management option. Since by definition a risk controversy is an area of competing visions about where an optimal resolution lies, competence in risk issue management should not be understood as seeking to "control" the outcome. Rather, it means generally being able to compete successfully with other influential stakeholders within the zone of controversy *in a way that is appropriate to the specific positioning of an organization and its lines of accountability within the larger social matrix.* Industry, ENGOs, and governments all have quite diverse positionings in this regard. Governments' positioning is defined primarily by its responsibility to define and defend the "public interest" as such, for example, to seek to be as "inclusive" as possible in relation to the spectrum of social interests.

Risk assessment and management are strictly subordinate activities within the field of risk issues. Sometimes the scientific assessment is definitive for the issue resolution and sometimes it is not. The outcome is often impossible to predict, and in any case depends primarily, in my view, on the specific pathway along which the issue evolves. It is possible that the former (i.e., where the scientific assessment is definitive) predominates over the whole range of issues, although the most high-profile cases may be those that fall into the latter camp. Where broad stakeholder consensus emerges, as it has now with a group of chemicals called persistent organic pollutants, the consensus is the product of a long and tortuous pathway filled with recriminations directed at some parties by others. In other cases (such as the case of Alar and apples or that of saccharin), some of those affected directly by the outcome remain convinced, years or decades later, that the wrong resolution occurred. In still others, such as bovine spongiform encephalitis (BSE), also known as mad cow disease, and British beef or health risks associated with radio frequency fields, the weight of massive and irresolvable uncertainties about the scope of exposure and potential harm hangs like a dark cloud over both the issue and its resolution to date. In all such cases, scientific assessment played or plays some role in the issue evolution, but only as one factor among many. What issue managers most need to know is how scientific assessment will "play" at different times in the evolution of risk issues, especially those (like dioxin or now endocrine modulators) that have a very long life span.

The divide between risk management and risk issue management affects none more seriously than governments. They must do both. Over the past thirty years, coinciding with the rise of the modern specialized field of health and environmental risk management, many governments, including Canada's, have developed outstanding expertise in risk assessment. They are not as good, by and large, at risk management, mainly because they experience difficulties (just as citizens do) in integrating multiple decision inputs of qualitatively different sorts into a coherent framework within and across issue types. These difficulties are compounded by Canada's institutional structure, which both decentralizes and multiplies jurisdictional responsibility over environmental policy issues and centralizes political authority within ministerial hierarchies in which environmental ministries are generally low in the pecking order. Canada's political institutions thus serve to magnify the difficulties of risk management while helping to create an integrity gap in environmental policy.

These and other characteristics of risk issues mean that involvement in them poses distinctive problems and challenges for Canadian organizations that either choose to become engaged with those issues (ENGOs, citizen groups) or are compelled by legal or other mandates to do so (business, governments). On a pragmatic level, the problems include: training and supporting competent personnel, allotting adequate resources, understanding the nature of the issues at all organizational levels, maintaining involvement over long periods of time, and relating fairly and effectively to other stakeholders. The challenges are quite severe; they include reacting responsibly to highly emotional situations, handling large uncertainties in decision-making frameworks, and taking into account the often very different values and perspectives that various stakeholders bring to risk issues.

There is very little in the health and environmental risk management literature explicitly dealing with managerial factors as such. A variable called "perceived managerial (in)competence" has been identified, however; it is defined as the "degree to which the public believes that a hazard implies that similar risks are being managed incompetently." The key finding is stated as follows: "Perceptions of managerial incompetence influence the public's response to a hazard to a degree approaching the scale of the event" (Renn et al. 1992; Burns et al. 1993). Here is a finding, derived from the well-known concept of risk amplification, that is directly relevant to the mission of risk managers. It means that managers have a lever with which they may be able to influence the outcomes of controversies over risks in society, helping to produce better resolutions to those controversies – as long as they are in a position to operate the lever.

Thus, managerial competence is a domain where improvement in risk issue management is or ought to be possible, to the extent that one can overcome Canada's institutional constraints. I believe that at least one primary limitation on doing a better job of working within existing institutional constraints is a faulty self-perception and self-representation of agencies charged with environmental and health risk management. To put the point succinctly, agencies like Environment Canada and the Health Protection Branch of Health Canada have conceived of themselves (over a long period of time) as experts in hazard characterization, and to a lesser extent in risk assessment, whereas what is needed from them above all is expertise in risk issue management. Naturally, those agencies also configured their professional staff complement in line with this conception. The commonest example of these faults can be found in the responses of such agencies over the years to public expressions of concern about hazards that fall under their mandates. All too often, the representatives of those agencies have addressed the hazard characterization (and have done so quite fairly, on the whole) but not the broader level of public concern. Such a focus on the scientific and technical dimensions of environmental risk can serve to amplify the public's perception of an integrity gap between government's (limited) actions to address environmental hazards and the (extensive) magnitude of concerns about them. What Canada needs above all, in order to close this dimension of its environmental integrity gap, is greater competence in addressing the unity of hazard-plus-concern in environmental risk issue management.[17]

Notes

1 A slightly different version of this chapter has appeared in sections of Chapters 1 and 7 in Leiss 2001.
2 According to the conventional scripting, public interest groups want to "tighten" control over environmental impacts, whereas industry wants to "loosen" them.
3 Pollster Doug Miller was reported to have presented the following analysis to environment ministers at the Canadian Council of Ministers of the Environment (CCME) meeting in Whitehorse in October 1995: "Although several polls have shown that the environment is no longer one of Canadians' top concerns, having fallen behind jobs and other economic issues, it remains 'a potent issue just below the radar screen'" (Matas 1995b).
4 As reported by Tom Spears in the *Ottawa Citizen*, 11 March 1998.
5 There is a useful review of developments in an earlier period in an article by Nemetz (1986).
6 Some of the results surfaced in a leaked memo reported in an article by Matas (1995a). The Canadian government has made a policy choice whereby biotechnology applications are assessed under a variety of statutory instruments, depending on the type of application (pharmaceutical, agricultural, forestry, etc.). The public credibility of this fragmented regulatory regime has been challenged (e.g., Saunders 1996).
7 Doern and Conway (1994) do not mention one other source of internal disarray, namely, the strong regional makeup of the department (divided into five regions: Pacific and Yukon, Western and Northern, Ontario, Quebec, and Atlantic). In areas such as pesticides, regional personnel have fought with their own headquarters staff, as well as with other federal and provincial departments, over policy issues.
8 This history is described and analyzed in Skogstad and Kopas 1992. See also Harrison 1994, 180ff. A good study of interjurisdictional confusion is Day and Gamble 1990.
9 For a sampling of coverage on Windy Craggy, see: "BC Copper Mine Faces US Review," *Globe and Mail*, 9 April 1992, B1, and 8 July 1993, B8. On the last acts in Kemano, see Howard 1995 and McInnes 1995.
10 There is a "harmonization" agreement between the federal government and the government of Alberta for conducting environmental impact assessments (EIAs) under the respective legislation of the two parties; see <http://www.ccme.ca/initiatives/environment.html> (16 December 2002). This is a great step forward (or, if what was said earlier in the text is correct, a progressive and beneficial step backward). Now all the public needs to see is an actual EIA carried out, credibly and completely for the first time in Canadian history, on an important proposed project where the provincial government has a stake.
11 For an overview, see Stavins and Whitehead 1992. Economic instruments themselves are a subset of a wider category of forms of "commercial activity which can further the interests of environmental protection" (Grabosky 1994).
12 House of Commons, Standing Committee on Environment and Sustainable Development, *It's about Our Health!* 86.
13 Doern and Conway (1994, 238) comment: "It [DOE] has failed over most of its existence to consider seriously the role of market instruments such as taxes, charges, and so-called tradeable-pollution permits to augment and complement its traditional regulatory urges." Fully *fifteen* years ago, Peter Nemetz (1986, 605) wrote: "The literature is replete with compelling demonstrations of the savings to society inherent in the adoption of market or quasi-market mechanisms for pollution control."
14 There are many individual exceptions to any general rule, including the one just stated. Also, there are major subsystems within Environment Canada as a whole to which the rule does not apply, the best example of which is the Atmospheric Environment Service, wherein general policy-making needs have been minimal (although global climate change issues are changing this context).
15 Environics "Environmental Monitor Survey," December 1993. These data are a bit old, but there are no more recent results, according to Environics (D. Miller, personal communication); however, Environics plans to include questions relevant to this measure in future surveys. D. Miller believes that the lineup in the 1993 chart still represents public thinking on the subject.

16 Over the past ten years, my colleagues and I have collaborated on in-depth studies of the following risk issues: Alar, pentachlorophenol and related fungicides, and electric and magnetic fields (power line frequencies) in Leiss and Chociolko 1994; bovine growth hormone, dioxins and chlorine, "hamburger disease," mad cow disease, PCBs, genetic engineering of food crops (environmental risks), and silicone breast implants in Powell and Leiss 1997; MMT (manganese-based gasoline additive), tobacco, pulp and paper mill effluent, and radio frequency fields (cellular telephone technologies) in Leiss 2001; climate change, and endocrine disruptors (ongoing).

17 In terms of professional complement, this means that such agencies should be staffed primarily by specialists in risk issue management, assisted by risk assessors, and only secondarily by scientists who have been trained in specialized fields of chemistry, biology, toxicology, and so on. In the previous generation, Health Canada's Health Protection Branch, for example, had a large complement of outstanding scientists whose professional advancement was determined in part by success in publishing a stream of original research in peer-reviewed journals.

References

Brown, P.M. 1992. Organizational Design as Policy Instrument: Environment Canada in the Canadian Bureaucracy. In *Canadian Environmental Policy: Ecosystems, Politics and Process,* edited by R. Boardman. Toronto: Oxford University Press.

Burns, W.J., P. Slovic, R.E. Kasperson, J.X. Kasperson, O. Renn, and S. Emani. 1993. Incorporating Structural Models into Research on the Social Amplification of Risk. *Risk Analysis* 13(6): 611-23.

Canada. Commissioner of the Environment and Sustainable Development. 1999. *1999 Report of the Commissioner of the Environment and Sustainable Development.* Ottawa: Minister of Public Works and Government Services. <http://www.oag-bvg.gc.ca/domino/reports.nsf/html/c904me.html> (16 December 2002).

Canada. House of Commons, Standing Committee on Environment and Sustainable Development. 1994. *It's about Our Health!* Ottawa: House of Commons.

Day, J.C., and D.B. Gamble. 1990. Coastal Zone Management in British Columbia. *Coastal Management* 18: 115-41.

Doern, G.B., and T. Conway. 1994. *The Greening of Canada: Federal Institutions and Decisions.* Toronto: University of Toronto Press.

Grabosky, P.N. 1994. Green Markets: Environmental Regulation by the Private Sector. *Law and Policy* 16(4): 419-48.

Harrison, K. 1994. Prospects for Intergovernmental Harmonization in Environmental Policy. In *Canada: The State of the Federation,* edited by D.M. Brown and J. Hiebert. Kingston, ON: Institute of Intergovernmental Relations, Queen's University.

Howard, R. 1995. Largest Project in BC Blocked. *Globe and Mail,* 24 January, A1.

Leiss, W. 2001. *In the Chamber of Risks: Understanding Risk Controversies.* Montreal and Kingston: McGill-Queen's University Press.

Leiss, W., and C. Chociolko. 1994. *Risk and Responsibility.* Montreal and Kingston: McGill-Queen's University Press.

Matas, R. 1995a. MPs Environmental Proposals Planned. *Globe and Mail,* 16 October, A3.

–. 1995b. Environmental Protection a Priority for Canadians. *Globe and Mail,* 24 October, A13.

McInnes, C. 1995. Autopsy Sure to Follow the Killing of Kemano. *Globe and Mail,* 30 January, A5.

Nemetz, P.N. 1986. Federal Environmental Regulation in Canada. *Natural Resources Journal* 26(3): 551-608.

Powell, D., and W. Leiss. 1997. *Mad Cows and Mother's Milk: The Perils of Poor Risk Communication.* Montreal and Kingston: McGill-Queen's University Press.

Renn, O., W. Burns, J.X. Kasperson, R.E. Kasperson, and P. Slovic. 1992. The Social Amplification of Risk: Theoretical Foundations and Empirical Applications. *Journal of Social Issues* 48(4): 137-60.

Robinson, A. 1999. Ottawa, NWT to Pay for Giant Cleanup. *Globe and Mail,* 28 August, B1.
Saunders, D. 1996. Test Potatoes Marketed before Approval. *Globe and Mail,* 6 February, A8.
Skogstad, G., and M. Kopas. 1992. Environmental Policy in a Federal System. In *Canadian Environmental Policy: Ecosystems, Politics and Process,* edited by R. Boardman. Toronto: Oxford University Press.
Stavins, R.N., and B. Whitehead. 1992. Dealing with Pollution: Market-Based Incentives for Environmental Protection. *Environment* 34(7): 7-11.
Vanderzwaag, D., and L. Duncan. 1992. Canada and Environmental Protection. In *Canadian Environmental Policy: Ecosystems, Politics and Process,* edited by R. Boardman. Toronto: Oxford University Press.

3
Canadian Environmental Policy and the Natural Resource Sector: Paradoxical Aspects of the Transition to a Post-Staples Political Economy
Michael Howlett

The Significance of Institutions for Understanding Public Policy Making

The role of structural variables in affecting policy decisions, structuring choice situations, constraining actors, and creating opportunities for action is now well established in the public policy literature (Clark 1998). Although the role played by socio-economic structures and political and cultural institutions in affecting policy outcomes is not a new insight (Hofferbert 1974; Simeon 1976), the manner in which earlier studies of institutional variables have been reconstituted into a reasonably coherent set of theoretical constructs in the guise of various forms of "neo-institutional" analysis is one of the hallmarks of public policy analysis in the past decade. At present, as Hall and Taylor (1996), Kato (1996), and Peters (1999) have argued, at least three currents of neo-institutional analysis coexist somewhat uneasily within the policy literature and inform the insights and analyses of many policy scholars.

It is beyond the scope of this chapter to address the nuances and different epistemological and pedagogical origins of the political, economic, and sociological versions of contemporary neo-institutional social theory. It is useful, however, in the context of sectoral policy studies to examine the general consequences of utilizing such a framework for analyzing public policy making, especially with respect to the overall assumptions and conclusions that can be drawn from these models about the nature of, and factors influencing, policy change and development.

The primary insight of neo-institutionalism, of course, is that institutions matter. That is, as Pontusson (1995) has argued, policy choices are seen not as being made in a random or unintelligible fashion but as the results of structured choice situations in which pre-existing decisions affect current choices, by limiting the range of options from which policy makers can choose.[1] The exact manner in which past decisions constrain choices is assumed to vary by policy sector, given the different trajectories and histories of past decisions in each. Generally speaking, however, neo-institutionalists point to such factors as the manner in which the domestic policy-making situation is linked to the international (Walsh 1994; Hobson and Ramesh 2002); the nature of political institutions for representation and interest intermediation (Hammond and Knott 1999; Scharpf 1994); the configuration of economic, social, cultural, and political resources and actors (Atkinson and Coleman 1989a, 1989b); and the structure of relationships existing between relevant policy actors (Knoke 1987; Laumann and Knoke 1987) as being significant structural factors predetermining certain aspects of policy choices and contents. In this regard, a key concept developed in the neo-institutional literature is that of a *policy regime,* or a relatively long-lasting set of ideas, actors, and political arrangements that structure policy debate and lead to a bias towards policy stability (Eisner 1994; Esping-Andersen 1985; Orren and Skowronek 1998-99).

In examining policy dynamics, then, a central question for neo-institutionalists is not why regimes endure but why they change. That is, as stated above, a principal neo-institutionalist assumption concerning the general nature of policy dynamics is that the propensity and possibility for policy change is limited by the combined structural effects of policy legacies that structure policy debate and policy choices so as to bias these towards the preservation of the status quo (Weir 1992). The emphasis on the key role played by policy legacies in this approach is a variant of the general concept of *path dependency* present in the neo-institutionalist literature – the idea that decisions made at earlier points in policy processes seriously affect the range of choices available to policy makers at later stages (generally, see Mahoney 2000; Pierson 2000; Arthur 1989; Wilsford 1994; Rose 1990). In the case of policy making, earlier decisions are seen to define the interests that actors pursue and create constellations of policy actors ("policy subsystems"), which, in turn, structure policy discourses and processes in such a way as to bias decisions towards the status quo (Hajer 1993; Singer 1990; Schaap and van Twist 1997; Baumgartner and Jones 1993).

This analysis does not rule out the possibility of regime change, of course, but focuses attention on several specific circumstances that can undermine regime structure and membership, and hence undermine policy stability (Castles 2001; Doern 1998). One such circumstance, as authors such as Sabatier (1993), Heclo (1976), and Wilsford (1985) have argued, is when stable regimes ("policy monopolies" or "advocacy coalitions") are faced with exogenous shocks that alter the configuration of actors, ideas, and interests that they contain.

In examining the potential for change and transition in Canadian resource and environmental policy, it helps to keep the elements and findings of neo-institutional policy analysis in mind. That is, a primary focus of the analysis should be upon the potential for shifts in background conditions to alter the nature of existing sectoral policy regimes.

The Political Economy of Canadian Resource and Environmental Policy

A neo-institutionalist analysis examines the way in which different interests are activated and impacted differentially by the embeddedness, or nesting, of policy processes in larger institutional and socio-economic structures. Although the presence of mediating institutions and regimes prevents a simple one-to-one correspondence between changes in background conditions and resulting policies, it is expected that polices will be affected by the nature and configuration of background conditions and structures (Hoberg 1998). In the case of environmental policy, as Hanf and Jansen (1998) argue, the "relevance of environmental quality issues and the agenda of specific problems facing [a] country will be, in some way, related to characteristics" such as

> its geographical location, exposure to imported pollution, peculiar ecological conditions influencing its vulnerability to environmental damage, its socio-economic structure (e.g., degree of industrialization/farming/tourism/urbanization/concentration of population) ... [which] gives a general idea of the type of environmental stresses or pressure to which [a] country (or particular part of it) is exposed and to which its policy process would have to respond. Such a description also suggests the kinds of social and economic interests that are likely to be affected by these problems and the environmental policy measures that are applied. This in turn suggests something of the socio-economic configuration of support or opposition to environmental measures.

Applying this framework to Canadian environmental policy making involves covering ground often referred to as the study of the political economy of Canada (Howlett et al. 1999; Carroll 1988; Marchak 1985; Cammack 1992). For students of Canadian political economy, historical and contemporary Canadian policy regimes are seen as having been constructed on the basis of geographical and demographic characteristics such as Canada's large landmass, northern location, and relatively small population (Innis et al. 1933; Buckley 1958; Watkins 1963). These conditions are argued to have led to the creation of specific types of economic and political structures, often referred to collectively in Canada as a "staples" political economy (Watkins 1977; Clark-Jones 1987).

Central to this mode of understanding Canadian policy making is an analysis of the overall structure and operation of the Canadian economy and the consequences it has for political life. As with neo-institutionalist analyses, in this approach the character of the Canadian economy, its regional differences, its status relative to international economies, and the pace and direction of its evolution are seen as being fundamental to understanding and predicting changes in policy content and policy-making styles (Pontusson 1995; Janoski and Hicks 1994). And, in this context, an apparent shift of the Canadian economy from a "staples" to a "post-staples" variant is seen as arguably the most significant factor affecting trends and developments in a large number of Canadian policy regimes, including resource and environmental policy (Hessing and Howlett 1997).

Staples and Post-Staples Political Economy
The term "staple" refers to a raw or unfinished bulk commodity product that is sold in export markets. Timber, fish, and minerals are staples, usually extracted and sold in external markets without significant amounts of processing and with very little control over the price exported goods receive in foreign markets (Innis 1930, 1933). The significance of having an economy based on exporting unfinished bulk goods lies not only in how it affects policy making by creating continuing issues with resource location and availability but also in how populations in staples-dependent areas react to their continued vulnerability to international market conditions. As Naylor (1972) and others (Hodgetts 1973; Stone 1984; Whalley 1985) have shown, the development of a staples-based economy, for example, triggers government investments in areas such as transportation and communications infrastructure designed to efficiently extract and ship goods to markets, as well as provision of export subsidies and credits designed to facilitate trade.

As most staples-based countries have a monopoly or near-monopoly on the production of only a very few resources or agricultural goods, producers must sell at prices set by international conditions of supply and demand. While international demand for most resources – outside of wartime – has increased at a relatively steady but low rate, world supplies of particular primary products are highly variable. A good harvest, or the discovery of significant new reserves of minerals or oil, or the addition of new production capacity in the fishery or forest products sectors can quickly add to world supplies and drive down world prices until demand slowly catches up and surpasses supplies, resulting in sudden price increases triggering a new investment cycle and subsequent downturn (Anderson 1985; Wilkinson 1985; Webb and Zacher 1988). As Cameron (1986) has noted, these fluctuations in international supplies account for the "boom-and-bust" cycles prevalent in most resource industries and, by implication, most resource-based economies like Canada's, and lead affected populations to press governments to provide a range of social, unemployment, and other types of insurance schemes as well as make large-scale public expenditures in the areas of job creation and employment.

The legacy of a staples political economy raises several overlapping problems for environmental policy making in Canada. In particular, a staples

economy pits economic interests and activities involved in resource harvesting and exploitation against environmental activities such as wilderness, species, and habitat preservation, and these types of conflicts have
been a hallmark of Canada's initial post-1960 experience with environmental regulation (Leiss 1979; Estrin 1975; Schrecker 1989; Swaigen 1980; Jeffrey
1984). In Canada, unlike in many other developed countries concerned
with issues such as urban pollution or toxic wastes, the key environmental
issues of the twentieth century were those related to resource management
involving conflicts over existing or potential resource extraction and transportation activities. These have included the designation and protection of
wilderness areas and other decisions to exempt lands from resource exploitation or related activities, such as pipeline and hydroelectric generation or
transmission; pollution regulation related to natural resource–producing
industries such as smelters or pulp and paper manufacturing facilities; pesticide and herbicide management issues related to intensive silviculture and
other forest industry–related activities; and disputes over harvesting and
extraction methods such as clear-cut logging; wolf, bear, and game hunting; fur trapping; deep-sea dragging; and offshore drilling, among others
(Artibise and Stelter 1998; Doern and Conway 1994; Emond 1985). Throughout this period, Canadian governments attempted to balance support for
resource mega-projects and existing resource industries with environmental protection, creating a policy regime focusing on environmental assessments and mitigation in so doing (Benidickson 1992, 1993; Bowden and
Curtis 1988; Mitchell and Turkheim 1977; Rees 1980).

This regime has not always proven successful in balancing these two interests. Canadian governments forced to choose between resource exploitation and preservation, for example, greatly favoured resource exploitation.
Only, as occurred in the harp seal harvest on the East Coast (Busch 1985;
Wenzel 1991) or rain forest logging on the West Coast (Wilson 1998), if
they were forced by international pressure, including consumer boycotts,
to abandon or reduce harvesting activities did they do so reluctantly. Similarly, park designations were often made only after resources had been removed, or the terms of reference for their establishment were written to
allow continued resource extraction to occur, or, as was frequently the case,
parkland designations represented trade-offs between ecological protection
in one area and increased harvesting and extraction in other, nonpark areas
(McNamee 1993). Many similar examples of the tension between extraction and protection in Canadian environmental policy can also be found.
These range from the preference for the sale of Candu reactors trumping
concerns related to the storage and disposal of nuclear waste, to the overweening concern for employment in Newfoundland that led to the complete collapse of the province's cod fishery in the early 1990s, and the
continuing concerns for employment and investment in the oil and gas

sector that characterize Canada's internal debate on the implementation of the Kyoto Protocol and the reduction of greenhouse gas emissions (Finch 1986; Apostle et al. 1998; Hutchings et al. 1997; Jaccard 2001).

The Fundamentals of a Post-Staples Political Economy

Most observers would agree that historically Canada can be characterized as a staples political economy and that this has had a significant impact on the evolution of Canada's environmental regime and practice. However, there is considerable disagreement over whether this depiction continues to characterize the economy and whether and to what extent it will continue to do so in future years. Earlier debates within the staples school itself centred on whether Canada had emerged as an industrial power in the wake of the wheat boom and manufacturing activities associated with the First World War (Bertram 1963; Richards 1985). While the failure of the manufacturing sector to grow outside of wartime led to the re-emergence of staples analysis in the 1960s and 1970s (Clement and Drache 1978; Williams 1983), current debates focus less on the impact of a transition from primary to secondary activities than on the undeniable growth in service sector employment and production in the post–Second World War era (Clement and Williams 1989; McKenzie 1987; Warton 1969; Grubel and Walker 1989). The idea that the economy has entered a new "post-staples" mode has led to a variety of debates in Canada concerning the consequences for government policy making (Niosi 1991a, 1991b).[2]

As Thomas Hutton (1994) has observed, "mature, advanced" staples economies have several common features that can be combined into a typical political economic profile. These include the substantial depletion of original resource endowments and consequent increasing pressure from "environmental" groups to inhibit traditional modes of resource extraction and stimulate development alternatives; the increasing capital- and technology-intensiveness of resource extraction processes and consequent decrease in employment in the staples sector; the evolution of development from "pure" extraction to increased refining and secondary processing of resource commodities; and the diversification of economic structure with growth in non-staples-related areas such as tourism and local administration and services (Hutton 1994).

While a mature staples political economy may still be characterized as resource-dependent, the economy is more diffused and diversified than in the past. As Hutton (1994) suggests, if this diffusion, diversification, and resource depletion continues, then an economy may make a further transition towards a post-staples one, in which severe pressures on resource sectors coupled with the prospect of even more substantial contractions in the near future lead to an internal reconfiguration of growth and development. Typically this would involve a significant increase in metropolitan shares of population and employment, the emergence of regional economic centres, and the decline of smaller resource-dependent communities.[3] As discussed below, the progression of parts of Canada towards a post-staples political economy both supports and contradicts key suppositions of the traditional staples analysis of Canada's future path of economic development, and has significant consequences for many policy areas, including that of the environment (Howlett 1996a).

The Overall Empirical Situation in Canada: Continued Resource Reliance

The late-twentieth-century development of the Canadian economy reflects an uneven and continuing process of economic diversification away from a classical staples orientation. Each province, however, reflects unique circumstances linked to resource availability, historical settlement patterns, and governance, resulting in an uneven mix of mature and post-staples political economies emerging at the provincial and regional levels.

The provinces of Quebec and Ontario, for example, have experienced the greatest industrialization, becoming the core or metropolis in the Canadian economy. Yet resource extraction continues to play a significant role even in the centre, and mega-projects of recent decades, such as the James Bay project in Quebec and nuclear power generation, fuel processing, and technology development in Ontario, reflect a continuing if shifting base of resource extraction consistent with a transition from a mature to a post-staples political economy. On the other hand, peripheral provinces have faced significant problems in making this transition and remain mired in crisis-ridden mature staples situations. From this perspective, the rapid decline in the Maritime and Newfoundland fisheries, culminating in the complete closure of the cod fishery in 1993, and the rapid declines in the timber industry and the salmon fishery in British Columbia are harbingers of a future transition in these provinces away from their current configurations (Howlett and Brownsey 1996; Tomblin 1995). An analysis of the sectoral structure of the Canadian economy supports the idea that Canada is involved in an uneven transitional process, moving from a mature staples to a post-staples state.

In most industrialized countries, the historical trend has been for economic activity to shift from the primary to the secondary sectors and finally towards the tertiary or service sector (Kuznets 1966). At first glance, this appears to have been the case in Canada over the last century, as the data in Table 3.1 indicate.

As these figures show, both the amount of goods and services produced in different sectors and the numbers of people employed in each sector have shifted decisively towards the tertiary or service sector. Over the last century, in fact, on a national basis, the primary and tertiary sectors have shifted

Table 3.1

Sectoral distribution of Canadian economic activity

	% GNP/GDP		% Employment	
	1880	2002	1891	2000
Primary	43.5	5.9	49.2	4.3
Secondary	18.9	16.9	14.7	15.3
Tertiary	37.6	77.2	36.1	80.2

Source: Statistics Canada, *Gross Domestic Product by Industry* (Catalogue no. 15-001-XIE) (Ottawa: Minister of Supply and Services Canada), available at <http://www.statcan.ca/english/ econoind/gdpm.htm>; Buckley and Urquhart 1965; Statistics Canada, *Labour Force Historical Review* (Catalogue no. 71F0004XCB) (Ottawa: Minister of Supply and Services Canada, 1965), available at <http://www.statcan.ca/english/Pgdb/People/Labour/labor10a.htm>.

locations as sources of economic production. This has been caused primarily by a rapid decline in agricultural activity and employment, which fell from 32 percent of GNP and about 46 percent of employment in 1880-91 to between 3 and 4 percent of each by 1983-84. Most of this economic activity and employment has been picked up in the tertiary sector, and especially in the provision of various kinds of services, which rose from about 37 percent of GNP and employment in 1880 to between 77 and 80 percent, respectively, by the year 2000.

This is not to say, however, that the Canadian economy is no longer reliant on natural resource–based production to generate wealth. Much of Canada's manufacturing base involves processing resource-based commodities such as lumber, pulp and paper, and various mineral and petroleum-based products that are commonly thought of as "primary production" but that the Standard Industrial Classification/North American Industrial Classification (SIC/NAIC) systems used by governments in North America (and elsewhere) categorize as "manufacturing industries."[4] The data in Table 3.2 show that by 2000 about one-fifth of domestic manufacturing capacity was accounted for by the wood, paper and allied, primary metal, non-metallic, and petroleum and coal products industries. An additional $27 billion was produced from electricity generation. In all, almost $100 billion, or about one-eighth of Canada's gross domestic product (GDP) in 2000, was still directly accounted for by these resource-related activities.

Other areas of economic activity are also closely related to these natural resource activities, such as rail, pipeline, highway, and marine transportation of resources and resource products and many resource-related construction projects. In addition, resource activities generate many indirect effects, from banking and financial arrangements associated with large-scale capital projects to the food, cars, and other expenditures made by workers and other consumers earning their salaries in the resource sector. In all, resource

Table 3.2

Resource component of the Canadian economy, December 2000

Economic activity	Component (in billions $1992)	% GDP
Primary SIC/NAIC (agriculture, fisheries, mining, forestry)	45,085	5.98
Manufacturing SIC/NAIC (wood industries, paper and allied, primary metal, non-metallic mineral products, petroleum and coal products)	24,486	3.25
Utilities SIC/NAIC (water, gas, electricity)	26,892	3.57
Total	96,463	12.8

Source: Statistics Canada. *Gross Domestic Product by Industry,* CANSIM Matrix no. 4680, available at <http://datacenter.chass.utoronto.ca/cgi-bin/cansim/cc_html?id=4680>.

and resource-based activities continue to generate as much as fifty cents out of every dollar produced in Canada (Department of Regional Economic Expansion 1977).[5]

Also congruent with a staples analysis is the fact that these resource products continue to be destined for foreign markets. That is, between 25 and 30 percent of Canadian GDP is earned from foreign trade, and exports of resource commodities continue to figure prominently in Canada's trade position. The data in Table 3.3 illustrate the extent to which Canada's positive balance of trade in merchandise items remains reliant on natural resource exports.

Table 3.3

Canadian merchandise trade balances, 2000

Product	Trade balance (in billion $)
Agricultural/fish products	9.0
Energy products	34.7
Forest products	38.3
Industrial goods	-5.8
Machines and equipment	17.1
Automobile products	18.8
Consumer goods	-25.4

Source: EStat, Table 380-0027, Exports and imports of goods and services, annual, available from Statistics Canada: <http://estat.statcan.ca/cgi-win/cnsmcgi.exe?LANG=E&USECII=1&ESTATTheme=1130>.

Table 3.4

Direction of Canadian export trade, 1900-2000, in percentages

	1900	1920	1940	1960	1980	2000
US	38.3	37.4	41.1	55.8	66.2	87.1
UK	52.3	39.4	35.5	17.4	4.0	1.4
Japan	0.1	0.6	2.5	3.4	5.4	2.2
Other Western Europe	2.9	13.8	6.3	8.3	10.7	3.3
Developing and transitional	–	–	–	7.9	11.9	4.2
Other (OECD)	6.4	8.8	14.6	7.2	1.8	1.8

Source: Webb and Zacher 1985, 88-89; EStat, Table 228-0003, Merchandise imports and exports, by major groups and principal trading areas for all countries, annual, available from Statistics Canada: <http://estat.statcan.ca/cgi-win/cnsmcgi.exe?LANG=E&USECII=1&ESTATTheme=1130>.

Forest and energy exports generate almost four times the trade surplus accumulated through automobile production. In fact, in 2000 the total primary processing sector generated an annual trade surplus of over $80 billion. This sum was sufficient to pay for all of the deficits incurred in importing highly manufactured machinery and equipment and consumer goods. This surplus also helped to cover part of the large deficit Canada runs every year on services trade – largely as a result of the large sums flowing out of the country in dividend and interest payments, as well as in areas and activities such as tourism.

And Canada continues to be a price-taker in these areas, now largely under the influence of the prices it receives for its products in the United States, which took almost 90 percent of Canadian exports by the year 2000 (see Table 3.4).

This continued reliance of the Canadian economy on resource extraction, harvesting, and processing puts it at odds with the situation in many other large, modern nation-states, especially the United States, East Asia, and Western Europe, and has very significant consequences for Canadian environmental policy making.

Incomplete "Post-Staplization" and Canadian Environmental Policy Making

There are three significant interrelated aspects of the contemporary structure of the Canadian political economy that affect Canadian environmental policy considerations. First, the fact that the production of wealth in Canada as a whole has been and remains dependent on resource extraction has coloured Canadians' attitudes towards the environment as well as influenced the configuration of actors involved in the formulation of Canadian environmental policy (Blake 2002; Bakvis and Nevitte 1992; more generally, see Altmeyer 1976). Second, not all the regions of the country are dependent on the export of the same resources, nor to the same extent, which has resulted in different patterns of environmental interests and actors in different parts of the country (Brownsey and Howlett 1992, 2000; Wallace 2000). Third, most resource commodities are exported to a single international market, that of the United States. This results in the existence of a small, open economy in Canada subject to international pressures in a variety of areas, including both resource trade issues and those concerned with environmental protection (Whalley 1986; Bennett and Anderson 1988; Dwivedi et al. 2001).

The Detailed Empirical Situation in Canada:
Uneven Development by Province and Region

Canada's regional variations in resources, population, and production have contributed not only to regional differences in wealth and power but also to different demands being placed on governments in different areas of the country (Markey et al. 2000; Statistics Canada 1995).[6] The data in Table 3.5 provide a breakdown of GDP per capita by province and the percentage of the national average that each province enjoys. With the exception of Saskatchewan, the Central and Western provinces enjoy per capita incomes

Table 3.5

Provincial per capita incomes, 2000

Province	Per capita income ($)	National average (%)
Newfoundland	20,576	76
Prince Edward Island	21,176	79
Nova Scotia	23,182	86
New Brunswick	22,664	84
Quebec	24,833	92
Ontario	28,977	108
Manitoba	24,993	93
Saskatchewan	22,756	85
Alberta	29,364	109
British Columbia	25,978	97
Yukon	31,210	116
Northwest Territories	37,426	139
Nunavut	19,319	72
National average	26,767	100

Source: EStat, Table 384-0012, Sources and disposition of personal income, annual, available from Statistics Canada: <http://estat.statcan.ca/cgi-win/cnsmcgi.exe?LANG=E&USECII=1&ESTATTheme=3764>; EStat, Table 051-0001, Estimates of population, by age group and sex, Canada, provinces and territories, annual, available from Statistics Canada: <http://estat.statcan.ca/cgi-win/cnsmcgi.exe?LANG=E&USECII=1&ESTATTheme=3867>.

Table 3.6

Distribution of sectoral economic activity by region, 1999

	% National GDP		
Region	Primary	Secondary	Tertiary
Atlantic	6.2	3.5	6.5
Central	24.2	79.7	60.9
West	69.5	16.8	32.5
	(100.0)	(100.0)	(100.0)

Source: EStat, Table 379-0003, Gross domestic product (GDP) at factor cost, by Standard
Industrial Classification, 1980 (SIC) and province, annual, available from Statistics Canada:
http://estat.statcan.ca/cgi-win/CNSMCGI.exe?Lang=E&CANSIMFile=EStat/English/CII_1_E.htm>.

above 90 percent or greater than the national average, while the provinces
of the Atlantic region have incomes below that percentage of the national
figure. In fact, even with substantial transfer payments included, the average per capita income in Newfoundland is only about three-quarters that of
the highest provinces, Ontario and Alberta (Ip 1991; Horry and Walker 1991).

Although the Canadian economy as a whole never experienced the shift
into manufacturing industries that orthodox theories of economic development envisioned, the economics of Ontario and, to a lesser degree, Quebec
did do so. As the data in Table 3.6 show, by the early 1980s there was a very
uneven distribution of both the overall levels of economic activities and
the sectoral nature of those activities between the regions of the country.
More specifically, the data in Table 3.7 show that provinces such as Newfoundland, Saskatchewan, and Alberta continue to rely heavily on their
natural resources and agricultural sectors to generate economic wealth, as
do the Northwest and Nunavut territories.

As these data indicate, the Western Canadian provinces continue to rely
upon agricultural and natural resource production to generate their wealth.
Central Canada, on the other hand, relies much more upon manufacturing
activities. These data, however, fail to include a significant component of
provincial manufacturing activity – in sectors such as oil refining, smelting,
sawmills, or pulp and paper production – that essentially adds value to resources. Table 3.8 shows the extent to which regional manufacturing was
reliant upon natural resources in the early 1990s; the numbers are high in all
jurisdictions, but especially in the cases of BC and the Atlantic provinces.

This reveals a distinct regional pattern of mature and post-staples political economies in Canada. As the tables illustrate, both the Atlantic region as
a whole and the west, especially British Columbia, have mature staples political economies and remain heavily dependent on resource activities for
their economic well-being. Only Quebec and Ontario have more diversified
post-staples political economies that are not entirely resource-dependent,

Table 3.7

Primary sector component of provincial GDP, 1999

Province	Total GDP	Primary sector components				Total primary	% GDP
		Agriculture	Fishing	Logging	Mining/oil		
Newfoundland	9,432.6	33.2	95.1	75.1	906.8	1,110.2	11.77
Prince Edward Island	2,537.4	122.8	43.9	9.3	8.9	184.9	7.29
Nova Scotia	17,923.7	199	194.7	60.8	219.4	673.9	3.76
New Brunswick	14,187.1	176.5	81.3	217.1	312.3	787.2	5.55
Quebec	158,517.3	2,467.9	44.6	896.7	1,312.8	4722	2.98
Ontario	313,509.8	3,445.9	30.5	431.9	2,138.4	6,046.7	1.93
Manitoba	25,244.0	808.3	12.4	42.1	454.7	1,317.5	5.22
Saskatchewan	23,886.2	1,971.2	3	85.9	3,126.1	5,186.2	21.71
Alberta	92,109.5	3,110.9	1.5	255.7	14,338.1	17,706.2	19.22
British Columbia	91,965.1	1,062.3	214	2,524.3	2,328.2	6,128.8	6.66
Yukon	970.5	1.3	0.1	0.2	57.4	59	6.08
Northwest Territories	1,828.1	0	1.3	0	375.8	377.1	20.63
Nunavut	670.2	0	0.6	0	121.2	121.8	18.17
Total	752,781.5						

Source: EStat, Table 379-0003, Gross domestic product (GDP) at factor cost, by Standard Industrial Classification, 1980 (SIC) and province, annual, available from Statistics Canada: <http://estat.statcan.ca/cgi-win/cnsmcgi.exe?LANG=E&USECII=1&ESTATTheme=3764>.

Table 3.8

Percent regional resource-based manufacturing activity, 1999

Region	%
Atlantic	51.5
Quebec	29.9
Ontario	21.4
Prairies	33.3
BC	52.3
Canada	27.8

Source: EStat, Table 379-0003, Gross domestic product (GDP) at factor cost, by Standard Industrial Classification, 1980 (SIC) and province, annual, available from Statistics Canada: <http://estat.statcan.ca/cgi-win/cnsmcgi.exe?LANG=E&USECII=1&ESTATTheme=3764>.

although even in those provinces substantial economic activity is still directly associated with resource extraction and processing.[7] Overall, this generates a national pattern of an uneven transition towards post-staplization.

This uneven pattern of development has been exacerbated by the institutionalization of free trade on a continental basis under the terms of the 1989 Canada-US Free Trade Agreement (FTA) and its successor, the 1993 North American Free Trade Agreement (NAFTA). These agreements helped lock in and accelerate many existing economic trends in Canada (Cadsby and Woodside 1993; see also Grinspun and Cameron 1993) and augmented many staples-era political relationships (Hurtig 1991; Cameron 1988; Harris 1998).[8] NAFTA has done this by both shaping and intensifying the competitive context in which rural resource extraction and production are undertaken. Although it has also increased the potential for intensified urban-based tertiary sector activities by facilitating enhanced trade in services, the increased demand for resources means additional pressure for more intensive extraction and harvesting. This is only partially offset by the creation of new North America–wide environmental institutions (Johnson and Beaulieu 1996).

Social and Political Implications of Uneven Development

This uneven regional pattern of mature and post-staples development is quite different from that associated with the earlier epoch of a fully fledged national staples political economy. In that system, it was expected that policy making would be affected by the existence of a specific type of nested "metropolis-hinterland" relationship between the centre and periphery in Canada and abroad. On one level, Canada existed as a resource supplier to the fully developed manufacturing centres in the US and Great Britain. On another level, within Canada, the Atlantic and Western provinces existed as peripheral to activities in Central Canada, first Quebec and then later Ontario, which served as the financial, cultural, and manufacturing centre for the rest of the country (Naylor 1972; Watkins 1977; Sacouman 1981). And, on a third level, rural areas outside major metropolitan centres within provinces and regions of the country served as resource producers for those urban entrepôt centres (Lucas 1971; Himmelfarb 1982). While the interests of these regions clashed in the sense that each wished to take full advantage of the position it held in these trade and production relationships, in a more general sense, they were united in their wish to maximize resource extraction, harvesting, and processing in the pursuit of wealth.

In those areas of the country with mature staples political economies, these relationships still exist. In the post-staples areas, however, many of these relationships have been altered. Hence, for example, the Central Canadian automobile industry is now thoroughly integrated into a continental system of production and is much more than a supplier of products to a captive domestic market, as it was in the classic staple state (Holmes 1996). And even though they continue to rely on resource exports, provinces outside of Central Canada have developed their own niches in the national and continental marketplace in service areas such as telemarketing, software development, filmmaking, insurance, and research and development.[9] In many provinces, this has resulted in a new form of internal urban-rural relations in which the two areas actually have very little to do with each other, as staples are exported directly from the province or region without having to be "processed" in the metropolis, while metropolitan areas themselves are increasingly integrated with other such areas on a national, continental, or international level and much less so with their immediately neighbouring non-urban areas.[10]

Implications of Uneven Structural Change for Canadian Environmental Policy

The legacy of a staples political economy for Canadian environmental policy is readily apparent in both a positive and a negative sense. On the one hand, as mentioned above, the existence of a staples political economy has meant that, generally speaking, land and animals have been viewed as objects to be exploited and ecological values and considerations have largely taken a backseat to the attainment of economic objectives linked to their harvesting or extraction. On the other hand, the lack of appropriate climatic conditions for large-scale agricultural production and reliance on other resources for economic development has meant that much land in Canada remains relatively untouched by humans, unlike the situation in many other parts of North America or the world, which have been completely transformed by farming. This has meant that significant ecosystem diversity and biodiversity protection measures remain a very real possibility in Canada

(Janicke and Jorgens 1997; Janicke and Weidner 1997). The existence of a hinterland-based staples political economy has also meant that Canada has avoided, or postponed, many of the sharp confrontations over issues such as urban pollution and degradation of the urban environment that have been the features of environmental policy in smaller or more populous countries.[11]

As long as resource extraction activities maintained a good deal of the labour force and generated much of the country's wealth, efforts at environmental protection or mitigation in Canada always began with the knowledge that resource harvesting or extraction enjoyed a potent blend of private (business and labour) and public (government) support (Schrecker 1985, 1984; Nord and Weller 1983). As a long-standing democracy, Canada has seen governments having to tread carefully in this policy area lest their environmental policy activities led to economic disruptions and electoral disfavour (Lyon 1992; Rabe 1997; see also Harrison 1999). Generally speaking, as a result of these geographic, demographic, economic, and political conditions, Canada developed an environmental policy regime that shared many characteristics with those of other countries with similar political economies, such as Norway, Sweden, Australia, or New Zealand.[12] As in some of these other countries, however, in Canada the growth of an urban-based tertiary sector associated with the transition to a post-staples state in some parts of the country has undermined elements of the existing environmental policy regime, altering public and regulatory priorities and creating a foundation for the emergence of alternative policies (Blake 1997, 2002; Clarkson 2001).

That is, in some areas of the country, especially in Central Canada, an increasingly large proportion of the population is employed in activities that are much less directly dependent on resource extraction than in the past. This has made them generally more supportive of environmental initiatives in areas such as wildlife and ecosystem conservation than more directly resource-dependent population groups in mature staples areas such as rural Western and Atlantic Canada (Blake 2002; Langlois 2001). The steadily increasing urban service sector component of the Canadian population can be expected to continue to support a wide range of general environmental initiatives, from biodiversity and habitat protection to fighting global warming, as well as more specific items related to the quality of urban life, such as smog, congestion, housing, and health-related issues (Blake et al. 1996).[13]

Conclusion: The Political Paradox of Post-Staples Canadian Environmental Policy

A variety of factors influence the adoption of Canadian environmental policy, from the nature of political institutions and political-administrative behaviour (Howlett 1994; Holland et al. 1996; Rabe 1997) to policy learning and lesson drawing from the experience of close neighbouring countries (Hoberg 1991) and the continued pressures for harmonization caused by international agreements and treaties (Toner and Conway 1996; Howlett 1996b). As neo-institutionalist policy analysts have argued, however, a very important determinant of public policy relates to the general physical, demographic, social, economic, and political structure of a country – in Canada, often referred to as a nation's "political economy."

Sectoral shifts in the structure of the Canadian economy, including a shift to services, tertiarization, and significant industrial expansion in regional centres has led to an uneven pattern of the internal reconfiguration of growth and development. A significant increase in metropolitan shares of population and employment and the decline of smaller resource-dependent communities has accompanied this shift (Coffey 1996; Coffey and Polese 1988). This has resulted in some shifts from resource-intensive production processes to more environmentally benign ones – even in resource-based industries, such as ecotourism – but this has not been uniform across the country (Janicke et al. 1993; Hutton 1994).[14]

Although incomplete, changes in industrial structure and labour markets have altered the nature of environmental concerns, the level of popular support for particular initiatives, and the interest in environmental issues among the Canadian public (Langlois 2001; Blake et al. 1996-97, 1997, 2002; Salazar and Alper 1999). In mature staples resource-based regions and rural areas, for example, support for basic environmental values such as wilderness protection declines when these designations are seen as contributing to the continuing decline of the traditional resource industries (Reed 1995; Donihee 2000). In post-staples regions and urban areas, on the other hand, there is much less opposition to activities such as wilderness park creation, which affect those areas much less directly than they do rural ones. Individuals in urban areas, however, are less likely to rank environmental issues as highly as issues such as crime or housing in terms of political salience, and may focus exclusively on high-level global or strictly local environmental issues in their thinking and activities (Grant et al. 1999; Roe 2000). Nevertheless, in urban areas quality-of-life issues such as air and water quality, urban green space, and urban sprawling land use do tend to rank highly among areas of public concern (Dunlap et al. 2001; Kahn 2000, 2002).[15]

Continued economic restructuring and associated population movement and settlement patterns in Canada in the near future are therefore likely to have a somewhat paradoxical impact on public opinion and government activism in the environmental sector. That is, overall, given the general decline of rural areas and the increase in urban populations over the past decades, diffuse general support for environmental issues is likely to increase at the same time that rural opposition to specific projects and proposals will intensify. This paradox poses a range of challenges to government policy makers seeking to manage economic development and mitigate environmental damage while retaining popular support (Baetz and Tanguay 1998).

Given this analysis, it is possible to develop two scenarios for the short- to medium-term future of Canadian resource and environmental policy in light of the contradictions and paradoxes of contemporary Canadian economic and political developments outlined above. In the pessimistic scenario, while the need for increased diversification and especially the growth of the tertiary sector implies the creation of more jobs with proportionally less direct resource reliance and negative impact, the creation of alternative employment is subject to global competition and may occur only very slowly, if at all. Stuck in a "mature staples trap," Canadian governments at both the federal and provincial levels may be forced to reinforce existing economic policy measures promoting increased resource extraction, and may fail to implement a new generation of more environmental protectionist policies, exacerbating the disjunction or "integrity gap" between ecological rhetoric on the one hand and non-ecological government actions and activities on the other (Kennett 2000; generally, see Howlett 2001a).[16]

A more optimistic scenario incorporates the potential for post-staplization to continue spreading and affecting environmental attitudes and behaviour throughout Canada, with a significant impact on future policy orientation and content (Howlett 2001b). The results of stronger environmental policies may, in a virtuous circle, in turn directly or indirectly foster the growth of emerging service and production-based industries. As Hutton (1995) suggests, a variety of environmentally benign environmental industries and services can develop in rural areas, related to resource restoration and recycling activities, such as fisheries enhancement, reforestation, and mine reclamation. Value-added resource industries and products such as custom wood products can also develop, along with the development of new products from industrial residues, such as fibreboard. And the potential exists for the development of alternative energy sources, such as the use of hydrogen fuel cells for public transit, as well as the further development of tourism and the convention industry (Hutton 1995). In this scenario, a more fully post-staples Canada moves slowly towards the situation in many other Western countries wherein environmental issues become more general and urban in nature and the gap between government rhetoric and policy action becomes less pronounced (Jordan et al. 1999).

While a detailed assessment of these scenarios awaits another day, both are derived from a neo-institutional perspective on the public policy process. That is, the analysis presented here underlines the manner in which conceiving of basic policy processes as being embedded in larger socio-economic or political economic structures allows some contemplation of how changes and alterations in those systems can reverberate throughout the policy process. As this discussion has shown, the manner in which such changes undermine existing policy regimes permits us to contemplate possible future resource and environmental policy configurations, both positive and negative, and helps us to better understand some aspects of the integrity gap in Canadian environmental policy formulation and implementation.

Notes

1 On the origins of this insight, see March and Olsen 1989, 1995, and Peters 1992.
2 Many of these discussions centre on the role of technology in driving service sector development.
3 Adapted from Hutton 1994.
4 On the origins and development of the concept of economic sectors and their incorporation into the UN SIC system, see Fisher 1966. On the strengths and weaknesses of this approach, see Singelmann 1978.
5 On the methods used to calculate indirect multipliers in the resource sector, see Department of Regional Economic Expansion 1977.
6 About 63 percent of Canadian economic activity takes place in the two Central Canadian provinces of Quebec and Ontario. The four provinces of Atlantic Canada account for only 6 percent of Canadian production, while the four Western provinces account for about 30 percent. See Statistics Canada 1995.
7 A large percentage of Central Canadian manufacturing is linked to an increase that has occurred in a single sector, that of automobiles, which accounted for about 23 percent of total Canadian trade in 2000. This sector is covered by special trading arrangements, including the Canada-US Auto Pact, the Canada-US Free Trade Agreement, and the North American Free Trade Agreement (NAFTA). Although significant in terms of exports, under the terms of the Auto Pact, large numbers of assembled automobiles and auto parts are also imported into the country.
8 While NAFTA formally provides only a continental linkage among trading partners, it is viewed by many to be responsible for the "deindustrialization of Canada," as some previously protected manufacturing jobs have been exported, and job creation in some traditional industrial sectors has tended to lag behind job losses. This is at least partly a function of Canada's harsh climate and diffuse population, which contribute to higher energy and transportation costs, which in turn restrict the competitive capabilities of Canadian manufacturers of standard consumer and producer goods. Regardless of its origins, however, the effect of such movements is to increase the reliance of the economy on primary (resource) and tertiary (service) sector activities, along with specialized, niche manufacturing.
9 Generally, see Industry Canada, Industrial Analysis Centre 2001. On specific initiatives in various provinces, see Brownsey and Howlett 2000. More generally, see Niosi 1998 and Clement et al. 1999.
10 On this phenomenon as it has occurred in British Columbia, see Barnes and Hayter 1992; Hutton 1997; Ley and Hutton 1987; and Davis 1993.
11 See the European case studies contained in Hanf and Jansen 1998 and Lafferty and Meadowcroft 1996.
12 Generally, see Radice 2000. For specific case studies, see Jansen and Mydske 1998 and Lundqvist 1998.
13 On the increased attention paid to non-resource-related environmental issues in Canada, see the reports of the Commissioner of the Environment and Sustainable Development, especially the 2000 annual report on smog, available at <http://www.oag-bvg.gc.ca/domino/reports.nsf/html/c000ce.html> (16 December 2002).
14 These trends should not be overexaggerated, though (see Trainer 2001).
15 On the US experience in these areas, see Dunlap et al. 2001 and Kahn 2000, 2002.
16 Harrison (1999) suggests that this is already occurring.

References

Altmeyer, G. 1976. Three Ideas of Nature in Canada, 1893-1914. *Journal of Canadian Studies* 11: 21-36.

Anderson, F.J. 1985. *Natural Resources in Canada.* Toronto: Methuen.

Apostle, R., G. Barrett, P. Holm, S. Jentoft, L. Mazany, B. McCay, and K. Mikalsen. 1998. *Community, State and Market on the North Atlantic Rim: Challenges to Modernity in the Fisheries.* Toronto: University of Toronto Press.

Arthur, W.B. 1989. Competing Technologies, Increasing Returns, and Lock-in by Historical Events. *Economic Journal* 99: 116-31.

Artibise, A.F.J., and G.A. Stelter. 1998. Conservation Planning and Urban Planning: The Canadian Commission of Conservation in Historical Perspective. In *Planning for Conservation,* edited by R. Kain. New York: St. Martin's Press.

Atkinson, M., and W. Coleman. 1989a. *The State, Business, and Industrial Change in Canada.* Toronto: University of Toronto Press.

–. 1989b. Strong States and Weak States: Sectoral Policy Networks in Advanced Capitalist Economies. *British Journal of Political Science* 19(1): 47-67.

Baetz, M.C., and A.B. Tanguay. 1998. Damned if You Do, Damned if You Don't: Government and the Conundrum of Consultation in the Environmental Sector. *Canadian Public Administration* 41(3): 395-418.

Bakvis, H., and N. Nevitte. 1992. The Greening of the Canadian Electorate: Environmentalism, Ideology, and Partisanship. In *Canadian Environmental Policy: Ecosystems, Politics and Process,* edited by R. Boardman. Toronto: Oxford University Press.

Barnes, T.J., and R. Hayter. 1992. Economic Restructuring, Local Development and Resource Towns: Forest Communities in Coastal British Columbia. *Regional Studies* 26: 647-63.

Baumgartner, F.R., and B.D. Jones. 1993. *Agendas and Instability in American Politics.* Chicago: University of Chicago Press.

Benidickson, J. 1992. Environmental Law Survey: Part I. *Ottawa Law Review* 24(3): 734-811.

–. 1993. Environmental Law Survey: Part II. *Ottawa Law Review* 25(1): 123-54.

Bennett, T., and D.L. Anderson. 1988. *An Inter-Sectoral Study of Canada's Resource Industries.* Technical Paper No. 8. Kingston, ON: Centre for Resource Studies, Queen's University.

Bertram, G.W. 1963. Economic Growth and Canadian Industry, 1870-1915: The Staple Model and the Take-off Hypothesis. *Canadian Journal of Economics and Political Science* 29(2): 162-84.

Blake, D.E., N. Guppy, and P. Urmetzer. 1996. *Being Green in BC: Public Attitudes towards Environmental Issues.* Vancouver: Fraser Basin Eco-Research Study.

–. 1996-97. Being Green in BC: Public Attitudes towards Environmental Issues. *BC Studies* 112: 41-61.

–. 1997. Canadian Public Opinion and Environmental Action: Evidence from British Columbia. *Canadian Journal of Political Science* 30(3): 451-72.

–. 2002. Personal Values and Environmental Attitudes. In *Citizen Politics: Research and Theory in Canadian Political Behaviour,* edited by J. Everitt and B. O'Neill. Toronto: Oxford University Press.

Bowden, M.A., and F. Curtis. 1988. Federal EIA in Canada: EARP as an Evolving Process. *Environmental Impact Assessment Review* 8(1): 97-106.

Brownsey, K., and M. Howlett, eds. 1992. *The Provincial State: Politics in Canada's Provinces and Territories.* Toronto: Copp Clark Pitman.

–, eds. 2000. *The Provincial State in Canada: Politics in the Provinces and Territories.* Peterborough, ON: Broadview Press.

Buckley, K. 1958. The Role of Staple Industries in Canadian Economic Development. *Journal of Economic History* 18: 439-50.

Buckley, K.A.H., and M.C. Urquhart. 1965. *Historical Statistics of Canada.* Toronto: Macmillan.

Busch, B.C. 1985. *The War against the Seals: A History of the North American Seal Fishery.* Montreal and Kingston: McGill-Queen's University Press.

Cadsby, C.B., and K. Woodside. 1993. The Effects of the North American Free Trade Agreement on the Canada–United States Trade Relationship. *Canadian Public Policy* 19(4): 450-62.

Cameron, D. 1988. *The Free Trade Deal.* Toronto: James Lorimer.

Cameron, D.R. 1986. The Growth of Government Spending: The Canadian Experience in Comparative Perspective. In *State and Society,* edited by K. Banting. Toronto: University of Toronto Press.

Cammack, P. 1992. The New Institutionalism: Predatory Rule, Institutional Persistence, and Macrosocial Change. *Economy and Society* 21(4): 397-429.

Canada. Commissioner of the Environment and Sustainable Development. 2000. *The Commissioner's Observations – 2000.* <http://www.oag-bvg.gc.ca/domino/reports.nsf/html/c000ce.html> (18 January 2003).

Canada. Department of Regional Economic Expansion. 1977. *Single-Sector Communities.* Ottawa: Department of Regional Economic Expansion.

Carroll, W. 1988. The Political Economy of Canada. In *Understanding Canadian Society,* edited by J. Curtis and L. Tepperman. Toronto: McGraw-Hill Ryerson.

Castles, S. 2001. Studying Social Transformation. *International Political Science Review* 22(1): 13-32.

Clark, W.R. 1998. Agents and Structures: Two Views of Preferences, Two Views of Institutions. *International Studies Quarterly* 42: 245-70.

Clark-Jones, M. 1987. *A Staple State: Canadian Industrial Resources in Cold War.* Toronto: University of Toronto Press.

Clarkson, S. 2001. The Multi-Level State: Canada in the Semi-Periphery of Both Continentalism and Globalization. *Review of International Political Economy* 8(3): 501-27.

Clement, N.C., G. del Castillo Vera, J. Gerber, W.A. Kerr, A.J. MacFadyen, S. Shedd, E. Zepeda, D. Alarcün. 1999. *North American Economic Integration: Theory and Practice.* Cheltenham, UK: Edward Elgar.

Clement, W., and D. Drache. 1978. *A Practical Guide to Canadian Political Economy.* Toronto: James Lorimer.

Clement, W., and G. Williams, eds. 1989. *The New Canadian Political Economy.* Montreal and Kingston: McGill-Queen's University Press.

Coffey, W.J. 1996. The Role and Location of Service Activities in the Canadian Space Economy. In *Canada and the Global Economy: The Geography of Structural and Technological Change,* edited by J.N.H. Britton. Montreal and Kingston: McGill-Queen's University Press.

Coffey, W.J., and M. Polese. 1988. Locational Shifts in Canadian Employment 1971-1981. *Canadian Geographer* 32(3): 248-56.

Davis, C.H. 1993. Is the Metropolitan Vancouver Economy Uncoupling from the Rest of the Province? *BC Studies* 98: 3-19.

Doern, G.B. 1998. The Interplay among Regimes: Mapping Regulatory Institutions in the United Kingdom, the United States, and Canada. In *Changing Regulatory Institutions in Britain and North America,* edited by G.B. Doern and S. Wilks. Toronto: University of Toronto Press.

Doern, G.B, and T. Conway. 1994. *The Greening of Canada: Federal Institutions and Decisions.* Toronto: University of Toronto Press.

Donihee, J. 2000. The New Species at Risk Act and Resource Development. *Resources* 70: 1-7.

Dunlap, R.E., C. Xiao, and A.M. McCright. 2001. Politics and Environment in America: Partisan and Ideological Cleavages in Public Support for Environmentalism. *Environmental Politics* 10(4): 23-48.

Dwivedi, O.P., P. Kyba, P.J. Stoett, and R. Tiessen. 2001. *Sustainable Development and Canada: National and International Perspectives.* Peterborough, ON: Broadview Press.

Eisner, M.A. 1994. Discovering Patterns in Regulatory History: Continuity, Change and Regulatory Regimes. *Journal of Policy History* 6(2): 157-87.

Emond, D.P. 1985. Environmental Law and Policy: A Retrospective Examination of the Canadian Experience. In *Consumer Protection, Environmental Law and Corporate Power,* edited by I. Bernier and A. Lajoie. Toronto: University of Toronto Press.

Esping-Andersen, G. 1985. Power and Distributional Regimes. *Politics and Society* 14(2): 223-56.

Estrin, D. 1975. Environmental Law. *Ottawa Law Review* 7(2): 397-449.

Finch, R. 1986. *Exporting Danger: A History of the Canadian Nuclear Energy Export Programme.* Montreal: Black Rose Books.

Fisher, A.G.B. 1966. *The Clash of Progress and Security.* New York: A.M. Kelley.

Grant, W., A. Perl, and P. Knoepfel, eds. 1999. *The Politics of Improving Urban Air Quality.* Cheltenham, UK: Edward Elgar.

Grinspun, R., and M.A. Cameron, eds. 1993. *The Political Economy of North American Free Trade.* Montreal and Kingston: McGill-Queen's University Press.

Grubel, H.G., and M.A. Walker. 1989. *Service Industry Growth: Causes and Effects.* Vancouver: Fraser Institute.

Hajer, M.A. 1993. Discourse Coalitions and the Institutionalization of Practice: The Case of Acid Rain in Britain. In *The Argumentative Turn in Policy Analysis and Planning,* edited by F. Fischer and J. Forester. Durham, NC: Duke University Press.

Hall, P.A., and R.C.R. Taylor. 1996. Political Science and the Three New Institutionalisms. *Political Studies* 44: 936-57.

Hammond, T.H., and J.H. Knott. 1999. Political Institutions, Public Management, and Policy Choice. *Journal of Public Administration Research and Theory* 9(1): 33-85.

Hanf, K., and A.I. Jansen. 1998. Environmental Policy – The Outcome of Strategic Action and Institutional Characteristics. In *Governance and Environment in Western Europe,* edited by K. Hanf and A.I. Jansen. New York: Longman.

Harris, R. 1998. Competitiveness and Complex Economic Integration in the North American Region. In *Innovation Systems in a Global Context: The North American Experience,* edited by R. Anderson, T. Cohn, J. Day, M. Howlett, and C. Murray. Montreal and Kingston: McGill-Queen's University Press.

Harrison, K. 1999. Retreat from Regulation: The Evolution of the Canadian Environmental Regulatory Regime. In *Changing the Rules: Canadian Regulatory Regimes and Institutions,* edited by G.B. Doern, M.M. Hill, M.J. Prince, and R.J. Schultz. Toronto: University of Toronto Press.

Heclo, H. 1976. Conclusion: Policy Dynamics. In *The Dynamics of Public Policy: A Comparative Analysis,* edited by R. Rose. London: Sage.

Hessing, M., and M. Howlett. 1997. *Canadian Natural Resource and Environmental Policy.* Vancouver: UBC Press.

Himmelfarb, A. 1982. The Social Characteristics of One-Industry Towns in Canada. In *Little Communities and Big Industries,* edited by R.T. Bowles. Toronto: Butterworth.

Hoberg, G. 1991. Sleeping with an Elephant: The American Influence on Canadian Environmental Regulation. *Journal of Public Policy* 11(1): 107-31.

–. 1998. Distinguishing Learning from Other Sources of Policy Change: The Case of Forestry in the Pacific Northwest. Paper presented to the annual meeting of the American Political Science Association, 3-6 September 1998, Boston, MA.

Hobson, J., and M. Ramesh. 2002. Globalisation Makes of States What States Make of It: Between Agency and Structure in the State/Globalisation Debate. *New Political Economy* 7(1): 5-22.

Hodgetts, J.E. 1973. *The Canadian Public Service.* Toronto: University of Toronto Press.

Hofferbert, R.I. 1974. *The Study of Public Policy.* Indianapolis, IN: Bobbs-Merrill.

Holland, K.M., F.L. Morton, and B. Galligan, eds. 1996. *Federalism and the Environment: Environmental Policymaking in Australia, Canada, and the United States.* Westport, CT: Greenwood Press.

Holmes, J. 1996. Restructuring in a Continental Production System. In *Canada and the Global Economy: The Geography of Structural and Technological Change,* edited by N.H. Britton. Montreal and Kingston: McGill-Queen's University Press.

Horry, I.D., and M.A. Walker. 1991. *Government Spending Facts.* Vancouver: Fraser Institute.

Howlett, M. 1994. The Judicialization of Canadian Environmental Policy 1980-1990: A Test of the Canada-US Convergence Hypothesis. *Canadian Journal of Political Science* 27(1): 99-127.

–. 1996a. De-mythologizing Provincial Political Economies: The Development of Service Sectors in the Provinces. In *Provinces: Canadian Provincial Politics,* edited by C. Dunn. Peterborough, ON: Broadview Press.

–. 1996b. Sustainable Development: Environmental Policy. In *Canadian Public Policy: Globalization and Political Parties,* edited by A. Johnson and A. Stritch. Toronto: Copp Clark Longman.

–. 2001a. The Implementation Gap: Rhetoric and Reality in Canadian Natural Resource and Environmental Policy. *Journal of Canadian Studies* 36(3): 159-70.

–. 2001b. Complex Network Management and the Governance of the Environment: Prospects for Policy Change and Policy Stability over the Long Term. In *Governing the Environment: Persistent Challenges, Uncertain Innovations,* edited by E. Parson. Toronto: University of Toronto Press.

Howlett, M., and K. Brownsey. 1996. From Timber to Tourism: The Political Economy of British Columbia. In *Politics, Policy, and Government in British Columbia,* edited by R.K. Carty. Vancouver: UBC Press.

Howlett, M., A. Netherton, and M. Ramesh. 1999. *The Political Economy of Canada: An Introduction.* Toronto: Oxford University Press.

Hurtig, M. 1991. *The Betrayal of Canada.* Toronto: Stoddart.

Hutchings, J.A., C. Waters, and R.L. Haedrich. 1997. Is Scientific Inquiry Incompatible with Government Information Control? *Canadian Journal of Fisheries and Aquatic Science* 54: 1198-1210.

Hutton, T.A. 1994. *Visions of a "Post-Staples" Economy: Structural Change and Adjustment Issues in British Columbia.* Vancouver: Centre for Human Settlements, University of British Columbia.

–. 1995. *Economic Implications of Environmental Enhancement: A Review and Interpretation of the Contemporary Literature.* Report prepared for the British Columbia Ministry of Environment, Lands and Parks. Vancouver: Centre for Human Settlements, University of British Columbia.

–. 1997. The Innisian Core-Periphery Revisited: Vancouver's Changing Relationship with British Columbia's Staple Economy. *BC Studies* 113: 69-100.

Industry Canada, Industrial Analysis Centre. 2001. *Identification and Preliminary Analysis of the Forces and Pressures Shaping the Canadian Economy – Overview Document to Support Industrial Analysis Research Final Report.* Ottawa: Industry Canada.

Innis, H.A. 1930. *The Fur Trade in Canada.* Toronto: University of Toronto Press.

–. 1933. *Problems of Staple Production in Canada.* Toronto: Ryerson.

Ip, I. 1991. *An Overview of Provincial Government Finance.* In *Provincial Public Finance,* edited by M. McMillan. Toronto: Canadian Tax Foundation.

Jaccard, M. 2001. Costing Greenhouse Gas Abatement: Canada's Technological and Behavioural Potential. *Isuma* 2(4): 45-52.

Janicke, M., and H. Jorgens. 1997. *National Environmental Policy Plans and Long-Term Sustainable Development Strategies: Learning from International Experiences.* Berlin: Freie Universität Berlin Forschungsstelle für Umweltpolitik.

Janicke, M., H. Monch, and M. Binder. 1993. Ecological Aspects of Structural Change. *Intereconomics* 28(4): 159-69.

Janicke, M., and H. Weidner. 1997. *National Environmental Policies: A Comparative Study of Capacity Building.* Berlin: Springer.

Janoski, T., and A.M. Hicks, eds. 1994. *The Comparative Political Economy of the Welfare State.* Cambridge: Cambridge University Press.

Jansen, A.I., and P.K. Mydske. 1998. Norway: Balancing Environmental Quality and Interest in Oil. In *Governance and Environment in Western Europe,* edited by K. Hanf and A.I. Jansen. New York: Longman.

Jeffrey, M.I. 1984. Environmental Enforcement and Regulation in the 1980s: *Regina* v. *Sault Ste. Marie* Revisited. *Queen's Law Journal* 10(1): 43-70.

Johnson, P.M., and A. Beaulieu. 1996. *The Environment and NAFTA: Understanding and Implementing the New Continental Law.* Washington, DC: Island Press.

Jordan, A., R. Brouwer, and E. Noble. 1999. Innovative and Responsive? A Longitudinal Analysis of the Speed of EU Environmental Policy-Making, 1967-97. *Journal of European Public Policy* 6(3): 376-98.

Kahn, M.E. 2000. The Environmental Impact of Suburbanization. *Journal of Policy Analysis and Management* 19(4): 569-86.

–. 2002. Demographic Change and the Demand for Environmental Regulation. *Journal of Policy Analysis and Management* 21(1): 45-62.

Kato, J. 1996. Review Article: Institutions and Rationality in Politics – Three Varieties of Neo-Institutionalists. *British Journal of Political Science* 26: 553-82.

Kennett, S.A. 2000. Meeting the Intergovernmental Challenge of Environmental Assessment. In *Managing the Environmental Union: Intergovernmental Relations and Environmental Policy in Canada*, edited by P.C. Fafard and K. Harrison. Kingston, ON: Institute of Intergovernmental Relations, Queen's University.

Knoke, D. 1987. *Political Networks: The Structural Perspective*. Cambridge: Cambridge University Press.

Kuznets, S.S. 1966. *Modern Economic Growth: Rate, Structure and Spread*. New Haven, CT: Yale University Press.

Lafferty, W.M., and J. Meadowcroft, eds. 1996. *Democracy and the Environment: Problems and Prospects*. Cheltenham, UK: Edward Elgar.

Langlois, S. 2001. The Contemporary Canadian State: Redefining a Social and Political Union. In *Leviathan Transformed: Seven National States in the New Century*, edited by T. Caplow. Montreal and Kingston: McGill-Queen's University Press.

Laumann, E.O., and D. Knoke. 1987. *The Organizational State: Social Choice in National Policy Domains*. Madison: University of Wisconsin Press.

Leiss, W., ed. 1979. *Ecology versus Politics in Canada*. Toronto: University of Toronto Press.

Ley, D.F., and T.A. Hutton. 1987. Vancouver's Corporate Complex and Producer Services Sector: Linkages and Divergence within a Provincial Staples Economy. *Regional Studies* 21: 413-24.

Lucas, R. 1971. *Minetown, Milltown, Railtown*. Toronto: University of Toronto Press.

Lundqvist, L.J. 1998. Sweden: From Environmental Restoration to Ecological Modernization. In *Governance and Environment in Western Europe*, edited by K. Hanf and A.I. Jansen. New York: Longman.

Lyon, V. 1992. Green Politics: Political Parties, Elections, and Environmental Policy. In *Canadian Environmental Policy*, edited by R. Boardman. Toronto: Oxford University Press.

McKenzie, R.B. 1987. The Emergence of the "Service Economy": Fact or Artifact. In *Conceptual Issues in Service Sector Research: A Symposium*, edited by H.G. Grubel. Vancouver: Fraser Institute.

McNamee, K. 1993. From Wild Places to Endangered Spaces: A History of Canada's National Parks. In *Parks and Protected Areas in Canada: Planning and Management*, edited by P. Dearden and R. Rollins. Toronto: Oxford University Press.

Mahoney, J. 2000. Path Dependence in Historical Sociology. *Theory and Society* 29(4): 507-48.

March, J.G., and J.P. Olsen. 1989. *Rediscovering Institutions: The Organizational Basis of Politics*. New York: Free Press.

–. 1995. *Democratic Governance*. New York: Free Press.

Marchak, P. 1985. Canadian Political Economy. *Canadian Review of Sociology and Anthropology* 22(5): 673-709.

Markey, S., J.T. Pierce, and K. Vodden. 2000. Resources, People and the Environment: A Regional Analysis of the Evolution of Resource Policy in Canada. *Canadian Journal of Regional Science* 23(3): 427-54.

Mitchell, B., and R. Turkheim. 1977. Environmental Impact Assessment: Principles, Practices, and Canadian Experiences. In *Managing Canada: Renewable Resources*, edited by R.R. Krueger and B. Mitchell. Toronto: Methuen.

Naylor, R.T. 1972. The Rise and Fall of the Third Commercial Empire of the St. Lawrence. In *Capitalism and the National Question in Canada*, edited by G. Teeple. Toronto: University of Toronto Press.

Niosi, J. 1991a. Canada's National System of Innovation. *Science and Public Policy* 18(2): 83-92.

–, ed. 1991b. *Technology and National Competitiveness: Oligopoly, Technological Innovation and International Competition.* Montreal and Kingston: McGill-Queen's University Press.

–. 1998. Canada's National R&D System. In *Innovation Systems in a Global Context: The North American Experience,* edited by R. Anderson, T. Cohn, J. Day, M. Howlett, and C. Murray. Montreal and Kingston: McGill-Queen's University Press.

Nord, D.C., and G.R. Weller. 1983. Environmental Policy and Political Support. In *Political Support in Canada: The Crisis Years,* edited by A. Kornberg and H.D. Clarke. Durham, NC: Duke University Press.

Orren, K., and S. Skowronek. 1998-99. Regimes and Regime Building in American Government: A Review of Literature on the 1940s. *Political Science Quarterly* 113(4): 689-702.

Peters, B.G. 1992. The Policy Process: An Institutionalist Perspective. *Canadian Public Administration* 35(2): 160-80.

–. 1999. *Institutional Theory in Political Science: The "New Institutionalism."* London: Pinter.

Pierson, P. 2000. Increasing Returns, Path Dependence, and the Study of Politics. *American Political Science Review* 94(2): 251-67.

Pontusson, J. 1995. From Comparative Public Policy to Political Economy: Putting Institutions in Their Place and Taking Interests Seriously. *Comparative Political Studies* 28(1): 117-47.

Rabe, B.G. 1997. The Politics of Sustainable Development: Impediments to Pollution Prevention and Policy Integration in Canada. *Canadian Public Administration* 40(3): 415-35.

Radice, H. 2000. Globalization and National Capitalisms: Theorizing Convergence and Differentiation. *Review of International Political Economy* 7(4): 719-42.

Reed, M.G. 1995. Implementing Sustainable Development in Hinterland Regions. In *Resource and Environmental Management in Canada,* edited by B. Mitchell. Toronto: Oxford University Press.

Rees, W.E. 1980. EARP at the Crossroads: Environmental Assessment in Canada. *Environmental Impact Assessment Review* 1(4): 355-77.

Richards, J. 1985. The Staple Debate. In *Explorations in Canadian Economic History: Essays in Honour of Irene M. Spry,* edited by D. Cameron. Ottawa: University of Ottawa Press.

Roe, E. 2000. Poverty, Defense and the Environment: How Policy Optics, Policy Incompleteness, fastthinking.com, Equivalency Paradox, Deliberation Trap, Mailbox Dilemma, the Urban Ecosystem and the End of Problem Solving Recast Difficult Policy Issues. *Administration and Society* 31(6): 687-725.

Rose, R. 1990. Inheritance before Choice in Public Policy. *Journal of Theoretical Politics* 2(3): 263-91.

Sabatier, P. 1993. Policy Change over a Decade or More. In *Policy Change and Learning: An Advocacy Coalition Approach,* edited by P.A. Sabatier and H.C. Jenkins-Smith. Boulder, CO: Westview.

Sacouman, R.J. 1981. The "Peripheral" Maritimes and Canada-Wide Political Economy. *Studies in Political Economy* 6: 135-50.

Salazar, D.J., and D.K. Alper. 1999. Beyond the Politics of Left and Right: Beliefs and Values in British Columbia. *BC Studies* 121: 5-34.

Schaap, L., and M.J.W. van Twist. 1997. The Dynamics of Closedness in Networks. In *Managing Complex Networks: Strategies for the Public Sector,* edited by W.J.M. Kickert, E.H. Klijn, and J.F.M. Koppenjan. London: Sage.

Scharpf, F.W. 1994. Community and Autonomy: Multilevel Policy-Making in the European Union. *Journal of European Public Policy* 1: 219-42.

Schrecker, T. 1984. *Political Economy of Environmental Hazards: A Study Paper.* Ottawa: Law Reform Commission.

–. 1985. Resisting Regulation: Environmental Policy and Corporate Power. *Alternatives* 13: 9-21.

–. 1989. The Political Context and Content of Environmental Law. In *Law and Society: A Critical Perspective,* edited by T. Caputo. Toronto: Harcourt Brace Jovanovich.

Simeon, R. 1976. Studying Public Policy. *Canadian Journal of Political Science* 9(4): 548-80.
Singelmann, J. 1978. *From Agriculture to Services: The Transformation of Industrial Employment.* Beverly Hills, CA: Sage Publications.
Singer, O. 1990. Policy Communities and Discourse Coalitions. *Knowledge: Creation, Diffusion, Utilization* 11(4): 428-58.
Statistics Canada. 1995. *Provincial Economic Accounts.* Catalogue No. 13-213. Ottawa: Minister of Supply and Services Canada.
Stone, F. 1984. *Canada, the GATT and the International Trade System.* Montreal: Institute for Research on Public Policy.
Swaigen, J. 1980. Environmental Law 1975-1980. *Ottawa Law Review* 12(2): 439-88.
Tomblin, S.G. 1995. *Ottawa and the Outer Provinces: The Challenge of Regional Integration in Canada.* Toronto: James Lorimer.
Toner, G., and T. Conway. 1996. Environmental Policy. In *Border Crossings: The Internationalization of Canadian Public Policy,* edited by G.B. Doern, L.A. Pal, and B.W. Tomlin. Toronto: Oxford University Press.
Trainer, T. 2001. The "De-materialization" Myth. *Technology in Society* 23(4): 505-14.
Wallace, I. 2002. *A Geography of the Canadian Economy.* Don Mills, ON: Oxford University Press.
Walsh, J.I. 1994. Institutional Constraints and Domestic Choices: Economic Convergence and Exchange Rate Policy in France and Italy. *Political Studies* 42: 243-58.
Warton, D.A. 1969. The Service Industries in Canada 1946-1966. In *Production and Productivity in the Service Industries,* edited by V.R. Fuchs. New York: Columbia University Press.
Watkins, M.H. 1963. A Staple Theory of Economic Growth. *Canadian Journal of Economics and Political Science* 29(2): 141-58.
–. 1977. The Staple Theory Revisited. *Journal of Canadian Studies* 12(5): 83-95.
Webb, M.C., and M.W. Zacher. 1985. Canada's Export Trade in a Changing International Environment. In *Canada and the International Political/Economic Environment,* edited by D. Stairs and G.R. Winham. Toronto: University of Toronto Press.
–. 1988. *Canada and International Mineral Markets: Dependence, Instability and Foreign Policy.* Kingston, ON: Centre for Resource Studies, Queen's University.
Weir, M. 1992. Ideas and the Politics of Bounded Innovation. In *Structuring Politics: Historical Institutionalism in Comparative Analysis,* edited by S. Steinmo, K. Thelen, and F. Longstreth. Cambridge: Cambridge University Press.
Wenzel, G. 1991. *Animal Rights, Human Rights: Ecology, Economy and Ideology in the Canadian Arctic.* London: Belhaven Press.
Whalley, J. 1985. *Canadian Trade Policies and the World Economy.* Toronto: University of Toronto Press.
–, ed. 1986. *Canada's Resource Industries and Water Export Policy.* Toronto: University of Toronto Press.
Wilkinson, B. 1985. Canada's Resource Industries. In *Canada's Export Industries and Water Export Policy,* edited by J. Whalley. Toronto: University of Toronto Press.
Williams, G. 1983. *Not for Export: Toward a Political Economy of Canada's Arrested Industrialization.* Toronto: McClelland and Stewart.
Wilsford, D. 1985. The Conjuncture of Ideas and Interests. *Comparative Political Studies* 18(3): 357-72.
–. 1994. Path Dependency, or Why History Makes It Difficult but Not Impossible to Reform Health Care Systems in a Big Way. *Journal of Public Policy* 14(3): 251-84.
Wilson, J. 1998. *Talk and Log: Wilderness Politics in British Columbia.* Vancouver: UBC Press.

4

International Institutions and the Framing of Canada's Climate Change Policy: Mitigating or Masking the Integrity Gap?

Steven Bernstein

The 1997 Kyoto Protocol establishes an international institutional framework for domestic responses to climate change that links emissions targets for developed countries to international market mechanisms. Despite the considerable and contentious compromises made to salvage the accord after the United States withdrew from it in March 2001, the protocol's major goals and instruments survived the negotiations towards a political agreement reached later that year on the rules of implementation and compliance. That success demonstrated the commitment of even recalcitrant developed countries, with the notable exceptions of the United States and perhaps Australia, to the protocol's major provisions, and the willingness of European Union (EU) countries, its strongest supporters, to make compromises to keep the protocol alive.[1]

Although the protocol takes only a small step towards altering the human impact on global climate, it represents a major breakthrough in the implementation of many of the broad principles and goals of previous efforts to respond to this complex and potentially costly global problem. The protocol goes well beyond the voluntary stabilization targets of the 1992 United Nations Framework Convention on Climate Change (FCCC). It commits developed countries to legally binding targets to limit or reduce greenhouse gas (GHG) emissions, and introduces three major market mechanisms that involve transferring "credits" for emissions to help countries meet their targets. Whereas these "flexible mechanisms" allow some leeway in how developed countries meet their commitments, the protocol also establishes a normative framework for the type of strategies pursued.

Drawing on insights from sociological institutionalism and constructivism in international relations (Finnemore 1996; Florini 1996; Adler 1997; March and Olsen 1998), I make the following two-stage argument:

1 The international climate change regime institutionalized in the FCCC and the Kyoto Protocol reflects and reinforces a prevailing set of global

environmental norms that I characterize as "liberal environmentalism" (Bernstein 2001). The norms of liberal environmentalism predicate environmental protection on the promotion and maintenance of a liberal economic order, as explained in more detail below.

2 As an embodiment of these norms and of concrete measures to implement them, the Kyoto Protocol enables and constrains responses to climate change in Canada. In sum, Canada's domestic climate change policy can be understood only in the context of this normative framework.

The main empirical outcome to be explained is Canada's climate change policy. Whereas international relations scholars have increasingly focused on why agents (primarily states and corporations) comply with international institutions or "regimes" (Chayes and Chayes 1993; Haas et al. 1993; Weiss and Jacobson 1998; Wettestad 1999; Young 1999; Simmons 2000; Checkel 2001), the focus here is not compliance per se but domestic and foreign policy development in an internationalized policy setting (Bernstein and Cashore 2000). Implicit in this approach is the assumption that when international institutions call for the implementation of specific policies formerly within domestic jurisdiction, those policies do not appear *de novo* when an international institution is created. Moving beyond a strict focus on how states react to rules, incentives, and sanctions once in place (compliance) opens up the possibility that compliance is not simply a reactive but also an interactive process between domestic policies and international pressures to move aspects of those policies along certain trajectories. Understanding policy development in such a context requires tracing the interactions of the international institutional context with domestic determinants of policy outcomes more commonly identified in the comparative public policy literature, such as domestic interests and institutions.

According to constructivists, institutionalized international norms can frame domestic policy discourse and strengthen domestic coalitions advocating compliance. The fit between international and domestic policy norms is especially important if policies promoted internationally are to be successful in promoting policy change domestically (Keck and Sikkink 1998; Bernstein and Cashore 2000). Thus, factors such as how well proposals for change link with other related policies, the changing positions of governments, and dominant ideologies or cultural discourse and practices can be important in determining whether and how states respond to international agreements. Furthermore, a country's concern for reputation can play a major role in determining whether it will respond to international normative pressure even before binding rules are in place, since international norms define appropriate identities and interests for membership in international society. According to Keck and Sikkink (1998, 29), countries most susceptible to transnational pressure "are those that aspire to belong to a normative community of nations" (see also Price 1998). While such factors do not necessarily override material interests, they may define how those interests are understood and shape responses to those interests.

These arguments also point to factors neglected in the mainstream literature in international relations on regime effectiveness and compliance, which, following a rationalist logic, focuses primarily on incentives and disincentives for compliance or on institutional design (e.g., Haas et al. 1993; Levy et al. 1995, 290-308; Zürn 1998; Wettestad 1999). Since both the compliance literature and the concept of an "integrity gap" introduced in this volume concern the attainment of policy (or treaty) goals rather than mere agreement on a goal or a promise to attain it, both could benefit from a greater attention to the framing and normative content of policies and institutions through which policies are made and implemented. Whereas the few compliance studies that acknowledge the importance of communicative action and learning address some of the factors identified above (e.g., Chayes and Chayes 1993; Weiss and Jacobson 1998; Underdal 1998), even the most overtly constructivist studies (e.g., Checkel 2001) pay less attention to how the normative basis of agreement can be a major determinant of compliance and effectiveness. Moreover, a focus on the substance of norms has the added advantage of providing insight into the content of policies. Such a focus is crucial in evaluating the effectiveness of a regime in achieving its overall goals, or the ways in which regimes shape, legitimate, and delegitimate particular policy responses.

This argument resolves a paradox in Canadian climate change policy. On one hand, as one of the largest emitters of GHGs per capita (and contributing about 2 percent of total world emissions),[2] Canada has promoted commitments and mechanisms on climate change consistent with its own domestic constraints, including limitations imposed by federalism, the energy sector, and domestic policy norms. Thus, critics of Canada's climate change policy rightly point to a weak policy response prior to 1997 and Canada's repeated efforts since then to modify the Kyoto Protocol to ease the rules on mechanisms and carbon "sinks" in a way that limits the requirements to cut domestic emissions. On the other hand, the multilateral negotiation process, emerging global environmental norms, and linkages to broader foreign policy goals and pressures have pushed Canada to commit to action well beyond what domestic constraints dictate. These outcomes suggest that international processes can lead to a narrowing of the environmental integrity gap, even if critics correctly point to compromises in the end goals of climate change policy.

Uncovering how these international institutional factors interact with domestic environmental policy is key to understanding the Canadian government's commitment to reduction targets and the Kyoto Protocol despite domestic interests that have pushed hard in the other direction. Its continued firm commitment to implement the Kyoto Protocol even after the US withdrawal is particularly puzzling from a rationalist perspective, since the Canadian government and powerful domestic economic interests had previously stated that international competitive concerns should prevent Canada from moving forward on Kyoto without the United States (Government of Canada 2001).

The rest of this chapter consists of four sections. The first shows how the norms of liberal environmentalism are reflected in the compromise of the Kyoto Protocol. The second section identifies the international and domestic institutional context for Canada's climate change policy and demonstrates the linkages between domestic and international environmental norms. Given this context, the third section briefly traces Canada's role and activities in global climate science and policy. The fourth section examines Canada's post-Kyoto climate policy to show how international processes have enabled and constrained domestic responses in line with dominant regime norms, pointing to lacunae in the literature on regime compliance and effectiveness.

Norms, Global Environmental Governance, and Liberal Environmentalism

Norms are shared conceptions of appropriate behaviour or action. In the context of global governance, they define, regulate, and legitimate state (and other key actors') identities, interests, and behaviour.[3] The importance of norms in policy comes from their *institutionalization,* which concerns the perceived legitimacy of the norm as embodied in law, institutions, or public discourse even if all relevant actors do not follow it (Jepperson et al. 1996, 54, note 69; Onuf 1997, 17). As such, norms are central to all governance structures since governance ultimately concerns the steering of actors towards collective or shared goals or values, whether or not they stem from a formal centralized authority with enforcement power (Rosenau 1995). In this regard, the institutionalization of norms has causal effects because it increases the likelihood of the behaviour they prescribe and decreases the likelihood of the behaviour they proscribe, transferring the burden of effort onto those who oppose the norm. While this may not guarantee that all behaviour will conform to the norm, it shifts the burden of effort and proof onto those actors who contest its validity, and empowers actors in conformity with the norm. Following such reasoning, Yee (1996, 97) argues that norms "quasi-causally affect certain actions not by directly or inevitably determining them but rather by rendering these actions plausible or implausible, acceptable or unacceptable, conceivable or inconceivable, respectable or disreputable, etc."

In this case, the Kyoto Protocol reflects and further institutionalizes a broader normative consensus on the appropriate or legitimate way to understand and address global environmental problems. Elsewhere, I have characterized this dominant set of norms that underpins global environmental governance as "liberal environmentalism." Most notably, the United Nations Conference on Environment and Development (UNCED), or Earth Summit, in Rio de Janeiro in 1992, and related negotiations, catalyzed the institutionalization of these norms in a wide range of international environmental treaties, in environment and development policies of international organizations, and, more broadly, in global environment and development discourse. Scholars may disagree on the merits of UNCED outcomes, but most acknowledge that a new regime or international law of sustainable development became institutionalized (Spector et al. 1994; Sand 1993; Pallemaerts 1996). My characterization is based on a larger study of global environmental norms that identified the set of specific norms that actually became institutionalized after the 1987 World Commission on Environment and Development (or Brundtland) report popularized the positive linkage of environmental protection and economic growth under the rubric of "sustainable development" (Bernstein 2001). This research found that global environmental governance post-Brundtland has viewed liberalization in trade and finance as consistent with, and even necessary for, international environmental protection, and both as being compatible with the overarching goal of sustained economic growth. The trend since then has been to attempt to implement these norms. This form of governance promotes market and other economic mechanisms (such as tradable pollution permits or privatization of the commons) over command-and-control regulations (standards, bans, quotas, and so on) as the best method of environmental management.

These norms are embodied most explicitly in the Rio Declaration on Environment and Development, "the one 'product' of UNCED designed precisely to embody rules and principles of a general and universal nature to govern the future conduct and cooperation of States" (Pallemaerts 1994, 1). For example, according to principle 12: "States should cooperate to promote a supportive and open international economic system that would lead to economic growth and sustainable development in all countries, to better address the problems of environmental degradation." In addition, the "polluter pays principle," embodied in principle 16 and as originally formulated within the Organization for Economic Cooperation and Development (OECD), is designed to internalize environmental costs so that they are included in the price of a product. It thus incorporates the basic logic behind market and other economic mechanisms that rely on price signals, and also promotes an end to market-distorting subsidies and, generally, a smooth operation of the market consistent with environmental protection.[4] While a wide variety of specific treaties and activities of international organizations involved in sustainable development have attempted to put these norms into practice, perhaps the best example of their institutionalization and attempted implementation is the Kyoto Protocol, as will be shown in the next section.

The focus on the normative underpinning of the protocol is important for the theoretical argument developed here, which builds on insights from the application of sociological institutionalism to international relations (Finnemore 1996; Weber 1994; Florini 1996; March and Olsen 1998). They demonstrate that the creation and function of international institutions – defined as relatively enduring and connected sets of rules and norms that define and prescribe standards of behaviour and structure patterns of activity among states, or that cross or transcend borders[5] – can often be better understood in reference to their "institutional" environment rather than their "technical" environment. The former views institutions as creating legitimate authority structures that make practices understandable and acceptable, and rewards behaviours judged as socially appropriate (Weber 1994, 7). This sociological understanding of institutions, following what March and Olsen (1998) have called a "logic of appropriateness," contrasts with rationalist accounts that view the functioning of organizations as dictated by efficiency and means-end rationality, or a "logic of expected consequences."

Extending this logic to the effects of international institutions on domestic policies, I argue that the "institutional" environment is an important determinant of the content of the policies implemented in the relevant issue area. Moreover, the compatibility, and interaction, of domestic policy norms and norms promoted in the international institution are significant determinants of compliance, potentially overriding or redefining domestic interests. Since international institutions, especially in the environmental issue area, ultimately are designed to promote changes in domestic policies or in the behaviours of government, substate, and corporate actors, and even individuals, the "fitness" with domestic policy norms is especially important. In practice, the relationship is two-way – domestic policy norms of major countries affect norms embodied in international institutions as much as vice versa (Ruggie 1983). The emphasis on "fitness" (Florini 1996; Bernstein 2001) puts greater emphasis on institutional structural factors than has been placed even by some other constructivist authors who focus more on how agents produce change through persuasion and argumentation (Checkel 2001).[6]

Canada has shown itself to be a fairly consistent proponent of, and participant in, policies that fit within a liberal environmental framework. However, while these norms are clearly reflected in how Canada has framed its policies for attaining its greenhouse gas reduction commitment under the Kyoto Protocol, as discussed below, actually reaching these objectives is a different question. For example, liberal environmentalism in practice may not be sufficient to meet environmental goals, especially when one considers that norms of free trade supported by liberal environmentalism are implemented in the context of institutions such as the North American Free Trade Agreement (NAFTA). The policy effect of NAFTA may be to create pressures for harmonization with US climate change policy, which can militate against action out of sync with that country. In that case, liberal environmentalism would actually contribute to an *environmental* integrity gap, as defined in this volume.

In addition, on the domestic level, institutions may embody policy-making norms that interact in unpredictable ways with the set of international norms I have described as liberal environmentalism. For example, decentralization of environmental responsibilities among the provinces, and the federal/provincial diplomacy that this entails, means that broad national policy norms are always open to negotiation and potentially compete with the distributional norms of a federal system. The interplay between Canada's engagement of liberal environmental norms and its efforts to live up to a 6 percent greenhouse gas reduction target could offer important insights into the relationship between international norms and domestic policy performance.

The Kyoto Protocol

The FCCC and, to an even greater degree, the Kyoto Protocol, with its link of binding commitments to market mechanisms, fit very well into the normative structure that I have characterized as liberal environmentalism. Whether or not one agrees that liberal environmental norms dominate global environmental policies to the degree that I suggest, the important argument here is only that Kyoto is a primary example of recent attempts to put into place concrete measures to implement them. Under Kyoto, developed states agreed to quantified emissions targets and a compliance system with potentially legally binding consequences[7] to collectively reduce GHG emissions[8] to 5.2 percent below 1990 levels by the period 2008-12[9] (compared with the mere voluntary "aim" of stabilizing emissions at 1990 levels in the FCCC). The inclusion of differential targets (see below) and mechanisms to help achieve them, and the subsequent successful negotiation of a detailed compliance system, also go far beyond vague references to policies and measures in the FCCC. Taken together, these provisions indicate that negotiators designed the agreement to be implemented, ultimately enforceable, and politically and economically acceptable, not a mere hortatory document.

Agreement on the protocol was the culmination of two years of negotiations, and came even though most OECD countries knew they would not reach even the modest FCCC stabilization goal. Business-as-usual scenarios predict that GHG emissions from developed countries will increase on average about 18 percent above 1990 levels by 2010, with some notable exceptions such as Germany and the United Kingdom.[10] The Canadian government estimated that GHG emissions in 2002 were about 19.6 percent *higher* than in 1990, and, under business-as-usual projections (i.e., with no changes in policies), would be 33 percent higher than Canada's Kyoto commitment by 2010 (Government of Canada 2002).

Despite this poor performance, Canada agreed to a 6 percent reduction target, in line with projected reductions required in other Group of Seven (G7) countries and major trade competitors. The US target is 7 percent, or roughly a 26 percent reduction from business-as-usual projections for 2010, although a US domestic plan announced in February 2002 as an alternative to Kyoto ignores that target and allows increases in emissions as the economy grows. The European Union[11] and central European countries agreed to 8 percent cuts and Japan 7 percent, or about 15 percent and 12 percent, respectively, from business-as-usual projections, although the EU and Japan are relatively energy-efficient, making reductions comparatively more difficult (Environment Canada 1999). Some countries negotiated increased emissions targets – Australia by 8 percent and Iceland by 10 percent of 1990 emissions – and others, such as New Zealand and Russia, must only stabilize emissions. Specific targets are not science-based but were negotiated in "a highly political process" (Grubb et al. 1999, 116).

The key to the agreement was the linkage between binding targets and "flexible" or market mechanisms. The main operative provisions of the original 1992 FCCC set the foundation for the compromise at Kyoto. Article 4(2)(a) and (b) spell out the obligation of developed states to "tak[e] the lead" in modifying their GHG emissions, but to do so while recognizing, among other things, "the need to maintain strong and sustainable economic growth." It further states that "Parties may implement such policies and measures jointly with other Parties" to achieve the stabilization target. This idea of joint implementation, explained further below, fits with the marketization of environmental protection and privatizing of the global commons typical of liberal environmentalism.

Another important provision of the FCCC and the protocol – the idea of common but differentiated responsibilities for developed and developing countries – is institutionalized in Article 3(1) of the FCCC to make it fully consistent with broader liberal environmental norms that promote economic growth, liberal trade, and market mechanisms, because it is linked to joint implementation. Like other norms in the agreement, common but differentiated responsibility was institutionalized at UNCED (for example, in principle 7 of the Rio Declaration) and is an important component of many recent multilateral environmental agreements.

Building on these basic ideas, the following three Kyoto mechanisms are the most ambitious attempts to date to implement market mechanisms at the global level:

- "Emissions trading" (Article 17) allows Kyoto Protocol Annex B[12] countries to trade emissions permits (i.e., portions of their national emissions budgets) among themselves.
- "Joint Implementation" (JI) (Article 6) allows individual emission reduction or carbon "sink" enhancement projects (discussed below) in FCCC Annex 1 countries to lead to international transfers of "emission reduction units" that would be counted towards reductions in the investing country. In effect, a project funded by one country that reduced emissions in another would count as an emission reduction in the investing country.
- The "Clean Development Mechanism" (CDM) (Article 12) allows the issuance of "certified emissions credits" for emission reductions (and potentially sink enhancements) produced by projects undertaken in non-Annex 1 countries. The principle is the same as JI, but investment would be from developed to developing countries.

The mechanisms all work on the same basic principle: that assigning property rights to emissions and creating a market that allows them to be transferred will enable emission reductions to be achieved where it is most efficient to do so. The impact on the atmosphere is the same regardless of where cuts are made. They can be considered "market" or "incentive-based" mechanisms because they rely on the establishment of a market for emission credits to create price signals, and thus incentives, for buyers, sellers, and investors, as long as abatement costs vary across countries.

Negotiations following the signing of the protocol focused on unresolved technical details of the mechanisms, compliance, financing for developing countries, and credit for carbon sinks or sequestration of carbon in forests or through other land-use or agricultural changes under Articles 3.3 and 3.4 (collectively known as "land use, land-use change, and forestry," or LULUCF, in negotiations). Canada and other members of the "Umbrella" negotiating group[13] made generous provisions for sinks a deal-breaker. This tactic paid off. The Bonn Agreement, reached at the resumed session of the sixth Conference of the Parties to the FCCC (COP-6 part 2) in summer 2001 not only makes LULUCF projects eligible under the CDM but also allows negotiated maximum credits in the First Commitment Period (2008-12), despite objections from the EU that these provisions threaten the protocol's environmental integrity. Ironically, the outcome on sinks, which also fits the overall compromise to support reductions in GHG concentrations in the most efficient or cost-effective way, would likely have satisfied the United States when

COP-6 negotiations were suspended over these issues six months earlier at The Hague, when Bill Clinton was still president.

Canada requires sinks to figure prominently in any implementation strategy because it fears high compliance costs, while it also possesses large land areas with actual or potential CO_2 absorption potential (Grubb et al. 1999, 76-80, 186-90). Reaching its target through emission reductions alone, even with other international transfers, will be difficult given Canada's energy-intensive economy and growing population (Grubb et al. 1999, 33).

The Political and Economic Context of Canada's Climate Change Policy

The international-domestic nexus of political and economic factors that impinge on Canada's climate change policy are outlined below to put the evolution of this policy in context. Identifying the material and ideational interests at play, as well as institutional constraints, provides the empirical foundation required to evaluate the arguments made in the next two sections. Especially significant is Canada's strong support for the concept of sustainable development and its promotion of norms associated with it internationally, which reflect what I labelled liberal environmentalism. These interactions illustrate the importance of the compatibility of international and domestic norms in explaining policy development in the direction of dominant international norms.

Canadian Foreign Environmental Policy

Canadian governments are traditionally strong supporters of multilateral institutions and a rule-based international order. As a middle power with an open economy, and geographically, economically, and politically in the shadow of the United States, Canada benefits immensely from rules to buffer direct US influence while promoting predictability in world economic and political affairs. This policy orientation also enables Canada to potentially play a leadership role disproportionate to its economic and military power. Its foreign environmental policy has offered many such opportunities because leadership can rest on scientific expertise and domestic financial and institutional support for such efforts, something Canadian governments have been able and willing to provide (Parson et al. 2001).

The Canadian government and individual Canadians have also been at the forefront of global environmental concerns and of sustainable development thinking. Government scientists or senior bureaucrats have held leadership positions in organized transnational or intergovernmental environmental activities, including the World Meteorological Organization (WMO), the United Nations Environment Programme (UNEP), and the World Climate Research Program (WCRP). Such leadership has been encouraged within the bureaucracy (Parson et al. 2001; Toner and Conway 1996). For example, Maurice Strong, who, among his many public and private positions, headed the Canadian International Development Agency (CIDA) in the 1960s, was the first head of UNEP; Elizabeth Dowdeswell, from Environment Canada, held the same position in the mid-1990s; and Gordon McBean, also from Environment Canada, has headed the WCRP. Strong was also secretary-general of both the 1972 UN Conference on the Human Environment in Stockholm and the 1992 Earth Summit in Rio de Janeiro. Canada is also home to the secretariat of the Convention on Biological Diversity (in Montreal), although, notably, it lost its 1995 bid to host the FCCC secretariat in Toronto, partly because it was perceived to lack leadership and domestic commitment; this offers some evidence of the international consequences of an integrity gap in Canadian environmental policy.

The Canadian government has also strongly supported sustainable development norms, and prominent Canadian individuals, most notably Jim MacNeill, secretary-general of the Brundtland Commission, and Strong, a commissioner, were instrumental in formulating and promoting those norms internationally. For example, Strong can be credited with bringing development concerns onto the environment agenda at the 1972 Stockholm conference with his organization of a meeting of twenty-seven developing country experts in Founex, Switzerland (*Founex Report* 1972). Even at this early stage, Strong promoted the idea that environmental protection required economic growth, and that the two could be mutually reinforcing.[14]

But it was the Brundtland Commission report that synthesized these ideas and brought them into the mainstream of global governance. Here, MacNeill, who wrote much of the report, played an instrumental role, bringing these ideas to the commission from the OECD in Paris, where he headed the Environment Directorate from 1978 to 1984. MacNeill identifies the "Environment and Economics" conference in 1984, which he organized, as the most important event to bring ideas associated with what I call liberal environmentalism into the mainstream of public policy (OECD 1985). The conference emphasized the desirability of strengthening the reciprocal positive linkages between environmental protection policies and economic growth, and the role of economic instruments, which it found were more efficient and more appropriate for preventative policies (OECD 1985). MacNeill "took with [him] into the Brundtland Commission" the conference's findings, which "formed a very large cornerstone of the Brundtland Commission's report and its conclusions with respect to sustainable development."[15] UNCED, or the Earth Summit, a direct outgrowth of the Brundtland Commission, institutionalized these ideas. Meanwhile, the commission also successfully promoted these ideas in the UN system, in the OECD, and within many governments, including Canada's.

A second important context for Canadian foreign environmental policy is that governments feel bound, for both political and economic reasons, not to stray far from US positions on major foreign policies. Canadian governments concerned with their international reputation of being at the forefront of global environmental concern and a good multilateral citizen who can broker compromises, and facing domestic pressure from civil society groups not to fall behind the United States on environmental issues, are keenly sensitive to any perception that Canada is losing its traditional role. Canada's poor domestic performance on climate change after 1992 raised awareness of an integrity gap between policy goals and performance, and, in line with earlier arguments about the importance of reputation in foreign policy, eventually became a major source of embarrassment internationally, which limited Canada's ability to play a leadership role.

Despite its early history of entrepreneurial leadership during international environmental negotiations, Canada's ability to make its view prevail is limited. Its influence instead rests largely on persuasion of its more powerful partners. Although Canada may often lead in identifying problems and supporting multilateral solutions, it is frequently unable to follow through in attaining its commitments because of domestic constraints, especially in policy areas that require multijurisdictional implementation across domestic sectors. These arguments suggest some support for the importance of the factors that Lee and Perl (in Chapter 1 of this volume) identify as possible causes of an integrity gap. As subsequent analysis will show, however, domestic-international interactions may alter expected institutional effects, especially if those expectations are based solely on a rationalist reading.

Domestic Normative Context

That norms of sustainable development influenced Canadian domestic policies should come as little surprise, given the crucial role of Canadians in promoting these ideas internationally (Parson et al. 2001). Domestic governments still needed to "learn" these norms, however, since many of the activities and programs incorporating these ideas occurred internationally first. The Conservative government of Brian Mulroney in the late 1980s and early 1990s was largely receptive. Just as these norms fit with broader trends in the international political economy towards the broad acceptance of global economic liberalism and market forces as the main engine of economic growth at the end of the Cold War (Biersteker 1992), they also fit better than previous formulations of environmental policy with prevailing domestic policy norms, which were also moving in a neoliberal direction.

By the late 1980s and early 1990s, sustainable development had become "a stated goal of Canadian environmental and economic policy" and a "primary goal in major pieces of environmental legislation, such as the Canadian

Environmental Assessment Act and the revised Canadian Environmental Protection Act" (Toner and Conway 1996, 110). The interpretation of sustainable development is consistent with ideas promoted in the OECD and at UNCED, where pollution prevention and the "polluter pays principle" is emphasized, environmental costs are to be internalized, and international free trade is promoted as consistent with environmental protection under policies such as eliminating subsidies in areas such as forestry and agriculture.

Round Tables on the Environment and Economy, initiated at national, provincial, and municipal levels following the Brundtland report, became the primary vehicle for the promotion of these ideas in Canada. These processes brought together politicians, officials, academics, and stakeholders at senior levels of industry and the environmental community. They grew directly out of the Brundtland Commission's visit to Canada in May 1986, when it met with the Canadian Council of Resource and Environment Ministers, the federal/provincial body that initiated the creation of the roundtables (Doering 1993).

While their direct influence is hard to discern, the National Round Table on the Environment and Economy (NRTEE), which reports directly to the prime minister, had good access to Mulroney. It provided detailed advice that fed directly into the UNCED process, and two NRTEE members served on the delegation (Doering 1993). In line with trends noted earlier, one major NRTEE initiative was an "economic instruments collaborative" in early 1992, which led to proposals for the application of such instruments to acid rain deposition, climate change, and ground-level ozone. In 1999 the NRTEE completed a series of technical papers on emissions trading systems, and released the report *Canada's Options for a Domestic Greenhouse Gas Emissions Trading Program.*

While it is difficult to follow the path of learning between such programs and the extensive analytic work done in the OECD (1994, 11-25) and the United States around the same period,[16] these processes have been mutually reinforcing in the case of Canada. The NRTEE process, which focused on domestic policy advice, complemented ideas being generated in policy shops such as the OECD, including the analytic work on emissions trading by the Annex 1 Expert Group of the FCCC, which influenced Canada's (and other countries') climate change policy and positions following COP-1 in 1995. Canada's position already fit well with the Expert Group's findings and support for emissions trading, whereas the EU and the Group of 77 bloc of developing countries (G-77) required greater convincing.[17] One indication of the policy synergy in Canada is that Doug Russell, Canada's chief negotiator at COP-1, chaired the Annex 1 Expert Group during some of its work on emissions trading.

Although the NRTEE appeared to wane in influence after the defeat of the Conservative government in 1993, after Kyoto it assembled a group of twenty-five prominent Canadians to examine climate change. They strongly supported early action, noting that the changes required would benefit the economy and society regardless of whether the threat turned out to be as serious as it appeared (NRTEE 1998). The logic of economic efficiency and win-win solutions typical of liberal environmental thinking continues to prevail in the NRTEE's work.

Institutional Constraints

The primary institutional constraints on climate change policy are conflict within the federal cabinet and federal/provincial relations. Environment Canada has traditionally taken the lead on climate change, although Natural Resources Canada leads on domestic implementation. The interests of these two ministries have often been at odds. Whereas Natural Resources Canada focuses more on the economic implications for the energy and resource extraction sector, Environment Canada often acts as an advocate for global action. The latter, however, has traditionally been perceived within the bureaucracy as lacking pragmatism and analytic ability outside of its scientific expertise.[18] Combined with a lack of prime ministerial leadership prior to 1997, these conflicts played havoc with Canada's international position. In practice, the personalities and strengths of ministers played a large role in determining the direction and coherence of Canada's position.

The complexity of Canadian federalism in crosscutting areas such as the environment further complicates the policy process. All provinces and territories and the federal government have environment ministries. Most environmental regulation occurs at the provincial and territorial level because provinces own the land and natural resources within their boundaries, and have exclusive jurisdiction over nonrenewable resources (since 1982). The federal government, however, generally leads in emissions policies and has jurisdiction over issues that fall under its constitutional powers to regulate trade and commerce and interprovincial transportation.

Since the federal government negotiates international treaties through the Department of Foreign Affairs and International Trade (DFAIT), a high level of federal/provincial cooperation is required if negotiated agreements are to be implemented. This is especially true with climate change, where many sectors directly implicated fall either exclusively under provincial jurisdiction (e.g., forests) or under complex joint federal/provincial policy mandates (e.g., transportation or agricultural policy). Even in the case of forests, however, the federal government (through Natural Resources Canada) provides policy and science-based research and advice, and, with DFAIT, leads on international forestry issues. Energy policies also have both federal and provincial aspects (Skogstad and Kopas 1992; Toner and Conway 1996). Since 1993, Joint Ministers' Meetings (JMMs) of federal and provincial ministers of environment and energy coordinate national climate change policy and provide advice on preparations for international negotiations. A National Air Issues Steering Committee and National Air Issues Co-ordinating Committee on Climate Change (NAICC-CC) provide analysis and advice to the joint ministers and overall direction in the management of the national policy process.

Economic Context

The Canadian economy is energy- and export-intensive, with trade in goods and services accounting for about 75 percent of GDP. These factors produce two types of economic constraints on abatement policies: external constraints posed by trade and competitiveness concerns, and internal constraints posed by the relative costs and benefits of abatement measures. Both constraints are complex, hotly debated, and not always independent in practice.

Since Kyoto, the debate over external constraints has focused mainly on whether the United States would ratify the treaty. Industry groups argue that the high level of economic integration with the United States means that independent action in Canada "could significantly put the cost structure for our industries out of line from what competitors in the US are facing."[19] While not disagreeing, environmental organizations and government officials also emphasize that relative inaction or a slow response in the context of US action risks the opposite danger, since US companies would have an advantage if incentives there promote innovations in energy-efficient technologies or renewable energy sources. Moreover, an ironic consequence of the US withdrawal that works to Canada's advantage is that the permit price of carbon in international markets under the mechanisms would drop substantially owing to decreased demand, reducing abatement costs for developed countries by over 80 percent according to some estimates. As a result, developed countries such as Canada are expected to rely even more heavily on Kyoto mechanisms and less on domestic reductions. Whereas compliance may therefore be enabled, *environmental* effectiveness is reduced (see den Elzen and de Moor 2002).

Global competitive pressures also work in both directions. Militating against aggressive action, Canadian manufacturers in energy-intensive sectors such as steel or auto manufacturing may compete against manufacturers in developing countries such as South Korea or Brazil, while energy supply companies may compete against operations in members of the Organization of Petroleum Exporting Countries (OPEC), none of which face mandatory emissions targets. Conversely, Kyoto may signal a broader shift to a less carbon-intensive global economy, which means that the marketplace will favour more carbon-efficient, eco-efficient, and energy-efficient companies.[20]

The economic and political meaning for Canada of US failure to ratify the protocol is also subject to two great uncertainties: whether it signals a lack of commitment by the United States to pursue a plausible climate change implementation strategy, and the reaction of the marketplace to moving out of sync with the United States. Whereas US ratification in the short term is a nonstarter, given the Bush administration's declared opposition, the United States has some history of refusing to ratify a treaty but complying with its most important provisions, as in the cases of Law of the Sea and, so far, the Comprehensive Test Ban Treaty.

In this case, President Bush, despite his initial stated skepticism of climate science and opposition to Kyoto, has in practice left in place or repackaged some major domestic initiatives that Clinton set in motion, including accelerated efforts to develop clean energy sources, tax incentives to promote clean energy technology, and increased research and development in efficient energy technology and renewable energy. Whereas Bush's proposed 2002 budget initially cut back on incentive programs, two months later he announced support for major new initiatives in these areas and the creation of a National Climate Change Technology Initiative to promote research and development of alternative technologies such as fuel cells. Moreover, his proposed alternative to Kyoto, announced in February 2002, builds on these programs with additional tax incentives, protection of transferable credits, and funding for carbon sequestration, increasing Clinton's commitment of about $4 billion over five years to about $4.6 billion (White House 2002). Because the proposal links emissions targets to GDP and occurs in the context of an expansive domestic energy policy, it will fall far short of the US's Kyoto target, assuming that economic growth occurs. Yet, it signals that even the Bush administration is unwilling to abandon an active climate change policy.

The apparent shift came in the face of congressional, international, and public pressure to support a more proactive climate change policy, and findings from a National Academy of Sciences panel report that reaffirmed the mainstream view on climate change was consistent with the consensus in the Intergovernmental Panel on Climate Change (IPCC), the major international scientific body established to research and report on climate change (Allen 2001; Pianin 2001). The abovementioned initiatives indicate that continued and even increased action directed by the US administration and Congress is possible even without ratification. Notably, like Canada's policy to date, it is largely voluntary and incentive-based and links mitigation strategies to economic growth and market mechanisms. It also signals that Washington is unwilling to close the door to future participation in the Kyoto mechanisms. In addition, some key state governments, such as California, are initiating their own climate change policies and programs ahead of Washington.

The internal economic debate in Canada revolves around the costs and benefits of meeting this country's Kyoto commitment, and their distribution. Analysis under Canada's post-Kyoto policy process suggests a compliance cost of Cdn$1.66 billion per year during the First Commitment Period (2008-12), based on "likely" estimates of the cost per tonne of CO_2 (Cdn$10, assuming that the US is out of the permit market) times the gap between business-as-usual projections for emissions and the Kyoto target.[21] This scenario assumes extensive use of Kyoto mechanisms internationally and a domestic trading system.

In macroeconomic terms, the government report estimates a reduction of 0-2 percent GDP by 2010. A 2 percent reduction in 2010 means that the economy would grow an estimated 29 percent over the next decade rather than 31 percent, the projected growth without Kyoto. The report also takes account of potential health benefits of about $300 to $500 million per year owing to reductions in some pollutants (although benefits decrease by using Kyoto mechanisms). Given the many assumptions embedded in the models and scenarios employed in these reports, these estimates are highly speculative. Furthermore, they "ignore the value of the benefits of avoiding climate change as well as any ancillary economic (e.g., lower energy bills) or environmental benefits ... that may be realized from lowering net greenhouse gas emissions" (Kyoto Mechanisms Table 1999, 40).[22] At the time of writing, provincial governments were demanding further analysis of an actual implementation plan and public consultations before they support ratification. The only certainty, as one official at Canada's Climate Change Secretariat (CCS) put it, is "that the longer you wait [to initiate action] the more expensive it gets."[23]

These macro-figures also hide the unequal distribution of marginal costs of abatement across sectors and regions. For example, growth in emissions from 1990 to 2010 in the provinces of Ontario and Quebec is expected to be about one-half that in Saskatchewan and Alberta, owing in part to the significant role of fossil fuels in the economies of the latter two provinces (Analysis and Modelling Group 1999, 62). Thus, political and economic constraints are linked in practice. A key principle of any national strategy is that "no region or sector [should be] asked to bear an unreasonable share of the burden" (Environment Canada 1997).

In summary, this section has highlighted that material interests in the form of economic costs and competitive concerns should militate against Canada pursuing an aggressive climate change policy. Canada's continued support of the Kyoto Protocol, especially in light of the US withdrawal, is thus particularly puzzling for a rationalist or interest-based explanation. Admittedly, the competing incentives, when material *and* ideal interests are taken into consideration, also suggest that a rationalist account can tell part of the story – the logic of responding to an ideational interest such as maintaining a good reputation acts as an external incentive or consequence just as material interests do, although the former is more difficult to quantify. Nonetheless, even under this expansive interpretation, a rational analysis is incomplete and very difficult to specify in advance of the context of the particular issue in question, especially an issue area as complex as climate change policy, where interest definition is highly uncertain. The following section explores how Canada's climate change policy actually evolved in light of the pressures identified above.

From Policy Entrepreneur to Political Laggard: The Evolution of Canada's Global Role in Addressing Climate Change

In this section and the next, I will show that although Canada was at the forefront of scientific and political efforts to put climate change on the international agenda, domestic political factors conspired to make it a laggard both internationally and in its domestic policy response after 1992. These factors included internal divisions within the federal cabinet and between the federal government and the provinces, a lack of attention from the prime minister, and resistance from powerful actors in the energy sector and industry more broadly. At the same time, Canadian domestic environmental policy began to reflect norms of liberal environmentalism, largely owing to the influence of the Brundtland Commission and the UN Earth Summit process.

This interaction between domestic and international factors, following the theoretical arguments made earlier, means that the normative compromise at Kyoto offers some hope for greater domestic action, thereby reducing an integrity gap. Even though Canada appears to have been dragged into the Kyoto agreement, the final outcome also fits with domestic policy norms on environment and sustainable development, making domestic opposition of the kind that paralyzed action on climate change between 1992 and 1997 more difficult. This conjunction of international and domestic environmental policy norms is not coincidental. It stems in part from an overlap of domestic Canadian and international policy communities and the Canadian government's strong support in the late 1980s for international efforts to promote sustainable development ideas and adopt them in Canada. Individual Canadians working through the OECD and the Brundtland Commission process played a major role in developing these norms, which then came back to confront Canadian domestic policy.

The Early Days: Science and Policy Activism

Environment Canada led Canadian climate change research and policy in the early days of global concern. Its role reflected the then-prevailing perception of climate change as a primarily scientific and environmental issue. Its science-based mandate and in-house expertise in atmospheric issues allowed its scientists to play important leadership roles in major international research initiatives, and in most of the key events and organizations that brought climate change to the global political agenda. Although Americans and Europeans were also prominent, Canadians and Swedes in particular displayed leadership disproportionate to their states' international position.

Three examples stand out. First, Jim Bruce, a scientist and assistant deputy minister at Environment Canada, chaired the October 1985 Villach Conference in Austria. It marked the turning point of a sustained transnational scientific research program aimed at generating consensus and promoting international political attention (Bolin et al. 1986).

Second, participants in that conference set up the independent Advisory Group on Greenhouse Gases (AGGG) in July 1986. Another Canadian, F. Kenneth Hare, chaired this small group of experts, prominent in various transnational research efforts and whose work had laid much of the basis for current climate change research.[24] The AGGG was mandated to monitor climate research data, conduct assessments of increases in GHG concentrations and effects, advise governments on possible mitigation measures, and possibly initiate consideration of a global climate convention. Its (and Canada's) influence culminated in the June 1988 Toronto conference on "The Changing Atmosphere: Implications for Global Security," which grew directly out of recommendations of a 1987 conference in Bellagio, Italy, also sponsored by the AGGG, among other organizations.

Conference Director Howard Ferguson of Environment Canada and Environment Minister Tom McMillan aimed to marshal the Villach and Bellagio findings to put forward a strong policy statement in Toronto (Agrawala 1999; Paterson 1996, 33-34). Among the members of the Canadian-dominated steering committee was Jim MacNeill, who had just finished his work on the Brundtland report, another direct impetus for the conference. The presence of Gro Harlem Brundtland, Canadian Prime Minister Brian Mulroney, and a number of ministers from a G7 summit held earlier at the same venue, among the 300 scientists and policy makers who participated, gave climate change science its most influential audience to that point. The main conference recommendation, that governments and industry should reduce CO_2 emissions by 20 percent from 1988 levels by the year 2005 "as an initial global goal," became a rallying point for proponents of a global convention, which the conference statement also recommended.

Meanwhile, a series of external events, especially a drought and unusually hot summer in 1988 in North America, elevated public concern and galvanized government responses to climate change. The increased media attention to environmental issues culminated in the famous Senate Energy

Committee testimony of NASA scientist James Hansen that the greenhouse effect was already occurring (Paterson 1996, 33; Boyle 1999).[25]

The work of the AGGG became sidelined and was eventually overtaken by the IPCC, which, as the "intergovernmental" modifier indicates, is more firmly under the control of governments. As explained by the secretary of the WMO Executive Council at the time, after a couple of years of the AGGG's work, "there was an unease that crept into some governments that this was an issue that was going to have enormous economic repercussions ... in particular the United States didn't like the idea of these free-wheeling scientists pronouncing on the subject."[26]

As climate change policy shifted towards economics and politics, Environment Canada scientists became more marginalized in the policy process, reflecting the wider trend in how the international community addressed the problem. Economic experts replaced senior atmospheric scientists and forestry experts on Canadian delegations after December 1991 in the final rounds of FCCC negotiations (Russell and Toner 1998, 6). Even within Environment Canada, the international affairs section responsible for climate change negotiations evolved to the point that it now consists completely of economists and/or international affairs specialists. These changes, especially since Kyoto, resulted from a perception that Environment Canada reflected too closely a concern with the environment rather than effective or pragmatic responses acceptable to governments.[27] The changes, which fit well with the treatment of climate change policy as consistent with economic imperatives, have enabled Environment Canada to take the analytic lead on policy issues such as emissions trading and sinks, but the sidelining of science also affected Canada's ability to lead in international negotiations.

A Laggard: Climate Change Policy, 1992-97
Domestic politics and a lack of federal leadership also caught up with Canada following the signing of the FCCC in 1992. Internationally, attention to the issue waned following Rio, gaining momentum again only at COP-1 in Berlin. Instead of pushing the agreement forward during this period, Canada – with its negotiating partners Japan, the United States, Australia, and New Zealand in the negotiating bloc known as JUSCANZ[28] – took a more cautious approach to future action than the EU. In the lead-up to COP-1, JUSCANZ countries indicated that they would agree that commitments under the FCCC were inadequate, but fought against negotiations towards targets and timetables until a last-minute deal on the "Berlin Mandate" committed states to negotiate a legally binding agreement by COP-3, with quantifiable emissions targets and dates (timetables), as well as policies and measures to achieve them (Rowlands 1995; Grubb et al. 1999, 47-48). Since Kyoto, the bloc evolved into the "Umbrella" group, adding Russia, Ukraine, and Iceland, with Kazakhstan as an observer, but losing Switzerland. Although the

bloc has no formal status, since Kyoto it has met regularly to map out a common position on key issues. Members' interests are most linked on issues such as sinks and the benefits of emissions trading and joint implementation. In practice, it acts as a counterweight to the EU+ group, which includes several central European countries, which pushed hardest for stronger commitments and limits to the use of market mechanisms and sinks.

Prior to Berlin, Canada put in place a weak and largely ineffective domestic implementation strategy. Canada's National Action Program on Climate Change consisted primarily of a Voluntary Challenge and Registry Program (VCR) and energy-efficiency initiatives. It aimed to fight climate change while "enhancing competitiveness and economic growth, facilitating innovation, and creating jobs,"[29] goals fully consistent with the new domestic environmental norms identified earlier. In 1995 the Joint Ministers' Meeting (JMM) also encouraged joint implementation as a strategy, even though the pilot phase of "activities implemented jointly" (AIJ) had not yet been confirmed at COP-1. Both independent and government reviews of the VCR suggest that despite some success stories, its impact on Canada's emissions is negligible, many companies' participation is limited to a letter of intent, and the program lacks sufficient incentives and penalties to be effective.[30]

The Berlin meeting revealed the deep divisions within the Liberal cabinet, which at times erupted into public warfare between Environment Minister Sheila Copps, who wanted to play a leadership role, and Natural Resources Minister Anne McLellan, who was doubly opposed to assertive action, being responsible for a ministry that worked closely with the fossil fuel industry and being the Alberta representative in cabinet (Russell and Toner 1998, 13). Combined with an uninterested prime minister, strong resistance to further commitments from many provinces led by Alberta (which is heavily dependent on oil and gas production and coal generation), and waning public interest in climate change in the early 1990s, McLellan's position prevailed.

The composition of Canada's delegations also began to shift to more closely reflect the challenges of domestic implementation. Whereas Environment Canada is still officially the lead department on international delegations (working closely with DFAIT), Natural Resources Canada now leads on many issues related to implementation. Delegations often include representatives from industry, finance, and agricultural ministries and from the Canadian International Development Agency (CIDA), as well as nongovernmental representatives from industry and environmental groups. Nongovernmental groups also participate through organizations such as the Climate Action Network (CAN), a transnational coalition of environmental groups that has played a significant role in global negotiations, or as part of transnational business associations. While delegations appear increasingly inclusive, many major environmental groups choose not to participate on government delegations or directly in government-sponsored policy processes domestically, in the belief that they can be more effective speaking independently or through transnational coalitions. Canadian delegations also increasingly include provincial representatives, eroding the traditional principle of consulting provinces but excluding them from multilateral negotiations.

A Follower: Kyoto and Beyond

Canada's poor performance domestically and confused position internationally took its toll on the federal government as momentum to negotiate a protocol gathered following COP-1. Prime Minister Jean Chrétien, previously unengaged, suddenly became acutely aware that Canada had fallen well behind even the US position. His forceful intervention that led to the abrupt policy change on the eve of the Kyoto meeting provides an excellent example of the importance of reputation in international affairs, a factor stressed by constructivists, especially for a country with Canada's foreign policy orientation. This is true even given strong domestic constraints.

The immediate causes of Chrétien's actions can be traced to pressure at the Denver Summit of the Eight in June 1997 and subsequent consultations with EU and American leaders. Officials noted a "surprising amount of direct contact" among heads of government on the issue, and intense and personal pressure on both Canada and the United States from European leaders, especially German Chancellor Helmut Kohl.[31] The final communiqué from Denver unequivocally supported climate change science indicating that human influence on the climate system would likely lead to "unacceptable impacts on human health and the global environment." It also committed the G8 to "take the lead" and forge an agreement "that contains quantified and legally-binding emission targets." Finally, it linked action to "flexibility" in reference to what would become the Kyoto mechanisms, as well as the need for developing countries to take "measurable steps" (Denver Summit of the Eight 1997).[32] The summit also came just prior to the UN General Assembly Special Session to assess progress on sustainable development since UNCED in 1992. Although it was not alone, Canada's poor environmental performance since Rio also caused embarrassment.

Whereas Canadian officials and industry opponents could dismiss the EU position of 15 percent emission cuts as unrealistic for Canada, they appeared unprepared when fellow JUSCANZ members moved to support binding reductions. Although the US position outlining the key compromise of binding targets linked to international market mechanisms took shape as early as the summer of 1996 at COP-2 in Geneva,[33] six months later a joint meeting of Canada's energy and environment ministers, although acknowledging that Canada would be 8 to 13 percent off its stabilization target, merely reaffirmed current domestic policies. These centred on the VCR, with only minor adjustments to strengthen reporting and encourage higher levels of action, primarily through information and education programs aimed at industry, municipalities, and consumers, and strengthened regulation of electrical motors, air conditioners, heat pumps, and transformers (Russell and Toner 1998, 15). The lack of change in either domestic or foreign policy following the JMM indicates that international pressure drove the prime minister to intervene to overcome domestic inertia.

In late October 1997, following the release of the American position, Chrétien suddenly made it a priority to "beat the US" on climate change. When he finally intervened directly in the policy process in November, he overrode, at some political risk, the 1997 JMM recommendations of merely a stabilization target at 1990 levels by the year 2010 (Environment Canada 1997). Chrétien responded with a series of speeches that forcefully stated his commitment to GHG emission reductions, gave an impassioned defence of climate change science, and compared skeptics to the tobacco industry, which denied the ill effects of smoking. He also argued that, contrary to opposition critics and industry, Canada would benefit from a global agreement owing to increased environmental and energy exports. Even then, the prime minister faced intensive lobbying from industry opposed to a legally binding agreement and a public campaign run by the Canadian Coal Association, which included fear-based advertisements warning of "economic suicide" if Canada signed a deal in Kyoto (Russell and Toner 1998, 16). Pushing in the other direction was a counter-campaign by the David Suzuki Foundation and polls showing that Canadians wanted the government to act on global environmental concerns (Smith 1998). In the end prime ministerial leadership prevailed in Canada's international position.

The last-minute intervention meant that the Canadian delegation did not receive its instructions until the Kyoto conference had already started, making it the last of the G7 countries to announce its position.[34] The new position called for a 3 percent reduction from 1990 emissions by 2010 and a further 5 percent by 2015, while endorsing the thrust of US proposals for binding targets and timetables to be linked to market mechanisms. In its press release, the Canadian government clearly indicated that the position resulted not only from domestic consultations with provinces and stakeholders but also from consultations with world leaders. The government also played up Canada's position between the US and the EU and its desire to "help find common ground in Kyoto," reflecting an attempt to reinvigorate Canada's role as a facilitator of global agreement and compromise. The press release contained lengthy quotations not only from Environment Minister Christine Stewart and Foreign Affairs Minister Lloyd Axworthy but also from Natural Resources Minister Ralph Goodale and Minister for International Cooperation Diane Marleau, indicating that Chrétien had brought cabinet ministers in line. When the US position moved to surpass Canada's commitment, following a last-minute intervention by Vice President Al Gore on 8-9 December, Canada followed suit by agreeing to a 6 percent reduction (Agrawala and Andresen 1999, 465). This shift in Canada's position indicates its increased adherence to evolving global environmental norms despite significant domestic constraints.

After Kyoto: Liberal Environmentalism and Domestic Implementation

The main argument of this section is that the institutional environment can enable action even though the structure of economic interests remains largely unchanged, a point missed in most compliance literature. Thus, the almost exclusive emphasis on institutional design, incentives/sanctions, and capacity in the compliance and effectiveness literature can obscure other important processes that explain why states follow or agree to major policy provisions and norms contained in the regime. Whereas institutional design and incentives are important to facilitate clear rules on mechanisms and to create international pressure through reporting for all countries, specific incentive measures to build capacity and transfer finance and technology will likely make less difference for a developed country such as Canada.

This argument is particularly relevant in the case of climate change since the challenge is first to get developed countries to meet their commitments. Their major challenge comes more from potential domestic opposition on economic grounds and issue characteristics that make it difficult for an international institution, no matter how it is constructed, to address the problem.

By most measures of effectiveness, the climate change regime would score low in the case of Canada before the formulation of its national climate change strategy in response to Kyoto. Why then, should we be more sanguine about the Canadian government's commitment to overcome its integrity gap in climate change policy in Kyoto's aftermath? The empirical evidence suggests that three effects consistent with the institutional environment or logic of appropriateness have mattered in explaining Canada's climate change policy, and offer some optimism for future implementation of policies consistent with the protocol.

First, as shown above, a concern with international reputation has played a significant role, making Canada's leaders vulnerable to international pressures for compliance. International reputation can be a strong motivating factor, especially for a country with a multilateralist and internationalist foreign policy that depends on areas such as the environment to make a mark. Canada aspires very much, as Keck and Sikkink (1998, 29) put it, "to belong to a normative community of nations." These findings demonstrate the importance of reporting, openness, and generating media and nongovernmental attention and participation, which are emphasized more in compliance literature less focused on rational choice analysis (e.g., Weiss and Jacobson 1998).

Second, in contrast to those who argue that domestic policy networks and institutions can be important constraints, it appears that international commitments such as Kyoto create opportunities to reframe domestic policy institutions and interests, enabling their closer alignment with international norms (Keck and Sikkink 1998). For example, the clientelist policy network of Natural Resources Canada and the natural resource and fossil fuel sector in Canada, which resisted significant compliance measures or input from non-industry groups, has been largely bypassed by the federal government's creation of a Climate Change Secretariat (CCS) and a more inclusive policy network and process, described below. Establishing the CCS to coordinate climate policy outside of both Natural Resources Canada and Environment Canada, and seconding senior bureaucrats from each, helped reframe the issue, thereby discarding some baggage carried by the narrower interests of each ministry. Thus unburdened, networks can be more fluid than sometimes portrayed in the policy network literature, especially in a parliamentary system. Here, material interests can be redefined by changing the frame through which actors perceive their interests.

Third, the norms of Kyoto have made it more difficult for those traditionally opposed to domestic action to launch counter-campaigns. The Kyoto Protocol, by reflecting and institutionalizing liberal environmentalism, provides an enabling environment for domestic implementation that was previously unavailable and that also fits well with Canada's own environmental policy norms, shifting the burden of effort onto those who oppose action. "Flexible" mechanisms are not merely flexible but reflect an underlying shift to market instruments and a notion of sustainable development that fits with free trade, market norms, "polluter pays," economic growth and competitiveness, and other elements of liberal environmentalism noted earlier. Even Alberta, traditionally the most resistant province to substantial commitments, has attempted to position itself to take advantage of new policy initiatives, and began to lead in pushing for early action (although it returned to an oppositional stand to the particulars of Kyoto as the ratification debate in Canada progressed). For example, it created Climate Change Central in 1999, a nonprofit corporation to create partnerships among various economic sectors, government, and academics to develop "technological advances that will lead to improved competitiveness and lower environmental impacts"; developed one of the more detailed provincial policies on combating climate change; and has attempted to position itself as a technological leader in clean energy production and sequestration technologies (Government of Alberta 2000).

The National Policy Response

Following Kyoto, the federal government committed $150 million in the 1998 budget over the three following years to develop a national action plan, programs on public education, and research into challenges and op-portunities for business. It also continued to give $70 million to Natural Resources Canada each year to improve business practices, $20 million for energy-efficiency initiatives, and $20 million each year to Environment Canada for climate change–related activities.

In April 1998 the federal government and provinces agreed at a JMM meeting to launch a broad consultative process overseen by the new CCS to design the National Implementation Strategy on Climate Change. The CCS reports to the joint ministers, and is a coordinating body independ-ent of, although working closely with, Natural Resources Canada and En-vironment Canada. Senior bureaucrats from those ministries, CCS, Finance, and the Privy Council Office (the prime minister's bureaucratic staff) also meet regularly in a CORE-4 group, and occasionally with other depart-ments, to ensure that the process is coordinated across the government. This initiative effectively broke open the clientelist policy network between Natural Resources Canada and the fossil fuel and resource sector. It also seems to have produced a redefinition of bureaucratic interests. Since Kyoto, a more cooperative atmosphere between the ministries and a sense of com-mon interest among the ministers is evident, especially since federal mon-ies devoted to climate change will largely flow through Natural Resources Canada.[35]

The main policy process involved the organization of sixteen "Issue Tables" made up of about 450 experts reflecting multiple stakeholder groups, in-cluding all levels of government, industry, environmental groups, commu-nity groups, and scientists. The tables analyzed the impacts, costs, and benefits of addressing climate change, and proposed options in response to the Kyoto Protocol.[36] The options papers produced fed into the process to form a national strategy, the first phase of which – the federal Action Plan 2000 – was announced in October 2000, just prior to COP-6. The plan is part of the First National Business Plan of Canada's Implementation Strat-egy, agreed to at a JMM that same month (with the exception of Ontario).[37]

Whereas uncertainties remain at this time over Canada's implementation strategy, by piecing together elements of the Action Plan, the 2000 federal budget, and findings of the tables process, the shape of Canada's response to Kyoto is starting to emerge. At the time of writing, the federal govern-ment put forward a discussion paper with four scenarios that reinforce the existing policy trajectory discussed below and that will be needed to bring Canada the rest of the way to its Kyoto target (Government of Canada 2002). The discussion paper identifies four policy options, with all but one includ-ing an extensive domestic trading system (although with different designs), and would depend on extensive use of sinks and varying degrees of use of Kyoto mechanisms. The options also involve a number of targeted measures and innovation and incentive programs. The one new feature is a proposal to get credit for "clean energy exports" to the United States, which are currently not eligible under the protocol.

The new proposals respond to the one clear signal from the tables' analysis, that voluntary measures are insufficient and that a "major intervention in the economy" will be needed if Canada is to meet its Kyoto target. The Kyoto mechanisms play a fundamentally important role here in shaping responses, since many countries, including Canada, will likely institute a domestic emissions trading system linked to an international trading regime (Government of Canada 2002). Two pilot trading programs are currently in place: Ontario's Pilot Emissions Reduction Trading Project (PERT), which recently became a nonprofit organization known as Clean Air Canada, and the national Greenhouse Gas Emissions Reduction Trading Pilot (GERT). Currently, these projects only allow participants to use the projects to achieve their own voluntary goals (for example, under the VCR), although the emission reductions might be recognized in any future formal trading regime. Since the federal government appears to fear widespread opposition to a carbon tax, it is increasingly apparent that alternatives to market interventions may also have to be found. These concerns account in part for Canada's growing emphasis, domestically and internationally, on carbon sequestration (sinks) and the Kyoto mechanisms, since other measures announced in Action Plan 2000 will fall far short of meeting Canada's commitments.[38]

The five-year federal plan aims to cut GHG emissions by 65 megatonnes per year for the First Commitment Period (2008-12), or one-third of Canada's Kyoto target, with steps to achieve the remainder left for future plans. The largest percentage of emission cuts will be achieved in the energy sector, primarily through a federal government plan to buy 20 percent of its electricity from "green" sources, such as wind or solar power, and from carbon sequestration in the agricultural and forestry sector. These two sectors each account for 20 percent of the proposed reduction, while another 25 percent will be achieved through international action (JI and CDM). Provinces and territories that agreed at the JMM are expected to cooperate with the federal initiatives and propose complementary actions. The federal action plan commits $500 million to these activities, which is in addition to the $625 million committed over five years in the 2000 budget (Environment Canada 2000). The budget is almost entirely devoted to international programs and private sector and research incentives for technological innovations. Included in that total is $125 million given to municipalities for energy-efficiency programs, transportation, and policy research.

The October 2000 JMM also approved the implementation of "baseline protection," effective 1 March 2001, under which companies can register their baseline emissions with the VCR. This initiative is crucial to removing disincentives to early action, and is a step towards crediting this action in the future. Whereas environmental groups see credit for early action as crucial to providing incentives to progressive companies, technical issues and splits within industry remain. Two difficulties present themselves: credits are hard to calculate independently of other market mechanisms being put in place, and early credit raises liability concerns for governments if they lack proper methodologies to ensure that incremental actions were indeed taken.

The debate over early action also reveals broader changes and diversity in the industry response to climate change. Even fossil fuel industries can no longer be treated monolithically. While many major industry associations still favour a go-slow approach, few still challenge the science, focusing instead on economic arguments concerning the effects of particular policies on trade and competitiveness. Companies that believe they can benefit from credit for early action or that see potential for relatively inexpensive or profitable efficiency gains, for example, have started to become more proactive and supportive of putting policy instruments in place that will allow them to build such credit into their planning and accounting. Prominent examples include the power companies TransAlta and Ontario Power Generation, which announced trades in emissions credits in October 1999 in the hope that credits bought now at low prices (between 40 cents and $5 per tonne of emissions) will be recognized when formal markets are in place and the price is much higher (Chase 1999). Whereas these trades occurred in an informal and unregulated market, making them risky ventures, they also provide an incentive for these companies to push for a formal credit system and for recognition of credit for early action. (Some environmentalists, however, worry that the quality of some credits is suspect.) Suncor, Alcan, and West Coast Energy are other examples of major companies interested in early action. Companies do not fall simply into proactive or resistant camps, however. Many companies, facing a variety of competitive and organizational pressures (such as costs/benefits of innovation) as well as consumer, shareholder, moral, and scientific pressures and influences, are still attempting to define their interests on this issue.

The debate in Canada reflects the wider debate in transnational industry, where some of the world's largest multinational corporations, many of which have subsidiaries in Canada, have adopted a more proactive climate change policy, including DuPont, Toyota, 3M, Boeing, Weyerhaeuser, and BP Amoco. In addition, major fossil fuel companies and automakers have left anti–climate change coalitions such as Global Climate Coalition,[39] and major energy companies, including BP Amoco and Royal Dutch/Shell, have launched internal carbon emissions trading markets to help them reach their pledge to cut emissions (*Financial Times* 2000). Opportunities to enhance effectiveness in Canadian environmental policy now exist where they did not previously, owing to the institutional environment created by Kyoto.

For example, blanket resistance to particular policy instruments or major interventions no longer prevails among industry associations, although most oppose the Kyoto targets because they view them as unrealistic.

The budget and policy responses to date indicate that Canada's domestic response will be almost entirely incentive-based and heavily dependent on Kyoto mechanisms and sink enhancement. These responses fit with the view that the final Kyoto agreement should "maximize the economic and trade opportunities for Canadian Businesses," and, as put by former Finance Minister Paul Martin, that "dealing with climate change provides opportunities for Canadian companies to make money and that developing new technology is key" (Environment Canada 2000; McIlroy 2000). From the foregoing evidence, the final national strategy will likely continue this trend of liberal environmental thinking, including a major economic instrument or instruments consistent with these norms.

Conclusion

As with liberal environmentalism more generally, the assertion that economic growth, liberal markets, and environmental protection can be made mutually supportive does not always easily translate into effective climate change policy. If more radical changes in practices are needed than can be accomplished by market mechanisms, incentives for technological innovations, or voluntary approaches consistent with the norms of liberal environmentalism, Canada may be hamstrung in its ability to meet its Kyoto targets. While enabling some actions, the downside of Kyoto is that it risks justifying inaction if tough regulatory choices are actually necessary to get the desired ecological effects. I conclude with some observations on the implications of the findings in the Canadian case for the literature on regime compliance and effectiveness and for the possibilities that international-domestic interactions might mitigate an environmental integrity gap, with the usual caveats regarding generalizing from a single case.

First, discussions of regime "effectiveness" should acknowledge that governing norms in the first instance define what effectiveness and compliance mean. On one level, the Kyoto norms and mechanisms may limit the ability of improvements to produce a "collective optimum" – one possible definition of effectiveness – if defined strictly in terms of ecological or sustainability criteria (Underdal 1997). This may even be the case if compliance – defined as the observance or adherence to regime commitments in practice – is enhanced (Weiss and Jacobson 1998). As Victor et al. (1998, 7) note, compliance does not necessarily lead to effectiveness, and may sometimes even be inversely related to it. Nonetheless, the fit of Kyoto with international and domestic environmental norms, combined with strong responses by Canada's major trading partners, does enable a range of practices that go beyond previous efforts. Effectiveness, if defined more modestly as a relative improvement compared with the absence of a regime or changes in behaviour that further the goals of the accord, may thus be achieved (Underdal 1997; Wettestad 1999).

Most of the regime and compliance literature glosses over or ignores the way regime norms define what effectiveness means, which is prior to questions of adherence to specific policy provisions. In this case, the ultimate goals of the FCCC and Kyoto are not simply emission reductions but also sustainable economic growth and equity. The institutionalization of these goals in norms of what I have labelled liberal environmentalism means that determining compliance and effectiveness must be sensitive to the substance of agreements and requires at least three steps. First, it means evaluating how the norms embodied in Kyoto have shaped the substance of climate change policy; second, whether those norms have shaped behaviour, as emphasized in most compliance and effectiveness literature; and, ultimately, whether that framing will sufficiently address the problem of climate change. The last question is not only a scientific one of whether the climate system has been stabilized but also a question of politics and values. In Canada the emphasis on the Kyoto mechanisms, incentive-based policies, sinks, and the possibility of domestic trading follows the pattern of compliance and effectiveness institutionalized in the FCCC and the Kyoto Protocol.

The second major implication is the importance of the institutional environment in enabling policy development along certain paths. Whereas policies such as emissions trading or the variety of incentive programs in Canada's national plan to date are not inconsistent with domestic interests in most cases, thus a "logic of consequences" tells part of the story, the institutional environment established by Kyoto and the norms of liberal environmentalism more broadly have enabled the kind of policies consistent with domestic interests and the goals of the agreement. For example, the Canadian insistence that any final agreement on Kyoto include significant latitude for credit for sinks enhancement under Articles 3.3 and 3.4 clearly reflects Canada's economic interest. Yet, the broader normative pressures have meant that even when domestic interests militate against continued support for Kyoto, the federal government has continued to search for ways to reconcile these interests with the environmental goals of the treaty. As detailed above, the reframing of technology and energy policies to incorporate environmental goals, and the way in which liberal environmental norms and the framing of climate change policies under Kyoto make it more difficult to argue that the treaty is anti-competitive or constrains economic growth, enable a range of policies consistent with it.

While somewhat speculative given the early stages of compliance, these findings suggest that compliance and effectiveness literature ought to pay more attention to the content of policies and not simply to the design of compliance mechanisms or incentives. This is especially true for developed countries, where the difficulty is usually not a lack of capacity or access to technology. It suggests that international institutions can play a positive role in closing environmental integrity gaps not simply through incentives or coercion but also by enabling the construction of policies that resonate with domestic norms and interests.

Canada's performance since Kyoto suggests just such a pattern, even though critics may rightly maintain that the broader integrity of Canada's position vis-à-vis environmental goals has been diminished in the process. As evidenced in the debate over the meaning of effectiveness, a definition of integrity gap that links *environmental* problem definitions with the measures to attain those objectives is likely to reveal a significant gap. This chapter has attempted to highlight that the move to liberal environmentalism has meant that environmental problems are no longer simply defined in environmental terms. Its more sanguine position on whether international institutions might facilitate the closing of that gap should therefore be read in the context of a set of values that may not always lead to problem definitions where ecological values are paramount, but rather where they are bundled or linked to other values. The merits of the concept of integrity gap over more social scientific terms such as "effectiveness" or "compliance" is that it highlights the value choices contained in any public policy and forces analysts to confront them rather than hide under technical measures.

Compliance and effectiveness, now understood as value-laden rather than value-neutral, do not result from a one-way relationship from an international institution to domestic policy implementation. They are better understood as interactive processes that include domestic policy ideas and trajectories interacting with international negotiations and institutions all through the process of proposal, creation, and eventual implementation of a regime. Thus, the focus here has been on domestic policy development within an internationalized policy environment, not compliance per se. Looking at this interactive process may tell us important things about why states comply that would be missed if the story started with an existing regime. In particular, how international policy and domestic policies fit or conflict with each other, and the interaction of the processes that create or change those policies, can be extremely important in understanding compliance, even with weak international institutions, if weakness is defined by the absence of enforceable rules. Design issues may be important in creating trust, information, and enforcement, but the initial agreement and commitment in principle to a regime, and the role that legitimating norms play in putting the onus on those opposed to regime goals, may be more important especially in the initial stages, and potentially count as much for compliance (or for reducing a domestic integrity gap) as more overt incentives and disincentives, although more research on this question is certainly warranted.

Acknowledgments
This chapter is a slightly revised and edited version of an article that appeared in *Policy Sciences,* and is reproduced with permission from Kluwer. Earlier versions of this paper were presented to the Forty-first Annual International Studies Association Conference, Los Angeles, 14-18 March 2000, and Canadian Studies conferences in Seoul, Korea, 24-25 February 2000, and Jerusalem, 25-29 June 2000. The author gratefully acknowledges helpful comments from conference participants, Benjamin Cashore, Dimitris Stevis, Linda White, and the editors of this volume; research assistance from Nicole Anastasopoulos and Christopher Gore; and financial support from a Connaught Grant at the University of Toronto.

Notes
1 Whereas US President George W. Bush's announcement in March 2001 that his country would withdraw from the Kyoto Protocol (signed by the US under President Bill Clinton) was a potentially serious setback, a breakthrough political agreement reached at the resumption of the sixth Conference of the Parties (COP-6) in Bonn in July satisfied Japan, Canada, and other states in the "Umbrella" negotiating group that had included the United States. Eighty-three states plus the EU have signed the protocol and 74 have ratified it as of mid-June 2002, including the EU and its 15 member states, Japan, and a growing number of economies in transition in Eastern Europe. Russia and Canada have stated a commitment to ratify, and a variety of developing countries have ratified or are in the process of doing so. The wave of ratifications came after most developed countries (with the exception of the United States) negotiated agreements on unresolved issues at COP-7 in Marrakech in October-November 2002. Since the protocol requires ratification by 55 parties that account for 55 percent of developed-country emissions in 1990 in order to come into force, US ratification (its emissions account for 36.1 percent) is important but not mandatory. Following Japan's acceptance of the protocol on 4 June 2002, the total emissions accounted for at the time of writing is 35.8 percent.
2 This estimate is based on data contained in Subsidiary Body for Implementation of the FCCC 2000.
3 For a review of norms literature in international relations, see Raymond 1997.
4 The argument is not that these norms are easily put into practice. Indeed, the tension between environment and trade/economic concerns is present in many forums. Rather, the argument is that the framing and understanding of appropriate behaviour on environmental issues stems from these norms. Moreover, to the degree that practical measures stray from them, agreement or ability to implement practical responses will be difficult and conflict-laden.
5 This definition draws from Keohane 1989; Wendt and Duvall 1989.
6 The emphasis on structure is not intended to deny agency. Constructivism rests on an ontology that struggles to privilege neither agency nor structure. However, this ontological position is difficult to maintain in empirical research. The balancing act here is to recognize that domestic and international social "structures," embodied in norms and institutions, are ultimately created and linked together through agents (individuals and groups) who reinforce, argue about, and communicate the norms that constitute these structures internationally and domestically.
7 At COP-7, negotiating parties agreed to establish a compliance committee with both facilitative and enforcement bodies, but deferred a decision on whether the enforcement branch would have legally binding consequences under international law to the first meeting of parties of the Kyoto Protocol following its coming into force (IISD 2001). A legally binding enforcement regime requires an amendment to the protocol.
8 The agreement covers six greenhouse gases: carbon dioxide, methane, nitrous oxide, hydrofluorocarbons, perfluorocarbons, and sulphur hexafluoride. The first three gases will be measured against 1990 levels. The last three can be measured against either a 1990 or 1995 base year.
9 Emissions can be averaged over the five-year period.

10 Efficiency gains in East Germany after reunification largely account for Germany's performance, while the UK has benefited from a shift from coal to gas-fired electricity generation.

11 Under Article 4 – the "bubble provision" – the EU target can be distributed internally among its fifteen members. At the extremes in the EU, Portugal will be permitted a 27 percent *increase,* while Luxembourg must *reduce* emissions by 28 percent.

12 With only a few exceptions, Annex 1 of the FCCC and Annex B of the Kyoto Protocol list the same countries: those that face reduction and limitation commitments under the Protocol (spelled out in Annex B). They include most OECD countries (except recent members Mexico and South Korea) plus economies in transition. Annex B also excludes Turkey because it had not ratified the FCCC when Kyoto was signed.

13 A loose alliance that has included Japan, the United States, Canada, New Zealand, Australia, the Russian Federation, Ukraine, Norway, and Iceland.

14 Maurice Strong, interview, Toronto, 19 February 1996.

15 Jim MacNeill, interview, Toronto, 11 December 1995. See also Hajer 1995, 97-99.

16 In the US, *Project 88* (1988) and *Project 88 – Round II* (1991) analyzed and promoted economic instruments.

17 John Drexhage, associate director of the international climate change team at Environment Canada, telephone interview, Ottawa, 29 March 2000.

18 Environment Canada officials, interviews, Ottawa, 24 January 2000.

19 John Dillon, Vice President, Business Council on National Issues, interview, Ottawa, 25 January 2000.

20 Robert Hornung, Pembina Institute, interview, Ottawa, 24 January 2000.

21 These figures are based on a 166 million tonne (MT) carbon "gap" between business-as-usual projections and the -6 percent Kyoto target, and a likely price of carbon (Cdn$10 per tonne), as estimated by the Analysis and Modelling Group of Canada's climate change policy process (Government of Canada 2002, 15-16). The 166 MT figure is equal to an estimated 240 MT gap minus projected LULUCF credits and emission reductions from government action taken to date.

22 Modelling costs and benefits is politically charged and filled with uncertainties, ranging from energy prices to technological innovations. For example, models that allow scope for cost-effective improvements in energy efficiency might translate into net benefits (i.e., no-regret measures). Whereas such models face criticism for underestimating the hidden costs of implementing new technologies, top-down models typically used in national forecasts tend to ignore such measures altogether, probably overestimating costs. See Grubb et al. 1999, 163-65 and Appendix 2.

23 Keltie C. Voutier, Senior Policy Advisor, Climate Change Secretariat, interview, Ottawa, 25 January 2000.

24 Other group members were Bert Bolin (later the first chair of the IPCC), Gilbert White, Syukuro Manabe, Mohammad Kassas, Gordon Goodman, and Gueorgui Golitsyn (Agrawala 1999).

25 Scientific consensus on this conclusion within the IPCC took another seven years.

26 Jim Bruce, interview, Ottawa, 18 June 1996.

27 Environment Canada officials, interviews, Ottawa, 25 January 2000.

28 The JUSCANZ bloc evolved, sometimes including Norway and Switzerland (JUSSCANNZ).

29 Smith (1998, 2), paraphrasing then Environment Minister Sergio Marchi's description (1996) of the program.

30 Campbell 1998; Hornung 1998; Pembina Institute 1998; NAICC 1996. The 1999 updated *Emissions Outlook* (Analysis and Modelling Group 1999) had to revise figures upward by almost 60 million tonnes because the 1997 *Outlook* had overestimated the potential of the VCR.

31 Interviews with officials and observers involved in Canada's Kyoto preparations, Ottawa, January and February 2000; Russell and Toner 1998, 15.

32 The US Congress had demanded meaningful developing country participation as a precondition for the US to sign any treaty. Although the United States dropped the demand in

the face of resistance from developing countries in the final negotiations in Kyoto, these pressures persist (Agrawala and Andresen 1999, 464-65).
33 Wirth 1996; Timothy E. Wirth, telephone interview, 13 March 1997.
34 Environment Canada officials, telephone interview, Ottawa, February 2000; Government of Canada 1997.
35 CCS and Environment Canada officials, interviews, Ottawa, January 2000.
36 Each of the following tables was co-chaired by a government and nongovernmental person: Analysis and Modelling, Transportation, Electricity, Kyoto Mechanisms, Technology, Sinks, Credit for Early Action, Public Education and Awareness, Agriculture and Agri-Food, Forest Sector, Buildings, Industry, Enhanced Voluntary Action, Municipalities, Science and Adaptation, and Tradeable Permits.
37 The Ontario government's opposition likely stems from a more general political jockeying over a range of issues in intergovernmental negotiations between Ontario and the federal government rather than from principled opposition.
38 A summary of the Action Plan is available at <http://www.climatechange.gc.ca/english/whats_new/pdf/gofcdaplan_eng2.pdf> (17 January 2003).
39 The Coalition also had well-known links to OPEC states. See Newell and Paterson 1998 and Rowlands 2000 on industry groupings and efforts to affect climate change policies.

References

Adler, E. 1997. Seizing the Middle Ground: Constructivism in World Politics. *European Journal of International Relations* 3: 319-63.

Agrawala, S. 1999. Early Science-Policy Interactions in Climate Change: Lessons from the Advisory Group on Greenhouse Gases. *Global Environmental Change* 9: 157-69.

Agrawala, S., and S. Andresen. 1999. Indispensability and Indefensibility? The United States in the Climate Treaty Negotiations. *Global Governance* 5: 457-82.

Allen, Mike. 2001. Bush Pledges Study of Climate Changes. *Washington Post,* June 11.

Analysis and Modelling Group. 1999. *Canada's Emissions Outlook: An Update*. Ottawa: National Climate Change Process.

Bernstein, S. 2001. *The Compromise of Liberal Environmentalism*. New York: Columbia University Press.

Bernstein, S., and B. Cashore. 2000. Globalization, Four Paths of Internationalization and Domestic Policy Change: The Case of Ecoforestry in British Columbia, Canada. *Canadian Journal of Political Science* 33(1): 67-99.

Biersteker, T. 1992. The "Triumph" of Neoclassical Economics in the Developing World: Policy Convergence and Bases of Governance in the International Economic Order. In *Governance without Government: Order and Change in World Politics,* edited by J. Rosenau and E.-O. Czempiel. Cambridge: Cambridge University Press.

Bolin, B., B. Döös, J. Jäger, and R. Warrick, eds. 1986. *SCOPE 29: The Greenhouse Effect: Climate Change and Ecosystems*. Chichester, UK: Wiley and Sons.

Boyle, R.H. 1999. You're Getting Warmer. *Audubon* 101(6): 80-87.

Campbell, K. 1998. From Rio to Kyoto: The Use of Voluntary Agreements to Implement the Climate Change Convention. *Review of European Community and International Environmental Law* 7: 159-69.

Chase, S. 1999. Firms Warm to Greenhouse Credits. *Globe and Mail,* 20 October, B1, 12.

Chayes, A., and A. Handler Chayes. 1993. On Compliance. *International Organization* 47: 175-205.

Checkel, J.T. 2001. Why Comply? Social Learning and European Identity Change. *International Organization* 55(3): 553-88.

den Elzen, M.G.J., and A.P.G. de Moor. 2002. Evaluating the Bonn-Marrakesh Agreement. *Climate Policy* 2: 111-17.

Denver Summit of the Eight. 1997. *Communiqué*. Denver, CO, 22 June.

Doering, R. 1993. Canadian Round Tables on the Environment and Economy. *International Environmental Affairs* 5: 355-70.

Environment Canada. 1997. Canada's Energy and Environment Ministers Agree to Work Together to Reduce Greenhouse Gas Emissions. Press release from Environment Canada. Regina, 12 November.
–. 1999. The Kyoto Protocol: Challenges and Opportunities.
–. 2000. Climate Change: Budget 2000 Overview. <http://www.ec.gc.ca/budget/cc_e.htm>. Last updated 29 February 2002.
Financial Times. 2000. Shell: Oil Group Launches International Carbon Emission Market. Climate-L [newslist]. 27 January. <climate-l@mbnet.mb.ca>. Posted 6 February.
Finnemore, M. 1996. *National Interests in International Society.* Ithaca, NY: Cornell University Press.
Florini, A. 1996. The Evolution of International Norms. *International Studies Quarterly* 40: 363-89.
Founex Report. 1972. Reprinted in *Environment and Development: The Founex Report on Development and Environment, with Commentaries by Miguel Ozorio de Almeida, Wilfred Beckerman, Ignacy Sachs, and Gamani Corea.* New York: Carnegie Endowment for International Peace.
Government of Alberta. 2000. Partnership Key to Alberta's Position Leading into Joint Ministers' Meetings on Climate Change. Press release and backgrounder from Halvar C. Jonson, Minister of Environment. Edmonton, 13 May.
Government of Canada. 1997. Canada Proposes Targets for Reductions in Global Greenhouse Gas Emissions. Archived at the Global Climate Change website, <http://www.climatechange.gc.ca/english/index.shtml> (27 November 2002).
–. 2001. Statement by Environment Minister David Anderson on Climate Change. Ottawa, 4 April.
–. 2002. A Discussion Paper on Canada's Contribution to Addressing Climate Change. Ottawa: Government of Canada.
Grubb, M., C. Vrolijk, and D. Brack. 1999. *The Kyoto Protocol: A Guide and Assessment.* London: Royal Institute of International Affairs, Earthscan.
Haas, P.M., R.O. Keohane, and M.A. Levy, eds. 1993. *Institutions for the Earth: Sources of Effective International Environmental Protection.* Cambridge, MA: MIT Press.
Hajer, Maarten A. 1995. *The Politics of Environmental Discourse: Ecological Modernization and the Policy Process.* Oxford: Clarendon Press.
Hornung, Robert. 1998. The Voluntary Challenge Program Will Not Work. *Policy Options* (May): 10-13.
IISD (International Institute for Sustainable Development). 2001. Summary of the Seventh Conference of the Parties to the UN Framework Convention on Climate Change: 29 October – 10 November 2001 (Marrakech). *Earth Negotiations Bulletin* 12, 189 (12 November).
Jepperson, R.L., A. Wendt, and P.J. Katzenstein. 1996. Norms, Identity, and Culture in National Security. In *The Culture of National Security,* edited by P.J. Katzenstein. New York: Columbia University Press.
Keck, M., and K. Sikkink. 1998. *Activists beyond Borders: Transnational Issue Networks in International Politics.* Ithaca, NY: Cornell University Press.
Keohane, R.O. 1989. *International Institutions and State Power.* Boulder, CO: Westview Press.
Kyoto Mechanisms Table. 1999. *Options Report.* Ottawa: Climate Change Secretariat. <http://www.nccp.ca/NCCP/national_process/issues/kyoto_e.html> (17 December 2002).
Levy, M.A., O.R. Young, and M. Zürn. 1995. The Study of International Regimes. *European Journal of International Relations* 1: 267-330.
McIlroy, A. 2000. $700 Million Falls Short of Goal. *Globe and Mail,* 29 February.
March, J.G., and J.P. Olsen. 1998. The Institutional Dynamics of International Political Orders. *International Organization* 52: 943-69.
Marchi, S. 1996. Speech delivered by the Honourable Sergio Marchi, Minister of Environment, Canadian Global Change Program – Climate Change Symposium, Ottawa, 6 November. Ottawa: Environment Canada.
NAICC (National Air Issues Coordinating Committee). 1996. *Review of Canada's National Action Programme on Climate Change.* Ottawa: NAICC.

Newell, P., and M. Paterson. 1998. A Climate for Business: Global Warming, the State and Capital. *Review of International Political Economy* 5: 679-703.

NRTEE (National Round Table on the Environment and Economy). 1998. *Declaration of the National Forum on Climate Change.* Ottawa: NRTEE.

–. 1999. *Canada's Options for a Domestic Greenhouse Gas Emissions Trading Program.* Ottawa: NRTEE.

OECD (Organization for Economic Cooperation and Development). 1985. *Environment and Economics: Results of the International Conference on Environment and Economics, 18th-21st June 1984.* Paris: OECD.

–. 1994. *Managing the Environment: The Role of Economic Instruments.* Paris: OECD.

Onuf, N.G. 1997. How Things Get Normative. Revised version of a paper presented to a conference on international norms, Hebrew University. Jerusalem, 26-27 May.

Pallemaerts, M. 1994. International Environmental Law from Stockholm to Rio: Back to the Future? In *Greening International Law,* edited by P. Sands. New York: New Press.

–. 1996. International Environmental Law in the Age of Sustainable Development: A Critical Assessment of the UNCED Process. *Journal of Law and Commerce* 15: 623-76.

Parson, E.A., A.R. Dobell, A. French, D. Munton, and H. Smith. 2001. Leading while Keeping Step: Management of Global Atmospheric Issues in Canada. In *Social Learning in the Management of Global Environmental Risks,* edited by W. Clark, J. Jaeger, J. van Eijndhoven, and N. Dickson. Cambridge, MA: MIT Press.

Paterson, M. 1996. *Global Warming and Global Politics.* London: Routledge.

Pembina Institute. 1998. *Corporate Action on Climate Change – 1997: An Independent Review.* Ottawa: Pembina Institute.

Pianin, E. 2001. Senate Budget Vote Rebuffs Bush on Global Warming. *Washington Post,* 7 April, A5.

Price, R. 1998. Reversing the Gun Sights: Transnational Civil Society Targets Land Mines. *International Organization* 52: 613-44.

Project 88: Harnessing Market Forces to Protect Our Environment: Initiatives for the New President. 1988. A public policy study sponsored by Sen. Timothy E. Wirth and Sen. John Heinz, Washington, DC.

Project 88 – Round II, Incentives for Action: Designing Market-Based Environmental Strategies. 1991. A public policy study sponsored by Sen. Timothy E. Wirth and Sen. John Heinz, Washington, DC.

Raymond, G.A. 1997. Problems and Prospects in the Study of International Norms. *Mershon International Studies Review* 41: 205-45.

Rosenau, J. 1995. Governance in the Twenty-First Century. *Global Governance* 1(1): 13-43.

Rowlands, I. 1995. The Climate Change Negotiations: Berlin and Beyond. *Journal of Environment and Development* 4: 146-63.

–. 2000. Beauty and the Beast? BP's and Exxon's Positions on Global Climate Change. *Environment and Planning C: Government and Policy* 18: 339-54.

Ruggie, J.G. 1983. International Regimes, Transactions, and Change: Embedded Liberalism in the Postwar Economic Order. In *International Regimes,* edited by S.D. Krasner. Ithaca, NY: Cornell University Press.

Russell, D., and G. Toner. 1998. Science and Policy when the Heat Is Rising: The Case of Global Climate Change Negotiations and Domestic Implementation. Paper presented to the CRUISE Conference on Science, Government and Global Markets: The State of Canada's Science-Based Regulatory Institutions. Ottawa, 1-2 October.

Sand, P. 1993. Kaleidoscope: International Environmental Law after Rio. *European Journal of International Law* 4: 377-89.

Simmons, B.A. 2000. International Law and State Behavior: Commitment and Compliance in International Monetary Affairs. *American Political Science Review* 94: 819-35.

Skogstad, G., and P. Kopas. 1992. Environmental Policy in a Federal System: Ottawa and the Provinces. In *Canadian Environmental Policy: Ecosystems, Politics and Process,* edited by R. Boardman. Toronto: Oxford University Press.

Smith, H.A. 1998. Stopped Cold: Action by Canada on Climate Change Has Been Blocked by Opposition Both Inside and Outside Government. *Alternatives* 24: 10-16.

Spector, B.I., G. Sjöstedt, and I.W. Zortman, eds. 1994. *Negotiating International Regimes: Lessons Learned from UNCED.* London: Graham and Trotman/Martinus Nijhoff.

Subsidiary Body for Implementation of the FCCC. 2000. National Communications from Parties Included in Annex 1 to the Convention: Greenhouse Gas Inventory Data from 1990 to 1998 (FCCC/SBI/2000/INF.13, 11 October).

Toner, G., and T. Conway. 1996. Environmental Policy. In *Border Crossings: The Internationalization of Canadian Public Policy,* edited by G.B. Doern, L.A. Pal, and B.W. Tomlin. Toronto: Oxford University Press.

Underdal, A. 1997. Patterns of Regime Effectiveness: Examining Evidence from 13 International Regimes. Paper presented at the 1997 International Studies Association Conference. Toronto, 19-22 March.

–. 1998. Explaining Compliance and Defection: Three Models. *European Journal of International Relations* 4: 5-30.

Victor, David, K. Raustiala, and E.B. Skolnikoff, eds. 1998. *The Implementation and Effectiveness of International Environmental Commitments: Theory and Practice.* Cambridge, MA: MIT Press.

Weber, Steve. 1994. Origins of the European Bank for Reconstruction and Development. *International Organization* 48: 1-38.

Weiss, Edith Brown, and Harold K. Jacobson, eds. 1998. *Engaging Countries: Strengthening Compliance with International Environmental Accords.* Cambridge, MA: MIT Press.

Wendt, Alexander, and Raymond Duvall. 1989. Institutions and International Order. In *Global Changes and Theoretical Challenges,* edited by J. Rosenau and E.-O. Czempiel. Boston: Lexington Books.

Wettestad, J. 1999. *Designing Environmental Regime Effectiveness: The Key Conditions.* Cheltenham, UK: Edward Elgar.

White House. 2002. *Global Climate Change Policy Book* (February 2002). <http://www.whitehouse.gov/news/releases/2002/02/climatechange.html> (17 December 2002).

Wirth, T.E. 1996. Remarks by the Honorable Timothy E. Wirth, Undersecretary for Global Affairs, on behalf of the United States of America before the Second Conference of the Parties to the Framework Convention on Climate Change. Geneva, Switzerland, 17 July.

WCED (World Commission on Environment and Development). 1987. *Our Common Future.* Oxford: Oxford University Press.

Yee, A.S. 1996. The Causal Effects of Ideas on Policies. *International Organization* 50: 69-108.

Young, O., ed. 1999. *The Effectiveness of International Environmental Regimes: Causal Connections and Behavioral Mechanisms.* Cambridge, MA: MIT Press.

Zürn, M. 1998. The Rise of International Environmental Politics: A Review of Current Research. *World Politics* 50: 617-49.

5
Energy Mixes and Future Scenarios: The Nuclear Option Deconstructed
Michael D. Mehta

The people of the Western world have an addiction problem – we are addicted to energy for heating our homes, running our vehicles, powering our televisions, and operating our industries. This addiction, like a dependency on drugs, alcohol, or caffeine, is difficult to notice at first, but nonetheless potentially harmful. For many years, the advantages of living in an industrial society appeared to eclipse the dangers created by unsafe industrial practices. Pollution and its effects on human health and ecosystems was treated as a necessary evil, a cost of doing business. Since the early 1970s, this attitude has been changing steadily with the rise of environmentalism and the increased scrutiny of a wide range of institutions, including governments.

Unfortunately, regulatory agencies such as Canada's former Atomic Energy Control Board (now known as the Canadian Nuclear Safety Commission) have shown an inability or unwillingness to deal with heightened public concern about the environment and human health. By maintaining a fortified position, the Atomic Energy Control Board systematically excluded the public from meaningful participation in policy debates on the risks associated with Canada's nuclear power program, and stifled discussion of its sustainability. As such, the regulation of nuclear power in Canada is a lesson in how technocratic decision-making cultures can create an integrity gap that erodes trust and damages the future development of a technology.

Why did this happen? Does Canada have other options for producing energy to meet future needs? What lessons can be learned from Canada's experience with nuclear power? Should other countries develop nuclear capacity? If so, under what conditions?

Energy Mixes: What Choices Are Available in the Developed and Developing World?
The energy options available to Canada are remarkable in their scope. With a relatively small population and large landmass, Canada has traditionally

taken advantage of an abundance of natural resources to provide for its energy needs. Large reserves of petroleum, natural gas, coal, uranium, and hydroelectric power have fuelled this nation's industrial development. Access to low-cost energy has stimulated economic growth, giving Canadians one of the highest standards of living in the world.

An examination of Canada's total primary energy supply for 1998 (International Energy Association 1998a) illustrates a reliance on fossil fuels. Approximately 76 percent of the energy supply comes from fossil fuel sources (oil, 34.7 percent; natural gas, 28.9 percent; coal, 12.2 percent).[1] Hydroelectric (12.1 percent), nuclear (7.9 percent), and commercial renewables (4.3 percent) make up the remainder.

Compared with other industrialized countries, Canada's reliance on fossil fuels is unremarkable. When we compare the energy mixes of developed countries with those of developing countries, however, some trends become evident. Figure 5.1 compares the energy mixes of two developed countries (Canada, USA) and four developing countries (Zimbabwe, Kenya, India, and China).

Canada and the United States have fairly similar patterns of energy use. Both countries rely heavily on oil and gas, have shifted away from a reliance on coal, and rely less on hydro, nuclear, and renewable energy sources. On the other hand, Zimbabwe, India, and China use coal to provide much of their energy. Also notable from this figure is the heavy use of renewable energy in developing countries, especially in Kenya. The most common source of renewable energy used in the developing world is biomass. Often,

Figure 5.1

Comparison of energy sources in sample developed and developing countries

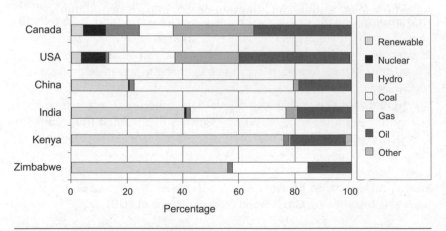

Source: International Energy Agency 1998.

wood and charcoal are used to provide energy for the developing world in a nonsustainable fashion. By contrast, the relatively small amount of energy from renewables in the developed world comes from the use of more technologically advanced sources, including photovoltaics, solar, wind, geothermal, and biofuels.

Clearly, developed countries can afford a more diverse mix of energy options and are able to devote resources to cleaner, less-polluting sources of fuel. In general, the developed countries of the world have moved from using wood to coal to oil to natural gas. With hydroelectric and nuclear power providing key support during these transitions, developed countries have maintained a consistent and growing supply of energy.

It is now commonly understood that such a pattern of development comes with certain environmental costs. Recent concerns about rising levels of atmospheric carbon dioxide and associated impacts on global climate patterns come to mind. In fact, there is a strong positive correlation between global economic trends and carbon dioxide concentration.[2] Figure 5.2 illustrates just how tightly coupled these two indicators are.

If we look at how atmospheric levels of carbon dioxide (measured at Mauna Loa, Hawaii) have increased over time, there is a striking relationship with gross world product. In fact, if we fit this data with a linear regression line, we are able to calculate how much economic value a tonne of carbon dioxide has in terms of economic growth. From the data, each tonne of carbon dioxide corresponds to approximately US$60 (1986) of economic activity.

The implications of this are striking. First, in order to develop economically, a country must be ready and able to exploit energy. Second, since

Figure 5.2

Global economic output and atmospheric CO$_2$ in parts per million concentration

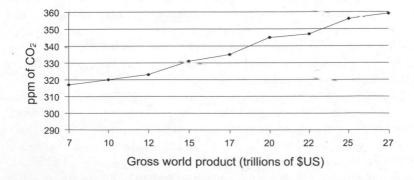

Source: Duffey 1999.

much of the development in the Western world has come from the nonsustainable use of carbon-rich fuels, the developed world has passed along the externalities of such practices to future generations in the form of pollution. Third, it is morally reprehensible to interfere with the growth of developing countries by limiting access to the very resources upon which the Western world nourished itself. The developed world must make efforts to change energy-use patterns without forcing similar constraints on the developing world.

This suggests that two parallel processes need to occur in order to optimize energy choices in both the developed and developing world. First, a de-carbonization of the economy is necessary. Not only should the economy be decoupled from fossil fuel usage but also externalities as derived from full-cost accounting procedures need to be more commonly used. Development should not come at the expense of the environment or human health. Second, developed countries need to shift energy production from carbon-intense sources to lower- or zero-carbon-content fuels. In a sense, this would enable the developing world to move through the chain of fuels (wood – coal – oil – gas) more quickly. While the developed world moves towards a more sustainable mode of energy utilization (e.g., a carbohydrate- or hydrogen-based economy), the developing world can hopefully leapfrog its way through these stages.

As the world's population increases and the developing world accelerates its use of energy, certain scenarios unfold. Many of these scenarios generate unpleasant outcomes from an environmental perspective. Again, if we consider atmospheric concentrations of carbon dioxide, the mix of energy sources used at a global level is germane. To see how different energy mixes influence atmospheric carbon dioxide levels, we turn our attention to how our six sample countries influence outcomes. It is worth noting that, on a global level, the following energy mix exists: oil (35.7 percent), gas (20.3 percent), coal (23.3 percent), nuclear (6.7 percent), and hydro with renewables (13.5 percent) (International Energy Association 1998b). In 1998 the world's total primary energy supply was 9.49 Gto$_e$ (or 9.49 billion tonnes of oil equivalent). This represents a significant increase from the 7.8 Gto$_e$ of 1993, 6.4 Gto$_e$ of 1981, and 6 Gto$_e$ of 1973 (Uranium Institute 1998). Using 1998 as a base year, this energy mix resulted in the release of 7.12 GtC (or 7.12 billion tonnes of carbon).[3]

If we adopt globally the energy mix used by Canada in 1998, the amount of carbon released decreases by almost 10 percent, to 6.43 GtC. The mix used by the United States maintains the status quo, with 7.21 GtC. Using the energy mix of China (1996), with its high reliance on coal, increases the global emissions of carbon to 7.41 GtC, a 4 percent increase. By comparison, a global energy mix matching that of India (1996) would see carbon emissions decrease by 27 percent, to 5.03 GtC. Even more extreme cuts in carbon emissions would be realized by adoption of a mix similar to that of Kenya (1996) (82 percent decrease, to 1.25 GtC) or Zimbabwe (1996) (36 percent decrease, to 4.44 GtC).

These calculations fail to illuminate two issues, however. First, they assume the status quo in which developing countries will not increase energy consumption even as population grows. Second, there is an assumption that lower carbon emission mixes are socially and economically feasible and sustainable. Obviously these assumptions do not hold, since both developing and developed countries push harder to use energy more intensively.

Other issues influence the choice of energy mix. For instance, it is necessary to take into account the resources readily available in a country. A reliance on imported fuel, especially for a developing country, can have a tremendous impact on balance of trade. Several countries have small or no reserves of fossil fuels. Many of these countries have small coal reserves and only minor opportunities for increasing electricity generation using hydroelectric power. While most of the developed world's energy consumption is stabilizing, and in some cases even decreasing, there is a core set of countries where energy demand is growing significantly.

On another level, the global reserves of low-cost oil are dropping. It is likely that the current trend of higher oil prices will continue as supply dwindles. Many experts believe that we have already surpassed the halfway mark in terms of using the world's "conventional" oil reserves. Table 5.1 shows oil reserves by region and type of reserve.

If we look at the "Ultimate reserves" column, it is evident that oil is not geographically distributed in an equitable fashion. Almost 40 percent of the world's ultimate reserves are in the Middle East. The most populous parts of the world, Africa and Asia, manage to garner only 15.1 percent of the global ultimate reserve.

Table 5.1

US Geological Survey estimates of oil reserves (in billions of barrels), 1 January 1993

Region	Cumulative production	Identified reserves	Original reserves	Undiscovered oil	Ultimate reserves
North America	199.0	112.0	311.0	90.3	401.4
South America	64.2	77.6	141.8	43.7	185.5
Europe	28.9	43.2	72.1	17.4	89.5
Former Soviet Union	119.1	125.1	244.2	100.0	344.2
Africa	56.5	76.5	133.0	37.7	170.7
Middle East	184.6	597.2	781.8	117.4	899.2
Asia/Oceania	46.3	71.2	117.4	53.2	170.6
World	698.6	1,103.2	1,801.8	470.7	2,272.5

Source: Masters et al. 1998.

With a world oil consumption rate of 30 billion barrels per year, it is likely that the halfway mark of the ultimate reserve will be met sometime between 2000 and 2008 (Lyman 1999). Now, this does not imply that the world will run out of oil in the near future. However, the cost of extracting and processing oil from nonconventional sources (e.g., oil sands, deep off-shore drilling) will likely be transferred to consumers. At this point in time, the wisdom of developing an energy sector based on a diminishing, nonrenewable resource is questionable.

The use of coal has its shortcomings also. Although global coal reserves are significant, the environmental and health implications are serious. Available data show that coal reserves are more equitably distributed on a global basis. The developing parts of the world, including Africa, China, and India, have large reserves of coal – approximately 38 percent of world reserves (World Energy Council 1998).

Like petroleum, coal is a dense and expensive energy source to transport. Countries without local supplies, or at least easily accessible supplies, pay a premium for transporting these energy sources. With natural gas, this problem is more acute. Unless directly serviced by a gas pipeline, the use of natural gas is prohibitively expensive. The distribution of natural gas closely parallels the distribution of coal and petroleum resources. Countries without these resources are at a distinct economic disadvantage. Table 5.2 shows where natural gas reserves are located geographically.

These scenarios suggest that there are only four types of energy worth considering in an intermediate time horizon of thirty or forty years:

- *Petroleum and natural gas,* although costs are likely to rise as reserves drop. Also, measures to mitigate carbon emissions are needed. This includes improving the efficiency of fuel use, shifting to fuels containing less carbon, and actively managing carbon dioxide emissions with sequestration. The use of petroleum and natural gas makes most sense for countries with reserves and established infrastructure. However, countries relying on such reserves should begin to search seriously for future alternative sources of energy.
- *Coal,* the use of which is recommended for parts of the world with significant reserves. Measures must be taken to minimize the environmental and human health costs, however. It should be noted that coal, like other fossil fuel sources, is nonrenewable. A country with low or unstable reserves of coal from imported sources should probably not invest too heavily in this energy source. Like oil and gas, coal may be part of a short-term solution for providing energy. Alternative sources of energy will eventually be required.
- *Nuclear power,* although it is not recommended as a source of energy. Countries with established nuclear reactors should apply full-cost accounting

Table 5.2

Estimates of natural gas reserves (in trillion cubic feet), 1997

Country	Reserves	% of world total
World	5,145	100.0
Top 20 countries	4,579	89.0
Russian Federation	1,700	33.0
Iran	812	15.8
Qatar	300	5.8
United Arab Emirates	212	4.1
Saudi Arabia	204	4.0
United States	167	3.3
Venezuela	143	2.8
Algeria	130	2.5
Nigeria	124	2.4
Iraq	110	2.1
Turkmenistan	101	2.0
Malaysia	82	1.6
Indonesia	72	1.4
Uzbekistan	66	1.3
Kazakhstan	65	1.3
Canada	64	1.2
Mexico	63	1.2
Netherlands	63	1.2
Kuwait	52	1.0
China	48	0.9
Rest of world	566	11.0

Source: Oil and Gas Journal 1997.

procedures to assess the costs of the entire fuel cycle, including waste disposal and reactor decommissioning. Nuclear power should be considered only for countries with large populations, high-energy growth rates, a small landmass, and minimal opportunities for developing sustainable sources of renewable energy. Additionally, a country must be able to afford a defence-in-depth approach for safely operating reactors from "cradle to grave." A country should consider importing electricity, if feasible, instead of developing a nuclear energy program, and exploiting renewable energy sources, including wind, photovoltaic, hydroelectric, geothermal, and biomass. This can also involve the use of hydrogen as a fuel source.

These assumptions boil down to one inescapable conclusion. Since fossil fuel resources (oil, gas, coal) are finite and therefore nonrenewable, a country that relies heavily on energy from these sources will eventually have to make some significant changes in its energy mix over time. This leaves open, at this moment in history, only two options: a greater reliance on nuclear energy or the development of renewables. The next section of this chapter critiques the nuclear option by relating how nuclear power has failed to provide for Canada's economic, social, environmental, or energy needs. It will demonstrate that Canada's experience with nuclear energy is consistent with this book's thesis of a divergence between goals and accomplishments in environmental protection, creating an integrity gap.

The Nuclear Option: What Happened to the Energy Source Once Considered "Too Cheap to Meter"?

Nuclear power symbolizes many of the problems of advanced, industrialized societies: rapid technological change, concentration of decision-making power, and incursion of government bureaucracy. The Canadian nuclear industry is even more concentrated, bureaucratic, and inaccessible than most due to its strong public sector character, protective legislation, and industry-government interlocks. Atomic Energy of Canada Limited (AECL), the Canadian developer of nuclear power plants, is a Crown corporation. The mining of uranium and production of heavy water, the former used as fuel and the latter as a heat moderator and coolant in Candu nuclear power plants, are both done by another Crown corporation, CAMECO, formerly Eldorado Nuclear Limited (ENL). The utility companies Ontario Hydro, Hydro-Québec, and New Brunswick Electric Power Commission are provincially owned and operated organizations. The regulation of all nuclear activities in Canada is done by a federal regulator, the Canadian Nuclear Safety Commission (formerly the Atomic Energy Control Board, or AECB). Several multinational corporations, including Babcock and Wilcox Co., play a role in the Canadian nuclear industry, manufacturing components such as control rods, pressure chambers, construction materials, and computer parts and software for power plants and their control rooms.

The regulation of nuclear power in Canada closely parallels the corporatist mode of policy making: complex interdependencies between manufacturers, suppliers, and regulators permit nuclear power to be promoted without serious concern for economic, environmental, or safety costs (McKay 1983). At present, the Canadian nuclear industry is in a state of crisis. A moratorium on new plant construction in Ontario and Quebec, weak sales of Candu reactors abroad, escalating costs associated with maintaining and repairing existing power plants, the huge debt of Ontario Hydro (recently restructured into Ontario Power Generation and other divisions), concerns about the disposal of an ever-increasing stockpile of radioactive waste, anxiety about who will be financially responsible for decommissioning costs incurred when closing power plants, and declining demand for electricity all conspire to make nuclear power less attractive. In addition, those involved with the industry must manage both the actual risks presented to society and public perceptions of such risks, in order to prevent this crisis from completely closing down the nuclear industry.

The crisis facing Canada's nuclear industry is more than a technical and an economic one. The regulation of nuclear power has failed to keep pace with changes in the political and social environment in which it must operate, while those who seek to expand its role in Canada's energy supply must now contend with an immense credibility problem arising from past policies.

One of the principal tenets of modern governance is that the role of the state had shifted from the authoritative allocator of resources to that of partner or mediator. Such a shift coincides with the sentiment that institutions matter. These institutions are often judged by their capacity to deliver results that are in line with their goals and objectives. Instead of institutions prescribing roles and expectations, institutions operating within new governance structures are expected to meet the expectations that the wider policy community develops based upon their policy commitments. In other words, these institutions are judged by the integrity of their policy performance.

This shift in emphasis suggests that government decision making must operate beyond the formal institutional rules of the past. Instead of relying upon bureaucratic structures and the expertise provided by technical experts, governments exist within neo-institutional environments where consideration of competing beliefs, cultures, paradigms, and traditional knowledge is important. In such an environment, institutions are expected to play a key mediating function, and their performance will significantly affect the legitimacy of governance arrangements. This new role is considerably different from the traditional constitutional notion of governance. By making a distinction between backroom politics and front-room policy making, neo-institutionalism allows us to shape the political process by accepting the validity of outside actors and assessing the legitimacy of traditional insiders. The Canadian nuclear industry and its regulator failed to notice a shift in this direction and have subsequently paid the price with a loss in credibility and trust.

Concerns about nuclear power have stimulated the formation of several public interest groups. Well-known groups in Canada include Durham Nuclear Awareness (DNA) (a branch of Nuclear Awareness Project), Canadian Coalition for Nuclear Responsibility, Greenpeace Canada, Ontario Energy and Environment Caucus, and Energy Probe. As well, labour unions have become part of the Canadian nuclear scene, particularly concerning the health and safety of uranium miners.

The Nuclear Establishment: A Policy Community
In Canada there is a "nuclear establishment," a relatively fixed set of relationships between members of groups and institutions that championed

and benefited from the development of nuclear power and other nuclear technologies (Jacob 1990). These groups and institutions are found at all levels of politics, ranging from local to international, and constitute the nuclear policy community. The community includes a regional coalition of jurisdictions, a national coalition of industrial interests (e.g., the Canadian Nuclear Association), an agency within the national bureaucracy (e.g., the Canadian Nuclear Safety Commission), and supportive committees within the Senate and the House of Commons.

The Canadian nuclear policy community is both historical and dynamic. It slices across the horizontal organization of society – institutions of state, economy, and civil society. Consequently, categories of private sector (economy) and public sector (state) become cloudy and porous. Private entities sometimes act as agents of the state, and public entities often assume the role of entrepreneur (Stevens 1993). The nuclear policy community also cuts across the vertical organization of society – individual, structural, and system levels. At the system level, the nuclear policy community is fortified by social arrangements that reinforce ideologies about social priorities and the norms of political behaviour. The power of the community is also structural – associated with the organization of institutions, procedures, and command of intellectual resources. Power dwells in an organization's network of external contacts. At the institutional level, power also emanates from a fundamental property of bureaucracies – the creation of procedure.

Another type of institutional power is access to, and monopoly of, intellectual resources such as technical expertise, professional opinion, research capability, and control over information. Technical expertise may delimit the language of political debate as organization confines targets of political activity and procedure channels it. Additionally, societal or systemic power is a form of control over widely held beliefs, concepts, modes of thinking, and expectations of political power or powerlessness (Richardson et al. 1993).

The organization and procedures of institutions within the nuclear policy community typify technocratic forms of decision making, variable tendencies towards fragmentation and centralizing of authority, a reluctance to consider nontechnical problems, and confidence in technical solutions. The role of organization and procedure becomes evident when one examines the nature of conflict between the nuclear policy community and its critics.

Regulating the Canadian Nuclear Industry

The Atomic Energy Control Act, first enacted in 1946, gave the Atomic Energy Control Board (AECB) authority to regulate and control atomic energy in Canada. The act gave the AECB a broad array of powers. Many of these powers were exercised through the agency's Atomic Energy Control Regulations. This included the power to license facilities using radioactive substances; regulate how such substances are used, stored, transported, and disposed of;

revoke or suspend licences for violations of regulations; form Crown enterprises; require that agencies operating under the auspices of the board submit reports and information about their operations; and give grants for research and development. All nuclear facilities, including commercial power plants, research facilities and reactors, particle accelerators, heavy water plants, medical irradiators, uranium-processing plants, radioactive waste disposal sites, and uranium mines, had to obtain a licence from the AECB. With the formation of the Canadian Nuclear Safety Commission in 1997, the Atomic Energy Control Act was replaced by the Nuclear Safety and Control Act.[4]

Canada's participation in the Manhattan Project, combined with a security-conscious environment following the Second World War (Finch 1986), explains the Atomic Energy Control Act's tendency to give the AECB a scope and breadth of powers that far exceeded those of other federal regulatory agencies. The act did not require public hearings at any stage of the AECB's regulatory activities. An independent environmental impact assessment requested by the federal minister of environment was the sole external mechanism for invoking public review.

In North America, the concept of environmental impact assessment (EIA) was introduced in the United States by the National Environmental Policy Act of 1969. In 1973 the Canadian government adopted a similar approach for assessing environmental consequences of construction projects, energy initiatives, and potentially hazardous facilities. The environmental assessment and review process (EARP) legislation was born. During the following decade, several provinces introduced their own environmental assessment processes, with Ontario's Environmental Assessment Act being the most comprehensive act by 1975. However, since all nuclear power in Canada operates under federal jurisdiction, according to the Atomic Energy Control Act, provincial legislation applied to non-nuclear projects only.

Environmental impact assessment is intended to scrutinize a development scheme while it is still early in the planning stage. In its early years, the concept of "environment" in EIA referred specifically to the natural world, but this was later expanded to include the social, cultural, and economic milieu (Richardson 1989). Thus, historically, concern with the social impacts of technology emerged from an analysis of effects on the natural environment. Beanlands and Duinker (1983), in a book on environmental impact assessment in Canada, stated: "Environmental impact assessment in Canada, as elsewhere, is a socio-political phenomenon. It is grounded in the perceptions and values of society, which find expression at the political level through administrative procedures of government. Science is called upon to explain the relationship between contemplated actions and these environmental perceptions and values."

There are some key differences in the concept of environmental assessment between Canada and the United States that can be explained by variations in political culture between the two countries. Sadler (1990) wrote: "Compared to the United States, the political culture in Canada is marked by a lesser degree of citizen activism, wide latitude traditionally granted to administrative discretion, and restricted rights to participate in decision making or to challenge the process in court." Essentially, environmental impact assessment in Canada is an administrative rather than a legislative process (Notzke 1994). Perhaps differences between Canadian and American versions of environmental impact assessment also have something to do with what Lipset (1985) observed. According to Lipset, Canadians are more likely than Americans to rely on the state, and are therefore less inclined to participate as individuals in the environmental policy process. Perhaps the EARP is an instance of this.

The EARP in Canada was administered by the Federal Environmental Assessment Review Office (FEARO) and reported directly to the federal minister of environment. The process was updated in 1977 and then reinforced in 1984 when the Environmental Assessment and Review Process Guidelines Order was issued by an Order-in-Council. This impact assessment process was primarily a self-assessment process with two phases: an initial assessment phase followed by public review by an independent panel (Kansky 1987). In the first phase, the government agency responsible for the project – in this case, the regulator (AECB) – reviewed a proposal. If the initiating department, agency, or regulator concluded that adverse environmental impacts were unlikely, there was no further review. The second phase of assessment was invoked if in the regulator's opinion, there was potential for significant environmental problems. In this case, the proposal was automatically referred to the minister of environment for public review.

According to Section 3 of the EARP Guidelines Order, agencies such as the AECB were to ensure that environmental implications of all proposals for which they had authority were fully considered. This section stressed that the self-assessment review process should occur early on so that irreversible decisions were made with full knowledge of their environmental consequences. Section 12 of the Guidelines Order specified the type of environmental consequences that required review by an environmental assessment review panel. They included such things as adverse environmental effects that were "significant" or "unacceptable." In essence, all significant or unacceptable environmental consequences of a specific proposal must be reported to the minister of environment. This reporting, however, did not mean that a public review was initiated.

Under Section 13 of the Guidelines Order, it was up to the regulating agency to determine whether or not public concern was *sufficient* to recommend a public review to the minister of environment. Unfortunately, this last requirement was ambiguously worded and may have been interpreted in various ways by agencies such as AECB. Unless a licensed nuclear facility posed clear and present danger, a public review of its safety was difficult to initiate. Section 13 of the Guidelines Order stated that a proposal for an environmental review could be suggested to the minister of environment if "public concern about the proposal is such that a public review is desirable." In other words, the AECB had to be convinced that public concern was significant enough to warrant recommending a public review. The AECB could grant an exemption from public hearings before a review panel if it deemed that the environmental impact of the project had not changed significantly from the previous relicensing period, or if expression of public concern about the proposal was not sufficient.

The AECB's interpretation of what constituted significant public concern, and how levels of concern were linked to the triggering of a public review, were both vague and frustrating. The board had complete authority to decide whether a referral was warranted, and, of course, the option to decide whether or not the granting of an operating licence or a renewal should be a matter of public review. It should be clear at the outset, however, that a nuclear facility required an operating licence no matter what the decision was. What is at issue, in this case, is whether or not this licence was contingent on public review.

An answer to the following question posed by David Martin, a founding member of the anti-nuclear group Durham Nuclear Awareness, in a letter of 27 April 1993 to the AECB requires further analysis. David Martin asked: "What specific quantitative and qualitative criteria does AECB staff use to judge the type and level of public concern that would make a review desirable or not?" This question addressed a variety of dimensions that I believe are more explicitly articulated in the following questions: How many letters must the AECB receive from the public in order to trigger a review? Do letters carry equal weight, irrespective of the status of writer, the gender of writer, the region in which the writer resides, or the pro-nuclear or anti-nuclear sentiments expressed in the text of the letter?

According to AECB staff member J.G. McManus, in a letter dated 7 May 1993, the AECB's staff "takes into consideration information received from many sources including elected officials at all levels, members of the public, special interest groups, intervenors and license applicants. Of particular interest are representations received from persons living in the vicinity of the facility in question, and anything offering new information." If "sufficient" public concern reached the ears of the AECB regarding the operating safety of Ontario Hydro's Pickering plant, then surely a public review should have been recommended. Durham Nuclear Awareness attempted to challenge the relicensing of the Pickering facility both by raising to the AECB specific technical concerns about the plant and by mobilizing public opposition. DNA endeavoured to convince members of the public to write letters of concern to the AECB demanding a public review. Incidentally, DNA and other public interest groups have unsuccessfully challenged the relicensing of Ontario Hydro's nuclear plants several times in the past.

Since the AECB can interpret Section 13 of the Guidelines Order according to norms and standards internal to the agency, is it possible that this regulator used what Doern (1976) referred to as a professionally open model of regulation? Doern described the professionally open model óf regulation as being distinguished by a high degree of trust. Its supporters avow that it is internally open, encouraging open criticism and evaluation among professional and technically qualified individuals. Advocates of this model intimate that regulators who use this approach are perceived by regulated industries as professionals trying to achieve collective goals: health and safety as well as production. As a result, professionals are more prone to divulge to their regulating peers what is working well and what is not. This model of regulation is also characterized by minimal reporting requirements and few, if any, public hearings. Here we see how the professionally open model of regulation fails to reflect the *perestroika* ushered in by neo-institutional arrangements. The public and other members of formal and informal policy networks have only a very marginal influence on decisions made in such an arena.

In Canada, opportunities for the public to be heard usually come from working on parliamentary committees, Royal Commissions, and environmental impact assessment hearings. Ashford (1990), in a paper on commissions of inquiry, wrote that public hearings are "symbolic rituals within the modern state, theatres of power" that legitimate states and allow them to "sit above society as the embodiment of the common good." Wynne views public hearings as rituals that can order and control the public by subverting their goals and values by showing internal contradictions and instability. Wynne (1982) wrote that the public falls victim to the hearing process technique because "language, including technical language, can tacitly guide people into seeing the world in certain ways, influencing what is regarded as an accepted value, and what is inevitable, possible, desirable, or at least tolerable." These critiques of hearings give the impression that the public is a passive, unwitting victim of state and corporate manipulation (Richardson et al. 1993).

The Canadian nuclear industry echoes the sentiments expressed by this professionally oriented model of regulation. The AECB's historical reliance on this model was an outcome of postwar security concerns that spawned the agency, the small size of the Canadian nuclear community, and the fact that most of the entities involved were state agencies with a typical Canadian penchant for secrecy. Much of this siege mentality was reflected in the regulation of nuclear power in Canada and revealed by an analysis of conflicts over nuclear safety.

Interventions by Anti-Nuclear Groups

Durham Nuclear Awareness intervened in the 1992 Pickering Nuclear Generating Station (Figure 5.3) relicensing bid. The operating licences (Pickering "A" and "B" were licensed separately but at the same time) expired on 15 October 1992. The AECB renewed both reactor buildings for a period of 26.5 months, but not without some opposition.

DNA expressed concerns about a variety of technical issues related to the plant's operating safety. Of particular concern was the lack of a second fast shutdown system at the four reactors in the Pickering "A" building. Newer reactors like those in the Pickering "B" building and the Darlington Nuclear Generating Station require a second line of defence against accidents resulting in a loss of coolant from the core. When reactors in Pickering "A" were first constructed – electricity generation began in 1971 – only one fast shutdown system was required by the AECB. DNA tried to convince the AECB to require Ontario Hydro to upgrade these reactors by including a second fast shutdown system as a licensing condition. Irene Kock of DNA said: "This is just one example of where Hydro can't meet the standards of its licence, but is allowed to keep reactors running" (Gerlsbeck 1992a). John Molloy, an official in the AECB's division of components and quality assurance, had said the following about the second fast shutdown system issue five years earlier: "We [the AECB] wouldn't license it unless we, and the Board members, felt it was safe enough" (McLaren 1987).

Figure 5.3

Ontario Hydro's Pickering Nuclear Generating Station

Photograph by Andrew Reedman.

DNA appealed to the AECB to hold public hearings according to the definition laid out in the EARP Guidelines Order. In order to achieve this goal, DNA questioned technical details associated with the safe operation of the nuclear plant, and worked towards mobilizing the public to write letters of concern to the AECB. DNA was concerned not only with the lack of a second fast shutdown system in Pickering "A" but also with the ability of the plant to withstand earthquakes (a fault line lying beneath the Rouge River valley just a few kilometres west of the plant had recently been discovered). DNA also expressed concerns about levels of radiation resulting from "normal" plant operation, and the adequacy of emergency planning and evacuation measures for the region surrounding the plant (Bobbit 1992).

Following media coverage of DNA's criticisms, there was considerable disagreement on the necessity of public review. Maurice Brenner, acting mayor of the Town of Pickering, welcomed public hearings. Brenner showed concern about the area's above-average rate of Down's syndrome (86 percent higher than the provincial average, according to a 1991 AECB study) (Johnson and Rouleau 1991). Gary Herrema, chair of the Durham Regional Council, refused to support a hearing into the plant's operating safety. Although concerned about a spill of tritiated water at the plant on 2 August 1992, he believed that a hearing would allow only "the uncomfortable few" and "fear mongers" to be heard. "You'd get a lot of bitching but little information," he said. With a different perspective, Jeff Brackett of DNA believed that a public hearing was essential because "[DNA is] tired of being lied to and we're tired of the nonsense" (Gerlsbeck 1992d).

Much of the controversy surrounding the 1992 relicensing centred on the major spill of tritiated water at the plant on 2 August. The nuclear station dumped nearly 3,000 litres of heavy water into Lake Ontario due to a crack in one of the 2,000 pressure tubes in the heat exchange system in reactor number one (Swainson 1992). This spill was arguably the largest ever at the Pickering station. Tritium, according to Section 4 of the 1992/ 1993 *Annual Report* of Ontario Hydro's Technical Advisory Panel on Nuclear Safety, is a

> radioactive isotope of hydrogen [that] occurs most commonly in the biosphere in the form of tritiated water. It decays with a half-life of twelve years to stable, inert helium, emitting a beta particle (an energetic electron) plus a neutrino in the decay process. Biological and physical studies have shown that nearly all the radiological hazard is due to the beta particle produced. The average range of these beta particles in water is less than one micro-metre. Because of the low energy and short range of the beta particles, tritium does not present an external radiation hazard. However, tritiated water is readily taken into the body by inhalation, ingestion or diffusion through the skin and consequently presents an internal radiation hazard.

DNA's concerns about the spill had to do primarily with the maximum dose levels of tritium allowed by the AECB. Candu nuclear reactors routinely release tritium in day-to-day operations.

The accident released the equivalent of 2,333 trillion Becquerels of radioactive tritium into the environment (Gerlsbeck 1992d). A Becquerel is a metric unit measuring radioactivity. It is equivalent to one radioactive disintegration per second (Lambert 1990). At that time, drinking water in Canada was considered by the AECB to be safe up to a dilution of 40,000 Becquerels per litre (Swainson 1992). Ontario Hydro officials were quick to point out that this amount of radiation represented less than 3 percent of the plant's monthly tritium release limit (*News Advertiser* 1992). While Irene Kock agreed with Ontario Hydro's claim that tritium levels were well within guideline limits, she believed that these guidelines were not strict enough. In her words, "There's no such thing as a safe emission. In my view, the only safe emission is zero discharge" (Swainson 1992). DNA was quick to point out that Canadian standards were fifty times less stringent than US drinking water standards, which have a maximum level for tritium exposure set at 700 Becquerels per litre of water. Stan Gray of Greenpeace suggested that Canadian radiation standards were based more on economic considerations than on safety. For Gray, these standards were "a political judgement the government makes on what is an acceptable death rate" (Gerlsbeck 1992c). In the same newspaper article, Norm Rubin of Energy Probe remarked that government standards on radiation were not realistic. Additionally, DNA was disturbed by the failure of Ontario Hydro officials to immediately notify the public about the spill. It believed that a public advisory should have been issued to tell people who depended on Lake Ontario water what the tritium levels were for several weeks following the accident.

In a letter to the AECB, dated 15 September 1992, protesting Ontario Hydro's reluctance to share information with the public, DNA stated: "People deserve to make a choice, whenever possible, about reducing their exposure to ionising radiation." Concern over tritium emissions had no noticeable effect on the subsequent relicensing of the Pickering plant. Ontario Hydro's facilities were not in contravention of any safety guidelines. The tritium issue would eventually reappear two years later, however, during a 1994 Pickering relicensing campaign (Mehta 2001).

Aside from issues dealing with the tritium spill and the absence of a second fast shutdown system at the Pickering "A" reactors, events surrounding the 1992 relicensing brought to the surface several issues that involved the concept of risk. For example, debates about the relative risks of ionizing radiation centred on comparing emissions levels and exposure limits to what individuals normally received from background radiation sources. According to the AECB, annual tritium releases from Canada's nuclear plants make up less than one one-hundredth of the dose received from naturally occurring sources of radiation (Gerlsbeck 1992b). Ontario Hydro's Technical Advisory Panel on Nuclear Safety (Ontario Hydro 1993) stated a similar sentiment:

Maximum radiation doses to the public resulting from the operation of Ontario Hydro's nuclear generating stations in 1992 were calculated to range from 3 micro-Sieverts at Darlington to about 23 micro-Sieverts at Pickering. Average doses to members of the public living within fifty kilometres of these stations were calculated to range from about 0.1 to 1.5 micro-Sieverts per year in 1992. All of these values are very low in comparison with the average of about 1000 micro-Sieverts per year ... all Canadians receive from natural sources of radiation every year of their lives. It is therefore expected that any health effects from radiation doses to the public ... are negligible and undetectable.

A Durham Nuclear Health Committee recommended that a monthly radiation exposure index combined with more comprehensive compiling of data on birth defects, stillbirths, and childhood cancer cases be initiated. The Durham Region health authorities likely intended to assuage the fears and anxieties of area residents through such reporting. There are, however, substantial differences in "acceptable" doses of ionizing radiation between countries such as Canada, the United States, and England. The average Canadian can be exposed to 5 milli-Sieverts per year of radiation (not including background levels or medical exposures), whereas levels in the US are twenty times lower at 0.25 milli-Sieverts per year, and ten times lower in England at 0.5 milli-Sieverts per year.

The AECB relicensed the Pickering plant in 1992 despite these concerns about safety. Public concern was not an issue in the decision. Only five letters, including one from DNA, were received by the AECB requesting that a public review be initiated. The only grounds for calling a public review would have to involve technical deficiencies. In an interview following the announcement regarding the relicensing, Hugh Spence, chief of the AECB's public information office, stated that "on balance, our staff concluded the plant was operated safely" (Haliechuk 1992). An AECB communiqué dated 14 October 1992 had the following to say about the AECB's decision: "The Board renewed the operating licenses for a period of 26.5 months until December 13, 1994. Although Board staff monitored and reviewed the state and operation of both plants and observed improvements in performance in a number of areas, it noted considerable improvement was needed before a fully satisfactory level of operation is achieved."

Durham Nuclear Awareness immediately denounced this decision. Irene Kock said, "We have a problem with the fact that the licences were extended at all at this time" (Haliechuk 1992). She continued, "We [DNA] have considerable concern about the AECB's ability to regulate. Perhaps they're too close to the [nuclear] industry." Such concerns about collusion were common in technocratic decision-making environments. Neo-institutionalism is less tied to formal organizational structures, and requires that institutionalized routines be decoupled from the actual practices of an organization (Meyer 1992). This decoupling enhances legitimacy by exposing the interconnectedness of formal state organizations and networks of actors (Peterson 1995).

This concern about the objectivity and neutrality of the Atomic Energy Control Board is a long-standing one. Because of this, the AECB's credibility was closely tied to its public image and public relations. A letter of 18 March 1981 from the AECB to Roy Henderson, City Clerk of Toronto City Hall, outlined how the AECB was attempting to be more open. The letter quoted an excerpt from a report of the Ontario Select Committee on the Safety of Ontario's Nuclear Reactors on the importance of opening public dialogue: "The Committee urged the Board to take all the steps it can to increase public awareness and public confidence in its proceedings by holding public hearings and, by making its decision, and reasons for decision, public."

A war of words – played out on a media battlefield – between the AECB and DNA illustrated just how easy it was to shatter trust between regulators, protesters, and the public at large. An interview in *Now Magazine* with AECB spokesperson Hugh Spence is one such example. Spence suggested that it was impractical to have an environmental assessment during a licence renewal hearing: "After all, it takes two to three years in many cases for one of these assessments to finish, and a license renewal is something that takes place over six months" (Cooly 1992). When asked about DNA's request for such a hearing, Spence said, "We take [DNA's] concerns seriously, which we do for all public groups, but they have a mission, and their agenda is doing away with nuclear power plants. Knowing where they're coming from, you know how to treat some of the things they say." In response, Jeff Brackett of DNA said, "That attitude is very unsettling," and "It's as if the AECB wants to keep [Ontario] Hydro from revealing to the public just what a financial and environmental disaster Pickering has been." DNA demanded an apology from the AECB in a letter of 10 September 1992 to then-president René Lévesque, indicating that Spence's comments were "completely unacceptable, coming from the chief public spokesperson of a supposedly neutral public agency." They never received one.

The decision to relicense Pickering also prompted heated exchanges between DNA and the AECB. A letter of 20 January 1993 from DNA to Secretary-General J.G. McManus questioned the AECB's decision not to require Ontario Hydro to upgrade its reactors in unit Pickering "A" with a second fast shutdown system: "It appears that AECB staff are making trade-offs between the cost of putting an independent fast shutdown system at Pickering 'A,' and public health and safety. According to BMD 93-07 [an AECB board member document], the cost of implementing a second fast shutdown system at Pickering 'A' will be $362 million. The cost should not even be a consideration for the AECB."

The AECB asked Ontario Hydro to consider alternative ways for achieving greater safety on shutdown options as a condition of the newly granted operating licence (changes to already constructed plants are known as "backfitting"). A letter from then-head of Ontario Hydro Maurice Strong to DNA justified Hydro's decision to install neutronic enhancement technology instead of a second independent fast shutdown system. Neutronic enhancement involves injecting neutron-absorbing gases into the core to slow down fission activity. Instead of shutting down the fission process instantaneously, as the insertion of control rods achieves, neutronic enhancement takes several minutes to control a runaway reactor. Strong stated in a letter of 5 April 1993: "As in the case of the shutdown system enhancement, any proposed solution undergoes intense scrutiny by the AECB. Numerous submissions providing exhaustive analysis and assessments and, in some cases, modifications to proposed solutions are required before the AECB is convinced that issues are being addressed satisfactorily." A letter of 25 February 1993 from Secretary-General McManus to DNA supported Ontario Hydro's proposal to use neutronic enhancement as a way of ensuring that Pickering "A" reactors were safer: "Modifications of this nature cannot have a deleterious impact on the environment. In this particular case, the only possible effect is a positive one: reduction in the possibility of an accident." This concurred with Strong's additional claim, in a letter to DNA dated 5 April 1993, that "[neutronic enhancement] is an option that provides the highest achievable assurance of public protection."

Concerns about the possibility of a "loss of coolant accident" (LOCA) at the Pickering plant were heightened when several examples of safety system unavailability became known. The emergency core cooling system was unavailable for fifteen months at reactor 2 in Pickering "A" until March 1989. The main containment chamber for all eight reactors was unavailable for seven years due to faulty seals. However, safety system malfunctions and subsequent periods of system unavailability were overshadowed by a host of serious accidents at the Pickering plant.

In November 1988, thirty-six fuel bundles were severely damaged in the reactor core due to operator error. A "loss of regulation accident" in July 1988 occurred when a worker removed the wrong fuse, thereby causing a computer in the operating station to increase power to the reactor. The tritium spill in August 1992 was the worst such spill in Ontario: A heat exchanger leaked contaminated heavy water into Lake Ontario. A flux tilt in reactor 3 at Pickering "A" caused an uncontrollable shift in the power level, forcing a shutdown state in October 1993. Besides these accidents, several thousand "significant events" have plagued the Pickering station.

Durham Nuclear Awareness also demanded a complete probabilistic risk assessment (PRA) of the Pickering reactors. Probabilistic risk assessment involves examining a host of possible compound system failures by aggregating risks across a system (Morgan and Henrion 1990). Such assessments attempt to predict the probability of safety failures in complex systems even in the absence of data for the system as a whole (Renn 1992). In other words, PRAs reveal the probability of compound error propagation. They have been particularly valuable in detecting deficiencies in complex technical systems.

Probabilistic risk assessment uses two approaches: "fault-tree" and "event-tree" analysis. Fault-tree analysis begins with an assumed consequence (fault), such as a loss of coolant accident, and then works back in time to examine the events that could lead to the fault. By contrast, event-tree analysis begins with a failure of a specific component (event), such as a rupture in a condenser tube, and then projects forward in time possible consequences of that event. Estimates from these different types of analysis allow probabilistic risk assessors to consider component failure and human error when calculating the probability of an accident. A 1992 study commissioned by DNA from an American research group, the Institute for Resource and Security Studies, pointed to the need for a complete probabilistic risk assessment of the Pickering reactors. In a letter to the AECB dated 15 January 1993, Gordon Thompson and Steven Sholly of this research group stressed the importance of this type of assessment. In a letter dated 20 January 1993, also to the AECB, DNA stated that "this information is a prerequisite to informed decision making on the matter of a second fast shutdown system at Pickering 'A.' DNA urges the Atomic Energy Control Board to require that Ontario Hydro complete the appropriate analysis as recommended by the Institute for Resource and Security Studies." In the end, no probabilistic risk assessment was requested of Ontario Hydro.

A probabilistic risk assessment was, however, conducted on the Darlington Nuclear Generating Station. In their letter to the AECB, Thompson and Sholly raised concerns about the quality of this assessment: "Our review of the Darlington PRA study revealed significant deficiencies. For example, the study was not subjected to thorough, independent peer review, although experience has shown that PRA findings are often substantially altered after such a review. This and other deficiencies lead us to conclude that the PRA process in Ontario does not meet standards that prevail in the United States."

This difference of opinion shows how risk experts have a fair degree of latitude in their assumptions when performing risk assessments. Perhaps the range of acceptable approaches reflects institutional biases or preferences. Perhaps AECB staff perceived the criticisms of Thompson and Sholly as motivated by a desire to contract out their services? In any event, this example illustrates how the institutional structures for assessing and managing risk are prone to organizational failures or deficits that may ultimately increase the level of risk to the public and environment. The corollary is that limited resources may be squandered in an attempt to reduce a risk that is low relative to others.

Probabilistic risk assessment is not perfect, however. It loses much of its value when common mode failures and simultaneous breakdowns occur as a result of human error or human-machine interactions. An assumption behind PRA calculations is that everyone is doing his or her job exactly as trained. Deviations from routine screening and remedial action often escape inclusion in the models used in PRA studies. As well, much of the data on the estimates for failure are incomplete, theoretical, or uncertain. PRA assumes that current reactor designs are adequate, overlooking possible design flaws. Lastly, PRA ignores major sources of reactor risk such as aging, earthquakes, sabotage, and terrorism.

The shortcomings of PRA are evident in a statement by US Nuclear Regulatory Commission (NRC) commissioner Kenneth Rogers at an international symposium on nuclear plant aging held in 1988. Although referring to the failure of pressure tubes in Westinghouse reactors, Rogers's narrative captures the sources of error usually unaccounted for in PRA studies: "The concern is with sudden multiple tube failures – common mode failures. For example, such failures could come about by having essentially uniform degradation of the tubes. Degradation would decrease the safety margins so that, in essence, we have a 'loaded gun,' an accident waiting to happen. Under those conditions, a pressure transient or a seismic event could rupture many tubes simultaneously" (International Atomic Energy Agency 1988). Consequently, a PRA represents the experts' answer to a host of uncertain interactions and events.

The January 1993 letter by Thompson and Sholly analyzed the probability of a severe nuclear power plant accident occurring. The estimates they gave for such an event (on a Chernobyl scale) were markedly different from those provided by Ontario Hydro. According to Thompson and Sholly, there was a 1-in-17 chance of a severe accident occurring over the next twenty or so years at one of Ontario Hydro's nuclear reactors. Ontario Hydro estimated that the probability of such an accident was closer to 1 in 437. In a letter to the AECB responding to the Thompson and Sholly analysis, David Martin stated that "this study shatters the myth of the superior safety of the Candu reactor. The risk of a major accident at Darlington, Pickering, or Bruce is about the same as it was at Chernobyl." Martin also stated that "the loss of life and the trillion dollar cost of a meltdown would be totally unacceptable, yet Ontario Hydro continues to operate twenty reactors."

The potential loss of life and property damage from a major nuclear accident in the southern Ontario region provoked anti-nuclear groups and nuclear critics to ask questions about the issue of liability. Canada's Nuclear Liability Act limited the responsibility of utility companies like Ontario Hydro to a maximum of $75 million for damage caused by their nuclear facilities and waste disposal activities. Needless to say, because of the locations of both Pickering and Darlington nuclear stations within some of the most densely populated regions of Canada, this amount of liability would be easily exceeded with even a small-scale accident. Loss of life, injuries to health, and damage to property and livelihood could cost trillions of dollars if an accident similar to Chernobyl occurred in this region.

This concern provoked criticism from the Toronto-based environmental group Energy Probe, which chastised the "nuclear risk-makers" for not taking full responsibility for the risks they generated (Energy Probe 1987): "Whatever else the computer models indicate, a worst-case scenario would clearly involve consequences that would greatly exceed the total liability of the risk-makers, leaving victims at the mercy of government agencies, federal Parliament, charitable organisations, family, and friends for whatever emergency assistance they were able and willing to provide. We believe that this situation is unfortunate, and are offended by the fact that it is the result not of accident, but of explicit government action – specifically the passage and proclamation of the Nuclear Liability Act." Energy Probe also castigated the nuclear industry for defining nuclear risk as "acceptable" to the public at large, but not a financial risk worth backing up. The report asserted that "[Energy Probe] cannot see how any conclusions can be credible that assert the 'acceptability' of a risk that will not be accepted by those who are most aware of the exact nature of the risk – and who profit by making the stations that create the risk."

In the United States, similar criticisms on the issue of industry liability have been made by anti-nuclear groups such as Critical Mass Energy Project (a division of Public Citizen) of Washington, DC. In a paper entitled "Consequences of a Nuclear Accident," Joshua Gordon and Mark Knapp (1989) of Critical Mass Energy Project point out that the American Price-Anderson Act exempts the nuclear power industry from all but $560 million of liability in the event of an accident. Although this limit is several times higher than the Canadian maximum, the amount covered is woefully inadequate. The *Reactor Safety Study* (known as WASH-1400) completed in 1975 by the newly created Nuclear Regulatory Commission (NRC) estimated that a major nuclear power plant accident could result in 45,000 fatalities and 70,000 injuries, and cause $17 billion in property damage (US Nuclear Regulation Commission 1975). Not included in the study are losses from lost wages, costs of evacuation, decontamination costs, lost farm crops, care for those killed, injured, or disabled, lost business revenue, lost taxation, loss of the nuclear power plant itself, and, last but not least, ecological damage.

Concerns about liability and financial responsibility are also part of a critique by DNA of the failure of Atomic Energy of Canada Limited (AECL) to adequately provide for decommissioning costs. AECL, a Crown corporation formed in 1952 through a provision in the Atomic Energy Control Act, has a variety of installations in Canada, including research laboratories (Chalk River, Ontario, and Whiteshell, Manitoba), two heavy water plants, and three nuclear power plants (Douglas Point and NPD in Ontario, Gentilly-1 in Quebec). These facilities are rapidly reaching the end of their engineered life spans. For this reason, reactors, radioactive waste, and contaminated equipment need to be dismantled and disposed of safely. This process, called "decommissioning" or "mothballing," is ideally intended to return nuclear sites to a "green field" condition. AECL's own estimates of decommissioning costs suggest that at least $200-300 million (in 1993 dollars) will be needed to clean up these sites. It should be noted that this conservative figure equals about half of AECL's equity.

The Auditor General of Canada has severely criticized AECL over the past decade for inadequately providing for the costs associated with decommissioning: "I wish to draw to your attention that as described in Note 11 to the financial statement, the corporation [AECL] is facing significant de-commissioning and site remediation expenditures which, under current funding arrangements, are financed mainly through parliamentary appropriations. These costs will continue to be incurred over the long term and their magnitude is such that there may be a significantly increased demand on government services" (Auditor General of Canada 1993). The report also noted that AECL's failure to log these costs as liabilities in its financial statements is a violation of generally accepted accounting principles.

In the United States, private utility companies are typically required by state law to put aside funds for decommissioning nuclear facilities. Critical Mass Energy Project provides a reactor-by-reactor assessment of decommissioning costs and funds in a 1990 report (Borson 1990). For example, the owner (Pacific Gas and Electric) of the Diablo Canyon reactors in California has set aside roughly 42 percent of the estimated $273 million decommissioning cost estimate. The Detroit Edison Company has in reserve approximately 32 percent of the costs for closing down the small Fermi research reactor in Michigan. Not all US utility operators are so committed to putting aside money for decommissioning, however. The Arizona Public Service Company has saved less than 4 percent of the funds required for its Palo Verde reactors. The owner of the infamous Three Mile Island facility, GPU Nuclear Corporation, has saved only 5 percent of the funds needed for decommissioning. Although these examples show how large a range exists in decommissioning funds across US nuclear facilities, compared with Canadian facilities there is a notable difference: no funds have been set aside for returning sites to their original "green field" condition in Canada. AECL and Ontario Hydro count on public funding for this large clean-up job. Consequently, the "true" cost of electricity from nuclear sources is much higher than what the consumer pays in monthly electricity bills.

Where Is Canada's Nuclear Industry at Now?

In August 1997, Ontario Hydro closed seven of its nineteen reactors. An independent consulting team brought in from the United States by Ontario Hydro's past president Allan Kupcis determined that safety was being compromised at many plants, including the Pickering plant, due to a rash of accidents and related safety problems. It is estimated that the costs associated with bringing these plants back into service could exceed $8 billion. Confronted with this immense integrity gap, nuclear power in Canada has finally begun a downward spiral from which it is unlikely to recover. Ironically, anti-nuclear activists, including members of DNA, were not the ones responsible for this development. A group of nuclear experts eventually recognized the integrity gap that had emerged between fundamental policy objectives (e.g., safety and economic efficiency) and the mounting evidence that many of Ontario's nuclear facilities were unsafe and therefore uneconomical.

Conclusions

Nuclear power has failed to provide a stable and low-cost source of electricity for the province of Ontario. In fact, nuclear power is declining in popularity in many parts of the Western world. With the exception of a few countries, including France, the nuclear option is no longer being seriously considered as a long-term, viable source of domestically produced electricity. If nuclear power is ruled out as an energy option, and a reliance on fossil fuels is limited by reserves and sustainability concerns, then what options remain? Clearly, the only real choice remaining for many parts of the world is the renewable energy option.

Countries with a large landmass and few energy choices should seriously consider utilizing biomass more efficiently. The commercial production of biofuels using low-value biomass fuel stocks and trees could yield high-quality biofuels, including bioethanol and biodiesel. For instance, large-scale hybrid poplar plantations can provide the fibre and the lignocellulosic material for bioethanol plants.[5] In other parts of the world, switchgrass and bluestem can provide abundant, high-quality forage for bioethanol production. With good cold tolerance and wide geographic adaptation, these grasses provide a high yield with low water and fertilizer inputs. Agricultural residues, including corn husks, rice husks, and alfalfa stems, can be used to produce biofuel too. Lastly, biodiesel can be made from renewable crops, including soybean and canola (rapeseed). At the moment, over a hundred cities worldwide have demonstration projects utilizing biodiesel. The use of renewable crops and trees not only provides much needed energy but also has the additional benefit of replacing carbon-intense fuels with carbon dioxide–neutral sources of energy.

Other forms of renewable energy need to be identified and developed. The use of micro-hydroelectric generators can tap into large energy reserves with minimal environmental impact. Wind generation and solar energy collection are two highly promising yet undervalued sources of energy. Finally, the creative exploitation of geothermal and wave sources of energy can provide for the basic needs of many parts of the world.

To conclude, the energy mix used by a country should reflect an awareness of the environmental, economic, social, and human health dimensions associated with it. Clearly, energy is a finite resource that can be tapped into in different ways with different impacts. The developed world should be responsible for fostering renewable energy development while allowing the developing world the opportunity to make progress with energy sources that are readily available. A shift towards a more sustainable energy future cannot occur unless energy is used more wisely. This entails stimulating energy efficiencies and changes in individual and collective behaviour. Moving away from large-scale, centralized energy programs, such as that ushered in by the nuclear industry, has the added benefit of better reflecting the needs of communities and incorporating the values and goals of a host of stakeholders. This shift in emphasis coincides with new models of governance that place a premium on integrity, a policy dimension that has much room for improvement at the intersection of Canadian energy and environmental concerns.

Notes

1 This does not include electricity trade.
2 "Vision of Energy Supply in the 21st Century: Managing the Global Bonfire." Paper presented at the Data Sources: World Bank, Statistics Canada, and US Department of Energy Carbon Dioxide Information Analysis Center (CDIAC) 1998. Linear regression equation taken from the work of Romney Duffey Climate Change and Energy Options Symposium, Ottawa, 17-19 November 1999.
3 These calculations are based on use of the Carbon Emission Calculation produced by the Uranium Institute (1997). This calculator has been replaced by one from the World Nuclear Association, and the calculations remain the same. <http://www.world-nuclear.org/conv.htm> (17 December 2002).
4 The Canadian Nuclear Safety Commission was formed with a separate mandate from the research and marketing mandate of Atomic Energy of Canada Limited. The Canadian Nuclear Safety Commission has an explicit mandate to establish and enforce national standards in the area of nuclear safety. The commission is a court of record, and a formal system is set out for review and appeal of commission orders and decisions. The commission is empowered to require financial guarantees, to order remedial action, and to require responsible parties to bear the costs of remedial measures. The commission and cabinet may incorporate provincial laws by reference and delegate powers to the provinces. Reference: <http://www.nuclearsafety.gc.ca> (17 December 2002).
5 A Canadian research network known as BIOCAP Canada is involved in exploring the use of poplars and other trees and agricultural crops to reduce carbon dioxide emissions through sequestration, and the use of these products and co-products for fuel, fibre, and industrial applications. For more information, consult BIOCAP's website at <http://www.biocap.ca>.

References
Ashford, A. 1990. Reckoning Schemes of Legitimation: On Commissions of Inquiry as Power/Knowledge Form. *Journal of Historical Sociology* 3: 1-22.

Auditor General of Canada. 1993. *Annual Report*. Sections 3.9-3.16. <http://www.oag-bvg. gc.ca/domino/other.nsf/html/99repm_e.html> (select 1993, then Chapter 3) (8 August 2001).

Beanlands, G.E., and P.N. Duinker. 1983. *An Ecological Framework for Environmental Impact Assessment in Canada*. Halifax: Institute for Resource and Environmental Studies, Dalhousie University, and Federal Environmental Assessment Review Office.

Bobbit, J. 1992. Nuclear Plant Probe Urged. *News Advertiser*, 21 August 1992, 4.

Borson, D. 1990. *Payment Due: A Reactor-by-Reactor Assessment of the Nuclear Industry's $25+ Billion Decommissioning Bill*. Critical Mass Energy Project Report no: C3342. Washington, DC: Critical Mass Energy Project.

Cooly, G. 1992. Nuke Review. *Now Magazine* 11(52): 23.

Doern, G.B. 1976. *The Atomic Energy Control Board: An Evaluation of Regulatory and Administrative Processes and Procedures*. Ottawa: Law Reform Commission of Canada; Minister of Supply and Services Canada.

Duffey, Romney. 1999. Vision of Energy Supply in the 21st Century: Managing the Global Bonfire. Paper presented at the Climate Change and Energy Options Symposium, Ottawa, 17-19 November, 1999. <http://www.cns-snc.ca/CNS_Conferences/conference_index. html> (17 December 2002).

Energy Probe. 1987. *Risks, Nuclear Safety, and the Ontario Nuclear Safety Review*. Report to the Ontario Nuclear Safety Review. Toronto: Energy Probe.

Finch, R. 1986. *Exporting Danger: A History of the Canadian Nuclear Energy Export Programme*. Montreal: Black Rose Books.

Gerlsbeck, R. 1992a. Pickering Nuke Plant Could Leak in Crisis. *Oshawa Times*, 18 June, 3.

–. 1992b. Anti Nuke Protesters Want Pickering Shut. *Oshawa Times*, 19 August, 1.

–. 1992c. Tritium Levels Soar in Water Samples. *Oshawa Times*, 17 August, 6.

–. 1992d. Feds Stall on Study of Tritium Effects. *Oshawa Times*, 5 August, 8.

Gordon, J., and M. Knapp. 1989. *Consequences of a Nuclear Accident*. Washington, DC: Critical Mass Energy Project.

Haliechuk, R. 1992. Two Nuclear Stations Get Renewed Licenses. *Toronto Star*, 17 October, B8.

International Atomic Energy Agency. 1988. *Safety Aspects of the Ageing and Maintenance of Nuclear Power Plants*. Reference: STI/PUB/759. Vienna: International Atomic Energy Agency.

International Energy Agency. 1998. *Energy Share of TPES in 1998*. <http://www.iea.org/stats/ files/selstats/keyindic/keyindic.htm> (14 August 2001).

International Energy Association. 1998a. *Key Energy Indicators in 1998*. <http://www.iea.org/ stats/files/selstats/keyindic/country/canada.htm> (8 August 2001).

–. 1998b. *Fuel Shares of World Total Primary Energy Supply for 1998*. <http://www.iea.org/ statist/keyworld/keystats.htm> (8 August 2001).

Jacob, G. 1990. *Site Unseen: The Politics of Siting a Nuclear Waste Repository*. Pittsburgh, PA: University of Pittsburgh Press.

Johnson, K.C., and J. Rouleau. 1991. Tritium Releases from the Pickering Nuclear Generation Station and Birth and Infant Mortality in Nearby Communities, 1971-1988. AECB report, INFO-0401.

Kansky, M. 1987. *Summary of the Federal Environmental Assessment and Review Process Procedures*. Prepared as a background paper for a project to determine Native Indian and Inuit concerns. Edmonton: Environmental Law Centre.

Lambert, B. 1990. *How Safe Is Safe? Radiation Controversies Explained*. London: Unwin Paperbacks.

Lipset, S.M. 1985. Canada and the United States: The Cultural Dimension. In *Canada and the United States: Enduring Friendship, Persistent Stress*, edited by C.F. Doran and J.H. Sigler. Englewood Cliffs, NJ: Prentice Hall.

Lyman, R. 1999. The Future of Oil Supply. Paper presented at the Climate Change and Energy Options Symposium, Ottawa, 17-19 November 1999. <http://www.cns-snc.ca/ CNS_Conferences/conference_index.html> (17 December 2002).

Masters, C.D., D.H. Root, and R.M. Turner. 1998. *World Conventional Crude Oil and Natural Gas: Identified Reserves, Undiscovered Resources and Futures*. US Geological Survey Open-File

Report 98-468. <http://energy.er.usgs.gov/products/openfile/OFR98-468/text.htm> (11 August 2001).

McKay, P. 1983. *Electric Empire: The Inside Story of Ontario Hydro.* Toronto: Between the Lines.

McLaren, C. 1987. Pickering Reactor Shutdown System Falls Below AECB Safety Standards. *Globe and Mail,* 24 July, A1.

Mehta, M.D. 2001. Regulating Nuclear Power: The Mismanagement of Public Consultation in Canada. In *In the Chamber of Risks: Understanding Risk Controversies,* edited by W. Leiss. Montreal and Kingston: McGill-Queen's University Press.

Meyer, J.W. 1992. Conclusion: Institutionalization and the Rationality of Formal Organizational Structure. In *Organizational Environments: Ritual and Rationality,* edited by J.W. Meyer and W.R. Scott. Newbury Park, CA: Sage Publications.

Morgan, M.G., and M. Henrion. 1990. *Uncertainty: A Guide to Dealing with Uncertainty in Quantitative Risk and Policy Analysis.* New York: Cambridge University Press.

News Advertiser. 1992. Opinion: How Safe Is Nuclear? 7 August, 6.

Notzke, C. 1994. *Aboriginal Peoples and Natural Resources in Canada.* North York, ON: Captus University Publications.

Oil and Gas Journal. 1997. Worldwide Look at Reserves and Production. *Oil and Gas Journal* 96(52): 38-39.

Peterson, J. 1995. Decision-Making in the European Union: Towards a Framework for Analysis. *Journal of European Public Policy* 2(1): 69-93.

Renn, O. 1992. Concepts of Risk: A Classification. In *Social Theories of Risk,* edited by S. Krimsky and D. Golding. Westport, CT: Praeger.

Richardson, M., J. Sherman, and M.A. Gismondi. 1993. *Winning Back the Words: Confronting Experts in an Environmental Public Hearing.* Toronto: Garamond Press.

Richardson, N.H. 1989. *Land Use Planning and Sustainable Development in Canada.* Ottawa: Canadian Environmental Advisory Council, Environment Canada.

Sadler, B. 1990. Impact Assessment in Transition: A Framework for Redeployment. In *Integrated Approaches to Resource Planning and Management,* edited by R. Lang. Banff, AB: Resource Management Programs.

Stevens, D.F. 1993. *Corporate Autonomy and Institutional Control: The Crown Corporation as a Problem in Organizational Design.* Montreal and Kingston: McGill-Queen's University Press.

Swainson, G. 1992. Reactor Spill Shuts Ajax Water Treatment Plant. *Toronto Star,* 4 August, A6.

United States Nuclear Regulatory Commission. 1975. An Assessment of Accident Risks in US Commercial Nuclear Power Plants. Reactor Safety Study. WASH-1400, NUREG-75 /014. Springfield, VA: National Technical Information Service.

Uranium Institute. 1997. *Nuclear Energy and the Environment.* <http://www.uilondon.org/co2gen.htm> (8 August 2001).

–. 1998. *The Contribution of Nuclear Energy to Limiting Potential Global Climate Change.* <http://www.uilondon.org/uifostat.htm> (8 August 2001).

World Energy Council. 1990. *Survey of Energy Resources.* <http://www.worldenergy.org/wec-geis/publications/open.plx?file=default/current_ser.htm> (11 August 2001).

Wynne, B. 1982. *Rationality and Ritual: The Windscale Inquiry and Nuclear Decisions in Britain.* Chalfront St. Giles, UK: British Society for the History of Science.

6

Participatory Management and Sustainability: Evolving Policy and Practice in a Mountain Environment

Fikret Berkes, Jay Anderson, Colin Duffield, J.S. Gardner,
A.J. Sinclair, and Greg Stevens

The case study described in this chapter, an interdisciplinary team project in southeastern British Columbia in a forested mountain environment, illustrates local and regional changes in sustainability planning in a multiple-use area. Change in local practice followed a major policy shift from a single-resource (logging) emphasis to multiple use. In the old management system, the forest industry used the forest with relatively little allowance for other uses. Under the new arrangement, the forest industry came under the control of an increasingly more stringent code, allowing for other uses and for the expression of environmental values in the form of more protected areas, conservation of major species, and biodiversity. This was accomplished through: (1) the incorporation of changing environmental values, (2) stakeholder participation in the normative planning stages, rather than post-decision involvement, and (3) ecosystem-based management in which resource users become participants in the process of monitoring ecosystem sustainability. This case illustrates the use of a diversity of information for sustainability planning, and the influence of rules and norms on policy making. It also shows, however, that a gap remains between policy and practice because of the inability to translate long-term participatory management into enduring policies at the various levels of decision making.

Introduction

Context
Sustainability can be examined from two different vantage points. Some of the chapters in this volume take a "macro" view, examining national-level policies and international agreements. Alternatively, one can take a "micro" view, looking at sustainability from the local level up. These two angles are complementary; they are part of a cross-scale approach to sustainability in which policies and practice may be examined across the scale of organization from the local level to the international (Berkes 2002). To understand

Canada's environmental successes and failures, we need to examine international forces as well as national and provincial policy. The cross-scale approach suggests, however, that we also have to know something about how environment and resource policies play out "on the ground" locally and regionally. In particular, we need to examine the dynamics of change and the evolution of policy and practice in response to various forces. This chapter takes a cross-scale view from the bottom up, and uses one detailed example, the examination of sustainability in a forested mountain ecosystem in British Columbia, to illustrate the application and evolution of science and policy from the local and regional to the provincial level.

The case study is offered not as an isolated story but as an example of the ambitious goals and some promising instruments that are being put into place for the conservation and management of the Canadian environment. Other case studies, corresponding to the various chapters of Agenda 21, could have been used just as easily to illustrate many of the same forces and processes. For example, a great deal of work is being done to implement biodiversity conservation (Chapter 15 of Agenda 21 [1992 Earth Summit]). Regarding indigenous peoples (Chapter 26), a number of land claims agreements have been signed between Aboriginal groups and the government since the Rio de Janeiro Earth Summit in 1992, including the Nunavut Land Claims Agreement of 1993 that changed the map of Canada by establishing a new northern territory. In the area of forest management (Chapter 11), the Canadian Model Forest network was created, with each model forest serving as a demonstration of partnerships to achieve sustainable forest management. Ocean protection (Chapter 17) is being addressed by the 1997 Oceans Act, which brings a new order and calls for ecosystem management and participatory approaches (Hanson 1998).

These changes in Canadian environmental management reflect a new dynamic of responses to the challenges posed by sustainable development and Agenda 21. A key characteristic of this new mode of environmental management is a widening of the policy network associated with ecosystem management (Coleman and Perl 1999). Can such initiatives for deliberation and action overcome the constraints and deadlocks that typify so much of Canada's previous environmental policy making? Or are there institutionalized constraints on the government's ability to deliver upon stated goals?

As the case study of British Columbia's approach to forest resource management will demonstrate, expanded policy networks have the potential to take into account a range of values that were previously ignored. They have the potential to create a kind of participatory science that supplements conventional scientific assessments done by government and industry. Such participatory management offers an institutional alternative to business as usual in Canadian environmental policy making that can contribute to the reduction of the integrity gap that has been noted throughout this volume. Institutionalizing participatory management requires moving beyond regional experiments, however, and creating the space to translate local alternative management approaches across the political scale into provincial and federal policy.

The Case Study

Research that supports sustainable development initiatives requires a broad approach, taking into account social, ecological, and economic factors. We started the British Columbia project with a special interest in the management of forested mountain environments, and in the use of participatory or people-oriented approaches to resource management. We adopted a view of sustainable development that explicitly included three elements:

- the environmental imperative of living within ecological means
- the economic imperative of meeting basic material needs
- the social imperative of meeting basic human and cultural needs.

Such an approach to sustainable development is concerned with much more than maximizing resource yields. It covers a broad range of environmental values as well as economic and social needs, and opens up the scope of decision making not only to a wider range of natural and social sciences but also to a range of stakeholders' interests affected by resource management decisions.

Under the overall goal of studying policy development with regard to the sustainable use of forested mountain ecosystems, case studies were developed in the Indian Himalayas and the Canadian Rockies. The objectives of the project were to develop integrated methodologies best suited for the comparative study of land resource management policies in forested mountain ecosystems; to study the successes and failures of mountain environment resource management policies and their social, economic, and historical context; to evaluate and develop criteria for assessing and monitoring sustainability in mountain environments; and to communicate policy implications to agencies and people concerned with sustainable development (Berkes and Gardner 1997). Parts of the study dealing with India (Berkes et al. 1998; Sinclair and Ham 2000; Sinclair and Diduck 2000) and with India-Canada comparisons (Duffield et al. 1998; Berkes et al. 2000) have been published elsewhere. This chapter is based on aspects of the Canadian case.

Following the introductory sections, the chapter has three major parts:

- the biophysical study, in which we sought to measure sustainability quantitatively, based on various databases

- the social study, in which we sought to assess sustainability qualitatively, based on indicators that were considered important by the people who lived there and used or managed resources of the area
- an analysis of the implications of our findings for improving the integrity of Canada's sustainability planning.

Concepts and Definitions

The sustainable development concept has been used widely as an organizing framework since the World Conservation Strategy (IUCN/UNEP/WWF 1980), the Brundtland report (WCED 1987), and the United Nations Conference on Environment and Development (UNCED), or Earth Summit, in Rio de Janeiro in 1992. The idea of sustainable development, as promoted in the World Conservation Strategy, referred to a broad range of objectives for meeting basic human needs while maintaining essential ecological processes and life-support systems, preserving genetic diversity, and ensuring sustainable utilization of species and ecosystems. The popularization of the term came with the World Commission on Environment and Development. Its report was long on problem descriptions and short on policy prescriptions, but it provided the standard definition of sustainable development as "development that meets the needs of the present without compromising the ability of future generations to meet their needs" (WCED 1987, 8).

The classical idea of sustained yields in resource management science goes back to a German forest scientist, Faustmann, who used the concept in 1849 to calculate the forest rotation period to maximize yields (Ludwig 1993). Applications of the sustained yield concept have been developed in fisheries, wildlife and rangeland management, and forestry, often with elaborate mathematical models that treat the target resource in isolation from the rest of the ecosystem. Since about the 1930s, maximizing sustained yields has been the goal in all areas of resource management. It was not until the 1970s that the concept first came under criticism from an ecological point of view, and, somewhat later, from the economic and social points of view.

The two kinds of sustainability are in sharp contrast. The maximum sustainable yield idea focuses on the resource as a commodity, with a prescription of the ways in which it can be efficiently extracted. By contrast, the second kind of sustainability – sustainable development – explicitly includes: (1) the environmental imperative of living within ecological means, (2) the economic imperative of meeting basic material needs, and (3) the social imperative of meeting basic social needs and cultural sustainability.

Thus, sustainable development is concerned with much more than maximizing resource yields. It covers a broad range of environmental values as well as economic and social needs, and opens up the scope of decision making not only to a wider range of natural and social sciences but also to a much wider range of stakeholders' interests affected by resource management decisions. A powerful but often ambiguous paradigm, sustainable development (SD) has been criticized for meaning all things to all people, and the institutionalization of SD has been interpreted as indicating a convergence of environmental and liberal norms (Bernstein 2001). Some authors have pointed out that it is more useful to consider SD not as a product but a process that does not have to be defined precisely in order to be useful. "Sustainable development is not a goal, not a condition likely to be attained on earth as we know it. Rather, it is more like freedom or justice, a direction in which we strive" (Lee 1993).

The Study Area
The study was carried out in the mountains of British Columbia along the Columbia River valley near the community of Nakusp (Figure 6.1). The Columbia River flows from north to south, widening to form the Upper and Lower Arrow Lakes. Water released from a series of dams built in the 1970s inundates the flatter parts of the river bottom and increases the size and depth of the Arrow Lakes. The dams were built for flood control and hydroelectric production, and the project was accompanied by considerable controversy at the time. Many families were forced from fertile valley bottomland as farms and towns were flooded. The area is sparsely settled; the town of Nakusp is the only sizeable community. It lies at the junction of the two roads that provide year-round access along the valley. In addition, there is an extensive network of resource roads (primarily logging roads) that allow vehicles ready access to all but the remotest parts of the watershed.

The diversity of the socio-economic history of the region reflects that of the mountain environment in which it is situated. Although no longer living there today, First Nations used the area before colonization, but were reduced by epidemics from the south in the mid-1800s. The Ktunaxa/ Kinbasket, the Shuswap and the Okanagan nations have overlapping land claims in the region (CORE 1995). Towards the end of the 1800s, there existed a mixed frontier economy in the area, based on silver and gold mining and timber extraction. The wood was used for railway ties, construction, boat building, fuel, telephone poles, and shingles. Some forests were burned to facilitate prospecting. During the early 1900s, the region was known for its orchards, but competition from the Okanagan and high transportation costs reduced production to a local scale. Hard times began in the mid-1900s, triggered by the collapse of the silver industry and high costs of transportation. This change in the local economy was compounded by hydroelectric development and the impacts of reservoir creation.

Despite local protests, the Columbia River Treaty was signed in 1964 and the Arrow Lakes were raised into reservoirs with the completion of Keenleyside Dam in 1969. Flooded private land was bought or expropriated, and the arrival of hydro workers brought a temporary economic boom

Figure 6.1

The study area, Nakusp, British Columbia

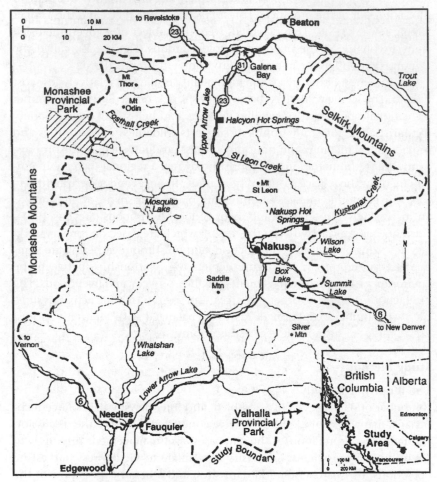

that faded by the early 1970s. In recent years, tourism has become a growth industry, and the population is beginning to increase as low land prices attract migrants from Vancouver, the Okanagan valley, and Calgary. Logging is still the backbone of employment in the area, however (Stevens 1997).

Starting in the 1960s, commercial forestry emerged as the major force in the region's economy. Tree Farm Licences (TFLs) and Forest Licences (FLs) were created to give security of timber access to large companies with pulp and lumber processing operations. Forest Licences are located in Timber Supply Areas (TSAs). Major companies in the region include Celgar, Slocan, and Pope and Talbot. Much of the actual timber cutting is done by independent local contractors. Regionally, the industry is stable with increasing employment, but in Nakusp it is more volatile and employment is declining. Forest harvest volumes, practices, and land-use planning are currently in a state of flux as a result of the provincial Forest Practices Code (FPC) and the Timber Supply Review (TSR). These changes were the subject of a government-led study involving all the major stakeholder groups (Figure 6.2), called the Commission on Resources and the Environment (CORE 1995).

The attraction of the area is the high quality of life and relatively low cost of land. The scenic wilderness beauty, hot springs, relaxed lifestyle, summer recreational opportunities, wildlife viewing, and heli-skiing draw a variety of tourists. The forest environment supports wilderness opportunities and provides local income from nontimber forest products such as mushrooms. In the 1990s, immigration and tourism spawned a regional increase in employment in the service, construction, trade, finance, and government sectors. The economic impacts of immigration and tourism are appreciated as an increasingly important component of local livelihoods (Stevens 1997). Current economic activities in the region, which are based on forestry, services, tourism, silviculture, construction, and mushroom gathering are summarized in Figure 6.3. The figure depicts the relationships between the environment, resource management activities, services, and livelihoods. The interactions of forestry, other resources, and socio-economic activities illustrate why timber extraction needs to be balanced with alternative forest uses for a more sustainable regional economy.

Study Methods

The Biophysical Study
A number of databases were assembled, and interviews with resource technicians, managers, and local users were conducted. Much of the discussion centred on interpretation of the databases, and management responses to environmental problems. Site visits were made to view forest harvesting operations, fish hatcheries, and dam sites, and a broad exploration of the local topography, economic activity, history, hazards, and land use was conducted. Some informal ground verification of satellite imagery was attempted, although most of the usable information was obtained from Geographic Information Systems (GIS) databases. Local contacts were a valuable source of information, identifying regional environmental concerns and providing leads to additional databases.

A Landsat 3 band Multispectral Scanner (MSS) image of the Columbia River valley, and two sets of air photos, one dating from 1970 and the other from 1987, were purchased, along with a selection of thematic and topographic maps. Eventually, an extensive and eclectic database was assembled from a variety of private, commercial, professional, federal, and provincial

Figure 6.2

Composition of the West Kootenay–Boundary regional negotiation table

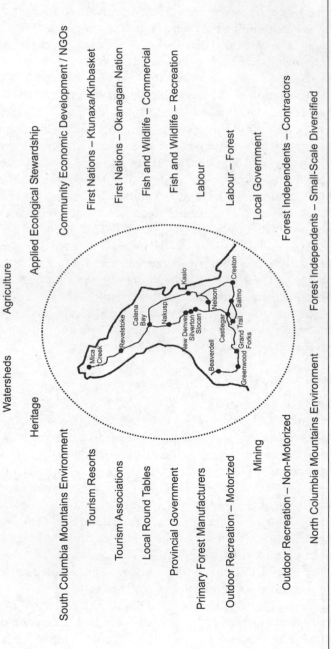

Agriculture

Applied Ecological Stewardship

Community Economic Development / NGOs

First Nations – Ktunaxa/Kinbasket

First Nations – Okanagan Nation

Fish and Wildlife – Commercial

Fish and Wildlife – Recreation

Labour

Labour – Forest

Local Government

Forest Independents – Contractors

Forest Independents – Small-Scale Diversified

Watersheds

Heritage

South Columbia Mountains Environment

Tourism Resorts

Tourism Associations

Local Round Tables

Provincial Government

Primary Forest Manufacturers

Outdoor Recreation – Motorized

Mining

Outdoor Recreation – Non-Motorized

North Columbia Mountains Environment

Source: CORE 1995.

Figure 6.3

A model of livelihoods in the Arrow Lakes region, showing relationships between the environment, resource management, socio-economic activity, services, and people's well-being

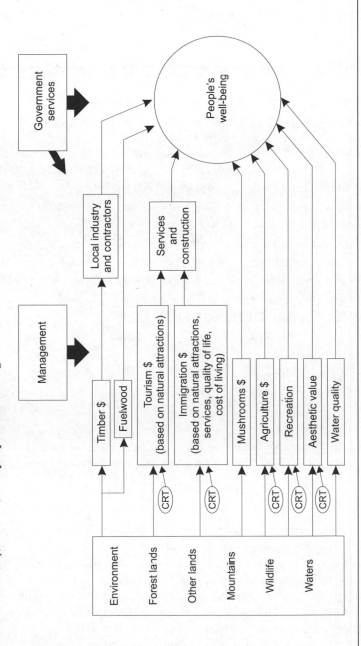

Source: Duffield 1997.

Table 6.1

Databases and data sources used for the study

Database	Comments and details
Satellite image	Landsat 3 band MSS image, 25 June 1992
Air photos	High-altitude coverage from 1970 and 1987
Hydrological data	Hydat CD-ROM dataset, Environment Canada
Climatological data	Environment Canada (B. Fehr)
GIS land-use data	BC Ministry of Environment, Lands and Parks (MoELP)
Land-use data	Commission on Resources and the Environment (CORE) report and background (CD-ROM)
Forest insect disease data	Forestry Canada
Caribou habitat data	Canadian Heritage, Parks Canada
Trapping harvest data	MoELP, Nelson, BC
BC fur auction price data	North American Fur Auctions, Winnipeg
Bull trout catch data	Glen Olson, Olson's Marine, Nakusp, BC
Kokanee catch data	MoELP, Grant Thorp, Senior Fishery Technician
Kokanee population data	MoELP, S. Sebastian
Arrow Lakes water quality	BC Hydro
Sewage discharge data	Environment Canada, Conservation and Protection
Air quality data	MoELP, Nelson, BC

Source: Adapted from Anderson 1997.

sources. We found twenty-one databases or data sets relevant to the study. Several of the data sets were redundant, however, as owners shared information with others. The most useful sixteen data sets were selected for study (Table 6.1).

The Social Study

To develop local indicators of sustainability, interviews were conducted with two groups. One group consisted of twenty-one natural resource management professionals in the Arrow Lakes region from Revelstoke, Nakusp, New Denver, Castlegar, and Nelson. The other group included twenty-two Nakusp stakeholders (local resident resource users and interest group representatives from Nakusp) drawn from the list of participants involved in the CORE (1995) process or related to it.

The interviews used a nonscheduled, structured technique based on four underlying questions. The questions evolved during the first few interviews, and the interviews themselves were highly flexible in style and pace depending on the person interviewed. Interviews ranged from half an hour to over two hours. The first three questions sought to elicit open dialogue and understanding of the major issues of concern, individual perspectives, and positives and negatives of living in the region. The last question targeted SD indicators by asking about signs and signals (and tell-tale signs and signposts) of SD. The aim was to encourage an easy flow of conversation. The interviews began with a brief introduction to sustainable development as something containing social, cultural, economic, and environmental dimensions. The four questions underlying the nonscheduled, structured interviews were as follows:

1 What are the issues, problems, and challenges concerning natural resources and the people in your area?
2 What drew you here; what do you like about living here; how do you make use of local natural resources?
3 How is your work linked to, or based on, natural resources? What natural resources?
4 What tell-tale signposts, signs, or signals come to mind that foretell a good or bad future for the people of this area, for the natural resources surrounding this area?

The Biophysical Study

Forests and Land Use

Two major provincial forest concessions make up the bulk of the study area: the Arrow Timber Supply Area (Arrow TSA) and Tree Farm Licence 23 (TFL 23). The TSA is a volume-based measure of tenure and is area-based. TFL 23 is leased by Pope and Talbot Limited. Much of the timber gathered from TFL 23 is processed at their sawmill in Castlegar. The Arrow TSA is divided among a number of harvesters, but the largest user is the Slocan Forest Company.

As summarized by Anderson (1997), the Arrow TSA has a total land base of 754,000 hectares, of which 201,000 hectares comprise the timber-harvesting land base. TFL 23 consists of an area of 555,000 hectares, of which 371,000 hectares are productive forest. The two are not distinct entities, as some of TFL 23 is included in the Arrow TSA. These two forestry administrations make up about 80 percent of the study area (the balance is in the Revelstoke TSA), although the study area itself comprises only about 21 percent of the land occupied by the TSA and the TFL together. The land base that is not part of the "productive forest" is made up of environmentally sensitive areas, private land, roads, steep slopes with unstable soils, inoperable land, unmerchantable timber, and other similar restrictions.

Forests in the study area are composed of stands of varying species and age. Within the Arrow TSA, Douglas-fir comprises 26 percent of the total; balsam, 24 percent; pine, 18 percent; and larch, 14 percent. Hemlock, spruce, cedar, and deciduous trees make up the balance. The study area is located within the interior wet belt, and includes the Interior Cedar-Hemlock (ICH) and Engelmann Spruce–Subalpine Fir (ESSF) biogeoclimatic zones. The ICH is found on lower slopes, while the ESSF is at higher and colder elevations. At the highest levels, the Alpine Tundra (AT) biogeoclimatic zone dominates.

At the heart of the issue of sustainable development in the forest industry is the size of the allowable annual cut (AAC), which is the government-permitted rate of timber harvest from a particular parcel of land. The focus of the calculation of the AAC is economic: the maximum number of trees that can be cut in a year and still guarantee a supply for industry in the future. It is a relatively short-term measure. Adjustments for other components of the forest ecosystem are a significant part of the calculation, but little or no attempt is made to examine the sustainability of these components in themselves. Instead, it is hoped that the forest set aside for nonharvest uses will be large enough to ensure their viability through the millennia.

Critical Sustainability Factors in the AAC

Approximately one-third of the study area consists of *watershed and visually sensitive areas*. In order to harvest these areas, cutting plans that are acceptable to the public must be developed. Local opposition to cutting of any kind often drags out the planning phase beyond ten to fifteen years. Only about 60 percent of the affected area has had a cutting plan accepted. This has the effect of deferring present harvests twenty to forty years into the future. In the modelling of the Arrow TSA allowable cut, riparian habitat protection zones were not subtracted from the land base since necessary information was not available at the time. This factor alone is estimated to reduce the harvesting land base by 2 to 4 percent.

With the increasing attraction of the Columbia River valley for retirement as the Canadian population ages and the Okanagan valley becomes crowded, pressures to refuse logging under any circumstances are bound to increase. Retirees and those not dependent on the forestry industry have no particular incentive to view logging as an acceptable alteration of the environment. Visual-quality restrictions are likely to increase, even in remote areas, as an increasingly mobile population seeks to visit "wilderness" areas. Environmental concerns and the social mood are likely to place significant demands on the forestry industry in the foreseeable future.

Minimum harvest age is an estimate of the time required for a stand to reach a merchantable condition. This factor is subject to market forces, silviculture, and technology, along with some uncertainty about actual growth rates of regenerating timber. Since it is subject to manipulation by technology, it is not unreasonable to assume that an earlier harvest age may be viable in future years. Stand volume estimates depend on surveys of the forest conducted over many years, generally assimilated into a GIS database. The accuracy of many of these surveys is questionable; Ministry of Forests officials suggested several times during our visits that the database held by Pope and Talbot was more reliable than that held by the government and on which the modelling was based. Arrow Forest Service staff have noted that the oldest forests in the region (20 percent of the land base) have many trees that are decayed and unmerchantable, and that actual timber volumes may be as much as 15 percent lower than assumed. In addition, much of the current harvest comes from younger trees, not the older ones that were assumed in the model, so that more area must be harvested to realize the same timber volume.

In all management areas, stands adjacent to recent cutovers cannot be harvested until a *"green-up" height* of three metres is attained by the regrowing forest, in order to provide habitat for wildlife. Due to brush competition, this green-up is often slower than assumed in the models. A companion issue is the *cut block adjacency rules,* which permit only 25 percent of an area to be cut at one time. Subsequent cutting cannot occur until green-up of the previous cut, a process that requires at least seventeen years. Most areas will thus require at least four passes spread out over nearly seven decades in order to remove all of the available timber. In actual practice, however, it is often impossible to cut the forest in 25 percent chunks, and often five or even six passes are needed to remove the timber.

The AAC calculations are extremely sensitive to adjacency rules and moderately sensitive to green-up rates. Taken separately, harvesting is already unsustainable with a six-pass restraint, and in need of reduction before the turn of the century with a five-pass restriction. If longer green-up times are needed, reductions to the long-term sustainable level will be required within twenty years. On the environmental front, ecological factors that impact the determination of the allowable cut and that were not included in the Arrow TSA analysis include land reserved for riparian habitat, old-growth requirements for caribou, cutting restrictions to accommodate use by wildlife, and the requirement that large pieces of woody debris be left for habitat on cutover sites.

Study of the GIS database obtained from the BC Ministry of Environment, Lands and Parks shows that less than 5 percent of the forest is 250 years or older within the study area. This is surprising because much of the land has been untouched by human hands, and has the general appearance of old-growth forest. The largest block of 250-year-old trees lies on the hills above Kuskanax Creek, on the north side. In fact, two-thirds of the timber harvest land base in the TSA is composed of immature trees between 80 and 120 years old, mostly as a result of forest fires that occurred in the late 1800s. Some of these fires were set by miners in the Slocan Lake area to expose the surface geology in their search for silver and lead deposits. In TFL 23, there is a moderate-sized component of the forest that has an age of 200 to 230 years, but the bulk of the licence area contains trees younger than 120 years.

As summarized by Anderson (1997), the forest industry in the study area and beyond is undergoing a series of changes brought on by several government initiatives, including the Forest Practices Code, the Protected Areas Strategy, and the CORE land-use proceedings. These programs are introducing a much stronger bias towards sustainable multiple use of the land and resource base. Declining employment in the forest industry, a renewed emphasis on tourism, and changing demographics have made local communities more receptive to alternative employment. In spite of these changes, substantial questions regarding economic sustainability remain. Many of these revolve around the assumptions used in the calculation of the annual allowable cut and the suitability of limits and obligations imposed by the Forest Practices Code. Overlying these concerns is the fundamental contradiction between viewing the forest as a wood-fibre farm rather than a matrix of a diversity of human users and natural values.

The question of harvest sustainability is sensitive to many factors. These factors are subject to many pressures for change, given the current social, political, and environmental climate, and the effects of the FPC, the CORE land-use recommendations, and a number of other government initiatives.

Wildlife

British Columbia has an impressive number of wildlife species, in large part because of the varied topography, climate, and biogeoclimatic zones that the province has to offer. The study area is not so well endowed, being restricted to species that prefer alpine and steep forested slopes. The loss of bottomland due to flooding has removed an area of high biological productivity and rich biodiversity from the region, probably resulting in the loss of some species from the area (such as the burrowing owl) and the migration of others to new habitats. The presence of human hands in this relatively uninhabited part of the central mountains has placed a number of other species in endangered or threatened status.

British Columbia assigns species and subspecies to "red" or "blue" lists that designate the level of threat to their continued survival in the province. Red-listed species are candidates for legal designation as threatened or endangered; blue lists are for sensitive or vulnerable species. Within the Central Columbia Mountain (CCM) ecosection, there are three red-listed species and twenty-two blue-listed species. Seventeen of the threatened species are birds. Not all of the species are found in the Arrow Lakes study area, as it encompasses only the western third of the CCM ecosection. Within the study area, the most prominent species are the mountain caribou *(Rangifer tarandus montanus)* and the grizzly bear *(Ursus arctos)*, both of which are blue-listed.

Mountain caribou are found mostly within the Southern Interior Mountains, numbering some 1,700 animals in all. Within the study area, they are found at higher altitudes on the east side of the Arrow Lakes, on the slopes of the Selkirk Mountains. They are a poorly studied population, and there is considerable uncertainty about their range and preferred habitats. Caribou are designated an "old-growth-dependent species" because much of their winter grazing depends on arboreal lichens that are most commonly found in the oldest forests, those greater than 250 years of age. Census information on mountain caribou in the Nakusp area is limited to a single study done in March 1994. This aerial survey showed significant caribou populations on the heights along Kuskanax and Gardner creeks in bands of 4 to 19 individuals. A total of 59 animals were sighted near the creeks, and a further 32 were found north of Halfway Creek. Animals in other locations nearby brought the one-day total to 131 sightings. Thirteen of the individuals sighted were calves, implying a healthy population.

A 1993 study of caribou habitat use in the Revelstoke area noted the variability in the use of the landscape by woodland caribou. During the late winter and summer, caribou tend to be found at higher altitudes; in the spring and early fall, they descend to lower slopes, although the spring descent appears to be relatively brief. Caribou preference for older forests is strongly expressed: forest age-classes 8 and 9 were selected by caribou on 80 to 95 percent of surveys throughout the seasons. Only springtime shows some slight tendency towards younger forests. In winter, caribou fed most often (46 percent) on the shrub falsebox *(Paxystima myrsinites)*. Forty percent of the diet consisted of old-growth lichens, and the balance consisted of food obtained by digging through the snow cover.

Caribou utilize old-growth forests over a large range. Home ranges from 169 to 215 square kilometres were calculated for the Revelstoke bands, with most movement occurring in spring. Preserving the habitat of the woodland caribou will have dramatic consequences for the forestry industry because the animal has a critical reliance on older forests, a wide distribution range from high to low elevations, small populations, a general intolerance of disturbance, and low fecundity. Clear-cut harvesting of mature forests is known to be incompatible with maintaining winter habitat for caribou (McLellan et al. 1994). As well, caribou are threatened by hunting and by fragmentation of populations by forest operations. Networks of roads that develop during forest harvesting operations allow snowmobiles into the alpine environments of the Selkirk Mountains during winter.

Grizzly bears are referred to as a "flagship species" because of their charismatic appeal to the public and as an "umbrella species" because of their wide-ranging habitat requirements, which, if protected, would provide living space for many other species. Grizzly bear populations in the Nakusp study area appear to be relatively stable, but other nearby areas, and North

America in general, have suffered extensive losses in the past century. Bears and their habitat are under considerable pressure from the human presence along the Arrow Lakes. And while increased access to wild areas, human–bear conflicts, and poaching threaten long-term survival, there are powerful environmental groups that have gathered to protect the bear's environment.

Grizzly bears are also highly mobile, varying habitat selection by season. Because of their omnivorous nature, nearly all habitats can be exploited by the bears, but the most important include riparian zones, avalanche chutes, mixed conifer and deciduous forests, meadows, alpine pastures, and winter denning habitat. According to CORE (1995), most grizzly bears feed intensively on huckleberry species to build the annual fat reserves required for hibernation. Grizzlies are thus extremely dependent on the maintenance of vegetative stages that support this important forage. Use of forage areas is also subject to the availability of adjacent thermal and security forest cover. Forest cover also provides movement corridors, edge habitat, and support of understorey forage species.

Grizzly populations in the West Kootenays are believed to consist of between 700 and 1,000 individuals (CORE 1995), a significant population size. Within the Selkirk Mountains, the estimated density of bears is 1 per 127 square kilometres. Current forest silvicultural practices attempt to bypass the shrub succession stage in the regeneration of marketable forests, depriving the bear of important berry food sources (CORE 1995). The extensive logging road networks that develop as a result of forestry operations bring humans into direct contact with the bears, presenting several problems, including habitat loss, harassment, displacement, human–bear conflict, poaching, and biological impacts such as reduced fecundity and survival. On the other hand, clear-cutting opens areas of the forest that can provide additional valuable habitat for the grizzly bear.

Local residents who come into regular contact with grizzlies treat the bears as a dangerous nuisance. For the most part, depredations in this area consist of attacks on cattle that graze the lower forests of the Selkirks. The number of people affected is very small, but encounters with grizzlies are certainly not rare in this prime habitat. A different attitude is held by the members of a variety of environmental groups who live in some other communities in the Selkirks. The centre of the local environmental movement lies in the communities of Silverton and New Denver, less than an hour south of Nakusp.

In summary, wildlife populations along the Arrow Lakes are subject to increasing stresses from human activities. Figures 6.4 and 6.5 illustrate how logging roads proceed into previously uncut areas and how cut blocks appear along the sides of these roads over a period of years. Logging has the most serious impact on caribou populations and will have to be managed carefully to preserve the Selkirk herds in a viable condition. The Forest Practices

Code will go some way towards providing these limits, but CORE documents suggest that the long-term survival of the caribou is still quite uncertain. Mature cedar and hemlock forests must be protected because of their heavy use in winter, especially those above Kuskanax Creek. Caribou in the Arrow Lakes area spend more time at low elevations than those elsewhere in the province, and the potential for conflict with the timber industry is very high. Grizzly habitat can most easily be protected by reducing contact between humans and bears. Much of this contact has been facilitated by the ready access to remote backcountry through the extensive network of logging roads. While many of these roads must now be rehabilitated according to the FPC, removing older roads will prove much more difficult.

Water Quantity and Lake Levels

Five hydrometric stations are located within the study boundaries; three were analyzed in detail for the purposes of this project. The issue of most concern to the local population was the extreme variation in water levels in

Figure 6.4

High-altitude air photo of the lower Kuskanax Creek, August 1970

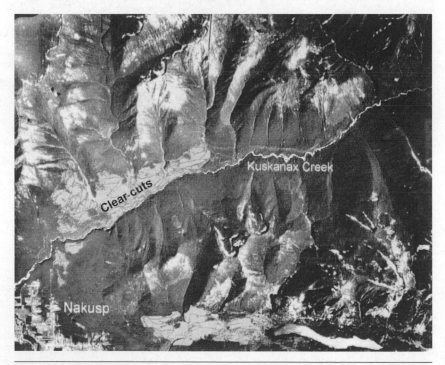

Source: Anderson 1997.

Figure 6.5

High-altitude air photo of the length of the Kuskanax Creek, July 1987

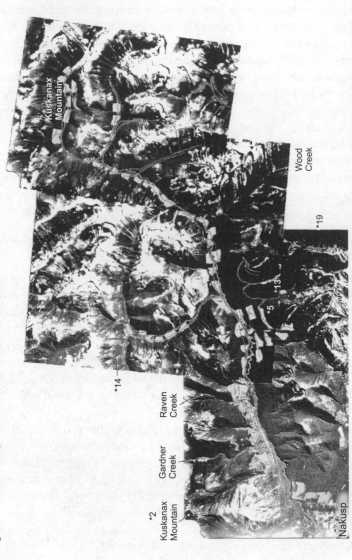

Notes: A string of clear-cuts extends almost the entire length of the Creek, and the roads leading off to new cutting areas. Asterisks (*) mark the locations of caribou sightings during a reconnaissance flight in 1994. Numbers beside the asterisks indicate the number of animals sighted.
Source: Anderson 1997.

the Upper and Lower Arrow Lakes from its management as a storage reservoir for downstream hydro dams. For the most part, this concern centred on aesthetic qualities, particularly within the town of Nakusp and at cottage sites along the nearby shoreline. During June, the level was at its seasonal low, revealing mud flats and sandbars along the shoreline of the town of Nakusp. Later, water levels had risen to a midsummer high, a rise on the order of ten metres. To study water quantity, two watersheds, Kuskanax Creek and Barnes Creek, were analyzed during the project using the Hydat database compiled by Environment Canada. No sediment measurements are available for these creeks, only streamflows. Sediment measurements would have been more useful, as the transport of particulate matter responds more directly to changes in the watershed and impacts fish populations more directly.

The Kuskanax Creek rises in the Selkirk Mountains northeast of Nakusp and flows southwestward to enter Upper Arrow Lake just above the town. The stream drops 1,490 metres within its 45-kilometre length. The watershed is relatively lightly logged, and settlement along the creek is dispersed and confined to the lowest 15 kilometres. Logging has been moving steadily back into the upper reaches of the watershed since 1970, and now extends along the major tributary as far as the headwaters. In general, only the area close to the stream bed is harvested. Narrow buffer strips protect all stream banks. The creek has two streamflow gauges, one 8 kilometres upstream from the mouth, and the other some 23 kilometres further along, 600 metres above the lake; both were analyzed for systematic changes in streamflow characteristics during the period of record that might reflect the influence of logging. Both sites showed a regular annual cycle dominated by snowmelt runoff in the spring, with spikes of higher streamflow resulting from significant precipitation events during the year. On average, runoff rises sharply in mid-April. Average streamflow peaks on 3 June and then declines slowly through the rest of the year.

The literature on watershed snowmelt suggests that removal of tree cover should result in a more rapid and higher peaked streamflow with a faster response to rising temperatures. Since snowmelt is highly related to temperature, the correlation between the two can be exploited to detect systematic changes that might be due to logging. This approach assumes that the correlation between streamflow and air temperature would rise as logging opened up more of the forest. Examination of the data did not show any statistically significant trend from 1964 to 1992. Correlation measures between temperature and streamflows also failed to show any significant trend. A similar analysis for the Barnes Creek, on the western side of the Columbia River valley, also did not show any statistically significant trend.

Changes in lake level are significant for sustainability. The Keenleyside Dam near Castlegar regulates lake levels for both the Upper and Lower Arrow

Lakes in response to demands for water from the state of Montana. Lake levels follow an annual pattern typical of temperate zone storage reservoirs – a gradual drawdown through the winter months to a minimum in early April, followed by a sharp rise to a peak in July. The average amplitude ranges from 425 to 438 metres above sea level with extremes at 420 and 441 metres. Before regulation, the Upper Arrow Lake varied between 417 and 429 metres. The original rise of the lake, present high-amplitude annual variation, and the slow winter discharge all have implications for sustainability. The original flooding destroyed a bottomland ecosystem of farms and forest, posing a considerable burden of human grief and displacing animals.

The single biggest loss to the Columbia River system is the disappearance of the Pacific salmon, due entirely to the construction of the Grand Coulee Dam in Washington state. The lake is now populated by kokanee, a landlocked, nonmigratory form of sockeye salmon, *O. nerka*. Since no data are available on fish populations before the dam construction began, only speculation remains to evaluate the effect on other fish species, bears, birds, and other consumers of the once-rich salmon resource. Discussion of the impact of damming and the annual wave of high and low water would not be complete without a discussion of the impact on human inhabitants. Emotions still rise when the subject of the original flooding and compensation is broached. Remaining members of the original families retain memories of farms long drowned, of graves hidden or moved, of a lifetime of work flooded. Compensation was meagre, often without substantial discussion. Still, many of the original families continue to inhabit the valley, with new jobs and roots.

In summary, two major watersheds along the Columbia River have been examined for streamflow changes that might result from an ongoing history of logging. No effects have been detected that deviate significantly from natural patterns. This does not completely eliminate the possibility that changes may have occurred in sediment loading and transport that are not reflected in streamflow trends, but the available evidence suggests that logging has had a relatively benign effect on the watercourses. Are the Arrow Lakes sustainable in the era of dams and fluctuating water levels? Apparently so, if a broad enough view is taken.

Fish

The Arrow Lakes contain a rich fishery, with kokanee salmon, bull trout *(Salvelinus confluentus)*, and rainbow trout (including the legendary Gerrard rainbow) attracting anglers from across North America. There is no commercial fishery. Local residents speak of readily available catches of bull trout, the most sought-after species, which are fished primarily in winter months, when the tourists have departed for home. Resource managers, however, talk of the fishery with a sense of unease, half-expecting a decline of fish populations in the coming years. The upstream dams have had a serious impact on the spawning grounds available for kokanee and bull trout, but the construction of a fish hatchery at Hill Creek, near the north end of the study area, has mitigated much of this loss. It would seem that concerns about the loss of kokanee are overstated, and current populations do not show a downward trend. Local fishermen give mixed opinions about kokanee populations, allowing at one moment that the fishery is "not good" and at the next moment that kokanee are "easy" in July and August. For the most part, they eschew kokanee and prefer bull trout.

Bull trout are another concern, with fisheries managers telling of significantly declining populations. Until 1995, bull trout could be fished freely, but catch limits were imposed for the 1996 season and beyond. Resource managers attribute most of the decline in the species to habitat destruction during logging operations and to overfishing. Local fishing opinion maintains that populations are healthy, but identifies increased effort and "knowing where to go" as important factors in fishing, a tacit admission of a decreasing catch per unit effort. Bull trout are particularly vulnerable to habitat loss in the tributaries of the Columbia River, as they occupy the steepest and highest parts of the stream courses.

In summary, fish populations are showing mixed responses to human development and presence along the Columbia River. While kokanee numbers are stable, in large part because of enhancement by the Hill Creek hatchery, bull trout numbers are declining from overharvesting and habitat loss. The Forest Practices Code (CORE 1995) requires riparian buffers that may go further than past practices in protecting spawning habitat. The jury is still out on the sustainability of fish populations, but no insurmountable barrier appears to have been reached besides the disappearance of migratory salmon species.

The Social Study

Signs and Signals of Sustainability

There are two approaches to measuring and quantifying sustainability. The biophysical part of this study examined sustainability using quantitative and objective data. This is only part of the story, however. Sustainability is also socially constructed – that is, people use their own values to make judgments about sustainability. We had previously explored the social dimension of sustainability by asking mountain villagers in the Himalayas about the indicators they thought were important for predicting a good future for themselves and their children. We repeated this approach in the British Columbia study (Duffield et al. 1998).

Results from the signs and signals question and content analysis of the first three questions were organized under the headings of environment, management, socio-economy, and healthy community. The signs and signals results were analyzed according to the two groups of respondents – Nakusp stakeholders and natural resources management professionals in the study region. To make the number of indicators more manageable, topics raised by one person that did not readily combine with other topics were not included. In several instances, combining signs and signals resulted in the "frequency sign/signal discussed" figure being greater than the number of people interviewed. For example, the Forest Practices Code and the Commission on Resources and the Environment were usually discussed together, probably because of their combined impact on forest and land-use management.

The most frequently mentioned sign or signal discussed by both groups was an "effectiveness of management process" indicator that considered forest and land-use rules and regulations, including the FPC and CORE. It is not surprising that the efficacy of forest and land-use management was given high priority as an indicator, since such management has the potential to safeguard sustainable development. Among professionals, only the forest and land-use management indicator stands above the rest in terms of frequency. In contrast, Nakusp stakeholders emphasized four additional signals above the rest: immigration linked to economic and commercial growth; health of the tourism industry; viability of the mushroom and other nontimber forest–based industries; and natural, aesthetic, wilderness attractions and recreational opportunities. The latter two signals were multiple-category indicators. Besides these top categories of signs and signals, several others were mentioned.

The additional indicators to monitor that were discussed by at least ten of the twenty-two Nakusp interviewees include: "youth opportunity" (embracing issues of education, credit, family planning, and role models); "community self-reliance" (ability of the community to meet its own needs for necessities and services); "local input and control" over management (an empowerment and management issue); ensuring that harvest is below the annual allowable cut (related to the Timber Supply Review); and quality of life.

The additional signs and signals to monitor that were discussed by at least ten of the twenty-one professional interviewees included: ecosystem-based management (a "mimic nature" approach used in land use and watershed restoration activities); ensuring that harvest is below the annual allowable cut; "wood utilization" (rules for harvest and processing exist and are improved); "land-cover pattern" (a key component of feedback for management); "local input and control" over management (critical to prevent future conflicts); "tourism industry health" (links to natural attractions and availability of services); "local value-added" (refers to adding value to locally extracted wood using local processing industries); "immigration linked to economic and commercial growth"; and "natural attractions."

The two pie charts in Figure 6.6 summarize and compare the frequency of indicators discussed by the two groups. The comparison is based on the percentage of signs and signals under headings of environment, management, socio-economy, healthy community and several mixed categories. The greatest differences between the two groups occur under headings of management (stakeholders, 19 percent; professionals, 40 percent) and healthy community (stakeholders, 20 percent; professionals, 8 percent).

Figure 6.6

Indicators of sustainability according to Nakusp area stakeholders and natural resource professionals

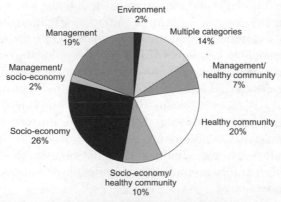

Local Nakusp stakeholder perspective

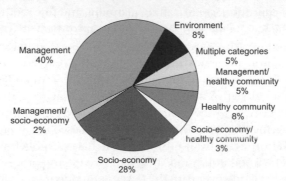

Natural resources professional perspective
in the Arrow Lakes region

Source: Duffield 1997.

Different job backgrounds probably account for the variance. The job description of professionals includes management, application of process, rules and regulations, and understanding of the interactions between management and effects on the environment. Local stakeholders also have knowledge of management, but their experience is more broadly focused on life in the community where they live. The stakeholders come from a variety of job backgrounds, many of which have a social, community development focus. It thus comes as no surprise that healthy community indicators of opportunity for youth, quality of life, sense of community, people's adaptability, tolerance for others, alcohol abuse, family abuse, and water supply and sewage issues are given greater consideration by Nakusp stakeholders than by professionals.

Figure 6.6 suggests that professionals give more weighting to environmental monitoring as a feedback signal for management; again, this is probably a result of job background. In contrast, the two groups give nearly equal overall weighting to indicators under the socio-economy heading. However, the stakeholder perspective is heavily based on the two indicators of immigration linked to economic and commercial growth and health of the tourism industry, whereas professionals identified a wider array of socio-economic signs and signals. Under the double-category headings in Figure 6.6, stakeholders placed more emphasis on socio-economy/healthy community indicators (stakeholders, 10 percent; professionals, 3 percent). Such signs and signals include community self-reliance, access to services, entrepreneurial spirit, and local investment. Stakeholders also discussed a greater diversity and slightly greater number of management/healthy community indicators (stakeholders, 7 percent; professionals, 5 percent). Their signs and signals include local input and control, environmental and social activism, and the resource management education level of the public.

A large weighting discrepancy occurs in the two indicators under the multiple categories heading of Figure 6.6 (stakeholders, 14 percent; professionals, 5 percent). This heading includes mushroom and nontimber forest industry viability, and maintaining natural attractions in the region. The large difference may result partially from the fact that interviews were conducted at the height of mushroom-picking season. As well, given that stakeholders receive the direct and indirect benefits of mushroom harvest and natural attractions (the latter relates to tourism, immigration, and well-being), locals may have a greater awareness of the importance of mushrooming and natural attractions to sustainable development.

Developing Criteria for Sustainability
Through the use of various databases, the project was able to make an overall *quantitative* assessment of sustainability with respect to the biophysical dimension of sustainability. A similar approach could not be used for the

economic and social dimensions of sustainability, however. Much less information was available on social and economic parameters. In a qualitative assessment of these parameters, CORE (1995) concludes that "economic and social indicators such as a reduction in resource industry jobs, lack of investor confidence, reduced community stability and conflicts among different resource users further emphasize a lack of sustainability, reflecting a general trend in Canadian resource-based communities."

Since part of the project objective was to involve the local people in resource management and sustainability assessment, we took the obvious but often-neglected step of *asking the local people* what sustainability meant to them. We asked a sample of local stakeholders for locally identified signs and signals that should be monitored in order to predict a good future, with the idea that these "signs and signals" may be considered as a proxy for sustainability indicators. For cross-verification, we asked the same question to a sample of natural resources management professionals working in the area. The responses were organized into five clusters: forest indicators; forest-linked indicators; forest management indicators; economic indicators; and social and community health indicators (Table 6.2).

Several conclusions can be drawn from the findings summarized in Figure 6.6 and Table 6.2. The first is that the two groups of respondents in the Arrow Lakes area had a great deal in common with each other, with about a two-thirds overlap in their responses. The managers placed more emphasis on management-related indicators and less emphasis on economic and social indicators than did the local population. Second, there was no single "key indicator," suggesting that meaningful indicators need to be context-specific. Indicators came in clusters, and the most robust cluster was the pervasiveness of good management, that is, using those indicators that provided feedback on management success. Third, both groups of respondents suggested signs and signals that covered the ecological, economic, and social aspects of sustainability.

Did this mean that the local people and the local managers knew their sustainable development theory, or did it mean that sustainable development theory is on the right track in terms of what local people and local management practitioners in fact recognize as important? The fact that our respondents in the Himalayas also provided sustainability indicators that covered ecological, economic, and social aspects suggests that the scientific concept of sustainability is consistent with the environmental understanding of people of mountain ecosystems (Duffield et al. 1998). In any case, our study demonstrated that *asking* the local people about sustainability generated sensible and meaningful indicators for a given area.

Implications for Sustainability Planning
The case study offers certain implications and insights regarding the integrity

Table 6.2

Categories of sustainability indicators based on interviews of local people and natural resources management professionals in forested mountain environments in Canada and India

Category	Indicators
Forest indicators	Quantity and quality of forest; amount of cover; tree species diversity; forest density; and availability of forest products. Few stakeholders mentioned old-growth forest. Several managers mentioned land-cover-related indicators: protection of riparian habitat, habitat fragmentation, biodiversity loss, and ecosystem health.
Forest-linked indicators	Avalanches and landslides; control of erosion; consistent water flow of streams, springs, and rivers; clean water; and consistent climate were mentioned by Himalayan villagers and managers but not by those of Nakusp. Nontimber forest products, water quality, and scenic beauty were mentioned.
Forest management indicators	Forest and land-use rules and regulations; harvest versus allowable cut; silvicultural success; ecosystem-based management; multiple-use. "Good management," using those indicators that provided feedback on the manager's ability to work for sustainability, was the most robust indicator.
Economic indicators	Economic growth and in-migration, as related to economic development. Both stakeholders and managers mentioned tourism, economic diversification, local value-added, road and rail access, and job creation per unit amount of wood harvested – all of them related to diversification and moving beyond a single-resource, extraction-based economy.
Social and community health indicators	Local input into decision making; youth opportunity, community self-reliance, quality of life, sense of community, and access to services. These were less frequently mentioned by managers, except decision-making input and quality of life.

Source: Adapted from Duffield et al. 1998.

of sustainability planning. We have concentrated so far on how provincial-level policy results in changes at the local and regional levels, even though there are implications at the national and international levels as well. In this section, we explore cross-scale implications of policy and practice more broadly. Changing resource and environmental policies may result in changing resource-use practice in three ways: the incorporation of new values and priorities, public and stakeholder participation in decisions, and ecosystem-based management. We deal with each in turn, after an examination of the context of the case study and before returning to the question of integrity.

The Context: Changing Resource-Use Policies
The CORE (1995) initiative, on which the case study builds, was predicated on the idea that resource demands have increased in British Columbia and that social values have shifted towards greater environmental protection (M'Gonigle and Wickwire 1989). These shifts, apparent not only in British Columbia but also across Canada, required new resource management and decision-making processes that reflected the full range of public values. The CORE exercise had included the analysis of timber supply sustainability in the area of the case study, as well as the sustainability of a range of other products and values related to the mountain forest; it defined sustainability as "the assurance that present land use decisions do not compromise the opportunities available to future generations" (CORE 1995).

The study team arrived in the case study area at a time when the single-resource-use approach was being replaced by one adapted to address multiple resource demands. For about three decades, the area had been managed largely for one product: timber from the forest. The area had in fact a history of shifting single-resource focus, from mining to agriculture to hydro-electric development to timber. Historical photographs of the area document these various phases and the boom-and-bust economy that went with them. In Howlett's terminology (Chapter 3), such an economy may be referred to as a "staples political economy," and the changes documented in the case study mark the transition to a "post-staples economy."

The debate under the CORE process (1992-94) was how to replace the single-resource focus with a planning process that allowed for consideration of many resources and values: agriculture, mining, forestry, tourism, recreation, aesthetic and spiritual enjoyment, fish and wildlife conservation, watershed protection, and biological diversity. The overall verdict of CORE (1995) was that resource use and management in the West Kootenay region had *not* been sustainable. Timber supply reviews conducted by the British Columbia Ministry of Forests had indicated that harvest levels had to be reduced by as much as 50 percent in some areas to achieve sustainable timber yields. Anderson (1997) subsequently calculated for the study area (which is a small part of the region considered by CORE) that current annual harvests needed to be reduced by about one-third to stretch out the timber supply into the future, that is, for long-term sustainable harvests.

Population data for two key indicator species, woodland caribou and grizzly bear, suggested that their long-term survival in the study area may be threatened if current practices continue. Caribou are sensitive to the reduction of old-growth forest, and very little was left of the oldest two age-classes of forest. Figures 6.4 and 6.5, based on two sets of air photos from 1970 and 1987, show the pattern by which a previously uncut forest area is developed. Figure 6.5 shows that caribou sightings were made in uncut areas; in fact, the largest concentration was found in the largest block of old-growth timber (Anderson 1997). The grizzly bear, by contrast, is a habitat generalist not readily affected by forest cutting. It is affected, however, by the construction of logging roads that bring the bears into conflict with humans. Some other species of wildlife may also have been affected through loss of habitat quality as a result of extensive logging, since large clear-cuts reduce landscape diversity. Yet other species are attracted to newly cut areas that tend to be productive with berries and edible shrubs.

On the whole, CORE (1995) concluded that water quality in freshwater systems that are critical for fish habitat as well as for human consumption has shown continuous signs of deterioration. The study team's interpretation of the data indicates a decline in one valuable species of trout (bull trout), while the population of the dominant landlocked kokanee salmon has been sustainable. There was some evidence, based on resource managers' observations (in the absence of actual data), that clear-cutting in the tributary watersheds has caused siltation, affecting some fish spawning areas and water quality in general. The analysis of the hydrological data has not shown a significant impact of forest cutting on water yields, however.

Figure 6.7 summarizes the available biophysical data to show those parameters that seem to be sustainable and those that are not (Anderson 1997). Note that the analysis is based on indicators for which quantitative data were available. Many parameters, such as the impact of forest cutting on water yields or erosion, cannot be shown because the data are ambiguous, insufficient, or nonexistent. The implications of our findings for new institutionalist approaches to policy development may be considered under three overlapping headings. The first concerns changing values and priorities in the use of forested mountain environments. The second involves improving public participation in management processes. The third involves the reconceptualization of ecosystem management to take account of people as an integral part of the system. Each of these will be considered in turn.

Changing Values and Priorities in Forest Use

The Arrow Lakes area is not an isolated case. A major change that has affected policy in recent years is a shift in social values towards greater environmental protection. Canada in general and British Columbia in particular have a history of rapid depletion of resources along a shifting resource frontier. The pattern of forest resource use has historically followed a sequence of exploitation from the more valuable to the less valuable species (Regier and Baskerville 1986). Under a resource management paradigm that emphasized commodification and economic growth, the decades-old "multiple-use

Figure 6.7

An OMOEBA diagram for the ecosystem of the Arrow Lakes study area

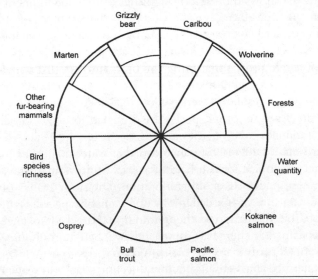

Notes: Resources that are used sustainably are represented by a sector that reaches the full radius of the circle. Resources that are not used sustainably have a sector length proportional to the degree of sustainability. The analysis is based on indicators for which quantitative data were available.
Source: Anderson 1997.

sustained-yield" approach guided the managers of public forests. An emerging forestry paradigm is challenging this traditional approach, however. Variously called forest ecosystem management, sustainable forestry, or multivalue forest management, the emerging approach establishes that the recognition of multiple values must be at the root of decision making in forest management. Bengston (1994) notes that this is resulting in the consideration of a whole series of new questions, such as: "What is the nature of forest values? Whose specific values are involved? How and why have forest values changed over time? What do changing forest values imply for ecosystem management?"

Resource users and managers in Canada are beginning to acknowledge the legitimacy of recognizing multiple values within the decision-making process. The CORE process in British Columbia attempted to bring stakeholders with varying forest values to the same discussion table. It achieved some success in motivating stakeholder participation in the process, and as a result, multiple-use and forest protection values were injected into the decision-making process. Other studies, including the Model Forest program, are underway in British Columbia and other Canadian provinces, to develop more detailed approaches and methodologies for

identifying and incorporating a broader spectrum of values within the decision-making process, including, for example, nontimber forest products and
Aboriginal values (Davidson-Hunt et al. 2001).

These competing values have yet to be reconciled, however. It is difficult
to say that CORE and model forest experiments have been successfully "scaled
up" into provincial- and federal-level policies to deal effectively with a reconciliation of values. As in other domains of Canadian environmental policy
making, the identification and study of alternative values is not in itself
sufficient to break the constraints of political institutions grounded in a
utilitarian tradition.

Public Participation: Moving to Normative Planning

Central to a respect for forest values emerging from broader recognition of
environmental values is the effective involvement of people within the
policy-making process. Often called public participation or multi-stakeholder
decision making, the focus in this process is on the diversity of people involved and the method of their involvement. In British Columbia, as elsewhere in Canada, public involvement in resource decision making usually
occurs through legislated environmental assessment processes. Such processes are supposed to provide an opportunity for public participation. Since
the environmental assessment process is project-driven, however, there is
usually little opportunity for stakeholders to be involved in the normative
planning stages. By this we mean a more inclusive mode of public participation, one that allows a broad range of participation *before* decisions are
made.

The CORE process is an example of normative planning. It involved some
twenty-four stakeholder groups on the round table (Figure 6.2). The CORE
(2000) report explains that negotiation was used as a means of attempting
to reach agreement among parties. Negotiation was carried out on the basis
of *interests* rather than predetermined *positions*. This is in contrast to positional bargaining, in which parties often perceive themselves as opponents
and bargain to achieve fixed all-or-nothing positions. Positional bargaining
tends to result in win-lose outcomes in which one party gains at the expense of others, as one finds in environmental assessment hearings. In interest-based negotiation, by contrast, parties communicate their interests
to one another and work towards win-win solutions that have a chance to
provide a balance and accommodate many interests.

Using this approach, the CORE process attempted to involve stakeholders
in normative planning about British Columbia forests *before* specific project
decisions regarding allocation were made by forest managers. This is different from post-decision involvement, which characterizes Canadian environmental assessment in general (Sinclair and Diduck 1995). CORE was not,
however, an unqualified success. Numerous questions were raised by

stakeholders about the process of involvement used by CORE, and there were concerns about the voices *not* heard, such as those of two Aboriginal groups. Further, as noted earlier, the full results of the CORE process were not adopted by forest managers in making allocation decisions, which underscores the point about the integrity gap.

Ecosystem-Based Management: Putting Humans Back into the System
Some very significant changes have been occurring in many parts of the world in the way people-environment relationships are being conceptualized (Berkes and Folke 1998). A key development is the focus on ecosystem-based management. Such management does not focus primarily on *resources* but rather on the sustainability of ecosystem structure and function necessary to *provide* these resources. According to the Ecological Society of America, ecosystem management must include the following components:

- long-term sustainability as a fundamental value
- operational goals
- sound ecological understanding
- understanding of complexity and interconnectedness
- recognition of the dynamic nature of ecosystems
- attention to context and scale
- acknowledgement of humans as ecosystem components
- commitment to adaptability and accountability.

All of these measures, and ecosystem-based resource management in general, have policy implications (Ecological Society of America 1995).

Current views of ecosystem-based management acknowledge the role of human societies, not merely as despoilers of the environment but as integral components of the ecosystem who must be engaged to achieve sustainable management goals. Of particular interest are local *institutions* of resource management, such as common property institutions, that regulate the use of shared resources. Such institutions function as repositories of local ecological knowledge and play a role in complementing government science. This kind of participation in management by community-based institutions goes beyond mere public participation. People who are living in an ecosystem and making a livelihood from it tend to have an understanding of that ecosystem and thus a key role in its management (Berkes and Folke 1998).

In the case study area, there was little evidence of ecosystem-based management with people, and no evidence of the use of local commons institutions for sustainable management. Internationally, examples of local groups creating their own "citizen science" and participating in management include watershed management groups in Minnesota (Light 1999) and lake management groups in Sweden (Olsson and Folke 2001). "People's

Biodiversity Registers" in India is an ecosystem assessment project in which entire regional networks of biodiversity users have been created in the countryside. The participants are rural people who are knowledgeable about and who use biodiversity in the form of food species, animal fodder, medicinal plants, and other such uses (Gadgil et al. 2000).

In conclusion, the case study reveals the evolution of resource and environmental policies to address three aspects of sustainable development: changing values and priorities, public participation, and ecosystem-based management. There are clear initiatives emerging in each of these three areas that have a potential to transform environmental policy-making processes, not only in British Columbia's forests but also in a number of other resource areas in various parts of Canada. Through Aboriginal land claims, model forests, and other experiments, people on the ground are being linked with resource managers and policy makers in ways that enable more effective, efficient, and equitable modes of resource and environmental management. Ecosystem-based management has the potential to close the circle by putting people back into the ecosystem, by valuing local knowledge, and by creating a "people's science." Such a science questions the top-down, managerial, expert-knows-best approach. Rather, people who make their livelihoods from an ecosystem become partners in the management of that ecosystem.

We began this chapter by identifying the potential for widening the policy network to deal with environment and resources, but we also questioned whether there were institutionalized constraints on the government's ability to deliver upon stated goals. The case study discussed here indicates that a gap remains between talk and action, and with respect to the scaling up of participation experiments across the levels of political organization.

Looking to the future, we can speculate about how Canada might change along the lines sketched out in Chapter 10 by Perl and Lee. The "citizen science" initiatives mentioned earlier complement Perl and Lee's three scenarios, particularly the third one, regarding international experience acting as a catalyst for institutional change. Such change is likely to come from progress at several scales at once. Higher-level international environmental initiatives (Chapter 4) are no doubt important, but they may be fragile in the absence of change towards sustainability at several levels across the scale of organization, including the regional and local levels.

References

Anderson, G. 1997. Biophysical Sustainability in a Mountain Ecosystem: Resource Use in the Columbia River Valley near Nakusp, British Columbia. MNRM thesis, Natural Resources Institute, University of Manitoba.

Bengston, D.N. 1994. Changing Forest Values and Ecosystem Management. *Society and Natural Resources* 7: 515-33.

Berkes, F. 2002. Cross-Scale Institutional Linkages: Perspectives from the Bottom Up. In *The Drama of the Commons,* edited by E. Ostrom, T. Dietz, N. Dolsak, P.C. Stern, S. Stonich, and E.U. Weber. Washington, DC: National Academy Press.

Berkes, F., I. Davidson-Hunt, and K. Davidson-Hunt. 1998. Diversity of Common Property Resource Use and Diversity of Social Interests in the Western Indian Himalaya. *Mountain Research and Development* 18: 19-33.

Berkes, F., and C. Folke, eds. 1998. *Linking Social and Ecological Systems: Management Practices and Social Mechanisms for Building Resilience.* Cambridge: Cambridge University Press.

Berkes, F., and J.S. Gardner, eds. 1997. *Sustainability of Mountain Environments in India and Canada.* Winnipeg: Natural Resources Institute, University of Manitoba. <http://www.umanitoba.ca/institutes/natural_resources/mountains> (17 December 2002).

Berkes, F., J.S. Gardner, and A.J. Sinclair. 2000. Comparative Aspects of Mountain Land Resources Management and Sustainability: Case Studies from India and Canada. *International Journal of Sustainable Development and World Ecology* 7: 1-16.

Bernstein, S. 2001. *The Compromise of Liberal Environmentalism.* New York: Columbia University Press.

Coleman, W.D., and A. Perl. 1999. Internationalized Policy Environments and Policy Network Analysis. *Political Studies* 47: 691-709.

CORE (Commission on Resources and the Environment). 2000. *The Provincial Land Use Strategy: A Sustainability Act for British Columbia.* Victoria: CORE. <http://www.luco.gov.bc.ca/lrmp/plus/> (17 December 2002).

Davidson-Hunt, I., L.C. Duchesne, and J.C. Zasada, eds. 2001. *Forest Communities in the Third Millennium: Linking Research, Business and Policy toward a Sustainable Non-Timber Forest Product Sector.* St. Paul, MN: US Department of Agriculture Forest Service.

Duffield, C. 1997. Signs and Signals of Sustainability, Arrow Lakes Region, West Kootenay, BC. In *Sustainability of Mountain Environments in India and Canada,* edited by F. Berkes and J.S. Gardner. Winnipeg: Natural Resources Institute, University of Manitoba.

Duffield, C., J.S. Gardner, F. Berkes, and R.B. Singh. 1998. Local Knowledge in the Assessment of Resource Sustainability: Case Studies in Himachal Pradesh and British Columbia, Canada. *Mountain Research and Development* 18: 35-49.

Ecological Society of America. 1995. *The Report of the Ecological Society of America Committee on the Scientific Basis for Ecosystem Management.* Washington, DC: Ecological Society of America.

Gadgil, M., P.R. Seshagiri Rao, G. Utkarsh, P. Pramod, and A. Chhatre. 2000. New Meanings for Old Knowledge: The People's Biodiversity Register Programme. *Ecological Applications* 10: 1251-62.

Hanson, A.J. 1998. Sustainable Development and the Oceans. *Ocean and Coastal Management* 39: 167-77.

IUCN/UNEP/WWF (World Conservation Union/United Nations Environment Program/Worldwide Fund for Nature). 1991. *Caring for the Earth.* A Strategy for Sustainable Living. Gland, Switzerland: World Conservation Union.

Lee, K.N. 1993. *Compass and the Gyroscope: Integrating Science and Politics for the Environment.* Washington, DC: Island Press.

Light, S., coord. 1999. *Citizens, Science, Watershed Partnerships and Sustainability: The Case in Minnesota.* Report. Minneapolis: Surdna Foundation; Minnesota Department of Natural Resources; Science Museum of Minnesota.

Ludwig, D. 1993. Environmental Sustainability: Magic, Science and Religion in Natural Resource Management. *Ecological Applications* 3: 555-58.

McLellan, B., J. Flaa, and M. Super. 1994. *Habitats Used by Mountain Caribou in the North Columbia Mountains.* Year 2, Preliminary Report no. 2. Revelstoke, BC: Parks Canada.

M'Gonigle, M., and W. Wickwire. 1989. *Stein: The Way of a River.* Vancouver: Talonbooks.

Olsson, P., and C. Folke. 2001. Local Ecological Knowledge and Institutional Dynamics for Ecosystem Management: A Study of Crayfish Management in the Lake Racken Watershed, Sweden. *Ecosystems* 4: 85-104.

Regier, H.A., and G.L. Baskerville. 1986. Sustainable Redevelopment of Regional Ecosystems Degraded by Exploitive Development. In *Sustainable Development of the Biosphere,* edited by W.C. Clark and R.E. Munn. Cambridge: IIASA/Cambridge University Press.

Sinclair A.J., and A.P. Diduck. 1995. Public Education: An Undervalued Component of the Environmental Assessment Public Involvement Process. *Environmental Impact Assessment Review* 15: 219-40.

–. 2000. Public Involvement in Environmental Impact Assessment: A Case Study of Hydro Development in the Kullu District, Himachal Pradesh, India. *Impact Assessment and Project Appraisal* 18: 63-75.

Sinclair, J., and L. Ham. 2000. Household Adaptive Strategies: Shaping Livelihood Security in the Western Himalaya. *Canadian Journal of Development Studies* 21: 89-112.

Stevens, G. 1997. Property Rights in a Canadian Mountain Ecosystem. MNRM thesis, Natural Resources Institute, University of Manitoba.

WCED (World Commission on Environment and Development). 1987. *Our Common Future.* Oxford: Oxford University Press.

7
Policy Communities and Environmental Policy Integrity: A Tale of Two Canadian Urban Air Quality Initiatives
Anthony Perl

Analyzing Canadian Air Quality Management Efforts Using Policy Communities and Policy Networks

During the 1990s, cities and metropolitan areas in developed nations renewed their efforts to address the problem of urban air pollution generated from transportation sources. Compared to the United States, where the Clean Air Act and its amendments created a national framework for regulating the vehicular emissions contributing to urban air pollution, Canadian provincial and municipal governments have experimented with more disparate policy approaches. Canada's varied initiatives and programs offer a good opportunity for comparative policy analysis. This chapter will use the analytical framework of policy communities and policy networks to assess the integrity gap that has been created by Canada's institutional constraints on formulating and implementing urban environmental initiatives.

Policy communities, and the policy networks that grow out of them, can help categorize the specific interactions among state and societal policy actors into patterns of functional relationships.[1] This allows for more effective interpretation of the influence that public officials, organized interests, governance structures, and other factors play in either constraining or facilitating urban environmental initiatives such as air quality management. The comparative correlation between policy communities and policy outcomes (or non-outcomes) can help explain why environmental initiatives carried out by urban and regional governments are just as likely to suffer from an integrity gap as their national and provincial counterparts.

Policy community analysis represents an analytical technique contributing to the "new institutionalism" in political science, sociology, and economics that calls attention to the influence of organized relationships among political and policy actors (March and Olsen 1989). Conceptually, institutions are defined to represent "the formal rules, compliance procedures, and standard operating practices that structure the relationship between individuals in various units of the polity and economy." The policy community perspective takes in the middle range of this institutional continuum, which ranges from organizational principles that are enshrined in constitutional law to the unwritten rules of bureaucratic and corporate culture. Between these extremes lies a range of structured deliberation and discourse over public problems that plays an important role in much policy making. Defining and exploring policy communities thus sheds light on the distinct patterns by which Canadian policy actors cluster together to exchange resources, including information, finances, authority, time, and legitimacy in pursuit of their preferred environmental outcomes.

Policy network dynamics arise from the distribution of power that state actors can use to influence and sanction the issues that are addressed within policy communities and the options that are endorsed by them. Unlike other policy actors, elected officials, bureaucrats, and judges have access to a very particular resource. When acting in their official capacity, the decisions of these policy community participants are considered binding upon all. Depending on the number of public sector participants and the way in which they exercise their authority, policy communities can give rise to policy networks that will exhibit distinctive modes of decision making and dispute resolution.

Table 7.1 distinguishes six such dimensions of policy network dynamics depending on whether state actors share political power with societal actors, and on the relative resource balance between private and public actors. This list is by no means exhaustive of policy network types, nor is it exclusive. It can, however, differentiate the policy network dynamics that have oriented air quality management initiatives in British Columbia and Ontario towards quite different administrative structures and substantive outcomes. It will also help to explain why the outcomes of Canadian urban air quality initiatives differ from those of the nine Western European metropolitan areas that were analyzed using the same conceptual framework in *The Politics of Improving Urban Air Quality* (Grant et al. 1999). With these analytical tools in hand, we turn to assessing and comparing the experience of Canada's two most populous English-speaking metropolitan regions in managing their air quality.

The Institutional Context for Canadian Urban Air Quality Policy

As in so many areas of Canadian public policy, jurisdictional responsibilities for urban environmental issues and problems tend to be well entrenched and resistant to alteration. The legal and institutional context described by Perl et al. (1999) thus remains little changed. Air quality management policies and motor vehicle regulation fall within a typically Canadian pattern of shared jurisdiction between Ottawa and the provinces. Following establishment of

Table 7.1

Types of policy networks

State–civil society relations / Balance of power between state and societal policy actors	Societal actors advocate policy options to state actors	Societal actors partner with state actors in formulating policy options
Balanced	Pressure pluralism	Corporatism
Favours state actors	State-directed	State corporatism
Favours civil society actors	Issue network	Clientelism

Source: Adapted from Coleman and Perl 1999.

the Canadian Environmental Protection Act in 1988, the federal government established national air quality objectives based upon federal/provincial negotiations (City of Toronto 1993). These federal objectives are not binding, and provincial governments may adopt federal levels as enforceable standards or simply develop their air quality regulations consistent with federal guidelines (Baar 1992). Policy responsibilities for regulating automotive emissions are also shared. Transport Canada, a federal ministry, establishes binding tailpipe emissions standards for new vehicles (City of Toronto 1993). Once those vehicles are on the road, provinces have the regulatory jurisdiction over emissions (Anderson and Woudsma 1996).

The jurisdictional intricacies of Canadian environmental policy do not stop with shared responsibilities between Ottawa and the provinces. Regional governments and municipalities further crowd the institutional landscape by developing and implementing environmental initiatives in Canada's urban areas. Regional governments like the City of Toronto (encompassing Canada's largest municipal government, responsible to an electorate of 2.4 million), the surrounding jurisdictions of York, Peel, and Halton, and the Greater Vancouver Regional District are distinctive institutions. These regional political entities, and their predecessors, have differentiated Canadian urban development from that of the United States (Goldberg 1986). While urban/suburban rivalry took a toll on many American cities during the 1960s and 1970s, Canada's regional governments oriented conflicts over taxation, physical infrastructure, and land-use planning in a different direction by depoliticizing policy choices. Unlike the American suburbs' contest to win economic development away from city centres, and American cities' counter-efforts to recapture employment and taxes, Canadian urban areas developed policy in a less adversarial policy community through the early 1980s. Societal interests had less ability to play one jurisdiction off against another, and thus more incentive to reach accommodation with regional governments. Perhaps the greatest drawback to Canada's more integrated municipal policy communities was that, by depoliticizing conflicts, regional governments have, on the whole, insulated policies from public engagement.

Until recently, Canada's regional governments have kept some distance from their citizenry. Provincial governments, which hold constitutional authority over municipal affairs, initially circumscribed the democratic participation in regional governments when legislating them into existence (Magnusson 1983). Given the urban concentration of Canada's population, the prospect of politicians being elected in regional municipalities with more votes than those cast for the premier of the whole province was both real and unwelcome to provincial elected officials. Regional governments were thus initially appointed or indirectly elected, leaving citizens with limited awareness of, and influence over, their activity. Only in 1997 did Toronto's 2.4 million inhabitants gain a directly elected leader, the mayor of the newly constituted City of Toronto. The Greater Vancouver Regional District remains an indirectly democratic governing body, with a board appointed from elected officials among its twenty municipalities and two unincorporated "electoral areas." With few exceptions, then, Canadian metropolitan governance fits comfortably into Canada's traditional political dynamic of elite accommodation (Tuohy 1992), in which the power to arbitrate policy differences is concentrated in the hands of a few political leaders who are insulated from public input.

Canada's multilayered institutional context raises both the administrative skill and the political stakes involved in addressing urban air pollution. For policies to move beyond the drawing board, governments must work to coordinate policy development across jurisdictional and geographical boundaries. When there is political will to address environmental problems, and when intergovernmental relations are managed skilfully, policy initiatives can be launched. But when politicians are reluctant to exercise leadership in addressing difficult policy problems and to risk visible failure, Canada's overlapping political jurisdictions and interwoven functional responsibilities provide plenty of room for cover. Thus, the linkage created by policy communities among and between policy actors can be critical in facilitating policy formulation. Policy communities can be conceived of as incubators of Canadian environmental policy, where ideas and interests grow together, yielding initiatives that would not emerge from more spontaneous interactions.

Harrison (1996) has noted that the intergovernmental division of policy responsibilities encourages a dynamic of "passing the buck." Policies that do get adopted also tend to suffer from undercontrol, a phenomenon where Canadian conventions of responsible parliamentary government give public officials considerable discretionary power, including the flexibility not to act upon broadly worded guidelines or statutes intended to protect the environment. In such a heterogeneous institutional context, the number of policy communities engaged in policy development can play a powerful role in orienting government's actions and inactions. The contrast between Toronto's diverse and discordant policy communities and Vancouver's more encompassing policy community highlights how different patterns of state/ society relationships have influenced Canada's major urban air quality management efforts, and how such initiatives still fall short of policy objectives.

Reconciling Three Discordant Policy Communities:
Toronto's Long Road to an Air Quality Management Plan
In the Greater Toronto Area (GTA), the extended and expanding metropolitan region surrounding Canada's largest city, recognizing the very existence of an air pollution problem provoked a lengthy and adversarial debate. Until 1995, the Ontario Ministry of Environment and Energy (OMOEE) emphasized the positive, claiming that that the GTA's air quality, along with that of the entire province, had been steadily improving over the last twenty years (OMOEE 1995). Where the federal and provincial governments have exercised their regulatory authority, pollution source levels of sulphur oxides, nitrogen oxides, and lead were shown to have decreased. For example, lead was banned as a motor fuel additive in 1990, and its ambient concentration was close to undetectable by 1994. Despite the official emphasis on progress, however, the levels of some serious pollutants were growing in the GTA's airshed during the 1990s.

Levels of ground-level ozone (GLO) and of particulate and fine particulate matter in the GTA's air had been increasing at the same time that other pollutants were declining. Studies by Burnett and co-workers (1994; 1998) identify ozone and particulates as serious threats to public health in the levels now found in the GTA's airshed. Between 1970 and 1990, 2 to 4 percent of deaths from heart attacks and respiratory disease in the GTA could be attributed to air pollution. By 1998, the renamed and reorganized Ontario Ministry of Environment (OMOE) recognized that air pollution was responsible for 1,800 deaths in the province each year (OMOE 1998). Most of these victims were living in urban areas, where most of the air pollution was generated by mobile sources in the transportation sector.

A study by Campbell and co-workers (1995) identifies the automobile as a major source of the GTA's air pollution. The OMOEE (1995) attributed 93.3 percent of the carbon monoxide, 63.4 percent of the nitrogen oxides, and 37.5 percent of the particulates in Toronto's airshed to motor vehicle emissions. Vehicle emissions can be reduced and new pollution-control technology has brought reductions of up to 90 percent (Deakin 1993). However, because the number of vehicles and the length of trips have outstripped technology improvements (Atkinson et al. 1991; City of Toronto 1993; Mennell 1995), cleaner cars have not translated into cleaner air for the GTA. This limit to what improving technology could actually deliver in terms of environmental outcomes demonstrates the need for policy instruments that reach beyond the automotive industry's deployment of technology.

While the provincial government and representatives of major polluting industries emphasized the public health improvements that already occurred from reduction of certain air pollutants, municipal governments, medical officials, and environmental advocates in the GTA demanded that more be done to counter the mounting health threat from GLO and particulates. For example, in 1998 the Ontario Medical Association (OMA) published a position paper on the health effects of GLO that called for decisive government action to manage urban air quality. In the transportation sector, the OMA called for adoption of California's standards for motor vehicle emissions, the most stringent in North America. The OMA also called for far-reaching efforts to alter the mix of public and private modes of transportation in the GTA (Ontario Medical Association, 1998):

> The OMA recommends that the Ministry of the Environment, together with the Ministry of Transportation and the City of Toronto, should develop and implement a comprehensive plan for public transit in the Greater Toronto Area. The OMA recognizes that such an undertaking is very challenging, and it is not clear that the political and near-term resources are present to accomplish such a task. Yet, without such a plan, the OMA is not confident that sufficient long-term emission reductions can be achieved from the transportation sector in this heavily impacted area.

What has emerged to date falls far short of the OMA's recommendations and the demands of urban governments and environmental nongovernmental organizations (NGOs). A first step towards air quality management was taken with Drive Clean, an urban vehicle emissions inspection program that was launched in 1998. By 2001 over 1 million inspections of passenger cars in the GTA had been carried out through licensed private service stations. The program reflects both an ideological orientation towards limited government and a close working relationship between the state and the automotive industry in its implementation through private service stations.[2] Toronto's air pollution policy debate and the initial phase of Drive Clean demonstrate how policy communities that are separated by jurisdictional and functional boundaries require political leaders to exercise the state's authority in order to launch a program in a contest among adversarial policy communities.

The first policy community to address urban air pollution in Ontario can be designated "environmental professionals," the set of scientists, engineers, lawyers, planners, and other experts who take an ongoing interest in environmental matters. Actors within this community work for municipal, provincial, and federal governments, as well as for NGOs and the private sector. Cohesion in this community is weak, with limited interaction between public and private sector participants (interview).[3] Despite the fact that many of these environmental professionals work for federal or provincial governments, public officials have rarely embraced the scientific or technical recommendations produced by their own experts. As a result, policy network dynamics within this community closely resemble the "pressure pluralism" category in Table 7.1. Nontechnical, process-oriented civil servants receive (and review) the technical input from researchers working for industry, academics, and public sector scientists. These environmental policy managers, in turn, pass along recommendations to their political masters, who are even more sensitive to public opinion and more focused on concerns of the business community than the generalist bureaucrats. The effect of this political-administrative chain of communication is to distance the environmental professionals from Ontario's environmental decision making.

At the heart of this community of environmental professionals are the employees of federal and provincial ministries. Environment Canada and the OMOE, where most of these professionals spend their careers, are both relative newcomers to Canada's bureaucratic context. Environment Canada dates from 1970, while the OMOE has focused exclusively on the environment only since late 1997, when it was extracted from the OMOEE, which had a dual responsibility for environmental and energy policies.

The OMOEE's staff size nearly doubled in the late 1980s and early 1990s, when a supportive Liberal government responded to growing public concern about the environment (interview). More resources meant a broader sweep of environmental policy making at the provincial level. Initiatives included tough enforcement of existing regulations against industrial polluters, instead of the previous undercontrol. New policy problems were also added to the OMOEE's responsibility, including reducing urban smog and its precursors (nitrogen oxides, volatile organic compounds, and particulates). However, rapid growth of the ministry and its technical capabilities was accompanied by a dilution of administrative effectiveness. The span of control from the deputy minister at the top to frontline staff extended in some cases through seven tiers.

A change of government in 1990 added to the confusion. When the social democratic New Democratic Party (NDP) government took power, former environmental activists who had clashed with the OMOEE from the outside suddenly became public officials. These environmentalists' ambitious agenda pulled policy making in disparate directions. For example, while the bureaucracy had one set of scientists and engineers working on air pollution issues, the minister's office had policy advisers developing parallel initiatives for both ground-level ozone and stratospheric ozone. This rapid growth of the policy community did not translate into an increased capacity for policy initiation.

The OMOEE's expanded air pollution research efforts created tension between bureaucratic and political participants within the community of environmental professionals. While the NDP politicians had asserted that poor urban air quality was affecting people's health, data from the ministry did not support these claims. Staff studies showed that air pollution was getting better, but that the ministry's standards were outdated, accepting pollution levels well above those in American jurisdictions (interview). Despite this identified gap between the OMOEE's standards and the state of best practices elsewhere, the government did not make updating these standards a priority.

In the early 1990s, Ontario's environmental professionals and politicians proved unsuccessful in forging an effective policy network dynamic with a second policy community that engaged in the debates and deliberations over urban air pollution. Ontario's "automotive policy community" comprises vehicle manufacturers, petrochemical producers, vehicle dealers, road construction contractors, financial institutions, organized labour, automobile associations, and a number of provincial and local government agencies (e.g., the Ministry of Trade and Industry). Members of the automotive policy community staunchly disputed the environmental professional community's efforts to intervene in limiting urban air pollution from transportation sources in the GTA. The environmental policy community's finding that motor vehicles generated the majority of pollutants in the GTA was challenged by the automotive policy community, which insisted that transboundary air pollution was the more significant policy problem. From this perspective, the 50 percent of Ontario's ground-level ozone precursors generated by sources in the US (Municipality of Metropolitan Toronto 1996) justified government's attention and action *before* measures to regulate or restrict transportation in the GTA were contemplated. The cost of acting to reduce the GTA's "homegrown" air pollution was seen as prohibitive, since unilateral regulatory or restrictive measures would derail the province's economic engine of growth – automobile manufacturing.

The auto industry's role in resisting regulatory interventions such as clean air legislation and fuel economy standards is well documented (Flink 1988; Crandall et al. 1986; Goddard 1994). Vehicle manufacturers have been even more strident in their opposition to economic instruments such as fuel taxes or road pricing that could be used to recover the social costs of automobility (Atkinson et al. 1991; Eck 1991). Rounding out the opposition to an increased user-pay system are car owners themselves (Sperling 1991; Dunn 1998). The automotive policy community is thus bound together by opposition to regulatory or pricing initiatives that would concentrate the automobile's environmental costs on either consumers or producers.

The economic weight and political muscle of Ontario's automotive policy community has yielded a clientelist policy network dynamic. As previously indicated in Table 7.1, clientelist policy networks feature a leadership role for certain societal organizations in policy formulation. In Ontario the reasons for such leadership are readily apparent. Automotive manufacturing is the single largest sector of the economy. The manufacturing, sales, and service of motor vehicles account for one out of every six jobs in the province. Given this considerable economic weight, it is not surprising that both the federal and provincial governments have aided the growth of Ontario's automotive economy and have been able to declare certain automotive air pollution options out of bounds. When a labour-backed NDP government came to power, the widespread employment in the auto, oil, and road-building sectors turned out to be as important for the government as the investment and profit levels had been for its predecessors. To appear fair to automotive interests, the NDP government exhibited considerable deference to their concerns, more than did its counterpart in British Columbia, where the automotive sector is minuscule.

The policy community working to preserve and protect Ontario's automotive industry could neither be ignored nor convinced to accept more than token air pollution policy initiatives. Two years into its mandate, the NDP government implemented its first steps towards controlling urban smog. These actions were deliberately modest and sought to lay the groundwork for future developments. For example, the government introduced new requirements for vapour recovery devices at gasoline transfer stations but then backed down from requiring vapour recovery technology to be installed at retail gas pumps. Oil companies argued that US automotive regulations would require vapour recovery modules to be installed on all 1997 model year vehicles, hence the cost of fitting gas pumps with parallel technology was excessive. Given the eight-year average age of Ontario's auto fleet, relying on in-vehicle vapour recovery technology would delay widespread deployment until well into the twenty-first century.

This tension between environmental and industry-based policy communities was cut short in 1995 when the NDP government was defeated. The new Progressive Conservative government had campaigned on a right-wing platform of tax cuts and smaller government designed to appeal to its traditional supporters in rural and suburban locations. Fiscal and programmatic restructuring quickly changed the OMOEE from an initiator of urban air quality policy into a follower of societal (e.g., industry) inputs (interview). Initiatives from the cabinet office and from the automotive policy community replaced the environmental policy community's ambition to clean the GTA's air.

While the change in provincial government tipped policy network dynamics towards automotive industry clientelism, a third policy community remained active in the locations where air pollution's costs are concentrated, the municipal and regional governments of the GTA. Despite this concentration of environmental burdens, GTA governments have presided over the sprawl of low-density housing, shopping centres, and office parks discussed in Chapter 8 that precipitated an explosion of urban mobility, mainly by single-occupant vehicles. GTA governments have tried to keep pace with growing automotive traffic by building more highways, while development of public transport has been limited by fiscal austerity (Perl and Pucher 1995). By the mid-1980s, rivalry between Canada's first regional government, Metropolitan Toronto, and surrounding jurisdictions in the GTA turned debates over urban smog into zero-sum trade-offs between the old centre, which had little to lose from limiting automobility, and the up-and-coming periphery, where automobility was seen as essential to continued growth and prosperity.

Ontario's public opinion, which Harrison (1996) sees as an important enabler of government action on environmental policy, appears closer to the suburban regional governments' reluctance to break away from the cycle of sprawl, increasing automobility, and economic growth. The government's polling revealed that while Ontarians ranked air quality relatively high as a concern, controlling toxic chemicals, water quality, and waste management were each given a higher priority than controlling air emissions. Furthermore, few respondents indicated that they would change driving and auto maintenance habits, even if this improved air quality. Ontarians' environmental preferences may be influenced by the region's geography, which offers no barriers to the arrival of US smog and also diffuses air pollution across southwestern Ontario. Such physical factors could create a cognitive constraint on taking action, since air pollution's causes can appear to lie beyond the reach of provincial or local policy.

The environmental nongovernmental organizations (ENGOs) that might have focused public concern on air pollution were paradoxically weakened by the environmentally conscious NDP's time in government. Key environmental and health policy advocates in Ontario spent most of the NDP's mandate inside government, engaged in internal struggles with the bureaucracy rather than mobilizing societal support for new policy initiatives. ENGO participants who remained outside government during the NDP's mandate lacked the political expertise to develop effective influence within the policy community of environmental professionals. When the Progressive Conservatives gained power and most transplanted environmental advocates returned to being outsiders, Ontario's government began its own multi-stakeholder consultation, engaging members of all three policy communities (professional, automotive, and urban/regional) but extending the clientelist dynamic in which auto industry priorities of voluntarism and incrementalism took precedence.

Such priorities yielded support for a very particular instrument of air quality improvement – a vehicle emissions inspection program delivered by private contractors, such as gas stations, garages, and auto parts store, on a for-profit basis. This system was introduced in stages, beginning with passenger vehicles in the urban centre of Toronto and expanding outward both spatially into the suburbs and functionally to include commercial vehicles such as trucks. Since Drive Clean's inauguration, both the vehicle-kilometres travelled by car and truck and total air emissions have continued to climb.

Ontario's approach to addressing urban air pollution suggests that the current clientelist policy network has limited the range of acceptable policy instruments to those that the automotive policy community will tolerate. When a government of the left was in power, and somewhat more attentive to the views of the environmental professional and urban policy communities, officials lacked the will to implement new policy initiatives. Now that a government of the right is in power, implementation is not a constraint, but the automotive policy community's preferences predominate. Exogenous factors, such as the health effects of increasing pollution levels and the need to gain popular support before an election, may yet challenge government to take measures presented by environmental and urban policy communities more seriously. Or a change in government could transform policy network dynamics. In the meantime, however, the GTA's air pollution appears likely to remain an unsolved environmental challenge with a gap between the chosen policy instrument of vehicle inspection and the objective of cleaning up a serious urban smog problem.

An Inclusive Policy Community Launches More Ambitious Policy in the Lower Mainland of British Columbia

The efforts of the Lower Mainland at controlling urban air pollution illustrate both the potential and the limits of an encompassing policy community in delivering relief from polluted air. The term "Lower Mainland" is the local definition of Vancouver's metropolitan region. More than elsewhere in Canada, policy actors in the Lower Mainland have been able to develop air pollution control policies that target the transportation problems of a metropolitan region. An inclusive policy community, shepherded by an active and engaged regional government, has facilitated these efforts. Even so, however, implementing a comprehensive policy program that links air quality to transportation and land-use goals has yielded limited results that fall short of stated policy goals. This overview of Vancouver's air quality management efforts will illustrate that while a fairly high level of received scientific knowledge and administrative experience are needed to initiate policy, they are not sufficient to deliver effective outcomes.

Vancouver's experience shows how the allure of technically precise solutions to politically sensitive problems, such as the significant air pollution impact of motor vehicles, will draw government into acting first on the least controversial end of the environmental policy continuum instruments. "AirCare," the Vancouver region's motor vehicle inspection and maintenance program, promised results through optimizing the emissions from existing automotive technology. AirCare's emission reductions have arrived more slowly than predicted, however, and at greater cost than estimated. Once AirCare became established, it created an organizational foothold in government for further and more ambitious transportation policy measures. While AirCare broadened the policy community concerned about the environmental effects of transportation in the Lower Mainland, however, it did not facilitate the adoption of more ambitious policy instruments that could effectively manage transportation demand. What has followed AirCare's launch is an example of "policy learning" (Bennett and Howlett 1992) about what transportation and air quality innovations were politically acceptable within the policy community.

Air pollution is not a new issue to governments, industry, or the general public in the Lower Mainland. As early as 1949, British Columbia's provincial government delegated the power to regulate commercial and industrial air emissions to the City of Vancouver. The city established a permit system for large point sources of pollution such as paper mills and cement producers. Baar (1995) notes that "visibility of emissions or awareness of the nuisance they create" was the guiding principle motivating the permit scheme, and that such a reactive approach "is consistent with mopping up the most visible manifestations of neglect." As a result, permits were issued without charge, with the primary criterion to keep smoke, odours, and other pollution impacts below the threshold of public perception, but no lower. Polluters typically negotiated a higher quota than their current output (interview), and unless there was public opposition (e.g., complaints or protests from neighbourhood associations), local government acquiesced.

Despite the limited scope and ambitions of Vancouver's air pollution permit system, the process launched a significant pattern of interaction on urban air pollution between business and local government. Vancouver's local government began building a capacity to monitor and regulate air pollution far earlier than either provincial or federal governments in Canada. A widespread conversion to natural gas for home, office, and industrial heating needs was begun in 1956, and wood-fired boilers powering sawmills along False Creek and the Fraser River were closed during the 1960s and 1970s.

Skocpol (1985) highlights the importance of state capacity as an explanatory factor in public policy development. Policy development is often limited by government's capability; thus, taking on regulatory responsibilities for air pollution early in the postwar years gave Vancouver's government an opportunity to build experience and know-how. In the same way, Vancouver's business community also entered a policy learning process regarding air quality management before counterparts elsewhere in Canada. While a part of this education took the form of industries learning how to minimize new regulatory burdens, such engagement in government's regulatory process did facilitate the emergence of a policy community where public and private stakeholders gained a common focus of attention and developed a shared vocabulary and norms.

By the early 1970s, Vancouver's air pollution policy community had gained enough experience to identify air quality management as a "common pool" problem that extended beyond the political boundaries of a single municipality. Both the City of Vancouver and its air pollution permit-holders could appreciate the inequity as well as the ineffectiveness of confining regulatory efforts within a narrow political jurisdiction. Accordingly, the provincial government amended the Pollution Control Act in 1972 to designate the Greater Vancouver Regional District (GVRD), a regional government with a much larger jurisdiction, as having responsibility for air quality monitoring and planning in Vancouver's metropolitan region (Tennant and Zirnhelt 1973). The GVRD's activity offers the opportunity to assess the workings of an inclusive (i.e., interjurisdictional and multisectoral) policy community in controlling pollution.

The scientific expertise that is being used to manage air quality in Vancouver has been developed by technocrats working for a regional government that is more remote and less familiar to most citizens than is its provincial or municipal counterparts. This insulation from the electorate may explain some of the reasons why the plans and recommendations of technocrats in the GVRD were not filtered, and discounted, to the degree found in the Ontario government's reaction to its environmental policy community. The GVRD is directed by mayors and councillors of twenty municipalities and two unincorporated "electoral areas" in the Lower Mainland, and they are appointed by their respective local governments. The link between residents and regional government is thus attenuated.

Political insulation could go only so far in facilitating the recommendations of environmental professionals, however. When the GVRD has considered controversial policy options, such as road pricing (Long 1993), provincial and municipal politicians have proven quite reluctant to embrace proposals that the public perceived as extreme, and in which the monetary costs appeared much more acute and immediate than the public health benefits. As a result, air quality management initiatives in transportation began with technically sophisticated yet politically palatable programs like motor vehicle inspection and maintenance.

During the 1980s, the regional government's monitoring and planning activities created an opportunity for introducing new policies to deal with air pollution in the Lower Mainland. New information, public awareness, and pressure on the province for some action by municipal governments converged to facilitate program creation. The new program embraced the goal of comprehensive airshed management and introduced regulatory measures to reduce pollution from point, mobile, and area sources.

Unlike the GTA, where local geography dispersed the social and economic impacts of air pollution, the Lower Mainland's geography both concentrated these impacts and raised the visibility of urban air pollution. The Coast Mountains to the north, the Cascade Mountains to the southeast, and the wind patterns associated with the Strait of Georgia to the west interact to inhibit the air circulation needed to disperse locally generated emissions (Bovar-Concord 1995; Mennell 1995; Farmar-Bowers 1996). These mountains converge at the eastern end of the Fraser Valley, effectively confining the region's air basin and concentrating air pollution impacts in Vancouver's eastern (suburban) periphery. Such a concentration effect gave regional officials added incentive to cooperate with the urban centre.

New information was also important in focusing both decision makers and the general public on air pollution as a policy problem. Data collection and analysis was one of the first steps that the GVRD took in pursuit of air quality management. The GVRD's first emissions inventory showed that a total of 602,400 tonnes of pollution had entered the Vancouver region's airshed in 1985 (GVRD 1994). This inventory also demonstrated that close to 75 percent of air pollution was produced by mobile sources (GVRD 1995a), a far higher level than had previously been estimated. These revelations were important catalysts for policy innovation. Industries with point-source emissions already controlled under the air pollution permit system gained the justification for advocating regulation of mobile sources, which caused far more air pollution (Vancouver Board of Trade 1991). The government was warned that any tightening of air pollution regulations that did not include mobile sources would face strong resistance.

Broadening the regulatory umbrella would give the industries whose point sources were already regulated an opportunity to shift the costs of subsequent remediation to other sources. De Spot (1994) notes that in 1993, 22 percent of all permit-holders contributed 80 percent of all permit fees. BC Hydro, the provincial electric utility, demonstrates behaviour within the policy community that typifies industry's response to this new information. BC Hydro sought to lead the transition to mobile-source initiatives by, for example, proposing to pay for van pools, bicycle paths, and buying back old cars in Vancouver as a more cost-effective alternative (per tonne of air pollution saved) to new control technology in its Burrard thermal generating station (BC Hydro 1993).

A key stream of new information introduced by the GVRD was an air quality index that provided Lower Mainland residents with daily updates on the level of air pollution. This index soon become a fixture of news-paper, radio, and television weather reports, giving the region's population a new perspective on the state of their environment. During the late 1980s, this news about local environmental deterioration in Canada's major cities coincided with reports on global environmental problems such as climate change, along with new initiatives to address them, such as the Brundtland Commission's advocacy of "sustainable development" (WCED 1987). Pub-lic concern about the environment was rising steadily during the late 1980s. Gallup polling found that concern for the environment peaked just before the recession of 1990, when close to a third of Canadians identified the environment and pollution as the most important problem facing the nation (Brooks 1998). The time was ripe for action on urban air pollution problems.

During the same period that these revelations about the precarious state of Vancouver's air and the environment as a whole were being publicized, the GVRD launched a consultation process on a new regional master plan. While this input revealed general concern about the environment, air pol-lution was among the highest-priority issues noted by residents of the Lower Mainland. The GVRD's summary of its new Liveable Region Strategic Plan states: "Early in the process, the public rejected a business-as-usual approach to regional growth that would spread population throughout the Fraser Valley. They rejected it because it would put development pressure on farm-land, increase the distance between jobs and housing, cost too much for public services and utilities, and result in worsening air pollution from in-creased automobile use" (GVRD 1995b).

Instead of business as usual, public input led the GVRD's board of direc-tors to adopt the following vision statement for their new regional plan (GVRD 1995b):

Greater Vancouver can become the first urban region in the world to com-bine in one place the things to which humanity aspires on a global basis: a place where human activities enhance rather than degrade the natural en-vironment, where the quality of the built environment approaches that of the natural setting, where the diversity of origins and religions is a source of strength rather than strife, where people control the destiny of their com-munity, and where the basics of food, clothing, shelter, security and useful activity are accessible to all.

Such a vision was to be achieved through five action plans for managing air quality, green space, drinking water quality, liquid waste processing, and solid waste disposal. In each of these domains, the GVRD sought to expand the boundaries of previous policy responsibilities. Addressing air pollution from mobile sources was the key innovation to securing better air quality. As early as 1985, the GVRD's board had begun to urge the province to launch a new air pollution control scheme to reduce emissions from mobile sources. The provincial government at that time, controlled by the rurally oriented and right-wing Social Credit party, did not act.

By late 1989, the GVRD, with support from regulated industry and municipal politicians, prepared to take the lead in policy development. Behind the scenes, regional officials informed their provincial counterparts that they would act unilaterally to introduce mobile-source emission regulation within the GVRD's boundaries (Baar 1996). The GVRD's threat of unilateral action was credible because it was backed by both the jurisdictional capacity and administrative competence to implement an air quality program (interview). Underscoring this capacity, the GVRD unveiled its Air Quality Management Plan (AQMP) in early 1990. That plan's mission statement stressed cooperation, noting: "The GVRD air quality management program will work co-operatively with the community to shape regional land use and transportation, encourage clean air lifestyles, and manage emissions from human activity so as to protect human health and ecological integrity both within the region, in neighbouring jurisdictions in the Lower Fraser Valley airshed, and globally" (GVRD 1994).

Vancouver's AQMP set ambitious targets for clearing the air. Emissions of sulphur and nitrogen oxides, particulates, carbon monoxide, and volatile organic compounds would be cut by 50 percent between 1985 and 2000. GVRD plans implied that emission reductions would have to come from more than just tinkering with existing technology. Vehicle inspections and maintenance would be followed by transportation demand management (TDM) measures such as "discouraging the unnecessary use of the automobile and encouraging use of ... walking, cycling, and ... public transportation" (GVRD 1994). Faced with mounting criticism from the opposition NDP and the prospect of action by the GVRD, the Social Credit government sought to claim credit for environmental protection by signing on to the AQMP initiative and agreeing to a vehicle inspection and maintenance program called AirCare (interview). AirCare quickly become the most visible component of Vancouver's air quality management program.

In moving from formulation to implementation of an air quality management program, policy makers had to make key choices on policy instruments. As in most urban transportation problems, policy options that promised the most effective results were perceived to be politically risky, while those that were politically palatable appeared less effective. Public officials in the GVRD knew that TDM measures could cut emissions more quickly and cheaply than establishing a vehicle inspection program, but they also knew that restrictions on automobility such as bridge or road tolls were politically controversial. The use of such pricing instruments might trigger a tax revolt, or at least significant intergovernmental conflict over the use of those funds (Bohn 1996). Finally, TDM measures would also distribute costs unequally within the region, possibly initiating a core-periphery conflict.

Provincial officials were even more averse to using government authority to limit or price mobility by motor vehicle, viewing such TDM restrictions as an infringement on people's liberty. Using TDM incentives would require heavy public investment in revamping Vancouver's public transit system to provide a viable auto alternative (*Vancouver Sun* 1996), representing an even higher cost than a vehicle inspection program. Provincial and regional elected officials viewed inspection and maintenance programs quite favourably because they appeared to represent a regulatory pill that the public was prepared to swallow. GVRD opinion polling revealed that a large number of residents supported a vehicle inspection program (interview). Furthermore, a publicly administered regulatory program would create jobs in both inspection and repair facilities that government could take credit for. Finally, there was evidence from nearby California suggesting that vehicle inspection and maintenance programs could mitigate mobile-source emissions without appearing to constrain mobility. Thus, the AirCare vehicle inspection program gained priority over more intrusive or costly TDM policy instruments in the GVRD's effort to manage emissions from motor vehicles.

Implementing an emissions inspection program that assessed every vehicle in the Lower Mainland proved to be a complex task. The GVRD had accumulated considerable administrative experience over regulatory programs that were similar in both magnitude and financial requirements to the AirCare program (interview). Vehicle safety inspections had originated at the municipal level in Vancouver, and the GVRD's staff had the most experience across the province with air quality measurement and modelling. Moreover, through managing emission reduction programs at large incinerators and steam generators, the GVRD also had experience in the management of capital-intensive projects.

Provincial endorsement of AirCare also brought provincial administrative leadership along with it, however. Although the same bureaucrats from various levels of government continued to meet throughout AirCare's design and introduction, functional responsibility came to rest in the British Columbia Ministry of Highways, Motor Vehicles Branch. In principle, this was the agency of government with the final say over mobile-source regulation in the Lower Mainland. In practice, it was not an agency with a great deal of experience in or knowledge of air quality management.

In meeting the new responsibility for vehicle emissions management, the Motor Vehicles Branch sought to supplement its limited experience with outside expertise. American consultants who had worked on inspection and maintenance programs in California were called upon to help design AirCare. However, importing expertise raised a problem with "policy learning" that Richard Rose (1993) has labelled "fungibility." Fungibility means the degree to which knowledge and methods developed to address a policy problem in one jurisdiction can be transferred to a different geographic and administrative context.

The American consultants' knowledge base was built upon California experience, bringing with it limitations that would hinder AirCare's initial effectiveness (Baar 1995). For example, California had a homogeneous fleet of vehicles to be inspected, in which all cars built in the same model year were mandated to have the same pollution control devices. Western Canada's fleet was heterogeneous. In Canada, auto manufacturers would sell a mix of US-specification vehicles and others that had been recalibrated to use different (and fewer) pollution control devices. Baar (1996) finds that 80 percent of 1984-85 model year vehicles had had their pollution control devices recalibrated to meet the lower Canadian emissions standards. This lack of standardization was not adequately addressed by the initial AirCare inspection protocols, which began with a visual inspection of pollution control devices to ensure that no tampering had occurred.

Because of these and other constraints arising from imported expertise, AirCare got off to a slow start in 1992, and has delivered the projected air quality improvements behind schedule and at a higher cost than forecast. This is not to deny AirCare's positive impact. The entire AQMP, of which AirCare is only part, has been estimated to deliver between $2.3 billion and $5.1 billion in net benefits to the Lower Mainland between 1994 and 2020 (Bovar-Concord 1995). Nonetheless, Bovar-Concord noted in their initial assessment that "there is a discrepancy in the timing of benefits and costs. The control costs tend to be incurred earlier in the time sequence, with major capital expenditures required in the mid-1990s when much of the control equipment is being introduced" (ARA Consulting Group 1994). Technically complex regulatory instruments may account for that higher cost in early years, while more cost-effective but politically controversial policy TDM measures were deferred until a later time.

That date of reckoning with more controversial and authoritative policy instruments in the Lower Mainland has been approached and then deferred once fiscal conservatives entered policy deliberations over charging drivers for their environmental damage and fomented a tax revolt. In 1998 the province created the Greater Vancouver Transportation Authority (GVTA), a single organization that consolidated financing, planning, and management responsibilities for transportation and air quality throughout the Lower Mainland. The GVTA took on operational responsibility for Vancouver's bus, rail, and ferry transit operations, for 2,100 kilometres of Vancouver's Major Road Network, and for AirCare.

Adopting the name "TransLink" in 1999, Vancouver's new transportation and air quality management agency developed a draft *Strategic Transportation Plan*. This document was unveiled on 12 January 2000 and, after public consultation, was finalized in April 2000 (TransLink 2000). Proposed TDM measures include major investments in public transit infrastructure and service improvements as well as new pricing instruments for motor vehicles. Pricing instruments included parking charges and an annual levy on vehicle ownership averaging $75, which would vary based upon both vehicle size and use, as well as transit fare increases. These are in addition to existing gasoline taxes and vehicle inspection and registration fees. For the first time in the Lower Mainland, an extensive public debate on alternatives to the unlimited growth of automobility was conducted with explicit reference to restrictive measures such as taxes and vehicle surcharges.

This discussion came to be dominated, however, by skeptics such as the fiscally conservative Canadian Taxpayers Federation (2000) and the market-driven Fraser Institute (Bixby 2000). Both organizations helped foment a tax revolt against TransLink's efforts to price mobility even partly based upon air pollution costs, citing a range of alleged inefficiencies and inequities in such a policy. Their tactics ranged from downplaying the magnitude of the air quality problem to denying the effectiveness of transportation demand management policy instruments. Support for TransLink's objectives began to ebb as the public focused on the short-term costs of the vehicle levy and other user charges. A poll conducted in October 2000 found that the public would only "grudgingly accept" TransLink's mobility pricing instruments (Ipsos-Reid 2000). For an unpopular provincial government facing an election campaign in 2001, this opposition was sufficient to make it back away from further implementation of mobility pricing and leave TransLink to face a fiscal crisis that has necessitated public transit cutbacks and contributed to a long and bitter strike by bus drivers. The capacity to achieve ambitious policy objectives involving urban livability and air quality in the Lower Mainland has thus been sharply constrained by this fiscal crisis.

Overall, the Vancouver region's AQMP has shown promise in making progress on its goals by utilizing technical policy instruments such as vehicle inspection. It has also demonstrated the potentials and pitfalls of policy learning, beginning with the challenge of adapting California's vehicle inspection experience and continuing with current efforts to recognize the need to move beyond technical fixes that fall short of cleaning the air. The Livable Region Strategic Plan set a target of reducing 1985 air pollution levels by 50 percent by the year 2000, but the GVRD's forecast performance for the instruments included in its AQMP estimates only a 32 percent reduction (GVRD 1994). From a technical efficiency perspective, there is something to be said for selecting policy instruments that require a less exacting design and administration than AirCare has needed. In terms of political efficiency, however, governments need to demonstrate that technical solutions in themselves cannot solve environmental problems before they enact any of the more contentious, yet more efficient, instruments, such as vehicle pricing, that could directly affect travel by automobile. Even such a demonstration has not yet been sufficient to enable the imposition of mobility pricing tied to regional air quality improvement.

Conclusion: Policy Communities as a Mode of Policy Learning

The air pollution policy deliberations of Toronto and Vancouver have shown the important role that policy communities can play in orienting program initiation. When a single policy community can encompass multiple political jurisdictions and economic sectors, and reach out to the larger society, launching new programs will be easier. Vancouver's AQMP and TransLink are the products of such an inclusive policy community. However, as problems with implementing AirCare and with financing TransLink's strategic transportation plan through a vehicle levy demonstrate, bringing disparate actors and interests into effective communication and interchange through policy communities does not guarantee the achievement of goals and objectives.

Exogenous factors, such as geography and the role of the automotive and energy industries in a region's economy, can make the path to formulating urban air pollution policy more or less arduous. Vancouver's inclusive policy community capitalized on geographic and economic conditions by engaging scientists, public officials, industry, and nongovernmental activists in a long-running dialogue on air quality. Sufficient consensus was reached so that the results of air quality measurement could be disseminated through the media. In turn, supportive public opinion has reduced the risk for policy makers (up to a point) in the Lower Mainland, while divided public opinion on how to attain clean air did little to embolden the GTA's decision makers. Thus, a gap remains between the stated goals of TransLink's Strategic Transportation Plan and the capacity to achieve these goals. Without such effective implementation, Vancouver's air quality and larger urban sustainability objectives will be increasingly threatened.

Timing is important. In the Lower Mainland, a conservative but populist government seeking re-election embraced a "green" policy issue like AirCare in the hope of attracting votes. By signing on to AirCare, the province became implicated in the larger AQMP, which has opened the door to the more authoritative TDMs that were proposed by TransLink. Subsequently, a social democratic government fearful of further antagonizing voters prior to an election backed away from charging drivers for a portion of their environmental impact. In the GTA, meanwhile, a left-wing government failed to enact significant measures on urban air quality before losing power – clearing the way for its right-wing successor to enact policy based on clientelist policy dynamics that addressed the preferences of the automotive policy community.

Compared with the GTA's three distinct policy communities, Vancouver's policy community demonstrated a high degree of integration, to the point that vehicle charges were about to be implemented. Internal consensus could be established regarding the significance of urban air pollution and on the desirability of mitigating its impacts through technological means (e.g., vehicle inspections). Such shared ideas complemented the participants' different interests and created a foundation for cooperative behaviour. The resulting agreement among Vancouver industries and the regional government to target mobile sources of air pollution allowed industry to shift remediation costs while at the same time enabling the GVRD to begin addressing social costs.

In the GTA, however, neither ideas nor interests were shared among the three disconnected and often adversarial policy communities. For example, with one policy community identifying the problem as a trans-boundary pollution issue and another viewing it as a product of the use of automobiles in the GTA, no consensus emerged on the cause of the air pollution problem. Policy community inclusiveness thus appears directly correlated with the macro-institutional framework within which these communities functioned. In the Lower Mainland, institutions such as the GVRD and TransLink promote a dynamic of cooperation and compromise that the provincial government legitimized. In the GTA, on the other hand, the presence of competing governments produced a dynamic of regional rivalry that was also legitimized by the provincial government.

Another difference between the GTA and the Lower Mainland was that the latter's policy community had reached a critical mass where broad-based, long-term engagement among policy participants enabled collaborative working relationships and demonstrated the benefits of such behaviour. Within this collective dynamic, participant linkages were numerous, bridging many differences of interest across the community. Such connections were evident among technical experts, industry, the public, and the state. In the GTA, where such a critical mass has yet to occur, the automotive industry remains a policy community unto itself and the government in power explicitly endorses the view that what is good for General Motors is good for Ontario.

Finally, successful policy formulation in Vancouver was a consequence of an active state supporting the work of policy entrepreneurs both within and outside government. Atkinson and Coleman (1989) have observed that, for an anticipatory policy like Vancouver's AQMP to be realized, the state must be able to coordinate policy community participants and support their entrepreneurial activities. The GVRD possessed both the incentive and the authority to play a leadership role within the policy community that fostered the AQMP's development and opened the door to TransLink. And as soon as government withdrew its support for TransLink's implementation of the vehicle levy, the policy community became constrained by fiscal feuding between anti-tax and pro-environment participants. In the GTA, the effective policy entrepreneurship occurred solely within one of three policy communities, the one devoted to advancing the automotive industry's interests.

By this point, it has become clear that policy network dynamics influenced the course of air quality management efforts in the Lower Mainland and the GTA. This analysis has revealed that, where an encompassing policy community could initiate politically palatable actions as a first step towards clearly defined outcomes, moving up the learning curve from the limited efficacy of technological "fixes" to measures that influence travel behaviour through pricing requires a willingness of state actors to reassert their authority to an extent that British Columbia's provincial leaders have been unwilling to either do themselves or delegate to TransLink. Introducing direct pricing for auto use, through tolls on roads or bridges, would almost certainly require a state-directed policy network to make the break from business as usual. Ontario's political leaders actually proved more willing to throw their authority behind the automotive policy community, leading to a clientele pluralist network based on the Drive Clean program.

The role of the state in these two examples of Canadian urban environmental policy reveals an important influence of government on policy architecture as the arbiter of policy community deliberations. Looking elsewhere in transportation, Dunn and Perl (1996) have identified an inventory of societal partnerships that state actors can cultivate to build the political infrastructure for new programs. Such political engineering can create new horizontal links between disparate communities and support policy entrepreneurship, as was seen in the Lower Mainland. Majone (1989) diagnoses an important attribute of the clientelist dynamic at work in the GTA when he suggests that institutional tinkering by the state can shift the balance of power within (and between) policy communities, and thus alter the comparative advantage held by certain interests.

In conclusion, although an encompassing policy community and shared public authority in a policy network may well be necessary to formulate an air quality management policy that reaches beyond technical tinkering with motor vehicles and considers more sustainable changes in land use and mobility, it is not sufficient to ensure the achievement of such objectives. In order to achieve the degree of change in vehicle use needed to truly clean the air in both the GTA and the Lower Mainland, regulatory and/or pricing measures extending beyond those even considered in TransLink's contentious strategic plan will be required. Difficult political choices will have to be made to introduce effective but controversial policy instruments. One factor that appears to aid in the adoption of such measures is policy learning. Despite all the intellectual pitfalls that Bennett and Howlett (1992) identify with this concept, policy learning can, sooner or later, demonstrate the limits and constraints that institutional arrangements contribute to an integrity gap between policy goals and outcomes.

As Canada's major urban regions consider air quality management options, a disjointed process of trial and error appears the most likely scenario for environmental policy development. Politicians, industry, NGOs, and the general public will need time to discover that politically innocuous policy options will not, in themselves, be enough to clean the air. As with most learning curves, the sooner that participants engage in air quality management efforts, the sooner they are likely to gain enough experience to realize this. In this race between collective policy-making capacity and the ecological capacity to absorb further urban sprawl and auto dependence, the existence of a policy community that can speed the progress of disparate actors up the policy learning curve could prove crucial to closing the integrity gap that exists between goals and results in Canada's urban environments.

Acknowledgment

This chapter is an updated and expanded version of "When Policy Networks Collide: The Institutional Constraint on Air Pollution Control Strategies in Two Canadian Cities," co-authored by Anthony Perl, Kevin Muxlow, and Jane Hargraft, which appeared in Grant et al. 1999 (pages 13-30).

Notes

1 For a theoretical discussion of policy communities and policy networks, and their contribution to the study of public policy in a globalizing world, see Coleman and Perl's (1999) article in *Political Studies*.
2 More details about the evolving vehicle emissions inspection program can be found at <http://www.driveclean.com>.
3 Interviews were conducted in 1997 and 1998, and the subjects were guaranteed anonymity.

References

Anderson W.P., and C. Woudsma. 1996. *Urban Transportation, Energy, and Air Pollution: A Comparison of Policy in the United States and Canada.* Hamilton, ON: McMaster Institute for Energy Studies.

ARA Consulting Group, Inc. 1994. *Clean Air Benefits and Costs in the GVRD.* Burnaby, BC: Greater Vancouver Regional District.

Atkinson, D., A. Cristofaro, and J. Kolb. 1991. Role of the Automobile in Urban Air Pollution. In *Energy and the Environment in the 21st Century*, edited by J.W. Tester, D.O. Wood, and N.A. Ferrari. Cambridge, MA: MIT Press.

Atkinson, M.M., and W.D. Coleman. 1989. Strong States and Weak States: Sectoral Policy Networks in Advanced Capitalist Countries. *British Journal of Political Science* 19(1): 47-67.

Baar, E. 1992. Partnerships in the Development and Implementation of Canadian Air Quality Regulation. *Law and Policy* 14(1): 1-43.

–. 1995. Economic Instruments and Control of Secondary Air Pollutants in the Lower Fraser Valley. In *Managing Natural Resources in British Columbia: Markets, Regulation and Sustainable Development*, edited by A. Scott, J. Robinson, and D. Cohen. Vancouver: UBC Press.

–. 1996. Marrying Science and Policy. Unpublished manuscript.

BC Hydro. 1993. *The Burrard Utilization Study Report*. Vancouver: BC Hydro.

Bennett, C., and M. Howlett. 1992. The Lessons of Learning: Reconciling Theories of Policy Learning and Policy Change. *Policy Sciences* 25(3): 275-94.

Bixby, M. 2000. The TransLink Levy: Taxing Patience More than Congestion. *Fraser Forum* (December). Vancouver: Fraser Institute. <http://www.fraserinstitute.ca/publications/index.asp?snav=pb> (17 December 2002).

Bohn, G. 1996. Road Tolls a Tougher Sell in Suburbs. *Vancouver Sun,* 17 September, B2.

Bovar-Concord Environmental. 1995. *Economic Analysis of Air Quality Improvement in the Lower Fraser Valley*. Burnaby, BC: Bovar-Concord Environmental.

Brooks, S. 1998. *Public Policy in Canada: An Introduction*. 3rd ed. Toronto: Oxford University Press.

Burnett, R. T., J.R. Brook, S. Cakmak, M. Raizenne, D. Steib, R. Vincent, D. Krewski, O. Philips, and H. Ozkaynak. 1998. The Association Between Ambient Carbon Monoxide Levels and Daily Mortality in Toronto, Canada. *Journal of the Air & Waste Management Association* 48: 689-700.

Burnett, R.T., R.E. Dales, M.E. Raizenne, D. Krewski, P.W. Summers, G.R. Roberts, M. Raad-Young, T. Dann, and J. Brooke. 1994. Effects of Low Ambient Levels of Ozone and Sulphates on the Frequency of Respiratory Admissions to Ontario Hospitals. *Environmental Research* 65: 172-94.

Campbell, M.E., B.A. Benson, and M.A. Muir. 1995. Urban Air Quality and Human Health: A Toronto Perspective. *Canadian Journal of Public Health* 86(1): 218-26.

Canadian Taxpayers Federation. 2000. *Axe the Auto Tax: CTF-BC Launches Campaign to Head Off $75 Auto Tax*. Victoria: Canadian Taxpayers Federation. <http://www.taxpayer.com/newsreleases/bc/May23-00.htm#Backgrounder/Relevant Information> (17 December 2002).

City of Toronto, Department of Public Health. 1993. *Outdoor Air Quality in Toronto: Issues and Concerns*. Toronto: City of Toronto.

Coleman, W.D., and A. Perl. 1999. Internationalized Policy Environments and Policy Network Analysis. *Political Studies* 47(4): 691-709.

Crandall, R.W., H. Gruenspecht, T. Keeler, and L. Lave. 1986. *Regulating the Automobile*. Washington, DC: Brookings Institution.

De Spot, M. 1994. *Air Quality Management Fees and Authorized Emissions in 1993*. Burnaby, BC: Greater Vancouver Regional District.

Deakin, E. 1993. Policy Responses in the USA. In *Transport, the Environment, and Sustainable Development,* edited by D. Bannister and K. Button. London: E & FN Spon.

Dunn, J.A. Jr. 1998. *Driving Forces: the Automobile, Its Enemies, and the Politics of Mobility*. Washington, DC: Brookings Institution.

Dunn, J.A. Jr., and A. Perl. 1996. Building the Political Infrastructure for High-Speed Rail in North America. *Transportation Quarterly* 50(1): 5-22.

Eck, T. 1991. Positioning for the 1990s – the Amoco Outlook. In *Energy and the Environment in the 21st Century,* edited by J.W. Tester, D.O. Wood, and N.A. Ferrari. Cambridge, MA: MIT Press.

Farmar-Bowers, Q. 1996. Air Quality Programs in Vancouver, British Columbia. *Road and Transport Research* 5(2): 51-56.

Flink, J.J. 1988. *The Automobile Age*. Cambridge, MA: MIT Press.

Goddard, S.D. 1994. *Getting There: The Epic Struggle between Road and Rail in the American Century*. New York: Basic Books.

Goldberg, M.A. 1986. *The Myth of the North American City: Continentalism Challenged*. Vancouver: UBC Press.

Grant, W., A. Perl, and P. Knoepfel, eds. 1999. *The Politics of Improving Urban Air Quality*. Cheltenham, UK: Edward Elgar.

GVRD (Greater Vancouver Regional District). 1994. *Overview: GVRD Air-Quality Management Plan*. Burnaby, BC: GVRD.

–. 1995a. *Livable Region Strategic Plan*. Burnaby, BC: GVRD.

–. 1995b. *Our Future*. Burnaby, BC: GVRD.

Harrison, K. 1996. *Passing the Buck: Federalism and Canadian Environmental Policy.* Vancouver: UBC Press.

Ipsos-Reid. 2000. *Strategic Transportation Plan Resident Survey – October 2000.* Vancouver: Ipsos-Reid. <http://www.translink.bc.ca/whatsnew/public-opinion-polls/final-stp-ipsos.pdf> (20 June 2001).

Long, R.A. 1993. *Transportation Demand Measures and Their Potential for Application in Greater Vancouver.* Burnaby, BC: Greater Vancouver Regional District.

Magnusson, W. 1983. Toronto. In *City Politics in Canada,* edited by W. Magnusson and A. Sancton. Toronto: University of Toronto Press.

Majone, G. 1989. *Evidence, Argument, and Persuasion in the Policy Process.* New Haven, CT: Yale University Press.

March, J.G., and J.P. Olsen. 1989. *Rediscovering Institutions: The Organizational Basis of Politics.* New York: Free Press.

Mennell, M. 1995. Air Quality Planning in One of North America's Fastest Growing Regions. *Environmental Manager* 1: 22-26.

Municipality of Metropolitan Toronto. 1996. *Bad Air Alert: It's Killing Us.* Blue Ribbon Committee Report. Toronto: Municipality of Metropolitan Toronto.

Ontario Medical Association. 1998. *OMA Ground Level Ozone Position Paper.* Toronto: Ontario Medical Association. <http://www.oma.org/phealth/ground.htm> (14 August 2001).

OMOE (Ontario Ministry of Environment). 1998. *Ontario's Smog Plan.* Toronto: Queen's Printer for Ontario.

OMOEE (Ontario Ministry of Environment and Energy). 1995. *Air Quality Report in Ontario: 1994 Comprehensive Report.* Toronto: Queen's Printer for Ontario.

Perl, A., J. Hargraft, and K. Muxlow. 1999. When Policy Networks Collide: The Institutional Dynamic of Air Pollution Policy-Making in Two Canadian Cities. In *The Politics of Improving Urban Air Quality,* edited by W. Grant, A. Perl, and P. Knoepfel. Cheltenham, UK: Edward Elgar.

Perl, A., and J. Pucher. 1995. Transit in Trouble: The Policy Challenge Posed by Canada's Changing Urban Mobility. *Canadian Public Policy* 22(3): 261-83.

Rose, R. 1993. *Lesson Drawing in Public Policy: A Guide to Learning across Time and Space.* Chatham, NJ: Chatham House.

Skocpol, T. 1985. Bringing the State Back in: Strategies of Analysis in Current Research. In *Bringing the State Back In,* edited by P.B. Evans, D. Rueschemeyer, and T. Skocpol. New York: Cambridge University Press.

Sperling, D. 1991. An Incentive-Based Transition to Alternative Transportation Fuels. In *Energy and the Environment in the 21st Century,* edited by J.W. Tester, D.O. Wood, and N.A. Ferrari. Cambridge, MA: MIT Press.

Tennant, P., and D. Zirnhelt. 1973. Metropolitan Government in Vancouver: The Strategy of Gentle Imposition. *Canadian Public Administration* 16(1): 124-38.

TransLink. 2000. *TransLink Strategic Transportation Plan, 2001-2005.* Surrey, BC: TransLink.

Tuohy, C.H. 1992. *Policy and Politics in Canada: Institutionalized Ambivalence.* Philadelphia: Temple University Press.

Vancouver Board of Trade. 1991. *Industrial Emission Reductions in the Lower Mainland: Report of the Vancouver Board of Trade Environmental Task Force.* Vancouver: Vancouver Board of Trade.

Vancouver Sun. 1996. Crossed Wires: Planners Want More Buses as BC Transit Plans Service Cuts. Editorial, 17 September, A14.

WCED (World Commission on Environment and Development). 1987. *Our Common Future.* Oxford: Oxford University Press.

8
Integrity of Land-Use and Transportation Planning in the Greater Toronto Area
Richard Gilbert

Formation of Metropolitan Toronto

Toronto was once a model of good regional governance, so good that in the 1960s, John Keith, a giant of regional planning in North America, used to bring decision makers from the New York region and elsewhere to Toronto "to show how it should be done." Dr. Keith – who died in March 2000 – served from 1969 to 1989 as president of the Regional Plan Association, a civic organization formed in 1922 to help secure orderly development of the thirty-one-county New York–New Jersey–Connecticut metropolitan area. His wife was from Port Credit, now part of Mississauga, the Toronto region's second largest city, and he knew the region well. He stopped bringing groups to Toronto in the 1970s because the Toronto region was evidently becoming yet another example of poor regional planning.

Toronto was a model in the 1960s because of the formation of Metropolitan Toronto in 1953. It was North America's first regional metropolitan government, created to provide urban services to the burgeoning suburbs around what was then the City of Toronto (see Figure 8.1). The surrounding rural townships and small towns were linked with the city in an upper-tier municipality – Metropolitan Toronto, also known as Metro Toronto or Metro – charged mostly with sharing the wealth of the city through provision of physical infrastructure in the suburbs. Later, Metro Toronto became for the most part a deliverer of human services, notably policing, welfare, and other social services, while retaining responsibility for major roads, water purification, sewage treatment, and disposal of solid waste.

At first, Metro Toronto had thirteen constituent local municipalities. In 1967 this was reduced by amalgamation to six, including the historic City of Toronto (incorporated in 1834). In 1998 these six local municipalities and Metro were amalgamated to form a single municipality – known as the (new) City of Toronto – combining upper- and lower-tier functions. The present city and the surrounding regional and local municipalities together form what has been known since the late 1980s as the Greater Toronto Area

Figure 8.1

Growth of Toronto, 1793-1961

1793 - 1834
1835 - 85
1886 - 1914
1915 - 45
1946 - 61

Lake Ontario

N

0   2 mi
0   2 km

Note: The inner solid line shows the approximate boundary of the City of Toronto during the period 1912-67. The outer dashed line shows the present boundary, which was the boundary of Metropolitan Toronto from 1953 to 1997 (see Figure 8.2).
Source: Base map, Roots et al. 1999; City of Toronto boundary, Baine and McMurray 1970.

Figure 8.2

The thirty local and five regional municipalities in the Greater Toronto Area in 1997

Note: On 1 January 1998, Metropolitan Toronto and its constituent local municipalities – East York, Etobicoke, North York, Scarborough, Toronto, and York – were amalgamated to form the present City of Toronto.
Source: GTA Task Force 1996.

(GTA), depicted in Figure 8.2 as it was just before the formation of the present City of Toronto.

Formation of the Four Surrounding Regions
In its early years, Metro Toronto had planning oversight over an adjacent area beyond its boundaries comprising 1,242 square kilometres, as well as its own area of 632 square kilometres (Baine and McMurray 1970). The Metropolitan Toronto Planning Area, as it was known, comprised about a quarter of the area of what is now known as the GTA but included over 80 percent of its population, including about a third of the population in what became the part of the GTA beyond Metro. In 1967 this part of the future

GTA had a population of almost 700,000, representing over a third of the population of Metro, mostly located in relatively densely settled towns and townships. Indeed, as shown in Table 8.1,[1] the overall residential density of the urbanized parts of the area outside Metro in 1967 was hardly less than that of Metro itself.

By the early 1970s, the contiguous urbanized area was beginning to spill beyond Metro's boundaries, and adjustments to the governing arrangements were required. The obvious rational adjustment would have involved extending the boundaries of Metro Toronto to include the newly urbanizing area and beyond, perhaps at least to the limits of the Metropolitan Toronto Planning Area. The Ontario government – which under the Canadian constitution has complete charge of municipal structure – was fearful of creating an overly powerful municipality. Thus, it instead created four upper-tier regional municipalities around Metro Toronto – Durham, Halton, Peel, and York – modelled on Metro. Figure 8.2 shows the four regions and their constituent local municipalities.

From their formation, the four regional municipalities surrounding what was then Metro and is now the City of Toronto became the main locus of growth in population and jobs. This is illustrated in Figure 8.3, which shows a clear slowing of population growth in what was then Metro after the formation of the regions. Thereafter, growth in the Toronto region occurred predominantly outside the boundaries of what is now the City of Toronto, that is, in what are sometimes known as the outer suburbs. The population outside the city passed that of the city in 1998 or 1999. If current trends hold, by 2008 most of the region's jobs will be located outside the city.

The growth in the Toronto region has been and continues to be fuelled mainly by the high rate of immigration to Canada and by the attractiveness of Toronto as a location for the settlement of immigrants. From 1991 to 1996, for example, over a million immigrants arrived, more than half from Asia, comprising 4.2 percent of Canada's 1991 population. Over 40 percent of these immigrants settled in the Toronto region, directly increasing the region's population by 12 percent over those five years. In 1996, 37 percent of Metro's population and 27 percent of that of the rest of the region consisted of what are known as "visible minorities" (Siemiatycki 1998). Current trends suggest that visible minorities will together comprise a majority of the region's population early in the twenty-first century.

Was it the formation of the four regions around Metro that shifted the focus of growth in population and employment away from Metro? Or would the focus have shifted even if the alternative model of regional governance – expanding the boundaries of Metro – had been imposed? The Canadian Urban Institute convened a meeting in April 1993 to mark the fortieth anniversary of the founding of Metropolitan Toronto.[2] The twenty or so participants represented some 500 person-years of planning and related

Table 8.1

Residential densities of urbanized portions of the Greater Toronto Area, 1967 and 1999

Year	Metropolitan Toronto/ (new) City of Toronto (Area = 632 km²)				Rest of (what became) the Greater Toronto Area (Area = 6,530 km²)			
	Urbanized area (km²)	Population (millions)	Density (residents/ km²)	Maximum density of added area*	Urbanized area (km²)	Population (millions)	Density (residents/ km²)	Maximum density of added area*
1967	345	1.92	5,577		137	0.69	5,020	
1999	595	2.50	4,208	2,319	1,046	2.56	2,447	2,059

* Estimated from differences in population and in urbanized areas. These are *maximum* values because they do not take into account redevelopment of existing urbanized areas and consequent possible increases in their population density.

Source: Based on Census of Canada data; Wright 2000; GHK 2002; IBI Group 2002.

Figure 8.3

Actual and projected numbers of residents and jobs in the City of Toronto* (circles) and the rest of the Greater Toronto Area (squares), 1956-2006

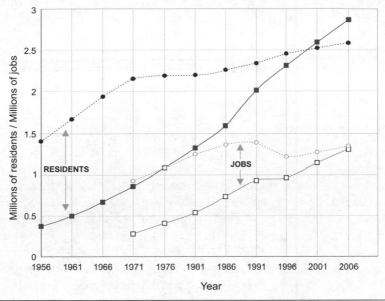

* The municipality as defined in 2002.
Source: Author's assessment of numerous estimates and projections of population and employment. For an authoritative presentation of some of the estimates and projections used, see IBI Group 2002.

experience in what is now the GTA. They were unanimous in assigning major responsibility for the woes of the GTA – particularly urban sprawl – to the provincial government's decisions in the early 1970s to create four regional governments around Metro rather than expand Metro's boundaries (and also to the provincial government's investments in water and sewer infrastructure in the area outside Metro).

Table 8.1 suggests that participants in the April 1993 meeting, who included the author, may have been wrong, at least with respect to the formation of the regions. From 1967 to the early 1990s, what were then Etobicoke, North York, and Scarborough – known as the *inner suburbs* (see Figure 8.2) – filled out with development that, according to the estimates in Table 8.1, may have been at a similar overall density to that in the outer suburbs.[3] Thus, Metro might have done just about as poorly as the new regional governments in containing sprawl during this critical period. This finding challenges the view that there would have been less sprawl if in the 1960s the boundaries of Metro had been expanded to include all or most of the region's newly urbanizing areas.

A word of caution should be offered about this conclusion. It relies on what may be fragile estimates of trends in the urbanized area of the GTA. Moreover, as indicated in the note to Table 8.1, the densities shown for the added areas are maxima; thus, the densities of the newly urbanized areas within Metro could have been – although are unlikely to have been – considerably higher than for those in the surrounding area.

If the data in Table 8.1 can be substantiated and even expanded, the conclusion that the formation of the peripheral regional governments caused sprawl will deserve re-examination. For the moment, it may be enough to point to the following possibilities:

- Sprawl would have happened anyway, no matter what the governmental arrangements. It was "in the air." By the 1970s, increased car ownership had made low-density suburban living possible because it obviated dependence on public transit, and desirable because it allowed relief from car-clogged central cities. Affluence was creating demand for new homes, fuelled by advertising and media reports. Low-density development occurred inside and outside Metro because that was what people were clamouring for. More of this development was located outside Metro because there was more lower-cost land that was easy for developers to assemble.
- Sprawl might have been constrained had Metro continued to make the planning rules; for many years, most growth could have continued to occur inside Metro. The new regional governments had no such ethic of land conservation, however, only what appeared to be unlimited low-cost land for development and strong needs to secure tax revenues from new development. The resulting fierce competition for development among municipalities inside and outside Metro changed Metro from being a land conserver to a land user.

These possibilities refer to the upper-tier municipalities, namely, Metro and the four surrounding regional governments. The local municipalities had at least as much and often more influence in planning decisions, however, and at least as much need for tax revenues from new development. The main contribution of the upper-tier municipalities lay in the provision and coordination of infrastructure.

Also important was the role of the provincial government. In the 1960s, the Ontario government began moving to restrain use of agricultural and other land for development in the Toronto region, a process that resulted in publication of the *Toronto-Centred Region Plan* in 1970. For reasons that are not clear but may have to do with the political weight of owners of potentially developable land, the Ontario government did not implement its plan but instead created the four regional governments. It also invested heavily in infrastructure that supported development, notably roads and sewage facilities, sometimes directly and sometimes through grant programs.

The complete story of how the Toronto region has evolved over the last forty years remains to be told.

The Main Issue: Urban Sprawl

In itself, the growth of an urban region may not be as much an issue for sustainable development as the nature of the growth. Urban regions in North America, and to a lesser extent in other rich countries of the world, have tended to grow by sprawling away from their centres. Urban sprawl can be defined as a condition where the rate of increase in the urbanized area of a region is substantially greater than the rate of increase in its population (Gilbert et al. 2000).

The difference between urban sprawl and other growth of an urban region is evident in a comparison of the urban regions of Mexico City and Los Angeles. The populations of both regions increased by close to 50 percent over the period 1970-90. The urbanized area of Mexico City also increased by about 50 percent (Losada et al. 1998), while that of Los Angeles increased by 300 percent, a sixfold greater rate. In many US urban regions, the ratio between the rate of increase in the urban area and the rate of increase in the population over the same period was higher: New York, 8 times; St. Louis, 10 times; and Chicago, 11 times. Some urban regions, such as Cleveland, recorded an increase in the extent of the urbanized area even though their population fell during that period.

The Toronto region's sprawl has been less extreme than that of many US urban regions, but has nevertheless been considerable. Table 8.2 shows that the relative growth in the Toronto region's urbanized area was well over twice the relative population growth during the period 1967-99.

The data and estimates in Table 8.1 (and Table 8.2) concern *gross* population densities, not the actual densities of the areas in which homes are located. Sprawl comprises land-intensive commercial and industrial development as well as residential development. It also comprises public land, including roads, associated with development. Commercial/industrial

Table 8.2

Sprawl in the Greater Toronto Area

Year	Urbanized area (km²)	Population (millions)	Increase in area	Increase in population	Ratio of increases
1967	482	2.61	240%	94%	2.6:1
1999	1,641	5.06			

Source: Based on Census of Canada data; Wright 2000; GHK 2002; IBI Group 2002.

development, in particular, may be making the strongest contribution to sprawl in the GTA. One study found that it takes seven times as much land to accommodate a worker in the GTA's outer suburbs than in the central city, but "only" four times as much land to accommodate a resident (IBI Group 1993).

Several features of sprawl are contrary to progress towards sustainable development:

- Sprawl results in more transport activity and thus more transport-related pollution and resource use. Figure 8.4 indicates that residents of the Toronto region's outer suburbs (namely, those of the four regions around what was then Metro) made longer motorized journeys on average in 2001 than urban residents (and mostly by private automobile). Transport-related pollution and resource use are mostly a function of transport activity. (Transport issues are discussed further below, under "A Closer Look at Transportation Trends and Impacts in the GTA.")
- Sprawl appears to be associated with larger homes and more resource use. Good data on dwelling-unit size in the Greater Toronto Area do not appear to be available, although there are strong suggestions that unit size increases with distance from downtown Toronto. Development at the edge of the urbanized area tends to occur at 10-15 units per hectare (uph), whereas development in long-settled parts of the GTA has mostly been within the range 28-26 uph. New development at the edge consists mostly of single-family houses, whereas new development in long-settled parts – almost all of it in and near downtown Toronto – consists mostly of apartments (Blais 2000). There are more people per household at the edge, but the unit sizes appear to be more than proportionately larger. Other things being equal – notably age of building and household income – larger units are likely associated with more resource use, particularly for heating but also for cooling, appliances, and even furnishing and provisioning.
- Sprawl results in higher infrastructure costs. An estimate for the GTA showed that current sprawl trends as opposed to more compact urban development will require 21 to 40 percent more expenditure on infrastructure over twenty-five years (Blais 1995). The amounts include capital, operating, and maintenance costs for roads, transit, water, and sewer services. Part of the higher cost is associated with more resource use.
- Sprawl usually results in loss of agricultural land. This has been particularly true in the GTA, where just about all the land that became urbanized between 1967 and 1999 had been Class 1-3 agricultural land, a total of 1,250 square kilometres or 28 percent of the amount of this class of land in the GTA in 1967. Moreover, by 1999 a further 992 square kilometres of Class 1-3 agricultural land had been approved or designated for urbanization (Wright 2000). If nearby agricultural land is lost to development,

Figure 8.4

Travel and car ownership in 1996 in concentric parts of the Toronto Region

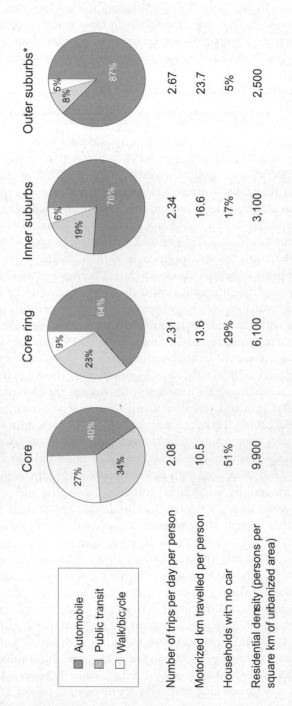

	Core	Core ring	Inner suburbs	Outer suburbs*
Number of trips per day per person	2.08	2.31	2.34	2.67
Motorized km travelled per person	10.5	13.6	16.6	23.7
Households with no car	51%	29%	17%	5%
Residential density (persons per square km of urbanized area)	9,900	6,100	3,100	2,500

* "Outer suburbs" refers to the Greater Toronto Area outside Metro Toronto.
Source: Based on Joint Program in Transportation 2002.

foodstuffs for an urban area must be imported from greater distances, with resulting increases in emissions. As well, countryside becomes farther from residents of earlier developments, causing them to travel greater distances when they leave the urbanized area for recreation and other purposes.

- Sprawl may affect species' habitats and migration paths, thereby reducing biodiversity. Biological diversity – of species and ecosystems – is essential for evolution and the continuation of life on earth. Even agricultural land in use, where one species is cultivated at the expense of others, can be a rich source of biodiversity. Urban development of any kind can reduce biodiversity by disturbing or eliminating species' habitats, including essential migration paths. Comprehensive data on the impact of urban development in the GTA on biodiversity are not readily available, but there are several indications of the potential effects of development, such as the impact on watercourses noted in the next paragraph. A point at issue for all urban regions is the relationship between biodiversity reduction and the density of development. Other things being equal, does a given human population reduce biodiversity more if the population's settlement pattern is scattered rather than compact? A scattered population affects a greater land surface, not least because of transport requirements, but may allow continued biological processes in the interstices of development.
- Sprawl causes other environmental effects through changes in land drainage patterns and albedo. The critical factor here is the amount of land that is paved or otherwise covered by impervious material. With larger areas of impervious surface, more water drains directly into watercourses, causing widening of stream beds, habitat disruption, and even flooding. For example, flow volumes in the lower reaches of Toronto's Don River rose by about 25 percent in relation to regional rainfall levels between the 1960s and 1990s. Besides causing more precipitation to be flushed into watercourses, land development involving large areas of impervious surface also allows the precipitation to reach watercourses more quickly. This removes opportunities for filtering and other treatment of water by natural features such as wetlands and vegetation. Flushed away with the rainwater and melted snow are the accumulated contaminants associated with human activity, particularly oils and chemical residues from transportation and pesticide use. As a result, some GTA watercourses are seriously stressed; others, even in suburban areas, have notably reduced levels of biological activity (Blais et al. 2001). Depending on the reflectivity (albedo) of surface material, development can change the extent to which sunlight is absorbed by surfaces in urban areas, causing local warming effects, resulting discomfort and more severe effects on humans and other species, and higher levels of energy use for air conditioning.

- Sprawl may have adverse social effects on inhabitants of the area. Data are scarce, including for the GTA, but arguments have been made that low-density development is inimical to community activity, in part because opportunities for face-to-face interactions are reduced, notably through high levels of automobile use. This is a debatable matter, in the GTA and elsewhere. There are also suggestions that high-mobility, automobile-based ways of living that are characteristic of low-density development are causing other social problems, particularly concerning children (Adams 1999; Burchell et al. 1998).

The types of concerns described above were placed in context by the authors of a comprehensive review of the literature on sprawl (Frank et al. 2000). The following conclusions were drawn, among others:

- Surprisingly little research has been done on the share of environmental harm that can be attributed to sprawling land-development patterns. Almost all of the research that has been conducted considers only the environmental impacts of transportation.
- Ninety percent of the environmental costs of transportation are related to impacts on air quality; impacts on water and habitat combined have been estimated at less than 10 percent of the environmental costs of transportation.
- Of the total environmental costs of transportation, less than 10 percent can be attributed to sprawl; most of the aggregate environmental costs of transportation would exist even if cities were more compact and transit-oriented.

These points may well apply to the GTA, although the data in Figure 8.4 suggest that within the GTA somewhat more than 10 percent of the environmental costs of transportation can be attributed to sprawl. Compared even with the inner suburbs, residents of the outer suburbs engage in an average of about 40 percent more motorized travel per day, with correspondingly greater environmental impacts.

Moreover, if the GTA's inner and outer suburbs had been developed at the density of the core ring (roughly the part of the inner three local municipalities of Metro Toronto that surrounded the broader downtown area), the urbanized part of the GTA would have about half its present area and would extend to an average of about twenty kilometres from downtown rather than thirty kilometres. Based on the data in Figure 8.4, the GTA's residents would likely be travelling on average up to 40 percent fewer kilometres each day.

A Closer Look at Transportation Trends and Impacts in the GTA
Contributing factors to the growth in the overall amount of travelling by

Figure 8.5

Changes in travel by personal vehicles and public transit in the GTA, 1986-2001, and contributing factors

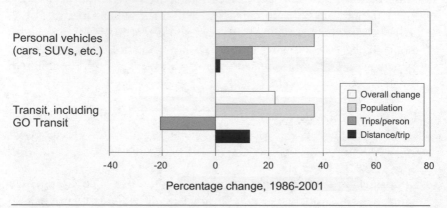

Source: Based on Joint Program in Transportation 2002.

car between 1986 and 2001 are shown in Figure 8.5, together with the corresponding changes for public transit. For travelling by car, the increase due to population was enhanced by additional trips per person and slightly longer trips. For travelling by transit, the potential increase due to population growth was strongly offset by a reduction in the number of trips per person, which in turn was offset by an increase in the average length of transit trips (due in part to an increase in commuting trips by rail from the outer suburbs to downtown Toronto).

Figure 8.6 shows the growth in automobile and heavy-truck traffic in the different parts of the GTA from 1986 to 1996. Overall, heavy-truck traffic appears to have grown at a rate similar to automobile traffic (28 versus 31 percent), that is, at more than the rate of population growth. As with automobile traffic, truck traffic has grown mainly in the outer suburbs, where the growth in economic activity has occurred (see Figure 8.3), although the growth rates for each have been different in different parts of the GTA. Truck traffic is of special importance because the emissions from trucks' diesel engines are more hazardous per unit of energy consumed than emissions from the gasoline engines used in cars and other personal vehicles (CST 2001).

Figure 8.7 shows changes between 1986 and 2001 in the purposes of trips made by GTA residents, in relation to what might have been expected from population growth alone. Work-related trips comprised a smaller portion of all trips in 2001; the growth in automobile activity was due to what are described as discretionary trips (shopping, social events, recreation) and to trips not involving the home, such as those from work to daycare.

Figure 8.6

Increases in automobile traffic and heavy-duty freight traffic in the GTA, 1986-96

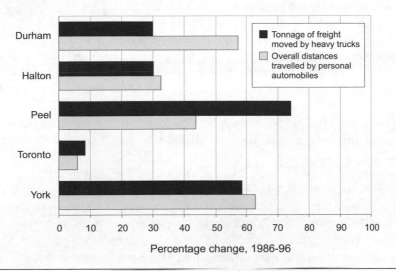

Source: Based on Joint Program in Transportation 2002; OGTA 1997.

Figure 8.7

Changes in trip purpose in the GTA, 1986-96

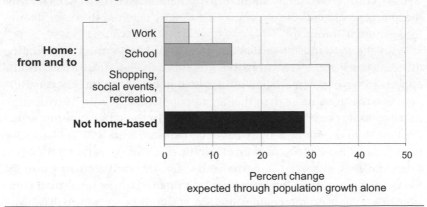

Source: Based on Joint Program in Transportation 2002.

This trend from work-based to discretionary and non-home-based trips was evident in every part of the GTA but was more pronounced among residents of what is now the City of Toronto. Work-related trips tend to be longer than other trips. Thus, the greater shift away from work-related trips in the City of Toronto accounts in part for the smaller growth in automobile traffic there (see Figure 8.6). It should also be noted, however, that the large growth in traffic in the outer suburbs occurred in spite of a shift away from work-related trips.

The greatest concern about air quality in the GTA and other urban areas in North America involves levels of ground-level ozone. Ozone is a highly reactive form of oxygen, damaging to living tissue (particularly those in airways) and to inert materials. It is the main component of summer smog. Ozone is formed by the action of sunlight on nitrogen oxides and volatile organic compounds, both of which result from transport activity and are pollutants in their own right. Unlike most other forms of air pollution, levels of nitrogen oxides and ozone have not been declining in the GTA; indeed, the incidence of "smog-alert" days increased slightly during the 1990s.

Because ozone takes time to form, and its formation is inhibited locally by other transport emissions, the highest ozone levels tend to occur down-wind of traffic. In the GTA, they occur at Stouffville, forty kilometres north-east of downtown Toronto and ten kilometres beyond the edge of the main urbanized area (Blais et al. 2001). Figure 8.8 shows that transport activity is the main source of nitrogen oxides in the GTA, and a major source of vola-tile organic compounds.

There is little information and less concern about resource use by trans-portation (and by other activities) in the GTA. In North America generally, there is growing concern about recent large price increases in vehicle fuel, natural gas, and electricity. These large price increases may be reflecting the beginning of the end of readily available, inexpensive fossil fuels (Bentley 2002; Campbell 2001). If costs rise further, and especially if supply short-ages develop, fuel use and availability of fuel will likely replace air pollution as the major issue associated with transportation. Suburban residents and businesses could be especially vulnerable to energy price increases and en-ergy shortages.

An associated issue is climate change, which seems to be occurring in part because of greenhouse gas (GHG) production from high levels of fossil fuel use (IPCC 2001). Canada, and by extension the GTA, has among the high-est per capita levels of GHG emissions (OECD 2000). Whether or not fuel shortages and resulting high prices occur, Canada and the GTA could come under pressure to reduce GHG emissions, which would mean reducing fos-sil fuel possibly through tax-based high prices or market-based rationing. Again, the special vulnerability of suburban residents and businesses could become evident. Global warming itself could benefit the GTA in relation to several other parts of North America. The GTA would not be subject to higher sea levels, the fate of coastal urban regions, or, because of Lake On-tario, to drought, the possible fate of many inland urban regions. There would be heat stress in summer and a higher incidence of disease vectors,

Figure 8.8

Emissions of volatile organic compounds (VOCs) and nitrogen oxides (NO$_x$) from transport and other GTA sources, 1980-95

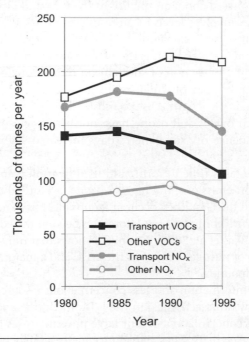

Source: Based on Energy and Environmental Analysis 1999.

but there would also be a longer crop-growing season and less need for energy to heat buildings.

Transport activity results in sprawl and is caused by sprawl. Suburban development began with and was stimulated at the beginning of the twentieth century by public transport, certainly in Boston (Warner 1978), London, England (Edwards and Pigram 1977), Los Angeles (Jackson 1985), and even Toronto (Stamp 1989). The development initially remained dense enough to allow convenient access to bus and streetcar stops and other rail stations. The ascendancy of the automobile in the 1940s and 1950s in North America, later elsewhere, stimulated development at much lower densities. This development was made possible by widespread personal motorized transport and created corresponding dependence on such transport. The pattern continues. Land at the periphery of the urban region is developed only in relation to its accessibility by road, and high levels of use of suburban roads are the result of the development. In the GTA, the main locus of road congestion is moving from the inner to the outer suburbs, with many

indications of impending paralysis if current trends continue (City of Toronto 2000).

Reducing Sprawl in the GTA: Planning without Integrity

A reasonable conclusion from the above is that there are strong imperatives
to reduce sprawl in the GTA, chiefly to reduce emissions, resource use, and
infrastructure costs, mostly by reducing the need for and the amount of
motorized transportation. There are also strong imperatives to continue
sprawl. The above-noted review of development in the US concludes that
"a surprising level of consensus appears to exist concerning the causes of
sprawl" (Frank et al. 2000), most of which would appear to apply to the
GTA. The indicated causes include the availability of low-cost land at the
periphery, population growth and reduced household size, affluence, competition among peripheral municipalities, de-industrialization of central
cities, zoning that favours low densities, and many more, including, of course,
the pervasive influence of the automobile. Strategies to reduce sprawl need
to address these causes.

The GTA's high rate of population growth provides opportunities to reduce sprawl by intensifying development in the outer suburbs and by ac-
commodating more of the growth in what is now the City of Toronto. The
next three sections will deal with the following topics: what has been hap-
pening in the outer suburbs; plans and prospects for the City of Toronto,
which now includes the inner suburbs; and directly reducing transportation activity, that is, reducing a facilitator of sprawl and the source of sprawl's
main impacts. The overall impression is that of much talk and little action
to reduce sprawl – of planning without integrity.

Reducing Sprawl in the GTA through More Intense Development in the Outer Suburbs

The late 1980s and early 1990s was a period of intense scrutiny of development trends in the GTA. To facilitate this scrutiny, the provincial government introduced the concept of "Greater Toronto," formed a provincial/
municipal coordinating body, the Greater Toronto Coordinating Committee (GTCC), and created the Office of the Greater Toronto Area, initially
with its own minister and deputy minister and then as a division of the
Ministry of Municipal Affairs and Housing.

The GTCC commissioned what became a landmark study: the Greater
Toronto Area Urban Structure Concepts Study (IBI Group 1990). This major
work compared three urban structure concepts for the GTA: *spread,* or continuation of sprawl; *central,* or concentration of about half of the projected
population growth until 2021 in what was then Metro; and *nodal,* or location
in the outer suburbs of as much of the growth as the spread concept but with
homes and jobs focused at compact nodes. Each concept was evaluated

according to forty-two criteria (e.g., concerning infrastructure costs and compatibility with sustainable development). The central concept was the easy winner. It rated first on twenty-three of the thirty-four criteria for which one concept was rated above the other two; spread and nodal each rated first on six of these thirty-four criteria. The nodal concept was nevertheless chosen by the GTCC as the guiding concept for development in the GTA, known as the *GTA Vision*.

In 1997, the Canadian Urban Institute reported on an evaluation of the performance of the GTA's municipalities in relation to the *GTA Vision* (CUI 1997). The CUI noted that by 1992 the regional governments had adopted new land-use and transportation plans "reflecting commitment to the *GTA Vision*." However, forty-seven rather than twenty-nine nodes had been designated and the resulting land-use pattern would be "closer to the spread model." The CUI found many inconsistencies with respect to designation of transportation corridors and "no evidence that infrastructure investment is being used strategically." Above all, the CUI found that the policies were "not yet having an impact on the private development sector," that is, they were not being implemented.

All in all, the selection of the nodal concept rather than the much higher-rated central concept, the actual adoption of what amounted to the spread concept, and the failure to implement even that concept amounted to a clear pattern of planning without integrity.

A more recent thorough assessment of development patterns in the GTA's outer suburbs noted that achieving "sustainable" urban development patterns has been a major thrust of provincial, regional, and local planning policy in the 1990s. The policies have sought to protect environmentally significant lands, support alternatives to the automobile, and make efficient use of infrastructure investment through reurbanization, compact development at the fringe, and nodal development (Blais 2000). The assessment concluded:

> Despite a body of planning policy with stated sustainability-related objectives, substantial amounts of development have proceeded and will continue to occur on significant greenfields lands, such as prime agricultural lands, the Oak Ridges Moraine [see below], and rural areas ... the regions' and local municipalities' own planning processes account for by far the greatest amount of development in the region. In other words, in terms of planning processes through which development is allowed to occur, "growth management" itself is probably the major contributor to loss of greenfields lands to development, including sensitive areas such as prime agricultural lands.

The assessment pointed to several contributing factors, notably policies of the provincial government that allow a municipality to justify urbanization on prime agricultural land if no viable alternatives are available within the municipality. It reinforces the conclusion drawn from the earlier assessment by the Canadian Urban Institute that the substantial mismatch throughout the outer suburbs between policy statements and plans on the one hand and practice on the other hand is an indication of planning without integrity.

Much of the action in the outer suburbs of the GTA has concerned the Oak Ridges Moraine, "a 160-kilometre long ridge of sand and gravel hills running along the northern part of the GTA ... the source of drinking water for over 250,000 people, and ... the headwaters for over 65 rivers and streams ... Since the 1980s, the urban population of the GTA has begun to advance northward, attracted to the wide vistas, rolling hills and verdant forests of the Moraine. The impact of urban sprawl is already evident in the number of fields and forests converted to urban malls and subdivisions, the headwater streams entombed beneath pavement, our historic villages and hamlets made redundant by strip malls, and the bumper to bumper traffic jams."[4] Blais (2000) indicated that the Moraine's population, which was 77,837 in 1991, is set to rise to 226,007 by 2021.

In May 2001, the Ontario government imposed a six-month freeze on development across the Moraine; this was replaced in November 2001 with an arrangement limiting development on the Moraine, and supplemented in April 2002 by the Oak Ridges Moraine Conservation Plan. The plan, said the Minister of Municipal Affairs and Housing, "will continue to steer development away from over 90 per cent of the Moraine." Between November and April, the government had approved up to 9,000 new homes on the Moraine, plus some commercial development, in addition to the 3,000 homes that had already been approved. These approvals aroused considerable local opposition; "betrayal" was a frequently used word. Moreover, concerns have also been expressed by the Ontario Federation of Agriculture that restrictions on development on the Moraine will mean that more prime agricultural land north and south of the Moraine will be used for development.

It may now be more difficult to build on the Oak Ridges Moraine, but the more fundamental issue of development on greenfield lands remains unaddressed, a further indication of planning without integrity.

Reducing Sprawl in the GTA by Increasing the City of Toronto's Population

The first three-year term of the council of the amalgamated City of Toronto saw the launch of an ambitious long-term planning exercise consisting of the development of an economic plan, a social plan, an environmental plan, and a land-use plan (known as the Official Plan), all linked together by an overarching strategic plan.

Only the Official Plan directly addresses the need to help reduce sprawl in the GTA (City of Toronto 2002). Initially, it proposed to plan for a City of

Toronto population of 3.5 million in 2031 rather than the projected 3.0 million (City of Toronto 2000). This could have the effect of reducing the population of the rest of the GTA from the projected 4.5 million to 4.0 million. Both city and outer suburbs now have populations of just over 2.5 million each (Figure 8.3).

Success on the part of the city would thus reduce the growth in the outer suburbs by about 25 percent and reduce the projected size of the GTA's urbanized area, at current development densities, by a little over 10 percent. It would raise the city's gross population density to just above the density of the part of the city that was urbanized in 1967.

Little was said in preliminary documentation (City of Toronto 2000) as to *where* this substantial increase in population should be located. There was mention of adding residential development in the downtown area, along the waterfront, around the former city halls of three of the pre-amalgamation municipalities, on abandoned industrial lands, and, with the greatest emphasis, along main streets. It is hard to see, however, how what was implied could add up to 1 million additional residents.

Possible reasonable estimates of the population that could be added to the City of Toronto in these places by 2031 are as follows: downtown, 50,000; waterfront, 100,000; former city halls, 50,000; abandoned industrial lands, 150,000; main streets, 100,000. These estimates total 450,000, about the same as the total expected without special intervention, and less than half of the proposed total of 1 million additional residents. Even these estimates could be optimistic, not least because of what appear to be prevailing attitudes among members of the current City Council. One columnist wrote about them: "The suburbanites who now run the city and set its planning policies, very often in blatant disregard of the professional advice our tax dollars afford them, hate development" (Barber 2001).

Perhaps because of the various difficulties in adding a million residents to the City of Toronto by 2031, this target is not in the version of the Official Plan adopted in October 2002 (City of Toronto 2002). The plan speaks only of taking the forecasted increase in population by 2031 as a "minimum expectation ... depending on the success of this Plan in creating dynamic transit oriented mixed use centres and corridors" (7). Moreover, the forecasted increase of 537,000 residents has been inflated by using a 1996 baseline even though 2001 census data had been published. A more appropriate thirty-year forecasted increase would be 341,000 residents, from 2.66 million in 2001 to 3.0 million in 2031.[5]

The watering down of the city's commitment to combat sprawl, evident in the absence of a target and in the way the projections are stated, is another example of planning without integrity. The watering down could perhaps be justified on the grounds that the plan as a whole was now more likely to be accepted, including several favourable aspects such as those concerning expanded transit facilities. Even with the watering down, however, the Official Plan aroused considerable opposition from residents groups and local politicians on the grounds that too much development was proposed. Moreover, expanded transit facilities may be justifiable only if there is a large population increase. The abandonment of the 1 million target could doom the Toronto region to car-oriented sprawl that will continue as long as there is oil to fuel it.

There are good words in the Official Plan: about improving the region's livability by reducing the pace at which agricultural lands and the countryside are urbanized, about reducing reliance on the automobile, and about meeting today's needs without compromising the ability of future generations to meet their needs. Without a firm target for a substantial increase in the City of Toronto's population, however, and a well-worked-out plan to meet the target, the Official Plan lacks integrity.

Several imaginative opportunities for development are not addressed in the City of Toronto's draft Official Plan. One would have a string of additional islands off Toronto's waterfront, mostly sculpted from the lakebed but also formed from demolition waste, that could house 200,000 to 400,000 people near the downtown area in car-free, largely sustainable developments. Another would transform the suburban campus of Toronto's second-largest university, and adjoining land, into an urban campus that serves as the key element in a corridor of intense development along an extension of the Spadina subway line to Vaughan City Centre. The corridor would house 200,000 people – 150,000 in the City of Toronto and 50,000 in York Region – and be the location of 100,000 jobs.

Reducing Levels of Transport Activity

The main adverse impacts of sprawl result from associated high levels of transport activity, which in turn help to sustain and enhance sprawl (see "A Closer Look at Transportation Trends and Impacts in the GTA"). Reducing these impacts by technological means – that is, emission controls and energy efficiency – could make sprawl more tolerable. However, the effect of making sprawl more tolerable in this way would be to enhance sprawl and bring to the forefront other adverse impacts of sprawl, such as its costs and its impacts on biodiversity. Reducing levels of transport activity, on the other hand, would reduce the impacts of transportation and would likely also reduce sprawl and its other impacts.

Land-use and other planning documents throughout the GTA speak of supporting alternatives to the use of the automobile, namely, transit, walking, and bicycling (e.g., City of Toronto 2000). The intention appears to be mostly that of replacing one transport activity with another, by making the other modes more possible and convenient. This is beneficial in itself when the alternative activity is less harmful. This is certainly true of walking and bicycling as alternatives to automobile use, and it is usually true of well-occupied transit. Whether enhancing the attractiveness of transit, bicycling, and walking in the outer suburbs will in itself reduce sprawl is doubtful. Indeed, improving such amenities and services could enhance the appeal of low-density development.

The reality in any case has been an increase in automobile (and truck) activity and a decline in the use of transit throughout the GTA, described here under "The Main Issue: Urban Sprawl." The reality too has been over-all declines in both transit service levels and transit investment in the GTA. Meanwhile, several new major roads have been constructed, and many more are planned. All in all, there is a substantial mismatch between planning intentions and reality, and thus another indication of planning without integrity.

Strategies that merely promote and enhance opportunities for transit, bicycling, and walking may be mostly doomed to failure. Except where there is pre-existing demand, improved transit may do little to raise ridership levels. A more effective strategy is to improve transit service *and,* simultaneously, restrain automobile use (World Bank 2000). Moreover, if fiscal restraints are used, the resulting revenue can be used to fund the transit improvements. Apart from minor physical restraints in residential areas (traffic mazes, speed bumps, road narrowings), there has been little interest in the GTA in complementing the expressed desire to increase use of alternatives to automobile with restraints on automobile use.

The Rise and Fall of the GTSB
Among the reasons given for the seemingly unyielding outward march of sprawl in the GTA has been lack of coordination at the regional level. The Greater Toronto Services Board (GTSB) was established in 1998 to provide such coordination. It consisted of GTA mayors, regional chairs, and several Toronto councillors.

The GTSB lacked the power to lay down rules about how land should be used and how transportation should be managed and funded. The lack of authority was welcomed by several GTSB members and served to exacerbate urban/suburban differences within the board. By mid-2001, there were signs of rapprochement and the development of a majority position within the GTSB to seek "teeth" for the body, particular on transport matters.

The main concern was traffic congestion. The GTSB developed proposals to relieve congestion by improving transit (e.g., GTSB 2000a), but very little was said about the need to restrain automobile use and thus make the transit improvements effective in increasing ridership. More was said about the need to increase road capacity (e.g., GTSB 2000b).

Perhaps concerned about the demands for power to effect change, the Ontario government abolished the GTSB at the end of 2001 and created the Central Zone Smart Growth Panel in February 2002. This is one of five Smart Growth Panels covering the settled part of Ontario. The panels are appointed bodies, including local politicians and other stakeholders, charged with advising the Minister of Municipal Affairs and Housing on the content and implementation of a Smart Growth Strategy to be developed by the government. The Central Zone includes the GTA and an additional area about four times the size of the GTA containing about half the GTA's population. The government's priorities for the Central Zone Smart Growth Panel are "unlocking gridlock," "promoting livable communities," and "re-thinking garbage." Proceedings of and materials developed for the panels are confidential.

It is difficult to determine whether replacing a forum for local politicians to discuss regional issues with a closed-door process for advising the only government that has power in the region is a step towards more or less integrity in planning for the GTA. The GTSB could have evolved into an effective regional government,[6] but such a government may have been effective only in worsening sprawl or in allowing sprawl to worsen.

How the Ontario Government Could Show Integrity

The present arrangement of Smart Growth Panels has the merit of clearly identifying the Ontario government as responsible for regional planning. Here is how the government could show integrity in its land-use and transportation planning for the GTA:

- Establish an unbreachable urban boundary at the envelope of the GTA's existing development, with cancellation of all approvals of development beyond the boundary and compensation for those affected in the form of tax credits for intensive development within the GTA.
- Foster intensive development within the urban boundary, particularly in the City of Toronto, including land created in Lake Ontario, to accommodate anticipated population growth.
- Reform municipal finances and property taxes to (1) reduce dependence of local governments on the revenue from new development, so as to relieve the pressure to encourage new development at any cost, and (2) shift the focus of taxation gradually from the uses of land to land itself, so as to encourage more intensive use of land.
- Impose strong fiscal restraints on automobile (and perhaps truck) use in the GTA, with the proceeds being used to finance improved transit in ways that balance increasing ridership and meeting the needs of those most affected by the fiscal restraints, all the while respecting the region's economic imperatives.

Given current perspectives, proposals for such actions are unlikely to be made by the Central Zone Smart Growth Panel. If they were made, the Ontario government would be unlikely to adopt them.

As long as the means of creating and sustaining sprawl are available, the GTA's entrenched system of sprawl production is likely to continue. One of the means, low vehicle fuel prices, seems about to become less available, as noted under "A Closer Look at Transportation Trends and Impacts in the GTA." Ideally, sprawl would be curtailed in a well-planned manner so as to reduce the impact of ever-increasing fuel prices. A more likely reality is that sprawl will be reversed haphazardly only because living in low-density areas will become unaffordable. This could be the painful outcome of decades of planning without integrity.

Acknowledgments

The author is grateful to Neal Irwin, Anthony Perl, and Don Stevenson for comments on earlier drafts of this chapter.

Notes

1 In Table 8.1 (and also Table 8.2), the 1967 data on urbanized areas are from Table 5 in Wright 2000, with the specific estimate for what was then Metropolitan Toronto being achieved by the author of this chapter's close measurement of the appropriate parts of Map 5 in Wright 2000. The same sources were not used for 1999 data as they are believed to be erroneous for that year. They have been superceded by the almost identical estimates in GHK 2002 and IBI Group 2002. The urbanized area data for 1999 in Tables 8.1 and 8.2 are a blend of the estimates in these two sources.

2 The 16 April 1993 meeting was an informal two-hour discussion structured around four questions, the second of which was "How might the Toronto region have developed if Metro's boundaries had been expanded in the early 1970s, instead of the creation of the regional governments around Metro?" According to comprehensive notes on the meeting taken by Don Stevenson, at the end of this part of the discussion, a poll was taken on the following question: "If expansion of the boundaries had taken place in the 1970s, would the development of the urban region have been more rational?" According to the notes, "the answer from the group was a loud and unanimous YES!" The whole of this part of the discussion was summarized as follows: "The creation of the surrounding regional governments was a mistake – it had led to further urban sprawl. The extension of Metro boundaries to cover the urbanizing area would have led to more compact, orderly development in the GTA. The Ontario Water Resources Commission's sewer and water pipes in Durham, Peel, and York were also major contributors to sprawl."

3 As indicated in the note to Table 8.1, the density estimates for the areas developed between 1967 and 1999 are *maxima*. If there had been an increase in the density in the land already urbanized in 1967, the actual density of the newly urbanized land could have been less, perhaps much less. Such intensification would have been more likely to have had such an impact in the area that was Metro Toronto in 1967, both because there was more urbanized land and perhaps because it had been settled for longer and thus may have been more susceptible to redevelopment. Accordingly, the density of the land urbanized between 1967 and 1999 in what is now the City of Toronto could have been *lower* than the density of the land urbanized during this period in the rest of the GTA.

4 The quote beginning with a description of the Oak Ridges Moraine is from *The Oak Ridges Moraine,* a brochure issued by the STORM Coalition and Earthroots, available at <http://www.stormco.org>.

5   The preliminary 2001 census information issued by Statistics Canada on 12 March 2002 (see <http://www.statcan.ca>) does not include correction for undercount, which will not be available until 2003. The preliminary population estimate has been increased by 3.0 percent to correct for undercount.
6   Evolution of the GTSB into an effective regional government seemed to be the intention of the Minister of Municipal Affairs and Housing (Al Leach) at the time the GTSB was created, but not perhaps of the provincial government as a whole. Mr. Leach did not seek re-election in 1999.

References

Adams, J.G.U. 1999. *Social Implications of Hypermobility*. Paris: Organization for Economic Cooperation and Development.

Baine, R.P., and A.L. McMurray. 1970. *Toronto: An Urban Study*. Toronto: Clark, Irwin.

Barber, J. 2001. Council's Antidevelopment Suburbanites Fend Off Revenue. *Globe and Mail*, 8 March.

Bentley, R.W. 2002. Global Oil and Gas Depletion: An Overview. *Energy Policy* 30: 189-205.

Blais, P.M. 1995. The Economics of Urban Form. Background paper for the Greater Toronto Area Task Force, Government of Ontario, 1996. In *Greater Toronto Report of the GTA Task Force*, GTA Task Force, January 1996. Toronto: Queen's Printer for Ontario.

–. 2000. *Inching Towards Sustainability: The Evolving Urban Structure of the GTA*. Report to the Neptis Foundation. Toronto: University of Toronto.

Blais, P.M., R. Gilbert, L.S. Bourne, and M. Gertler. 2001. *State of the GTA 2000*. Toronto: Greater Toronto Services Board.

Burchell, R.W., N.A. Shad, D. Listokin, H. Phillips, A. Downs, S. Seskin, J.S. Davis, T. Moore, D. Helton, and M. Gall. 1998. *Transit Cooperative Research Program Report 39: The Costs of Sprawl Revisited*. Washington, DC: National Academy Press.

Campbell, C.J. 2001. Peak Oil: A Turning Point for Mankind. *Hubbert Center Newsletter* (2-1): 1-4. <http://hubbert.mines.edu> (24 November 2002).

City of Toronto. 2000. *Toronto at the Crossroads*. <http://www.city.toronto.on.ca/torontoplan/crossroads_change.htm> (24 November 2002).

–. 2002. *Toronto Official Plan*. City of Toronto (as approved in November 2002). <http://www.city.toronto.on.ca/torontoplan/official_plan.htm> (23 January 2003).

CST (Centre for Sustainable Transportation). 1998. *Sustainable Transportation Monitor No. 1*. Toronto: CST.

–. 2001. *Sustainable Transportation Monitor No. 4*. Toronto: CST. <http://www.cstctd.org> (24 November 2002).

CUI (Canadian Urban Institute). 1997. *GTA Urban Structure: An Analysis of Progress towards the Vision*. Toronto: CUI.

Edwards, D., and R. Pigram. 1977. *Metro Memories*. London: Midas Books.

Energy and Environmental Analysis. 1999. *An Updated Look at VOC and NO_x Emission Trends in Selected Canadian Metropolitan Areas*. Report prepared for the Canadian Automobile Association. Arlington, VA: Energy and Environmental Analysis.

Frank, N., S. White, Z.R. Peng, K. Harris, and W. Sanders. 2000. *Exploring Sprawl: Findings of a Comprehensive Review of the Literature Related to "Sprawl" or What Do We Really Know?* Presented at a meeting of the Association of Collegiate Schools of Planning, Atlanta, GA, 2-5 November 2000. <http://www.uwm.edu/~frankn/Sprawl_Frank.htm> (9 May 2001).

GHK International (Canada). 2002. *Growing Together: Prospects for Renewal in the Toronto Region*. Prepared for the City of Toronto. Summary available at <http://www.city.toronto.on.ca/moraine/pdf/2002summary.pdf> (24 November 2002).

Gilbert, R., H. Wood, and J. Brugmann. 2000. *Urban Land Management and Global Sustainability*. Report prepared by the International Council for Local Environmental Initiatives, Toronto, for the 8th session of the United Nations Commission on Sustainable Development. <http://www.iclei.org/csdcases/csdstudy/index.htm> (24 November 2002).

GTA Task Force. 1996 (January). *Greater Toronto Report of the GTA Task Force*. Toronto: Queen's Printer for Ontario.

GTSB (Greater Toronto Services Board). 2000a. *How Coordinated Transit Can Reduce Congestion.* Background paper for the Greater Toronto Area Strategic Transportation Plan. Toronto: GTSB.

–. 2000b. *Congestion and Economic Competitiveness.* Background paper for the Greater Toronto Area Strategic Transportation Plan. Toronto: GTSB.

IBI Group. 1990. *Greater Toronto Area Urban Structure Concepts Study.* Summary report prepared for the Greater Toronto Coordinating Committee. Toronto: IBI Group.

–. 1993. *Urban Travel and Sustainable Development: The Canadian Experience.* Report prepared for the Canada Mortgage and Housing Corporation. Toronto: IBI Group.

–. 2002. *Toronto-Related Region Futures Study: Interim Report: Implications of Business-as-Usual.* Report to the Neptis Foundation. CD-ROM. Toronto: IBI Group. Summary available at <http://www.neptis.org/report.asp> (24 November 2002).

IPCC (Intergovernmental Panel on Climate Change). 2001. *Summary for Policymakers: A Report of Working Group I of the Intergovernmental Panel on Climate Change.* <http://www.ipcc.ch/pub/spm22-01.pdf> (24 November 2002).

Jackson, K.T. 1985. *Crabgrass Frontier: The Suburbanization of the United States.* New York: Oxford University Press.

Joint Program in Transportation. 2002. Database for the 1986-2001 Transportation Tomorrow surveys. Toronto: Data Management Group, Joint Program in Transportation, University of Toronto. <http://www.jpint.utoronto.ca> (24 November 2002).

Losada, H., H. Martinez, J. Vieyra, R. Pealing, and J. Cortés. 1998. Urban Agriculture in the Metropolitan Zone of Mexico City: Changes over Time in Urban, Suburban, and Peri-Urban Areas. *Environment and Urbanization* 10(2): 37-54.

OECD (Organization for Economic Cooperation and Development). 2000. *OECD Environment Data: Compendium 1999.* Paris: OECD.

OGTA (Office of the Greater Toronto Area). 1997. *Strategic Overview of Goods Movement in the GTA.* Toronto: OGTA, Government of Ontario.

Roots, B.I., D.A. Chant, and C.E. Heidenreich. 1999. *Special Places: The Changing Ecosystems of the Toronto Region.* Vancouver: UBC Press.

Siemiatycki, M. 1998. *Immigration and Urban Politics in Toronto.* Paper presented to the Third International Metropolis Conference, November-December 1998, Zichron Yaacov, Israel. <http://www.international.metropolis.net/events/Israel/papers/Siemiatycki.html> (24 November 2002).

Stamp, R.M. 1989. *Riding the Radials: Toronto's Suburban Electric Streetcar Lines.* Erin, ON: Boston Mills Press.

Warner, S.B. Jr. 1978. *Streetcar Suburbs.* 2nd ed. Cambridge, MA: Harvard University Press.

World Bank. 2000. *Study on Urban Transport Development.* <http://www.worldbank.org/transport/utsr/yokohama/day2/padeco.pdf> (24 November 2002).

Wright, R.M. 2000. *The Evolving Physical Condition of the Greater Toronto Area: Space, Form and Change.* Report to the Neptis Foundation. Toronto: University of Toronto.

9

Toronto's Exhibition Place: Closing the Integrity Gap between a Nineteenth-Century Fairground and a Sustainable Twenty-First-Century City

David Gurin

Introduction: Urban Change, Institutional Inertia, and Environmental Integrity

Cities are always changing. Structures built as factories become apartment buildings; shady residential streets become commercial thoroughfares; entertainment areas fall in and out of favour. The institutions that cities set up sometimes change more slowly than urban buildings, streets, and parks, however. As a result, important parcels of urban land administered by municipal institutions are sometimes not adapted to new needs or used for environmental and social benefits. This chapter explores one such example in the heart of Canada's largest metropolis. Exhibition Place in Toronto offers a case of past policy goals having been institutionalized into an administrative structure that continues to pursue them long after economic, environmental, and social changes have rendered their premises questionable. Exhibition Place is a microcosm of Canada's environmental integrity gap. It is a place that is supposed to generate economic vitality and enhance quality of life in Toronto and its environs, but it falls short of its potential in generating both economic and environmental benefits. This shortfall actually places constraints on the revitalization of Toronto's waterfront.

Exhibition Place presents a very valuable urban opportunity for Toronto. The site is quite large, commanding eighty hectares on the Lake Ontario waterfront. It is a place one enters through a classical triumphal arch from the east or under a broad modern archway from the west. Much of it is open space, and twenty major buildings (many architecturally and historically significant) and many smaller ones are venues for recreational events. The National Trade Centre houses business promotion activities. There are elaborate fountains and gardens, and grand views of downtown skyscrapers and Lake Ontario. Despite these amenities, however, Exhibition Place is in serious trouble. Attendance at its most important annual event, the Canadian National Exhibition, has been declining for years. The impressive grounds are empty for much of the year. Moreover, this vast waterfront property languishes while nearby neighbourhoods with fewer natural amenities (such as green space and waterfront access) redevelop into thriving commercial and residential communities.

This chapter identifies an institutional constraint on governing Exhibition Place that has set it apart from planning efforts and initiatives that have reshaped a good part of Toronto's waterfront and nearby neighbourhoods over the years. In Toronto, as in other waterfront cities, railway yards, warehouses, and piers once dominated the waterfront. The transfer of goods between freight cars and ships was the chief waterfront activity. Because this business has both declined and moved elsewhere within the Greater Toronto Area (GTA), waterfront lands have become available for redevelopment as housing, recreation, and commercial spaces. In fact, however, building on the newly available land has been a slow undertaking.

Toronto waterfront redevelopment is still ongoing, even after decades of efforts by planners, city council, and developers. For many years, change on the lakeshore has been the pre-eminent project of Toronto city planners. It has produced Harbourfront, a project that includes residential towers along the lake (not entirely beloved, as many critics feel they block the view for those who don't live in them) and Queens Quay Terminal, an office/residential/entertainment complex in a renovated warehouse on a pier. It will eventually produce City Place, a major residential project in construction on former railway lands. The Harbourfront streetcar, which connects Exhibition Place and Union Station, and the Martin Goodman Trail, a foot and bicycle trail the length of the waterfront, are other products of planning along the waterfront. But at Exhibition Place, where land use was never as far removed from commercial and recreational uses as that of former railyards and warehouses, change has been slower and less successful than in other lakefront areas.

Why is Exhibition Place not living up to the potential of its magnificent site? How could so precious an urban asset become a problem? The explanation stems in part from Exhibition Place's management structure, which, by its nature, remains insulated from the social and economic forces that have precipitated change in other waterfront or nearby lands controlled by the private sector. Exhibition Place stands apart from these redevelopment efforts in large part because it is organized as a public entity. Moreover, it is a public entity that exists at arm's length from government.

Exhibition Place is owned by the City of Toronto, but its management is delegated to a Board of Governors that lacks both the direct democratic accountability of a city agency and the entrepreneurial freedom of a private corporation. This board was established to operate Exhibition Place as a hybrid of park space and commercial activity, and has moved slowly and tentatively in adapting this original mission to economic and environmental changes in the surrounding city that render the hybrid vision increasingly contradictory (Board of Governors of Exhibition Place 1999). The Board of Governors has overseen some impressive new construction on the site (principally the National Trade Centre), but Exhibition Place still contributes far less to Toronto's life than would be expected from a place so central in the city's geography and history.

According to the province's City of Toronto Act, the board has the mandate "to provide an opportunity for business stimulation and economic development in the community and across the country and provide a focus for public celebrations and events, while preserving the architecturally and historically significant structures on the grounds." At first glance, the governing arrangement for Exhibition Place would not appear to place a significant constraint on achieving this mandate, by adapting specific policies and priorities to Toronto's changing circumstances. The Exhibition Place Board of Governors has thirteen members appointed by City Council, including five councillors, the mayor or his designate, three Canadian National Exhibition Association members, the association president, and four others who may be either city councillors or citizen appointees. The board's current structure was established in 1983 as part of the Municipality of Metropolitan Toronto, and continued when Metro was amalgamated into the new City of Toronto in 1998. At present, Toronto's mayor and five councillors are the only elected officials on the board, insulating Exhibition Place from the direct political demands and expectations that would face a city agency such as the parks department.

The board's composition broadens its governance beyond typical municipal politics, but its financial administration works to constrain economic responsiveness. The board submits its budget to Toronto City Council each year and operates Exhibition Place according to general principles adopted by Council. The board cannot enter into any agreement that will allow use of the property for more than three years without Council approval. And the board needs Council approval for all capital expenditures. This means that the board cannot, without Council approval, get a bank loan for capital improvement, even if it is clear that such improvements will earn profits sufficient to repay the loan. In other words, it can't operate with the same kind of ledger as a private business. The board does contract with a private company to manage the National Trade Centre, however.

As these administrative attributes illustrate, the Exhibition Place Board of Governors is a municipal variant of Hodgetts's (1973) "structural heretic," a public agency that is run at arm's length from responsible government. Thomas and Zajcew (1993, 116) write that such administrative entities fit "uncomfortably within our constitutional framework." But the environmental integrity gap that has emerged at Exhibition Place stems from more than this political anomaly. The combination of political and economic constraints that has been institutionalized in Exhibition Place's governing arrangements ensures that its Board of Governors cannot act as effectively as a private business out to maximize profit, and it cannot act as effectively as a parks department, which normally makes its product freely available. The result is that it performs neither role well enough to realize the combined opportunity of its location and assets.

Public agencies at all levels of government can run parks magnificently. They can also build and operate water and sewer systems and much else with admirable efficiency. The difficulty at Exhibition Place is public ownership of land for which there is no public purpose, beyond doing business as usual. This is a problem because the use of land in a city sometimes has to change dramatically with changes in demography, technology, and values. City governments may want to regulate that process of change, and that is a reasonable role. But they are rarely capable of actually leading such changes in urban land use. The real estate market seems to be good at innovation; local government seems to be good at conservation. Both are necessary roles, but it is difficult for one institution to perform both simultaneously.

The Board of Governors, acting on behalf of Exhibition Place's owner, the City of Toronto, has responded to pressures to revive Exhibition Place by encouraging more development of the same sort of activities that have always typified it. I will argue the opposite case, that the combination of trade promotion and recreation embodied by Exhibition Place is obsolete in contemporary Toronto. I do not mean that amusement or the encouragement of trade is obsolete, but rather that segregating these functions into an isolated institutional setting is not working well for the city.

Worse, Exhibition Place is not the only enterprise on Toronto's waterfront constrained by institutional inertia. Ontario Place, its entirely contiguous neighbour to the south, is in similar decline. There has been analysis and argument within government circles about joining Exhibition Place with Ontario Place. From a geographical and functional point of view, the linkage is natural: Ontario Place is entirely devoted to entertainment, Exhibition Place to entertainment and trade promotion. In the weeks that the Canadian National Exhibition takes place, a single admission entitles people entry to both facilities. Some parking facilities are shared. The two places have many of the same interests and problems. However, the provincial government built Ontario Place and continues to own and operate it, while the City owns Exhibition Place. Despite the similarity of their functions the two places remain under completely separate management. The province managed to amalgamate seven municipal jurisdictions (against their expressed will) to create the new City of Toronto, but, ironically, the province has been unable to amalgamate two extremely similar public enterprises located alongside each other (a union not likely to arouse any public ire).

Addressing this integrity gap that has emerged on Toronto's waterfront is justified because Exhibition Place is a potentially magnificent district of

Toronto. It doesn't live up to its potential because it remains tied to a policy framework that the surrounding city has left behind. The next section will explore what this framework for Exhibition Place represents, and how it came to be so firmly grounded in the organization's administrative structure.

The Institutional Legacy:
From Agricultural Fair to Urban Amusement Park

The roots of administrative organizations can go very deep. Exhibition Place's roots are in the tradition of agricultural fairs. In European towns and villages, the fair was a seasonal enhancement of the normal marketplace, usually in the heart of the settlement. In North America, where spread-out farmsteads rather than farming villages have been the rule, the agricultural fair was usually held in a large open space on the fringe of the town or city that served as marketplace for an agricultural area. This pattern still persists for local, county, and state or provincial fairs across North America. In Toronto the fair began as early as 1846, with the formation of the Provincial Agricultural Association, Canada West. The association organized the first Provincial Agricultural Fair in Toronto; subsequent fairs were held in various Ontario towns and cities. In 1878 Toronto defeated Guelph and Ottawa in bidding for the fair.

This bidding process of a century and a quarter ago seems astonishingly familiar, as Toronto recently bid for the 2008 international Olympics. Hoping that the fair would be held permanently in Toronto, the city leased more than fifty acres (twenty hectares) of military land, the nucleus of the present Exhibition Place, from the Dominion government of Canada. The central building of the 1878 fair was the Crystal Palace, fashioned of cast iron and glass. In all, the city spent $75,000 to build twenty-five structures in three months, "despite the fact that this expenditure had twice been voted down by the ratepayers" (Firth 1983). This is early testimony to the persistence of official rather than popular enthusiasm for expenditure on big public exhibitions, at least in their formative stages. Contemporary Toronto officials aggressively pursued the Olympics when public opinion was neutral to negative on the idea, according to newspaper polls conducted in late 1999.

When the 1879 Provincial Agricultural Fair was awarded to Ottawa despite Toronto's great efforts and expense, the Toronto City Council organized a rival "Industrial Exhibition." Despite its name, its emphasis was still agricultural, reflecting the nature of the province, and its popularity grew annually. It could boast a significant number of first-time exhibits of machinery and inventions. In 1882 it was the first fairground in the world lit by electricity. In 1885, when street railway cars in the cities of the world were still pulled along tracks by horses or mules, the exhibition was the site of one of the first demonstrations of electric streetcars. This new mode of transportation, which was eventually to become emblematic of Toronto, made such a big impression on a visiting American that he promoted the first electric street railway system, in Montgomery, Alabama (Miller 1960).

In 1904 the Industrial Exhibition became the Canadian National Exhibition, and by 1912 its site had twenty-three permanent buildings, including the Dairy Hall, Agricultural Hall, Horticultural Hall, Carriage Building, Hatching House, Stoves Building, and a 5,000-seat grandstand. In 1922 the Coliseum was built on the site, in part to house the Royal Agricultural Winter Fair, which continues to be a well-attended November event. Grandstands and a stadium were built and expanded to accommodate the Toronto Argonauts in the 1950s and the Toronto Blue Jays in the 1970s. The teams eventually left for the SkyDome, and Exhibition Stadium was demolished in 1998.

Beginning in the nineteenth century, Toronto built up its exhibition as an event combining economic development, technological progress, and social amenity. The success of these early exhibitions served to entrench an organization that would continue delivering this particular package of commerce and entertainment long after Toronto had moved on to newer modes of amusement and begun facing new opportunities for its waterfront land. Those responsible for Exhibition Place appear not to have recognized the immense opportunity that a role change could create. Both Pierson (1993) and Skocpol (1992) remind us that policies feed back into society to reorient politics by motivating certain actors, both within and outside government, to support the governing arrangements that generate benefits for them. Thus, the Canadian National Exhibition, the Molson Indy, and other long-term institutions at Exhibition Place resist change and the Board of Governors responds to their interests. The result is the integrity gap that will be summarized in the next section.

Urban Integrity Gap: From Amusement Park to Parking Lot
There are 8,200 parking spaces (including 1,294 indoor spaces at the National Trade Centre) at Exhibition Place. The site may have grand and historic architecture as well as the impressive, modern National Trade Centre, but its dominant aesthetic is that of parked cars, or bare asphalt when the cars aren't there. This situation has been true for quite some time now. *The Redevelopment of Exhibition Place,* a 1982 report of the City of Toronto Planning and Development Department, included a section entitled "Exhibition Place Today – from Park to Parking Lot." The report recalls that "Exhibition Place was originally conceived as a lakeside park to host an annual fair. Today, the easterly two thirds of the site could be more accurately described as a parking lot interrupted by exhibit buildings" (City of Toronto Planning and Development Department 1982).

Similar findings are reported in *Future Uses of Exhibition Place,* published by a Metropolitan Toronto Executive Task Force on the subject in 1987.

These findings were further acknowledged in 1996 when the Metropolitan Toronto Planning Department published *Guidelines for Public Access, Circulation and Open Space Improvements at Exhibition Place.*

Since these reports, even more parking has been added on the sites of demolished buildings and grandstands. Today about 20 percent of the site is occupied by permanent buildings, less than 20 percent by grass and landscaping, and the remaining more than 60 percent mostly by roads and parking lots.

Amid the winter desert of asphalt or the summer sea of parked cars – choose your season and metaphor for the sterility of a landscape overwhelmed by the needs of automobile storage – there are splendid buildings at Exhibition Place. These include seven buildings and structures designated under the Ontario Heritage Act and seventeen buildings and structures listed by Heritage Toronto. Shows, exhibits, and bazaars, including the Royal Agricultural Winter Fair, take place in these buildings during different parts of the year.

The National Trade Centre (NTC) is the newest, biggest, and most expensive building at Exhibition Place. Completed in 1997, it cost $180 million, partly paid by Metropolitan Toronto, then owner of Exhibition Place, and partly paid by federal and provincial grants. The NTC comprises over 1 million square feet of exhibition space for trade shows. It has been linked to the adjacent Coliseum in an ingenious way that preserves the historical façade of the older building as a beautiful interior wall in the combined structure. It is also connected to the Automotive Building by means of a tunnel. It is the largest trade show facility in Canada, with all the necessary state-of-the-art communications and conduit systems. It has been deemed a success because of its multiplier effect in the Toronto economy. It brings in visitors who spend money. But the National Trade Centre has had little effect on its surroundings, either within Exhibition Place or outside its gates.

It is worth noting a few of the other buildings at Exhibition Place because of their historic and aesthetic appeal, and, in some cases, the new uses to which they have been put. The Horticultural Building (1907) is an ornate, domed neoclassical structure. The Music Building (1907), similarly fanciful, was built by the CNE and the railway companies of that time. It was initially called the Railways Building and exhibited rail transportation developments. It was recently upgraded and rented to Immersion Studios, an interactive educational programming and design company.

The Arts, Crafts and Hobbies Building (1912), another glass-domed edifice, was built to house exhibitions sponsored by the provincial government. The building was first known as the Dominion Government Building, then the British Empire Building, then the Travel and Tourism Building. Its name changes appear to reflect changes in Canadian taste and priorities over the century. In its current incarnation, it is the rented home of Medieval

Times, a dinner theatre. Medieval Times has invested almost $5 million to renovate and upgrade the building.

The Ontario Government Building (1926) is a two-storey stone beaux arts structure with a triangular floor plan surrounding an open courtyard. It offers a cloistered serenity in the Spanish or Arabic style. Courtyards of this sort are rare in Toronto, but unfortunately few people get to enjoy it, as the building has hardly been used in recent years. The Horse Palace (1931) is one of the best equestrian facilities in Canada, and among the finest art deco buildings in Toronto. It is used for the CNE, the Royal Winter Agricultural Fair, a riding school, and the mounted unit of the Toronto Police.

Many of these buildings are architectural gems, but they have not become urban gems because they aren't really part of the city. Their range of functions is very narrow: entertainment and trade shows. No one lives nearby. No one passes these buildings on the way to someplace else. No one is likely to pass them accidentally. They don't serve multiple functions, as, for example, apartment buildings with shops on the ground floor, or office districts that also contain department stores and specialty shops. They are very far from what city planners like to term "mixed use."

To borrow from the language of ecology, Exhibition Place is a monoculture, and lack of diversity can endanger the health of a large swath of urban geography just as surely as it upsets a natural system. This monoculture contrasts sharply with the urban ambitions and achievements of Toronto. The same city government that owns Exhibition Place has made a name for itself in North America by facilitating the kind of mixed-use, vibrant, and sustainable urban community that is so clearly lacking on this stretch of waterfront. As the following section will demonstrate, Toronto has done better in revitalizing the stretches of its waterfront that it does not own than it has done on the land it does own at Exhibition Place. This is the essence of an urban environmental integrity gap.

Waterfront Renewal and Urban Sustainability

The study of urban waterfronts has been a growth industry among planners. This is understandable, considering that the lakefronts, riverfronts, and oceanfronts of the cities of the industrialized world are potentially so attractive yet often so miserably neglected. These waterfronts weren't seen as problems when they were abuzz with shipping and industry, but changes in technology made the old functions obsolete and waterfronts became derelict. Soon planners saw opportunities for new waterfront functions: housing, parks, marinas, beaches, and restaurants with a view. Exhibition Place is on the waterfront, but even though it embraced an industrializing nation's philosophy of blending commerce with entertainment, its physical form and function were already post-industrial. Nonetheless, it has to be understood in the context of changes on the waterfront. And Toronto's waterfront has been studied, planned, and debated with fervour, as is usual in so many cities that grew inland from their waterside origins. This introspection has taken many forms, the most significant of which has elaborated a vision for the waterfront based upon ecological sustainability.

In 1988 the Canadian federal government and the province of Ontario jointly created a Royal Commission on the Future of the Toronto Waterfront, headed by David Crombie, a very popular former mayor of Toronto. In 1992 the Royal Commission published *Regeneration: Toronto's Waterfront and the Sustainable City*. The report, more than 500 pages, advocated "watershed planning" and an "ecosystem approach" as the guiding principles of Toronto's waterfront renewal. It was geographically thorough, tracing hydrological systems back from the lake to the headwaters of the rivers and streams that empty into it. It examined fish life and the water pollution that threatens it. It studied Toronto's history of "shoreline modification," a term for the city's long history of creating artificial land in the lake (Royal Commission 1992).

The report spoke in terms of the Toronto "bioregion" and pointed to the inadequacy of most official planning protections for ecologically vulnerable parts of the region. It noted that development applications are just as likely to be filed in non-urban areas as they are in areas designated as urban on official plans, a telling criticism of Ontario's land-use planning system. The report advocated "greenways," pedestrian and bicycle paths along the water's edge. *Regeneration* saw the waterfront as the place where city meets nature in a relatively fixed and clear way, unlike the ever expanding and nature-threatening suburban sprawl. The report makes a strong case that Toronto's waterfront is a clear boundary with nature and a good place to take a stand for sustainability. On the waterfront, sustainability means accessible and swimmable beaches (those that are not closed due to polluted water), drinkable water, and uninterrupted views.

Regeneration discussed at length the notions of urban "place" and "corridor," and the fact that these two very different uses of city space are often in conflict. This is especially true along the Toronto waterfront, where land that ought to be place (parks, houses, commerce) is corridor instead (the elevated Gardiner Expressway, Lakeshore Boulevard). But the report never got to the point of making concrete recommendations about the Gardiner. Many had expected the Royal Commission to recommend tearing down the Gardiner because it is an eyesore and it impedes the city's connection to the waterfront, but its report just noted the various replacement alternatives: at grade, underground, or transit. The commission presented these choices largely in terms of the central sections of the Gardiner, downtown. It didn't specify options in the Exhibition Place vicinity.

The Royal Commission had the wisdom to deal with Exhibition Place as part of a larger area, which it labelled Garrison Common and which includes

Ontario Place, the railway lands to the east, and the Liberty-Niagara neighbourhood to the north. It noted that "one of the paradoxes of Garrison Common is that it has exceptional transportation facilities, but limited accessibility" (Royal Commission 1992). This is a comment on the fact that the area is cut by two major highways (Gardiner and Lakeshore) and a major railway, which splits in two directions in Garrison Common, part going north to Milton and Georgetown, part going west to Hamilton. The Royal Commission tried to mend some of this chopped-up quality of the area by proposing a rail consolidation that would shorten the rail route and free up land for development and better street connections to the north and east of Exhibition Place. However, the federal government, probably the only possible source of the large amounts of money needed to consolidate the lines, was more intent during that period on privatizing the railways than on dealing with the problems their routes created for a particular Toronto neighbourhood. This is an example of the larger issue of the federal government's unwillingness to spend money on fixing urban environmental problems.

Regeneration also proposed a system of local streets extending the city grid pattern in the area to the east of Exhibition Place. This system would be crowned with a public square at Princes' Gate to celebrate that lovely gateway. "Inside the gates, Princes' Boulevard would continue westward, providing a strong organizing element for the structures and activities to be established there" – thus, the report refers to the building of the National Trade Centre, still only a plan when *Regeneration* was published.

The Crombie report did well to point out the natural features of Garrison Common, and to recommend as far as possible the restoration of the buried Garrison Creek and the cleaning up of the lake. These recommendations need to be taken seriously in any renewal of Exhibition Place. Parts of the site should be naturalized and allowed to revert to their original lakeside nature where possible. The Waterfront Regeneration Trust, which grew out of the Royal Commission on the Future of the Toronto Waterfront, produced a *Preliminary Master Plan for Garrison Common*. It makes excellent urban design recommendations. For example, it proposes that the city's traditional grid be spread into the areas north and east of Exhibition Place. These would have residential and commercial activity.

Within Exhibition Place, the master plan shows a grand, straight tree-lined boulevard from Princes' Gate through the grounds. Aside from the CNE crowds, however, it doesn't tell us who would stroll along this boulevard or why anyone would be there outside of a few weeks in August. It works Exhibition Place into a grid, but there are no indications of any changes in the diminishing activities within that grid. Nor is there a piercing of the rail and highway barrier to the north. On the south, Lakeshore Boulevard remains, but there is a suggestion in the scale of the drawing that Lakeshore might be a somewhat narrower and therefore "tamer" road.

Regeneration is a marvellous text, with sincere respect for nature and an intelligent approach to the urban fabric. It understood the need to study Exhibition Place in its larger geographic context. However, it missed the dynamic changes in the Liberty-Niagara neighbourhood to the north of Exhibition Place. This is understandable, as these changes were only beginning when the Royal Commission's studies were underway. In Liberty-Niagara, old industrial and commercial structures have been rehabilitated for altogether new purposes. This kind of transformation is more often helped by a laissez-faire attitude on the part of city officials than by any kind of formal plan, but it is a kind of transformation that can help us understand how to improve Exhibition Place (Waterfront Regeneration Trust 1993).

The same former mayor Crombie who headed the Royal Commission took charge of promoting Toronto's bid for the 2008 Olympics, and he viewed the Olympics as a means of implementing some of the recommendations of the Royal Commission. The official Olympics Bid proposed that a new Olympic Stadium, aquatics centre, and velodrome be located at Exhibition Place and Ontario Place (Toronto City Council 1998). There was, however, considerable internal debate between advocates about using the Olympics as a means of reviving the west waterfront of Toronto, which would include Exhibition Place, and the east waterfront, which would have allowed revival of the city's port lands, a far more derelict area. The Bid also listed potential transportation improvements that would have had major impacts on Exhibition Place: waterfront streetcar extensions, removal of the Gardiner Expressway through the central part of the city, Front Street extension (for better access to the Gardiner from downtown), and a transit link to Pearson airport.

Even without the Olympics, Exhibition Place could be parkland for the large numbers of residents who will be living in City Place, which is now under construction on the railway lands site. To do that effectively, however, Exhibition Place would have to be much more of a park and less of a parking lot. For that to happen, its institutionalized policy priorities would have to be revisited and sorted out. The site's park function and its management would need to be separated from the trade and exhibition functions in order to close this gap in Toronto's waterfront regeneration efforts.

Transportation: Emblem of Degeneration at Exhibition Place

As elaborated elsewhere in this volume, a third to a half of greenhouse gas emissions are automotive in origin; automotive vehicles also emit about half of the volatile organic compounds and nitrogen oxides that combine to form ozone, the principal poison in urban smog. It is also worth emphasizing that automobiles take up an enormous amount of valuable urban space. It is already a commonplace that cars destroy the urban environment, but very few municipal governments have had the political courage to contain the relentless growth in the number of cars on their streets. Exhibition Place is emblematic of the serious transportation problem that tears at Toronto's environmental integrity.

Before the dramatic growth in Ontario car ownership in recent decades, most people went to all events at Exhibition Place on the Bathurst streetcar. A majority still do go to the "Ex" itself by transit, but the parking lots are nonetheless filled, even though the price of parking is more than doubled during the August Canadian National Exhibition. For other events, the majority arrive by private car, and Exhibition Place's vast parking fields accommodate not only these visitors but also those going to Ontario Place. Because of changes in the way people travel, Exhibition Place has in some respect taken on the form of a suburban shopping mall, an island of human activity in a sea of asphalt.

The destination sign on the front of the Bathurst streetcar reads "Exhibition." It is a charming experience to be on the line during the Ex, when in the morning or afternoon many streetcars are filled with happily expectant children going to the CNE. Later in the day, the cars are bringing home the same kids and their parents, satisfied and exhausted. At these times, the Bathurst streetcar becomes an extension of the Ex's amusement park merriment. This streetcar used to go into the Exhibition grounds, but it had to be relocated for construction of the National Trade Centre. Before this construction project, officials of the Metro Planning Department argued for using the relocation as an opportunity to extend the line to Ontario Place. This could have been done in a variety of ways: under the National Trade Centre, through Exhibition Place, or around the edges of Exhibition Place.

Burying the line in the basement of the National Trade Centre would have made the trade centre into a kind of extension of downtown. Underground construction is always more expensive than at grade, but it would have put the trade centre on the transit map in a significant way. Instead, the basement of the National Trade Centre was used for parking cars. Another alternative would have been to extend the Bathurst streetcar line through Exhibition Place grounds and across a bridge over Lakeshore Boulevard. This was rejected because managers of the CNE and of the Molson Indy thought it would interfere with pedestrian and automotive circulation during their events. This is an interesting objection in view of the fact that streetcars easily traverse streets through other intense urban activities, but it is symptomatic of planning processes followed for Exhibition Place, which is considered separate, off the urban grid, and unable to operate by the same rules as the rest of the city. The third alternative, to run the streetcar down the east side of Exhibition Place and then to the south of it, between Ontario Place and Lakeshore, was rejected because of the cost and because in crossing Lakeshore at grade it would diminish the capacity of the highway somewhat.

All these proposals to enhance public transportation were given short shrift during the planning period for the National Trade Centre. The Exhibition Place administration pursued a single-minded focus on getting the NTC built on time and within budget. The idea of combining it with a public transportation improvement was viewed as getting in the way of a public enterprise trying to prove that it could operate as efficiently as a private entity. The promotion of transportation options became, in this context, an impermissible "political" agenda. The Toronto Transportation Commission, with responsibility for development and operation of all public transport within the city, was, as usual, operating under serious budgetary constraint. It therefore went along with the cheapest alternative, which relocated the terminal station of the Bathurst streetcar line to the back of Exhibition Place, out of sight and less convenient than it used to be.

Exhibition Place has the rail, transit, and road infrastructure to be a transportation hub in a city that badly needs alternatives to congested existing facilities. But it would be reasonable for it to become a hub only if it contained numerous all-year destinations. The National Trade Centre is a good start as the nucleus for such destinations, but more is needed. The Exhibition Place area would be a good location for a secondary commuter station to Union Station. A private report (IBI Group 1995) advocated the building of a Union Station West, but it would need a sufficient mixture of commerce and residence located around it. If the proposed rail relocation took place and if a line operated to Pearson airport, the new station would be the first downtown stop for a train coming in from the airport.

There have been many plans for new streetcars, commuter service operated by GO Transit, and even an aerial tramway from Union Station to Exhibition Place, but these have all faltered. Instead, the Bathurst streetcar, which once plunged into the site, is now at its edge. There is a covered walkway leading into the site from the streetcar station, but it is a far cry from plans for a major transportation hub. These can become real only if there are more people coming to Exhibition Place for a greater variety of reasons throughout the year. If just part of the land at Exhibition Place were developed in ways that reflect the value placed on some surrounding urban land, then it would become uneconomical to retain so large a portion of the area as surface parking. Other, more lucrative uses would bid for the space. Redevelopment possibilities for Exhibition Place become clearer when the experience of surrounding neighbourhoods is taken into account.

Redevelopment Lessons from Surrounding Neighbourhoods
Exhibition Place has four neighbouring districts: Ontario Place, Bathurst-Strachan, Liberty-Niagara (also called Garrison Common North), and Parkdale. Their experience offers a lesson for revisiting the objectives behind Exhibition Place's current governance.

Ontario Place, just south of Lakeshore Boulevard and connected to Exhibition Place by three pedestrian bridges, is an amusement park built in 1970 on stilts and on three artificial islands in Lake Ontario. According to *Regeneration* (Royal Commission 1992), it was the "Province's answer to Expo '67" and was "described by William Dendy and William Kilbourn (1986), writing in *Toronto Observed* as being 'designed to amuse rather than impress.'" But Ontario Place is both amusing and visually exciting. Its architecture is playful; it looks like it has been assembled from a giant version of Tinkertoy or some other children's building kit. Besides amusements, it has a large-screen movie theatre and an amphitheatre for pop concerts. In recent years, however, Ontario Place, like Exhibition Place, has been suffering a decline in attendance. While its architecture still amuses, it has also become somewhat worn in appearance. Ontario Place needs sprucing up. This could take the form of renovation as an amusement park or, as in the case of Exhibition Place, it might profit from a more complete re-evaluation of its singular land use and its relationship to the rest of the city.

Such reconsideration is unlikely to occur without an analogue to the institutional change that is needed at Exhibition Place. Ontario Place and Exhibition Place can be thought of as organizational twins, both tied to their past by an institutionalized insulation from both political and market signals. Change in the governance arrangements for either entity might well spur change at its neighbour, as the opportunities of moving beyond institutional inheritance become more apparent. Of course, the most promising opportunities might require some coordination between reorganization initiatives.

To the east of Exhibition Place, the Bathurst-Strachan area is scheduled for intense residential development. A plan for blocks and streets in the area follows the city's basic grid. This may lead to pressures for making Exhibition Place into more of a park, but new residents will also have Harbourfront and its recreational activities, as well as the open space of Coronation Park and closer areas of the waterfront. Bathurst-Strachan's redevelopment could also affect the transportation options for Exhibition Place by generating more travel demand. To the west of Exhibition Place is Parkdale, a neighbourhood with housing and social problems, which appears to derive little benefit from its proximity to Exhibition Place. Future change in this area does not appear likely to lead, or greatly influence, the options for change at Exhibition Place.

The Liberty-Niagara neighbourhood to the north is an industrial district that is transforming itself into an area attractive for both living and working. This is being done with no assistance from government. The transition has been going on for about a decade. It is a healthy re-use of industrial structures that would remain empty if not for the rapidly growing community of mostly young artists, filmmakers, small industrialists, and computer start-up operations that have transformed a dying nineteenth-century industrial district into a thriving neighbourhood. Railway tracks and the Gardiner Expressway create a barrier between this community and Exhibition Place, but a newly completed pedestrian tunnel under the tracks may help pierce the barrier.

It may be that Exhibition Place has more to learn from Liberty-Niagara, which has undergone a significant metamorphosis, than from anyplace else. It has taken a nineteenth- and early twentieth-century urban fabric and made it into a thriving community of the twenty-first century. This change highlights the policy question facing Exhibition Place: can a nineteenth-century fairground also be renovated to satisfy twenty-first-century urban desires and opportunities?

The Future: An Inconsistent Official Vision

In recent years, the CNE has attracted a declining number of people. This decline represents an even more steeply declining share of the growing population of southern Ontario. Residents of the province will frequently express great affection for the CNE, or the Ex, but they go there less and less. This decline in CNE attendance and the loss of the Toronto Blue Jays, the Argonauts, and numerous popular music concerts all contribute to serious financial shortfalls at Exhibition Place. This has led the Board of Governors to some short-term strategies for raising money, such as a twenty-seven-metre-high electronic sign that advertises products to passing motorists on the Gardiner Expressway.

But the board has also focused on longer-term ways of reviving Exhibition Place. The grandest strategy was for using it as part of the site of the 2008 Olympics. The draft "bid book" prepared by TO-Bid, the agency charged with winning the 2008 Olympic Games for Toronto, proposed that many existing public waterfront locations be used as venues for Olympic events. TO-Bid saw the construction of these new sport venues as permanent additions to the city, a legacy from the Olympics that "revitalizes the Exhibition Place/Ontario Place area as a year-round destination." An Olympic Plaza would have been built on the parking lot where Exhibition Stadium used to stand (TO-Bid 1998).

The expansion of the National Trade Centre and more comprehensive services for trade show visitors are also goals of the board. A hotel to serve trade show visitors on the site was not always encouraged; the pre-amalgamation City of Toronto was cool to the idea of a hotel on a site designated as a park and outside the central business district. But a hotel is now among the uses being sought.

To judge proposals by private entrepreneurs, the Board of Governors approved proposal evaluation criteria. These are important both for what they prohibit and for what they encourage. Offices, shopping, industry, and institutional and residential uses are all forbidden as primary activities. The board will accept proposals only for the sorts of uses traditional for the site, or allied uses, such as a hotel for National Trade Centre participants. The evaluation criteria require:

- *Public accessibility:* Outdoor areas are to be "available to the public as a park at all times." Indoor activities must have "high levels of attraction and popularity."
- *Year-round use:* "Traffic-generation and other types of synergy with existing activities" are favoured. Festivals like the CNE are encouraged.
- *Image:* Beauty, historical character, and a "strongly public" image are to be preserved.
- *Tourism:* The project must be attractive to visitors.
- *Uses:* "Appealing, exceptional ... should have a special reason for locating in so prominent a waterfront site. There should be some thematic connection to the site's history, tradition ... present the face of Toronto to the world."
- *Economic development:* High value-added, permanent employment must be generated.
- *Financial:* The project should relieve Exhibition Place of the need for major capital investment (Board of Governors of Exhibition Place 1998).

In my view, the evaluation criteria are contradictory. They prohibit shopping, industry, and institutional and residential uses but express the desire that "uses and activities should contribute to a diversity of experience, theme and environment." I think it would be difficult to achieve diversity without inviting in some of the prohibited uses, and, so far, there has been little success in attracting new uses that do measure up to the criteria. In early 2000, the Toronto Waterfront Revitalization Task Force released a report about the future of the waterfront. One of its suggestions was that housing units be built in Exhibition Place. The Board of Governors quickly rejected the idea, however, on the grounds that the housing would be in the way of the Molson Indy and other events on Exhibition Place grounds. The institutional inheritance discussed above leads the board to prohibit certain kinds of uses, even though such restrictions constrain, and perhaps undermine, the expressed desire to have diversity.

Reconciling the Official Vision with Development

That Exhibition Place remains a public space under government ownership is an unstated assumption in the Board of Governors' criteria for evaluating proposals for use of Exhibition Place. This is not surprising, as the public would not easily give up a prime piece of real estate designated as a park. Exhibition Place is not really a park in the same way as High Park, two kilometres to the west along the waterfront. It isn't even a park like the much narrower Aquatic Park and Coronation Park, which border it to the west and east. There are, however, parklike areas within the site and, more significantly, there are rich, fanciful, elegant, and historic pavilions and other architectural creations, mostly on the western end of the grounds. In the words of the *Preliminary Master Plan, Garrison Common,* these are "wonderful and unused" (Royal Commission 1991).

That is the difference between the Exhibition Place grounds and other parks – the grounds are mostly unused, even in fine weather. Because the land is publicly owned, there is little pressure for its use, which in private ownership would be measured in financial terms. If Exhibition Place is to remain public and not be a drain on the public treasury, it has to find uses for these buildings and space, and they must at least pay for themselves and for general upkeep of the grounds. The same argument doesn't apply to other parks because they are well used, so that even if they don't themselves provide revenue, use of public funds is justified. Public ownership at Exhibition Place may continue to work, but it has to move beyond an institutional legacy that limits innovation and flexibility in the use of resources to attract users. The test of future organizational efforts will be whether they have the capacity to close the gap that has emerged at Exhibition Place by making it "wonderful and used."

Wonder and use, or in language less poetic and more bureaucratic, "environmentally sustainable and financially viable" proposals, may be achievable within the limits of the board's evaluation criteria if they are applied imaginatively. Enterprises that would meet the criteria include: a festival marketplace; a community college or other educational institution; visual arts workplaces; film, television, and video production and presentation facilities; and any cultural, educational, or environmental institutions with broad appeal to the public. Probably, however, the key place to begin is to build on the success of the National Trade Centre, by expanding it and by developing a new hotel to serve it.

Two kinds of shows use the NTC: consumer shows and trade shows. About 80 percent of the NTC's business consists of consumer shows. These are aimed at local audiences and thus do not offer many economic spin-off benefits for the general Toronto economy, such as hotel room nights and restaurant spending. Most of the $200 million in secondary economic benefits generated by the NTC comes from the 20 percent of its use as a trade show venue. More space is needed for trade shows, especially additional meeting room space, the scarcity of which restricts the NTC's ability to attract trade shows that include conferences and seminars.

While the NTC has succeeded in capturing a broad range of trade shows, there is an irregularity in the flow of business. This could be improved, according to a University of Toronto graduate student report (Workshop in

Planning Practice 1999), by adding a permanent "trade mart," a place where manufacturers and wholesalers in a particular industry operate permanent showrooms aimed primarily at corporate buyers. A trade mart allows buyers to visit a large number of competing businesses in the same line of production under one roof. Manufacturers find trade marts useful because, by clustering with competitors, they can attract a greater number and wider range of buyers than by operating independent showrooms. Trade marts in some American cities are very big and attract many separate clusters of industries. A Canadian trade mart at the NTC could, for example, represent Canada's strength in building materials and residential design, and companies in this industry participating in the trade mart could take advantage of the services provided by the TradeLink office already at the NTC. TradeLink provides a permanent information centre for export-import activities. It is a resource centre designed to help local manufacturers who want to export.

I go into detail about the NTC because it has become a primary generator of traffic to the Exhibition Place area, and in the normal course of city development, such primary generators attract secondary uses. For example, it would be part of the natural course of urban devlopment for a hotel to have opened near the NTC. I suspect that if privately held land were across from the NTC this would already have happened. This is not to say that the Board of Governors is recalcitrant, just that the process is different from the experience of most hotel developers. Rather than the invisible hand of the market, it is the task of the Board of Governors to get proposals for a hotel. The hotel could be jointly marketed with the NTC, and it should also appeal to families with children young enough to be attracted to the amusements of Ontario Place.

A festival marketplace, a mix of retail and entertainment uses, is another possibility within the official guidelines that was examined by University of Toronto students (Workshop in Planning Practice 1999). Festival marketplaces usually offer the same merchandise as in a department store or shopping mall, but arranged in a more interesting setting and supplemented with unique local crafts or produce. Granville Island in Vancouver is an example of a festival marketplace that might be appropriate for Exhibition Place; closer to home, Queens Quay Terminal at Harbourfront in Toronto is a smaller example. Queens Quay is not fully rented nowadays, however, so a proposal of this sort is not guaranteed success. A festival marketplace needs some special draw, like a superbly central location where people want to be or have to be. The festival marketplaces at the railway stations in Philadelphia and Washington are examples. So are the marketplaces in Boston and Baltimore. Granville Island is centrally located and offers the special quality of an island location and converted old buildings. It would take good architectural imagination to use some of the Exhibition Place buildings in this way. And the off-centre location of the site would still be a problem.

Reconciling the Official Vision with the Environment

A large public property such as Exhibition Place has the potential to be a model of environmental soundness in energy, transportation, water use, and recycling. Some similar public places are trying to create such a model. The Tivoli Gardens amusement park in Copenhagen is making its heating and lighting systems models of energy efficiency, converting its vehicles to electricity, turning its kitchen waste into feed for 1,400 pigs, monitoring the watering of many hectares of flowers and lawns, and clearing up its algae-choked lake (Hoge 1999). In Sydney, Australia, the 2000 Olympics were designed to be the "Green Olympics," with renewable electricity (from rooftop photovoltaics and wind power), energy-efficient buildings, solar hot water, waste and water recycling, rail connections, and a bicycle- and pedestrian-friendly layout. Unfortunately, Exhibition Place is not nearly so synonymous with environmental sustainability.

Emblematic of the problem is the annual Molson Indy, an automobile race that sends cars careening around the grounds at high speed and with accompanying cacophony and noxious exhaust that detracts from the health and tranquillity of neighbourhoods many kilometres away. All plans for improvements must first be made to conform to the needs of the Indy for a track. For example, trees planted in conjunction with the building of the National Trade Centre had to be put in movable containers so they could be lifted out of their pits and moved to another place when the race is on. The Molson Indy represents the antithesis of environmental sustainability. As long as the Molson Indy remains as both a symbolic and quite concrete manifestation of the automobile's primacy as a cultural and recreational priority, it is difficult for Toronto to claim that environmental values guide its waterfront development.

The CNE itself misses the opportunity to emphasize the environmental value of local agriculture. The food stands at the annual fair are an emporium of everything a consumer could get anywhere else. Food pavilions that could market the bountiful products of Ontario agriculture instead sell ordinary fast food. The CNE would be a good place to begin to demonstrate sustainable agriculture and the relationship between rural planting, suburban sprawl, and urban eating.

The Exhibition Place site could be cleansed of contaminants, and a closed-system approach to stormwater management and sewage could be installed gradually as part of the redevelopment process. Existing buildings could be retrofitted with energy conservation technologies and alternative energy sources (solar, wind). The internal road network could be changed to add safe spaces for walkers and bike riders. "Traffic calming" could make Lakeshore Boulevard narrower and safer to cross, ensuring a better connection between Exhibition Place and Ontario Place.

Because of all the parking space, less than one-fifth of this "park" is permeable, allowing for very little infiltration of water back into the soil. There is a need for more planting and naturalization, returning little-used grassy areas back to more natural conditions, with native trees, shrubs, and wildflowers. This means shifting from lawns and shrubs to chemical-free areas that support diverse native plants and animals. Grounds as large as Exhibition Place are also an excellent place to experiment with "living machines" to cleanse sewage. Grey water recycling systems can minimize the production of sewage. Planting on the large, flat roofs of Exhibition Place buildings can reduce stormwater runoff, moderate indoor temperatures, and save energy (Workshop in Planning Practice 1999).

Conclusion: An Integrative Vision for Exhibition Place

Exhibition Place is a kind of urban vacuum. Old tenants for sport and entertainment slip away and new uses get installed only after years of government deliberation followed by big infusions of public money. The National Trade Centre was built with grants from three levels of government. It appears to be succeeding in producing some profitable spin-off effects for the Toronto economy in general, but it hasn't inspired any additional development at Exhibition Place itself. The problem is that Exhibition Place is an urban anomaly. It is a park by official designation, but a park that is expected to earn revenue through a specific combination of entertainment and economic development functions. This is a contradiction that prevents Exhibition Place from being either a successful commercial venture or a satisfying park.

To restore the integrity of this urban vacuum, Toronto could decide that Exhibition Place is either a park or a parcel of marketable real estate like any other in the city and change its administrative arrangements accordingly. Or it could decide that certain portions of the site are parkland and others are to be opened for development by the private sector. In those parts that are park, there should be no expectation of revenue, or no more than is generally expected from parks. The maintenance of parks is a crucial government function and one especially desirable in important geographic locations such as lakefronts. In those parts of the site not designated as parkland, restrictions on use should be re-examined. Why not open the site to residential and commercial use? Why not increase the availability of apartments near the lake? Why not have a twenty-four-hour population and a lakeside neighbourhood of shops, offices, and hotels amid the splendid fountains, flowerbeds, and fanciful architecture of Exhibition Place? This would attract people from the entire region.

This kind of development can happen while historic buildings are maintained, or even improved by renovation for new uses, just as old factories are being renovated for residences in the neighbourhood to the north of Exhibition Place. The entrepreneurial spirit and creativity of the Liberty-Niagara area is needed inside Exhibition Place. A fine-grained plan of streets and blocks is required. The preliminary master plan for Garrison Common is a good start, but it assumed the same restrictions on the kinds of uses as in the Board of Governors' evaluation criteria. If those restrictions were removed, and if some of the physical barriers that isolate Exhibition Place were pierced, there could be a surge of desirable lakefront development at Exhibition Place. Such development could occur at the same time that parkland on the site was being improved. The major environmental issue has to do with eliminating the parking spaces and naturalizing the area. With year-round use, more underground parking, and improved public transportation, the remaining green space should have no more parking space chewed out of its territory.

In our system, planning is a regulator of the marketplace, mostly through official plans and zoning. But when the government owns land, the planner becomes less the regulator (setter of the framework) and more the architect on a large scale. In places like Exhibition Place, government can make direct investment rather than set the stage for private investment, and this is an appropriate role when there are governmental functions for which development is needed. But when the governmental purpose dims, governments flounder as developers. This has happened at Exhibition Place as the CNE has waned.

It wouldn't be possible to hold the Molson Indy in an Exhibition Place rebuilt as either a true park or a mixed-use area, but it would probably be possible to have an annual CNE of some measure in the parkland. The actual space taken up by the outdoor activities of the CNE is small compared with the amount needed to park cars for it. The CNE would have to become an attraction that people came to almost exclusively by public transportation. This would be an environmental model of major consequence to the region and the world. The nature of the CNE really needs re-examination too. What is the reason for a fair that offers the same food and sundries available everywhere else? In the most successful cities, the streets themselves are the fairs. They are full of variety and bustle. This is a spirit and an activity not to be cherished just in one site in August but through the town all year. The CNE needs a thorough twenty-first-century re-examination, one that can break with its nineteenth-century institutional legacy.

It may seem contradictory, but I believe that environmental salvation for Exhibition Place actually resides in its becoming more intensely developed – with residence, commerce, and entertainment, and public transportation attractive enough to render obsolete the thousands of parking spaces on the site. Lakeshore Boulevard should become less of a barrier, either by being decked over or by being tamed into a narrower roadway that is easier to cross. Many more people should be coming to the grounds or living there all year, and the money generated should provide for more luxuriant and natural parks and gardens. I think the same principles can be applied to Ontario Place, and the two places ought to be integrated into a vibrant neighbourhood by the lake.

The best way to rescue Exhibition Place would be to pierce the walls of railway and highway that segregate the site from the rest of the city and from Lake Ontario. As Newman and Kenworthy (1999) have amply demonstrated, environmental sustainability in cities relates (paradoxically perhaps) more to high density and land-use diversity than to acreage of parks. The long-standing and exclusive emphasis on amusement and trade in Exhibition Place should be abandoned, and housing and commerce permitted within the grounds. The place should be integrated with the surrounding urban fabric and better connected with Lake Ontario, the city's dominant natural feature and defining environmental challenge in the pursuit of sustainable urban development.

References
Board of Governors of Exhibition Place. 1998. *Program and Development Concept.* Toronto: Board of Governors of Exhibition Place.
–. 1999. *Workshop on the Future of Exhibition Place.* Toronto: Board of Governors of Exhibition Place.
City of Toronto Planning and Development Department. 1982. *The Redevelopment of Exhibition Place.* Toronto: City of Toronto Planning and Development Department.
Dendy, W., and W. Kilbourn. 1986. *Toronto Observed: Its Architecture, Patrons, and History.* Toronto: Oxford University Press.
Firth, E.G. 1983. *Toronto in Art: 150 Years through Artists' Eyes.* Toronto: Fitzhenry and Whiteside, in cooperation with the City of Toronto.
Hodgetts, J.E. 1973. *The Canadian Public Service 1867-1970.* Toronto: University of Toronto Press.
Hoge, W. 1999. Samso Journal: In This Energy Project, No Tilting at Windmills. *New York Times,* 9 October, A4.
IBI Group. 1995. *Toronto Core and Waterfront Economic Renewal and Transportation Strategy.* Toronto: IBI Group.
Metropolitan Toronto Executive Task Force on Future Uses of Exhibition Place. 1987. *Future Uses of Exhibition Place.* Toronto: Municipality of Metropolitan Toronto.
Metropolitan Toronto Planning Department. 1966. *Guidelines for Public Access, Circulation and Open Space Improvements at Exhibition Place.* Toronto: Municipality of Metropolitan Toronto.
–. 1997. *Garrison Common Transportation Plan.* Toronto: Municipality of Metropolitan Toronto.
Miller, J.A. 1960. *Fares Please! A Popular History of Trolleys, Streetcars, Buses, Elevateds, and Subways.* New York: Dover Publications.
Newman, P., and J. Kenworthy. 1999. *Sustainability and Cities.* Washington, DC: Island Press.
Pierson, Paul. 1993. When Effect Becomes Cause: Policy Feedback and Political Change. *World Politics* 45(4): 595-628.
Royal Commission on the Future of the Toronto Waterfront. 1991. *Preliminary Master Plan, Garrison Common.* Toronto: Royal Commission on the Future of the Toronto Waterfront.
–. 1992 *Regeneration.* Toronto: Royal Commission on the Future of the Toronto Waterfront.

Skocpol, T. 1992. *Protecting Soldiers and Mothers: The Political Origins of Social Policy in the United States*. Cambridge, MA: Harvard University Press.

Thomas, P.G., and O.W. Zajcew. 1993. Structural Heretics: Crown Corporations and Regulatory Agencies. In *Governing Canada,* edited by M. Atkinson. Toronto: Harcourt Brace Jovanovich.

TO-Bid. 1998. *Toronto 2008 Olympic Bid*. Toronto: TO-Bid.

Toronto City Council. 1998. *Report, Toronto 2008 – The Olympic Bid*. 4-6 March.

Waterfront Regeneration Trust. 1993. *Garrison Common Implementation Plan*. Toronto: Waterfront Regeneration Trust (Ontario).

Workshop in Planning Practice. 1999. Exhibition Place. Graduate Student Reports on Economic Development, Environment, and Transportation. Toronto: University of Toronto.

10
Conclusion
Anthony Perl and Eugene Lee

The preceding chapters have identified two increasingly discordant characteristics of Canadian environmental policy that developed during 1990s. On the one hand, Canadian environmental policy ambitions have expanded to embrace both domestic and international concerns about the risks of climate change, unsustainable development, resource depletion, ecosystem destruction, and decay in various attributes of the quality of urban life, among other issues. National, provincial, and municipal governments have each made commitments to preserve environmental quality where possible, and to remediate environmental degradation where necessary. And yet, Canada increasingly appears to be falling behind in the attainment of its policy goals, in both absolute terms and in comparison with the accomplishments of most other advanced industrial economies. A recent comparison of twenty-five environmental indicators ranked Canada's overall performance as second worst among twenty-eight Organization for Economic Cooperation and Development (OECD) member nations, followed only by the United States (Boyd 2001). The study's author, David Boyd (2001, 34), concluded that his findings offer "compelling evidence that Canada is a laggard, not a leader, with one of the poorest environmental records in the industrialized world." Boyd's findings demonstrate the seriousness of the integrity gap in Canadian environmental policy that has emerged at the beginning of the twenty-first century.

This concluding chapter will offer an interpretation of the nature and extent of that integrity gap by drawing upon the preceding chapters' evidence regarding the nature and magnitude of constraints that contemporary institutions place on Canada's ability to translate environmental policy goals into outcomes. It will then consider ways in which those institutions might be changed and go on to assess how those changes might facilitate greater reconciliation of environmental ambitions and outcomes in Canada. Potential changes will be developed in three scenarios that link institutional restructuring to differing political origins of such a renewal.

Characterizing the Integrity Gap in Canadian Environmental Policy
Evidence for the integrity gap in Canada's environmental policy is unmistakable in the contributions to this volume. Each contributor has touched upon institutional constraints that worked to cause a divergence between Canadian environmental policy outcomes and their objectives. To better understand what is causing this integrity gap, we need to consider five attributes that emerge from the findings in preceding chapters:

- Canada's political institutions are ill suited to resolving the conflict and controversy generated by contemporary environmental challenges.
- Canada's natural resource sector plays a much larger role in the national economy than is the case in Europe, Japan, or the United States, resulting in disproportionate political influence for natural resource industries that tend to oppose bearing either the constraints or the costs associated with environmental protection.
- Canadian environmental policy is constrained by conflicting tendencies in its foreign policy. On the one hand, Canada seeks to be a part of multilateral initiatives to advance sustainable development, such as the Kyoto Protocol. On the other hand, Canada embraces a continental (and perhaps eventually hemispheric) free trade regime that ties the nation's prosperity ever more closely to exporting to the United States.
- Canada's own technocratic elite, for the most part, lacks sensitivity to the environmental risks generated by government's own activities, thus forfeiting the chance to lead private industry by example.
- Canadian federalism divides environmental responsibilities between two or more levels of government. These overlapping jurisdictions often amplify political conflicts over environmental policy.

Let us consider each attribute in turn, based upon the contributors' own findings.

William Leiss is the first in this volume to illuminate how a part of Canada's integrity gap arises from the lack of fit between our environmental challenges and the problem-solving capacity of existing governmental institutions. He explains why the institutional constraints on Canada's environmental policy capacity are so significant. These constraints originate from the fact that environmental problems are a latecomer to Canada's policy agenda. The need to address such challenges emerged only after the figurative concrete of Canada's governmental institutions had been poured. These institutional forms were designed to support quite different public problem-solving efforts from those associated with implementing effective environmental protection. Yet it has proven exceptionally difficult to modify Canada's governmental structures to deal with environmental and other new problem areas during the 1990s.

The division of powers between Ottawa and the provinces has not been adjusted to accommodate the broad, horizontal scope of environmental issues and challenges. It has proven no less difficult to create room for environmental initiative within Ottawa's own administrative structure. There, central agencies, financial guardians such as the Ministry of Finance and Treasury Board, and even traditional line departments such as Natural Resources and Industry defend their turf and guard their influence based upon long-standing legitimacy and a good fit within the organizational framework of cabinet government.

The structural constraints that Canadian federalism and administrative organization place upon meeting new policy challenges are not unique to environmental protection. Health care is another policy domain where both federal and provincial governments share jurisdiction, and where fiscal constraints and bureaucratic rivalries in Ottawa also intrude on policy development. However, after growing evidence of an integrity gap between the stated policy of universal accessibility to adequate health care and the reality of an overloaded and declining health care delivery capacity during the 1990s, Health Canada is taking strides to close the gap.[1]

One key difference between Ottawa's responses to capacity problems at Health versus Environment arises from the differing perceptions of these policy domains among Canadians. In Health Canada's annual report for 1999-2000, Minister Allan Rock stated that the principles of a universal and effective public health care have achieved "iconic status for Canadians." He went on to state that "Canadians expect the federal government to live up to its responsibilities under the [Canada Health] Act and to take such steps as are necessary to ensure the sustainability of our Canadian universal, portable, accessible, comprehensive and publicly administered health care system" (Health Canada 2000). Government's unequivocal embrace of leadership in health policy contrasts with a much more tentative commitment to environmental policy objectives. This dichotomy reflects public opinion in these policy domains.

In a culture that is recognized as being particularly risk-averse, Canadian concerns regarding environmental hazards are to some extent offset by worries regarding the economic risks of policy intervention. This pattern of conflicting concerns leaves government less inclined to take preventive actions. Whereas support for preserving the integrity of health care is clearly tied to an expectation that Ottawa ought to implement the Canada Health Act's objectives and vision, public perceptions regarding the environment do not motivate comparable leadership efforts in Ottawa.[2]

Leiss suggests that the much higher uncertainty regarding causal connections in environmental risk assessment encourages the portrayal of indecision by government and obstruction by industry as caution and prudence, two values that are prized in Canada's pragmatic political culture. For example, there is a clear connection between the number of medical specialists at work in a hospital and the immediate saving of lives. This contrasts with the less obvious relationship between the number of regulators and scientists working for an environmental agency and the prevention of ecological damage that would impact Canadians' future well-being. Such dissonance between perceived costs and benefits is perhaps greatest when it comes to policy efforts to prevent the worst effects of climate change.

Michael Howlett is the first contributor in this volume to raise the second attribute of Canada's integrity gap in environmental policy, the pronounced political influence of industry engaged in natural resource exploitation. Environmental uncertainty and indecision about managing risks through more effective environmental policy contrast sharply with the certainty of economic gains that Canadians perceive to be generated by natural resource extraction, agriculture, and energy production. Howlett explains how Canada's maturing staples economy plays an ongoing role in generating political opposition to environmental regulations and preservation initiatives. In large parts of the country, particularly in the Western provinces, the less certain and more diffuse benefits of environmental protection lose out to concrete fears about job losses and economic deprivation that would emerge from constraining Canada's historical generator of national wealth, the extraction and export of natural resources.

Even though the Canadian economy is maturing, with uneven movement towards a "post-staples" economy, Howlett sees no inevitable decline in the potency of anti-regulatory arguments and resistance to policy intervention put forward by resource and manufacturing industries. While a "greening" of public opinion can be traced to the growing number of largely urban citizens who no longer see their livelihood as dependent upon direct exploitation of the land, that same economic transformation works to raise the fear and loathing of environmental initiatives among the non-urban population. Outside of Canada's urbanized areas, livelihoods remain tied to a natural resource base that is declining in relative, and in many cases absolute, economic importance. Thus, the growth of pro-environmental public sentiment is offset by spatially distinct anti-environmental concerns in natural resource–dependent communities and regions. Critiques of Canada's initiatives in health care policy such as those published by the Fraser Institute and the Atlantic Institute for Market Studies (Walker et al. 1999; Fraser Institute 1998; Crowley et al. 1999) are not received amid such a fragmented and diverse range of attitudes and interests, and have therefore been unsuccessful in raising a comparable level of public doubt about the benefits of government action outweighing the costs.

Howlett's analysis suggests that Canada's particular configuration of political and economic attributes yields a very difficult challenge for proponents of environmental action. Politicians who seek a national political base will find it difficult, if not impossible, to draw support from the regions where the primary production of natural resources yields opposition, or at best indifference, to environmental protection efforts. Government thus has a far greater incentive to work on resolving the institutional constraints posed by federalism and bureaucratic structure in order to advance health care policy, among other initiatives, than it does to address these same obstacles to greater integrity in environmental policy. In the latter domain, declarations of principle and stopgap measures to mitigate damage usually suffice to assuage urban environmental activists, while under-implementation and inaction on measures that would inhibit resource exploitation will avert the ire of staples-dependent constituencies. While Canada's institutional structures do not lend themselves to an easy adaptation in the face of new policy challenges, this turns out to be a symptom, not the root cause, of our integrity gap in the environmental domain. Thus, an important question is what influences of politico-economic structures or political processes would generate the will among Canada's leaders to change those institutions.

Leiss emphasizes the opportunity to change the political dynamics of Canada's environmental policy development from within, by developing new modes of communication and public engagement. He suggests that effective risk issue management could enhance the Canadian public's ability to connect real environmental hazards to the policy opportunities for effectively mitigating them. Risk issue management, centred on risk communication efforts and activities, could reduce the antipathy of primary resource-producing constituencies. This would occur through the building of awareness that business as usual is actually a higher-risk strategy than natural resource conservation and other protective measures. The dramatic examples of the collapse in Canada's Atlantic fishery followed by the steep decline in the Pacific fishery could be translated through risk communication into a cautionary tale for other resource sectors. Such risk issue management efforts would likely have an even greater impact on mobilizing the greener segments of Canada's population to demand more from their leaders, especially on global risks such as climate change.

Better risk issue management efforts would likely stimulate the effective political demand for building greater environmental policy capacity. It could raise the Canadian public's ability to judge the claims about environmental risk with as much or perhaps even greater sophistication than is exhibited in assessing claims about economic risk. Thus, the techniques of risk issue management can be expected to play an important role in overcoming the political inertia that now confronts efforts to reduce or remove institutional constraints on Canadian environmental policy.

Howlett calls attention to the potential for globalization and increased trade with the United States to transform Canada's political economy. Such change could transform contemporary governments' discomfort with environmental activism, at both federal and provincial levels. The more such economic restructuring fosters tertiary (service) sector development, the more a shift in the balance of power between pro-environment and pro–resource development policy communities would be likely to occur. Regional fragmentation in attitudes and priorities concerning the environment may be the first symptom that the traditional environmental antipathy of the staples-economy era is approaching a political realignment. The influence that risk communication initiatives and structural change in Canada's economy could exert on government's approach to environmental policy will likely depend upon Canada's international environmental (and other) policy engagements, a topic that Steven Bernstein brings to light in his chapter, which draws out the third dimension of Canada's integrity gap, the conflict between multilateral and continental influences in our foreign affairs and trade policies.

Bernstein uncovers the interplay of domestic institutions, international norms, and executive leadership as forces responsible for the contrast between Canada's leadership in environmental policy design efforts and laggardness in their implementation. Our environmental policy capacity is often constrained by the conflicting desires to foster a logic of sustainable development through multilateral cooperation, on the one hand, and the embrace of economic growth as the top policy priority that is part of our American-led trading regime, on the other. This tension has increased since the United States became an explicit dissenter from collective efforts to advance global sustainability, such as the Kyoto Protocol.

Bernstein extends the findings of Leiss to the international arena by showing how Environment Canada's considerable technical capacity enabled our scientists and bureaucrats to play a leading role in contributing to and orchestrating the scientific consensus on climate change as a significant global risk. Canadian policy experts working in international organizations such as the OECD and the Brundtland Commission also took the lead in forging the consensus on "liberal environmentalism," a doctrine that sought to overcome the zero-sum conception of an inherent conflict between environmental protection and economic development. The green market mechanisms that would be stimulated through policy were intended to reward the firms and sectors that incorporated environmental sustainability into their business practices while highlighting the costs that firms and sectors doing business as usual imposed on their communities and the global ecosystem. According to Bernstein, linking sustainable development with the marketplace through mutually supportive policy instruments has a distinctly Canadian flavour.

While Canada has exercised disproportionate influence over the development of the liberal environmental norm embodied in the Kyoto Protocol, which holds considerable influence over environmental deliberations in Europe, the United States has become a conspicuous dissenter. As would be expected, American skepticism towards the particular market mechanisms that predominate in Kyoto's policy instrumentation had been reverberating among Canadian economic interests and political institutions long before the Bush administration formally announced that America would walk away from its commitment to ratify the Kyoto Protocol.

Corporate America's profound aversion to the imposition of costs associated with environmental protection, through market mechanisms or otherwise, has never been far from Canadian economic consciousness. With so much of our economy now dependent on trade with the US, American resistance to Kyoto has translated into demands from Canadian business interests to "go slow" or "wait and see" what alternative approach to greenhouse gas reduction the Bush administration will put forward. Bernstein concludes that domestic skeptics and opponents of government action on climate change or other environmental risks have used the institutional constraints imposed by federalism and the balance of power among ministries in Ottawa to block action *except* when leadership from the very top intervened to spur some initiative. This occurred when Prime Minister Chrétien acted to advance Canada's climate change commitment at Kyoto and to follow it up through a new Climate Change Secretariat that would (ostensibly) reconcile internecine rivalry among Ottawa's ministries.

Bernstein shows how this fairly modest institutional change has had consequences in federal/provincial approaches to the formulation of climate change policy that *could* remove some obstacles to effective implementation. For example, Alberta appears to have changed its policy strategy from opposing action on climate change policy to seeking an application of market mechanisms that would favour (or at least not penalize) the energy sector. Prime ministerial leadership thus made a difference in overcoming the policy impasse on climate change that had developed prior to Kyoto.

The lesson of how Canada's environmental initiatives interact with the global dynamics is that leadership from on high in Ottawa can make a significant difference in closing the integrity gap between policy and practice, at least to the point of formulating a national action plan on climate change. That leadership appears to be inspired by a prime minister who is concerned about keeping Canada aligned with the largely European consensus on liberal environmentalism. And that consensus bears the imprint of considerable involvement on the part of Canadian scientists and experts who found more attention and support for their work outside this country's policy institutions than within them.

Canada's actions on climate change show that it is possible to overcome the impasse arising from domestic resistance by industrial and resource networks that seek to align our environmental policy with the skepticism towards liberal environmentalism that currently prevails in the American government. Bernstein's analysis points to a paradoxical reconciliation of Canada's environmental integrity gap, whereby strong leadership can break the logjam of resistance by domestic interests that are more closely tied to America's environmental unilateralism than they are to proposals that Canadian experts have shepherded through a multilateral consensus. But this way of addressing Canada's environmental integrity gap at the intersection of international and domestic politics is contingent upon a prime minister who wishes to balance global (and now European-led) coalitions on climate change policy with the NAFTA trading regime's identification of economic growth as the centrepiece of all legitimate public policy.

Michael D. Mehta's exposé of the nuclear industry points to a fourth attribute of Canada's environmental integrity gap, the insensitivity of technocratic elites working in government and public enterprises to the environmental risks that they generate. Mehta highlights how some of Canada's most contentious environmental challenges arise from the use of energy, both at home and abroad. World prosperity is correlated with the consumption of fossil fuels, raising substantial equity considerations about how less carbon-intensive energy production could impact economic growth. To deny such growth opportunities to less developed nations after having profited from the combustion of fossil fuels ourselves would be "morally reprehensible," in Mehta's words. Such hypocrisy would widen the ethical dimension of Canada's environmental integrity gap. But nuclear power, Canada's most controversial alternative to energy generated by fossil fuels, both for domestic production and as an export technology, embodies many of the worst attributes of this country's institutionalized indifference to sustainable development.

Mehta demonstrates that the institutional arrangements that have fostered and regulated nuclear power in Canada were not up to the task of honestly assessing its costs and risks. Nor did institutions such as the Atomic Energy Control Board, Ontario Hydro, and CAMECO (formerly Eldorado Nuclear Limited) live up to a standard of accountability that was appropriate to their status as public entities responsible for various aspects of high-risk energy supply. Instead, these organizations relied upon the technical and administrative guidance of staff who were well insulated from both democratic input and economic signals regarding risk and cost. John Kenneth Galbraith (1967, 60-71) identified this model of organizational leadership by a cadre of experts as the Cold War economy's "technostructure." Such insular and self-referential leadership yielded self-justifying policy options that are at ever-greater odds with the post–Cold War reconfiguration of policy networks that has occurred in many other areas of governance. Instead, Canada's nuclear establishment continues to operate as a guardian of the status quo, offering little to recommend the pursuit of this particular energy source as a sustainable environmental policy option. Government's own denial of the need for full public accountability regarding environmental risks provides the advocates of business as usual in the private sector with further support for resisting change.

Fikret Berkes and his colleagues suggest a possible antidote to bureaucratic indifference regarding environmental risks by pointing to the opportunity for a bottom-up enhancement of institutional capacity that could occur from Canadian environmental initiatives at the local and regional level. Looking at the evolving collaboration between professionals and local community stakeholders that have been brought together in dialogue over British Columbia's forest management, Berkes and his colleagues seek to elucidate both ecological and socially constructed measures of sustainable development. Noting that the understanding of ecological change as being more or less sustainable depends upon the values and objectives that communities apply to interpreting change, Berkes and his colleagues sought to delineate what the signs and signals of a sustainable ecosystem were to managers and stakeholders, and why these were perceived to be important.

The good news is that both resource managers (e.g., the representatives of forestry companies engaged in logging the British Columbia interior) and community stakeholders identified environmental, economic, and social criteria among their understanding of sustainable development. The bad news is that the two populations interpreted the potential for sustainability rather differently. Resource development managers viewed the *process* of resource development as the single most important indicator that revealed prospects for the future. For them, the technical and administrative dimensions of extracting natural resources would determine the future sustainability of these efforts. While community stakeholders also identified resource development practices as important to attaining sustainability, they perceived other indicators as sending more important signals. Immigration linked to the health of the local economy, tourism activity, the viability of nontimber forest–based activities such as mushroom harvesting, and the aesthetic qualities of wilderness recreation were each identified by community stakeholders as important attributes of sustainable forestry.

Although both resource managers and community members could identify the same universe of indicators that would suggest the state of the environment in areas where timber extraction was ongoing, they looked to different measures for evidence of the sustainability of logging practices. While managers identified pursuit of appropriate administrative and technical procedures as the best way to judge the prospects for sustainability, community residents sought measures of ecological and social outcomes that verified the results of such practices. Integrating these process- and results-oriented perspectives into a common and mutually recognized understanding of what it takes to attain sustainable development of a natural resource in a particular ecosystem is certainly possible, given the finding that all participants in the Berkes study did recognize the same range of indicators. And while it would not occur automatically, such accommodation might well proceed more easily at the frontline of environmental challenges than it would at a national level, given the entrenched institutional constraints on this larger scale. Berkes thus raises the hope that local innovation could lead to policy breakthroughs that would percolate upward within Canadian political institutions and help reduce their environmental integrity gap. However, he also confirms the second attribute of Canada's environmental integrity gap, raised by Howlett. Berkes's survey documents show that the structural influence of natural resource extraction translates into different environmental understandings and values of people sharing the same ecosystem.

While local and regional initiatives do indeed show promise for building the capacity for enhanced environmental policy, several contributors, including Perl, Gilbert, and Gurin, draw out the fifth dimension of Canada's integrity gap, which arises from the fact that multiple jurisdictions have environmental policy responsibilities. Anthony Perl demonstrates how value differences, and the policy conflicts arising from them, have been amplified by the multiple jurisdictions engaged in air quality management initiatives in two of Canada's large urban centres. Both the Greater Toronto Area (GTA) and the Lower Mainland of British Columbia face serious air pollution problems, and both have developed policy initiatives in response. The goals and instruments of these approaches turned out to be quite distinct, reflecting different configurations of public and private actors that engaged in defining the urban air pollution problem in each community. These policy communities each came up with a program to address the largest source of local air pollution, emissions from motor vehicles, but that is where the similarity ends.

In the GTA, deliberations were influenced by a clash between three policy communities that took different positions on the nature of the problem and the appropriate solution. Environmental professionals, automotive interests, and municipal governments each sought their own solutions to Ontario's air quality problem. In a province where one out of six jobs is tied to the manufacture, sale, and upkeep of motor vehicles, it should come as no surprise that government took the automotive policy community's solution most seriously.

One result of this contention among three policy communities was that a provincial policy on urban air quality management took longer to emerge in the GTA than it did in the Lower Mainland. Another consequence was that policy options were limited to those accepted by all three policy communities, yielding a lowest-common-denominator consensus on a motor vehicle emissions inspection program known as Drive Clean, which was launched in 1999. Drive Clean aims to solve the GTA's smog problem by inspecting cars, trucks, and buses to ensure that the pollution control devices on vehicles meet their design specifications.

In British Columbia's Lower Mainland, air quality management proceeded along a different trajectory because a single, encompassing policy community brought public and private participants together in pursuit of a more ambitious solution. This policy community was shepherded by an active and engaged regional government, the Greater Vancouver Regional District (GVRD), something that the GTA still lacks on a scale to match its environmental problems, as pointed out in Richard Gilbert's chapter. While differences remained among various stakeholders in the Lower Mainland, the pace of environmental policy innovation was quicker and its scope broader. AirCare, the GVRD's air quality management program, was launched in 1992, seven years before Drive Clean. As suggested by their names, AirCare emphasized attaining an environmental outcome (clean air), while Drive Clean focused on controlling one pollution source (motor vehicles). This difference suggests the diversity that could arise when communities and regions take the lead in developing environmental policy initiatives.

Despite their differences, neither of these bottom-up initiatives has succeeded in closing the integrity gap between environmental objectives and outcomes. Drive Clean is probably incapable of doing this by relying solely upon current emissions control technology. And while AirCare has grown into a more ambitious initiative to advance the sustainability of transportation and land use in the Lower Mainland, this effort is far from bearing fruit. TransLink, the organization that was created to implement new forms of automotive pricing and investment in transportation alternatives throughout the Lower Mainland, has had very limited success. An anti-tax backlash has stymied TransLink's implementation of pricing mechanisms for parking and road use that could enhance the prospects for sustainability. Thus, whether their ambitions were limited or expansive, air quality management initiatives at the local and regional level have fallen well short of measures that would effectively clean the air in Toronto and Vancouver.

Richard Gilbert's chapter on the integrity gap in land-use and transportation planning in the GTA considers both why and how jurisdictional adjustments in Canada's largest urban area have not helped in attaining the sustainability goals that were established in successive regional plans. Gilbert notes that Toronto's apogee of integrating transportation, land use, and efficient urban development efforts occurred between 1953 and the early 1970s, before the words "sustainable development" had ever been uttered in sequence. What enabled Toronto to attain such success as it did in bucking the North American trend of sprawl and auto dependence was an alignment of all the planning and administrative capacities needed to coordinate land use with transportation. Many of the criteria that informed planning and development of Toronto's urban growth during this period would fit comfortably within today's sustainable development framework.

Toronto's urban development was sufficiently dynamic in both economic and political terms that Ontario's government used its constitutional discretion over municipal affairs to clone the metropolitan governmental structure in 1971. Provincial leaders worried that expanding the boundaries of Metro Toronto might create a supercharged governing institution with more economic and political power inside its jurisdiction than existed in the rest of Ontario combined. Establishing four regional governments surrounding metropolitan Toronto had the intended consequence of balancing Toronto's political and economic growth with that of surrounding municipalities within the GTA as a whole.

As Gilbert notes, it is debatable whether the GTA's jurisdictional subdivision *caused* the sprawl that is now the region's single greatest sustainability challenge. There is little doubt, however, that the governments responsible for the region's land-use and transportation planning have found it difficult to work together in solving these problems. Gilbert's review of current plans for reducing sprawl and auto dependence in the GTA points out that even if these plans were fully implemented, they would not reach their target of concentrating 500,000 newcomers in the City of Toronto's current, expanded boundaries. Based upon past experience, development policy conflicts between contending jurisdictions make even attaining the upper end of Gilbert's estimate of what could be done to enhance sustainability within existing plans appear unlikely.

If the talk about sustainable development vastly outpaces action to achieve it at the level of the GTA as a whole, David Gurin's analysis shows that the pattern is little different even at the level of one of Toronto's most promising urban redevelopment opportunities. Gurin's analysis of what is occurring at the prime waterfront site known as Exhibition Place demonstrates that jurisdictional amplification of the integrity gap can also occur within a very focused geographic space. He demonstrates how Exhibition Place has languished in both economic and environmental terms, especially compared with the redevelopment of nearby former industrial lands that are being transformed into thriving communities. The private redevelopment initiatives beyond the boundaries of Exhibition Place come closer to embodying sustainable development principles because they enable residential, commercial, and tertiary industry (e.g., design and multimedia production studios) to coexist in an "urban village" setting. Gurin suggests that stagnation of the Canadian National Exhibition (CNE) site results from the stewardship of a special-purpose governing body.

In a microcosm of the integrity gap, the CNE's Board of Governors has embraced the goal of reviving the site's fortunes but has been unable to break with past practices to implement innovative solutions that would yield a successful and sustainable redevelopment initiative. Half-measures arising from an institutionalized aversion to resolving incompatible policy objectives that exist in so many domains of Canadian environmental policy constrain efforts to transform Toronto's Exhibition Place into a flourishing urban space. In the absence of a megaproject like the city's failed 2008 Olympics bid, which had envisioned generating massive public sector re-investment, Gurin doubts that Exhibition Place will be able to attain its considerable potential under current institutional arrangements.

The independent findings of researchers who contributed to this volume clearly demonstrate that Canada's integrity gap in environmental policy is both real and significant. This raises the question of how seriously to treat such a problem. Before considering different scenarios through which the status quo could change, it is worth briefly reflecting on what might be justified in order to improve the integrity of Canada's environmental policy.

How Seriously Should One Take the Integrity Gap in Canada's Environmental Policy?

Changing current institutional arrangements to enhance Canadian environmental policy capacity is certainly a daunting prospect. Should such measures even be tried? The answer likely depends upon how one interprets the attributes of this integrity gap in Canada's contemporary environmental policy efforts. A somewhat provocative interpretation that would justify immediate action is worth considering.

Upon close inspection, Canada appears to be a country that has yet to introduce effective institutional arrangements for attaining many (perhaps most) of its environmental policy goals. Furthermore, our economic structure still orients political leaders towards prioritizing natural resource extraction, excessive energy use, and dependence upon motorized mobility over conservation and sustainable development initiatives. In the international arena, Canada resembles a nation seeking to have its cake and eat it too. Our external relations pursue recognition for leadership in global sustainability while also actively reaping the rewards of ever-closer economic integration with the United States, a country that increasingly behaves as if global sustainability was someone else's problem. And rather than finding evidence of any concentration in misguided or compromised leadership at the top of Canada's governing institutions, closer examination shows that the failings behind our integrity gap appear to involve much more widespread policy lapses. Crown corporations, regional and municipal governments, and specialized administrative bodies all appear to regularly avoid, evade, or undermine opportunities for protecting communities from environmental harm.

Those who accept this interpretation of our findings should consider one key implication: such a widespread gap between the goals that environmental policy proposals embrace and what is *actually being done* to local, regional, and global ecosystems cannot occur without the collective indifference of Canadians. At the beginning of the twenty-first century, Canadians from all walks of life appear to be in a state of denial regarding the costs and risks of the integrity gap in our environmental policy. However, before proceeding further along this line of reasoning, which would underscore the necessity of major efforts at institutional change, we ought to briefly consider the other side of the story.

Skeptics might not accept this interpretation of our findings as indicating a serious policy problem. Some would reject the need for ambitious environmental policy goals in the first place, making the significance of any gap between intent and outcome a moot point. It is fairly obvious where such an understanding of this country's environmental situation leads. Others might recognize the need to do something about environmental risks and challenges and go on to acknowledge Canada's gap between environmental policy goals and outcomes, but then argue that such shortcomings are inevitable in the implementation of public policy.

Those who question whether it is reasonable to expect more from Canada's environmental policy than the contributors to this volume do could point to the gap between other nations' rhetoric and achievements on the environmental front. They could interpret such a gap as being the reflection of balance between popular expectations regarding employment and economic growth and sentiments in favour of environmental protection and sustainability. Or they might point to an inevitable lag time in implementing solutions to complex interjurisdictional policy challenges and identify the signs of Canada's limited environmental progress as evidence that the gap will eventually close, at least in relative terms, without radical institutional redesign.

Such arguments might be persuasive regarding efforts in other policy domains such as health, where shortcomings can be corrected after the fact, at least on a systemic level. As Leiss has noted, however, the nature of environmental risks and challenges makes relying upon their resolution through the incremental adaptation of current institutional arrangements a risky proposition indeed. Moving Canada's economy and society closer to sustainable development will require bold departures from current environmental policy shortfalls. Something about the way that Canadians pursue environmental objectives will have to change in order to reduce the prospect of significant harm arising from the way in which government manages its responsibilities in this domain. The following section contemplates three scenarios whereby institutional change could significantly enhance environmental policy capacity.

Institutional Alternatives for Closing the Integrity Gap in Environmental Policy: Three Scenarios

A number of triggers could launch a redesign of Canadian institutions, resulting in the strengthening of environmental policy capacity and the closing of some of the integrity gap identified in this volume. Considering the nature of such change is, inevitably, a speculative venture. It can provide a sense of the possible origins of such initiatives as well as the directions in which they might go, but to expect detailed forecasting of their outcomes is unrealistic. Three scenarios that characterize the dynamics of institutional change according to their political origin will be sketched out here. As summarized in Table 10.1, relevant institutional change could arise as a result of the feedback from existing environmental policy, it could grow out of a more widespread (and profound) departure from domestic governing arrangements, or it could come about through Canada's efforts to meet new international environmental commitments. These paths to institutional renewal are neither mutually exclusive nor wholly independent of one another, but they will be discussed in turn under the assumption that only one of them would be likely to launch the necessary institutional changes.

Scenario 1: Explicit Initiatives to Change Institutions

The first scenario explores what a purposeful initiative to renew institutions that influence environmental policy might look like. Here, feedback from the shortcomings of existing or future environmental outcomes triggers a

Table 10.1

Possible scenarios for institutional restructuring

Scenarios	Possible origins
1 Explicit initiative to change environmental institutions	• Feedback from crisis or significant policy failure • Transformation to post-staples political economy • Electoral realignment • New leadership and/or ideology.
2 Spillover from domestic political reform not directly connected to environment	• Changed intergovernmental relations resulting from constitutional restructuring of federalism • Fiscal/administrative renewal of governments and policy responsibilities • Constitutional change in individual rights vis-à-vis the state.
3 Responding/adjusting to international engagements and obligations of multilateral regimes	• NAFTA • Kyoto Protocol

conscious effort to change administrative structures and jurisdictional boundaries in order to enhance environmental policy capacity. A direct attempt at institutional redesign to improve environmental policy delivery could be precipitated by several political triggers, such as a significant and publicly recognized failure of one or more existing environmental policies. The environmental equivalent of the recent blood scandal, in which Canadian health protection institutions were demonstrated to have been worse than negligent in safeguarding the medical integrity of the nation's blood supply, could prompt analogous efforts to dramatically restructure policy responsibilities.

Such policy failure would have to occur on a large scale and be well documented by a public inquiry. The findings of the Commission of Inquiry on the Blood System in Canada (the Krever Commission) presented a damning assessment of the government's oversight of the Red Cross (Public Works and Government Services 1997 and made it impossible to put off fundamental institutional transformation. Such a public indictment helped end a dysfunctional policy process in which "decisions were made by elected officials (and their public servants) more concerned with short-term spending than with disease prevention, by a Red Cross board of directors that had more life-guards than public-health experts, and by a myriad of committees whose experts wore so many hats they were in perpetual conflicts of interest" (Picard 1996, 32). The Krever Commission's findings were instrumental in compelling the Red Cross to withdraw from managing Canada's blood supply, and in creating two new organizations, Canadian Blood Services and Hema-Quebec, to take up the responsibility for restoring confidence in Canada's blood supply.

Even a contentious policy failure in which a commission of inquiry itself gets embroiled in political conflict can lead to institutional change. Such was the case with the Commission of Inquiry into the Deployment of Canadian Forces to Somalia, whose 1997 report, *Dishonoured Legacy: The Lessons of the Somalia Affair,* was based upon an investigation cut short by a government that was preparing for an election in 1997. That commission concluded that "authority in the Canadian Forces is not well defined by leaders, nor is it clearly obvious in organization or in the actions and decisions of military leaders in the chain of command. Moreover, we found that governments have not carefully exercised their duty to oversee the armed forces and the Department of National Defence in such a way as to ensure that both function under the strict control of Parliament" (Public Works and Government Services Canada 1997).

Although the government acted to sidestep a military scandal in the run-up to an election, it also subsequently disbanded the Canadian Airborne Regiment in response to evidence of its problematic structure and the military's inability to remedy these deficiencies from within.

Ontario's commission of inquiry into the contamination of Walkerton's water supply has produced the most recent call for change following a high-profile policy failure. Justice Dennis O'Connor's report (2002a, 2002b) called for a radical overhaul of the management and oversight of Ontario's drinking water. The report proposed upgrading the financial, institutional, and legal resources devoted to assuring Ontario's water quality, through the enactment of new legislation. A new Safe Drinking Water Act would establish a comprehensive legal framework for drinking water management. This act would be the first of its kind in Canada, and would establish a legal right to safe water for all Ontarians.

Justice O'Connor's report (2002b, 18-30) also recommended developing new administrative and analytical capacity within Ontario's environment ministry. New branches would be given responsibility for planning and overseeing water systems, while a new chief inspector for drinking water systems would take over the regulation of agricultural discharges from the Ministry of Agriculture. These changes would substantially reverse the Ontario government's prior policy of privatizing water-testing laboratories and establishing arm's-length regulation and oversight (Mackie 2002b; Harris and Brennan 2002). If carried out, these recommendations would lead to significant institutional adjustment, closing the integrity gap in Ontario's drinking water management policy.

The Walkerton inquiry triggered a public outcry in favour of introducing new standards of transparency and accountability into Ontario's technocratic approach to drinking water management. Demands have been voiced for an implementation plan that would be open to public scrutiny; for example, the Ontario Public Service Employees Union stated that "the Walkerton inquiry created an open process that shone the light of day onto the workings of the Ministry of the Environment ... The implementation of the report should be just as open so Ontarians see what their government is doing" (*Toronto Star* online 2002a). Ontario Premier Ernie Eves agreed to legislate the Safe Drinking Water Act proposed by the opposition New Democratic Party, and pledged to implement all ninety-three recommendations of the Walkerton report (*Toronto Star* online 2002b). At this writing, the potential for significant institutional change in this part of Ontario's environmental policy institutions appears great, although doubts linger about the Tory government's commitments to enact its pledges (Mackie 2002a; Perkel 2002).

While the conclusion of the story of this tragic failure of environmental policy remains to be written, such public exploration of policy shortcomings shows a real potential for facilitating substantial institutional change. Future Canadian environmental catastrophes are certainly conceivable under current arrangements, which would add further impetus for institutional restructuring.

A scenario of institutional realignment that removes constraints on effective policy could also be brought about by less dramatic, although no less momentous, changes in environmental politics. An electoral realignment at the national, provincial, or even municipal level could introduce future leaders to a new set of environmental priorities or, less likely, introduce a new set of leaders who give the environment a high priority. A further transformation of Canada's political economy towards a post-staples economy of tertiary production could stimulate such realignment or leadership change. An environmentally influenced crisis in a staples sector such as farming on the Prairies or forestry in BC – caused by drought or other effects of climate change – could trigger such a political realignment. Other phenomena associated with post-staples restructuring, such as the weakening of the political power of provinces that are highly dependent on natural resources, breakthroughs by major environmental engineering or service industries, or rapid acceleration of urbanization, could also alleviate the cost-distribution problem that currently constrains environmental policies. Either way, environmental protection initiatives would gain political muscle, which would be flexed in overcoming the institutional constraints that limit current policy capabilities.

Although a Green Party holding the balance of power in Canada's parliament or even a provincial legislature would appear far-fetched, it is possible to imagine local governments being influenced by councillors who are green in all but party affiliation. Even without winning elections, Green candidates and campaigns can influence the disposition of mainstream parties in government, by raising environmental priorities in the same way that Social Credit and Christian Heritage parties do for fiscal and moral fundamentalism.

A third trigger for institutional reconfiguration intended explicitly to enhance environmental policy capacity could come from the courts, which have been open to supporting claims arising from an integrity gap between what statutes enable in the area of regulation and enforcement and what the federal government currently delivers. Deimann (1998, 928-29) contrasts the difference between the Chrétien government's willingness to relinquish environmental powers to the provinces, as embodied in the Canada-Wide Accord on Environmental Harmonization, with the Supreme Court's judgment in *R. v. Hydro-Québec* [3 S.C.R. 213, 151 D.L.R. (4th) 32], which asserted concurrent jurisdiction over environmental matters and bolstered Ottawa's capacity to enforce the Canadian Environmental Protection Act.

What, then, might the institutional changes arising from such triggers of a purposeful effort to enhance environmental accountability look like? They would almost certainly be centralizing in nature, giving greater jurisdictional weight to national and regional convergence and coordination in implementation, enforcement, and evaluation over provincial and local diversity and disharmony in these matters. One reason for such a direction is that these matters could hardly be less decentralized, and constrained by jurisdictional overlap and conflict than they are today.

Barry Rabe characterizes Canada's decentralized environmental governance as a mode of policy making that has produced nothing in the way of innovation and little more in terms of effectiveness. He writes that "most provinces adhere to medium-based, pollution control–oriented regulatory systems constructed in the 1970s, appear eager to bend existing regulations to satisfy the overriding imperative of economic development, provide minimal enforcement or monitoring of regulated parties, and engage in minimal policy learning or idea diffusion with neighboring provinces or the federal government" (Rabe 1999, 290). In breaking with this pattern, the limited organizational boundaries for existing environmental agencies in Ottawa and the provinces would likely be expanded to include some of the fiscal and regulatory turf that is now claimed (though not necessarily exercised) by ministries such as Finance, Treasury Board, Natural Resources, and Industry.

In terms of bureaucratic influence, national agencies such as Environment Canada and the Canadian Environmental Assessment Agency would be the likely winners, as would regional agencies pursuing environmental initiatives, such as TransLink in British Columbia's Lower Mainland. The most likely losers would be provincial environment ministries as well as public/private partnerships that are currently charged with implementing certain environmental initiatives. Canada's Voluntary Challenge and Registry, Inc. comes to mind as one underperforming environmental policy body that would be out of business soon after a reassertion of government responsibilities for environmental protection.[3] These organizations would see their piecemeal efforts, and in many cases underenforcement and limited implementation, eclipsed by more encompassing organizations with higher ambitions.

These institutional adjustments would cumulatively have the effect of enabling national, provincial, and regional agencies to carry out environmental mandates with fewer jurisdictional, administrative, or fiscal constraints. Such a scenario would not necessarily result in bigger and more commanding bureaucracies. This is because some of the same constraints that have blocked effective implementation and enforcement of government regulations have also precluded the introduction of certain market instruments, such as pollution pricing, or hindered the deployment of others, such as tradable emissions credits. In sum, the institutional changes motivated by a desire to enhance environmental effectiveness would most likely yield *better* environmental governance in Canada, but not automatically require *bigger* government in this area.

Scenario 2: Spillover from Domestic Political Reform

The second scenario under which institutional change could enhance environmental policy capacity begins from the premise that redesign of jurisdictional boundaries and bureaucratic organizations occurs out of a desire to upgrade some fundamental attributes of Canadian government. In other words, Canada's environmental policy capacity could be improved as a by-product of more ambitious domestic institutional redesign. Such reforms could range from adjustment of the constitutional relationship between Ottawa and the provinces to judicial review of governing arrangements that expand rights to challenge a government's exercise of policy responsibilities. While this is not the place to launch a detailed investigation of Canada's macro-political restructuring options, that topic has been of considerable interest to political and legal specialists in recent years.

Whether by attempting formal amendment, negotiation among the prime minister and provincial premiers, or unilateral initiative, the varied approaches to managing intergovernmental relationships since the patriation of Canada's constitution in 1982 have each been motivated by one overarching objective: enhancing national unity within a fractured federation. Most, but not all, of this effort has been directed towards creating a workable means for Quebec to participate fully in Canadian federalism. Following divisive and unsuccessful efforts at formal constitutional amendment through the Meech Lake and Charlottetown accords, which unleashed waves of mega-constitutional politics yielding little more than frustration among their participants (Russell 1992), attempts at enhancing unity through institutional redesign have shifted to efforts where the stakes of failure are lower.

Ottawa's varied decentralization initiatives across a number of policy domains represent a form of "mini-constitutional" politics that has succeeded in, if nothing else, frustrating the winning conditions that Quebec sovereigntists hoped to capitalize upon following the demise of efforts to recognize a distinct constitutional status for that province. It has also led to considerable variation in the role of national and provincial governments across different policy domains. Simeon (2000, 238) characterizes this present mode of federal/provincial relations as an era of "collaborative federalism." Today's effective governance is seen to depend upon coordinated policy activity between Ottawa and the provinces. Such coordination must contend with long-standing conflicts, such as the quest for sovereignty by Quebec's government and the search for fiscal and ideological autonomy by Alberta and Ontario. The 1996 Canada-Wide Accord on Environmental Harmonization was the product of this dynamic. This accord has yet to yield an effective application of coordinated environmental powers, however.

Lucas and Sharvit (2000, 133) claim that the Canada-Wide Accord on Environmental Harmonization falls well short of the threshold at which coordinated implementation could begin: "In the end, we find that the standards sub-agreement errs on the side of generality. While it is thus likely to be relatively secure from constitutional challenge, it is unlikely to be interpreted as a legally binding commitment for either the federal or provincial governments." Thus, collaborative federalism has yet to yield its definitive expression of environmental policy capacity.

While a decentralizing trend is apparent in the overall direction of today's mini-constitutional approach to national unity, that trend has yet to see provinces take the lead in implementing environmental policy responsibilities. Unlike labour market training, for example, where provinces were clearly put in charge as part of a deal on nonconstitutional federal restructuring (Fafard 1998, 217), the environment remains part of a second tier of policy domains where collaboration has been declared in principle while the administrative and legal details needed to implement many policies remain to be dealt with.

The environment thus falls into a zone of federalist limbo. Through the Canada-Wide Accord on Environmental Harmonization, new intergovernmental relationships remain under development, unlike defence or fiscal policy, which remain firmly under control at the centre of Canadian government (Savoie 1999, 135-37, 170, 192). As a result, environmental responsibilities still remain in the murky middle of policy coordination, where it can often appear that nobody is in charge. What further efforts to enhance national unity would be likely to change this ambiguous status?

One possible change would be to harmonize Quebec's policy autonomy across all or more of the domains than have been delegated up to this point. This would result in a much clearer focus on the environmental accountability of at least one province (Quebec), depending on the degree of asymmetry in future jurisdictional rearrangements. If efforts to enhance national unity beyond Quebec were seen to justify institutional change, the environmental dimension of jurisdictional realignment would likely be greater than if these moves were focused on Quebec. That is because the value of autonomy in environmental matters is likely to be most prized by Canada's Western provinces, where natural resources loom large in the economy and any form of federal policy initiative appears to threaten right-wing ideologues.

Following the Liberal government's increased majority in the 2001 federal election, a "gang of six" prominent conservative intellectuals issued a public letter calling for Alberta to erect a "firewall" to protect the province from Ottawa's anticipated policy depredations. They warned that "as economic slowdown, and perhaps even recession, threatens North America, the government in Ottawa will be tempted to take advantage of Alberta's prosperity, to redistribute income from Alberta to residents of other provinces in order to keep itself in power" (Grace 2001, 11). This call to public policy resistance proposed that Alberta opt out of the Canada Pension Plan and establish its own provincial plan, as Quebec has done. It also recommended that the province's contract with the Royal Canadian Mounted Police be allowed to lapse, and that a new provincial police force be created to assert control over law enforcement within Alberta's boundaries. Such an attack on Ottawa, followed by proposals for fiscal and legal autonomy, caught the eye of international media (Carlisle and Bagole 2001) and drew the Liberal government's attention.

Ottawa's subsequent signal that it wished to placate Western concerns over environmental constraints on expanding oil and gas development to meet America's insatiable appetite for energy illustrates how the attempt to combat provincial alienation outside Quebec could spur environmental policy decentralization. In an April 2001 speech to the Canadian Association of Petroleum Producers, Prime Minister Chrétien gave his full support to expediting the development of Canadian energy resources in the Northwest Territories and the Mackenzie River delta. He stated that "the Government of Canada will do what is required to ensure that the proper regulatory regimes are in place to facilitate the earliest possible movement of Canadian and American gas from the North to southern markets" (Prime Minister of Canada 2001).

Whether environmental concerns are nearer or further from the surface of a national unity initiative that realigned jurisdictional arrangements, providing provinces with a clearer measure of authority over environmental policy would remove at least one constraint on initiative. This stimulus for action would come about because opportunities for buck passing and blame avoidance that today's concurrent jurisdiction with murky organizational boundaries facilitate would be much reduced.

The established pattern of provinces placing economic development ahead of environmental protection might change if provincial accountability for environmental impacts became as clear to citizens as the provinces' role in economic growth appears to be. Thus, if decisive decentralization were to come about, it could trigger a new wave of environmental accountability, focused on provincial governments that have not usually had to bear the brunt of criticism and pressure from those opposed to unsustainable development. In the relatively few instances where pressure has been brought to bear on provincial governments, international economic boycotts have motivated these governments to impose regulatory or other policy requirements to enhance the sustainability of the industries in question.

Boycotts of British Columbia wood products to protest logging of old-growth rain forests or Newfoundland fish products to protest seal hunting did yield policy initiatives where domestic protests had failed. Indeed, such international efforts to make government live up to domestic environmental obligations can be seen as a barometer of this country's integrity gap in environmental policy. The greater the gap between our stated goals and our actions, the more likely that environmental activists outside our borders will hold us to account. Given the regional differentiation in Canada's staples economy, boycott campaigns could exert more impact on provincial governments than on Ottawa. Gunton (1998) demonstrates how environmental NGOs were able to mobilize governments in both Europe and the United States to consider banning imports of British Columbia forest products during the 1980s, and how this had a direct effect on changing provincial environmental and forestry policies. Alper (1997, 362) presents similar findings and states that "it is clear that transnational environmental groups have become a major force in ecoforestry decision making in BC."

While one can develop a plausible scenario of mini-constitutional change yielding decentralization negotiated by first ministers, another government actor could lead institutional redesign in a very different direction. The Supreme Court of Canada has signalled its willingness to intervene in recasting macro-institutional arrangements regarding the rights of individuals against government in general, and the right of particular political communities such as the First Nations and Métis of Canada. Regarding the former, the court has upheld giving communities and nongovernmental organizations standing to demand that governments enforce their environmental policy objectives, as in the case of federal and provincial environmental assessment.

Hoberg (1993, 326) notes that the federal judiciary has advanced the scope of "legalism" as an environmental dispute resolution mechanism. The Federal Court upheld third-party claims that compelled government agencies to implement environmental assessment guidelines for the Rafferty and Alameda dams in Saskatchewan and the Oldman River Dam in Alberta [*Canadian Wildlife Federation* v. *Canada (Minister of the Environment)*, 4 C.E.L.R. (N.S.) 287; *Friends of the Oldman River Society* v. *Canada (Minister of Transport)*, Action no. A-395-89, Federal Court of Appeal, 13 March 1990]. This trend has fallen short of turning the Canadian Charter of Rights and Freedoms into an environmental Magna Carta, at least for the moment, but it has opened the door to using legal means to enhance environmental policy capacity.

Another area of constitutional jurisprudence that the Supreme Court has been even more active in is the structural implications of Aboriginal tenure and the institutional protection that must be afforded to such land rights. In its *Delgamuukw* decision (*Delgamuukw* v. *British Columbia*, [1997] 3 S.C.R. 1010), the court linked Aboriginal tenure and environmental issues by holding that such tenure endures because of, and through, stewardship of the land to sustain Aboriginal peoples. Any government initiative that might undermine such sustainability (for example, through industrial development or resource extraction) was held invalid, because under Aboriginal tenure, development was "subject to the ultimate limit that [land] uses cannot destroy the ability of the land to sustain future generations of Aboriginal peoples" (*Delgamuukw, supra* note 1 at para. 166). Henderson and co-workers (2000, 363) write that "this sustainable development component of Aboriginal tenure affirms the tenure as a proprietarian order – an idea that is coming to be recognized as an incident of all land tenures." Elaboration of this doctrine as a guiding principle in reorganizing Canada's governing institutions would enable, indeed necessitate, a profound change in environmental capacity in order to provide the sustainability safeguards that have been held to be inherent in Aboriginal title to large segments of Canadian territory.

Thus, whether it arises from political efforts to enhance national unity or jurisprudence that advances individual or Aboriginal rights, institutional reorganization would have the collateral effect of influencing the effectiveness of environmental policy making. And while the consequences of change could undermine effectiveness in unexpected ways, there is considerable reason to expect that some of the constraints behind the current integrity gap would be set aside. At the same time, both national and provincial governments might face new demands for environmental accountability, both from the courts and through the court of public opinion.

Scenario 3: Responding to External Factors

In the third scenario through which Canadian institutional change could enhance environmental capacity, the impetus for such adjustment arises from international political and economic relationships. Formal commitments could focus on environmental issues such as the United Nations Framework Convention on Climate Change, or they could require an alignment of domestic institutions with other types of agreements, such as those on security or trade, that have only tangential concern with the environment. In either case, Canada's long tradition of multilateral engagement, and domestic adjustment to meet international obligations, suggests that institutional transformation could definitely occur through such means. Informal international coordination could also exert a similar influence, particularly that arising from the Canada-US relationship.

With respect to environmental accords per se, the Kyoto Protocol's future remains uncertain following the Bush administration's withdrawal of support in March 2001 (Fialka and Cummings 2001). In the aftermath of vigorous domestic and international protests, President Bush has been seeking to fill this environmental policy void that has left his administration politically vulnerable. Environmental advocacy groups lost little time in attacking the President as a global despoiler. Even some major industries and business interest groups have voiced concern over the current lack of an effective climate change policy, fearing a global backlash and boycotts of US exports

(*BusinessWeek* 2001; Panchak 2001). One administration insider told a *New York Times* reporter that the decision to abandon Kyoto was "made in an appalling vacuum of information" (Revkin 2001, A10).

The Bush administration has promised a made-in-the-US policy alternative to address climate change. The plan emphasizes a supply-side solution to increasing energy supplies of all fossil fuel groups. The recommendation to expand nuclear power production is portrayed as an environmentally sensitive measure, because nuclear fuel is depicted as a zero-emission energy source. High-technology strategies to conserve energy or mitigate the effects of greenhouse gas emissions are given more limited attention, but they are at least recognized in the plan (National Energy Policy Development Group 2001). Should such a plan yield actual environmental policy innovation, such as the introduction of tax credits for emission-reducing motor vehicle technology or the stimulation of large-scale emissions trading among manufacturers and electricity producers, Canada might face a situation where fast action to harmonize with US initiatives would appear necessary.

Like many European nations, Canada is now waiting to see what, if any, actions on climate change the Americans will actually implement. Under similar circumstances, such as the immediate aftermath of America's earlier support for the Kyoto Protocol, Canada has launched a rapid institutional response to keep up with, or even try to stay ahead of, its closest neighbour's environmental agenda. Both Bernstein (in Chapter 4) and Paehlke (2000) identify Ottawa as the conduit through which international environmental initiatives can dramatically realign political and economic institutions in Canada.

There are, however, other international relationships that create opportunities to restructure Canadian governing institutions, including those influencing environmental policy capacity. The most significant has been the adoption of a North American Free Trade Agreement (NAFTA). Canada's trade commitment with the US and Mexico builds upon a free trade commitment with the US that opened the door to a continental market in natural resources, including energy. Makuch (1994, 423) objected to that agreement's lack of concern for environmental consequences, noting that "unrestricted trade rules for natural resources virtually guarantee that they will be unsustainably utilized with little concern for conservation." In part to counter such types of "race to the bottom" criticism, NAFTA included side agreements on both environmental and labour standards.

Kirton (1997, 480-81) suggests that environmental standards got linked to free trade out of political necessity: "In the first instance, the [Commission on Environmental Cooperation], and the broader NAFTA environmental regime, were the product less of any fundamental enduring commitment to environmental values on the part of the three governments in North

America than of a temporary need of a Republican, and then Democratic, president to secure sufficient domestic support to ensure legislative passage of a historic free trade agreement."

The North American Accord on Environmental Cooperation, which led to the creation of the North American Commission on Environmental Co-operation (NACEC), was designed to facilitate each nation's environmental enforcement, not establish a supranational authority over such policies. As such, it offers a multilateral route to identifying and closing integrity gaps in the environmental policies of all three NAFTA signatories.

Richardson notes that the NACEC is empowered to investigate complaints from individuals or nongovernmental organizations within NAFTA that a government is failing to adequately enforce its existing environmental laws. She suggests that "Articles 14 and 15 of the NACEC represent a critical institutional mechanism to encourage the effective enforcement by the Parties of their domestic environmental law" (Richardson 1998, 193). Appeals to NACEC challenging integrity gaps in Canadian environmental policy could come from a wide range of environmental policy participants.

While environmental NGOs would have an obvious motive to seek redress of such integrity gaps, industry and labour interests seeking protection from "unfair" Canadian competition could also protest any environmental shortcomings that they perceive north of the border. Vogel and Rugman (1997) examined ten cases of environmental enforcement claims brought under General Agreement on Tariffs and Trade (GATT), Free Trade Agreement (FTA), and NAFTA dispute resolution procedures and found that nine of them involved a "baptist-bootlegger" coalition dynamic, whereby an industry appealed to the environmental provisions of the North American Accord on Environmental Cooperation, not out of support for the principle of sustainable development but to advance its own economic interests over competitors located in another NAFTA nation. In these nine cases, they note that "a domestic bootlegger industry can be identified as benefiting from the environmentally based trade barrier placed in the path of its foreign rival" (Vogel and Rugman 1997, 286).

Whatever the motive behind such complaints, the linking of trade and environmental policies within a multilateral agency that can intervene to investigate lax enforcement could stimulate institutional changes within Canada that enhance environmental policy capacity. Because of NACEC, an integrity gap in Canada's environmental policy could become a significant economic liability in our trading relationships with American and Mexican competitors. Efforts at institutional redesign could thus be justified as valuable measures to defend the benefits that Canada derives from open trade, a powerful argument given today's North American economic integration. Hoberg (1997, 359) suggests that the likelihood of such change will depend upon what specifics the rulings of NAFTA dispute resolution panels add to the environmental dimension of the larger trend towards North American economic convergence.

Closing Thoughts on Canada's Integrity Gap in Environmental Policy

To date, the integrity gap in Canada's environmental policy has not come to the fore as a significant problem that those in government must deal with. Regardless of how serious such a gap might appear to the contributors to this volume, one should never dismiss the possibility that Canada's leaders will generally prefer to muddle along, adopting ad hoc and partial measures to ameliorate symptoms rather than actually cure problems (for example, implementing smog crisis plans rather than urban growth boundaries in major urban areas). If our readers are left with only one idea from the preceding pages, however, it should be that *Canada can do much better regarding the environment if institutional arrangements are changed.*

From Ottawa's opportunity to enforce national environmental standards, to provincial governments' potential to enforce regional urban development plans, to municipalities' ability to uphold their own planning regulations and oversee their special-purpose agencies, redesigning key Canadian political institutions can enhance environmental policy capacity in important ways. While that change may seem daunting to those inured to, or immersed in, the constraints that today's institutions impose on environmental policy making, the reality is that such organizational change is actually far easier in Canada than tackling the constraints on environmental policy capacity faced elsewhere in the world. For the most part, we do not lack the scientific skills, the technological know-how, and the economic resources that stand out as the *real* constraints on environmental policy capacity on a global scale. Compared with developing nations, for example, Canada has only political self-restraint standing in the way of immediate adoption of more sustainable environmental policies across a wide range of issues. Sooner or later, something is bound to spur action to diminish, or even eliminate, the self-restraint that Canadians are known for.

Patience with a government that "talks green," that possesses state-of-the-art scientific and technological skills to address environmental problems, and that presides over one of the most affluent economies on the planet will certainly grow thin – both at home and abroad – when the physical (as opposed to policy) integrity of the environment becomes a more obvious problem. Whether such a realization will occur in Canada before, during, or after a critical mass of sentiment regarding environmental priorities develops on a global scale is an interesting but actually secondary point. The fact that Canada has the opportunity to remove its self-imposed institutional barriers to environmental policy capacity means that we can take up the relatively less difficult task of improving upon the sustainability of our natural resource management, energy consumption, and urban development ahead of countries faced with much greater constraints. It is even possible to predict that, once the institutional causes of our integrity gap are addressed, Canada will accomplish a great deal compared with nations facing more serious economic and social obstacles to what is almost certain to be the greatest policy challenge of the twenty-first century.

Notes

1 Reinvestment in health care spending and the recent creation of a task force led by former Saskatchewan premier Roy Romanow are two of the most visible signs of such efforts to renew policy capacity. For coverage of the task force, see Bellavance 2001 and Kennedy and Bryden 2001. For other health care renewal efforts, see Harrigan 2000 and Gray 2000.
2 Evidence of this dichotomy abounds in recent federal and provincial election campaigns, where both governing parties and their adversaries promised to "fix" the health care delivery system while largely ignoring matters of environmental risk.
3 Information about Voluntary Challenge and Registry, Inc., which grew out of government's effort to encourage Canadian industry's self-regulation and progress towards reducing contributions to climate change, can be obtained at <http://www.vcr-mvr.ca/vcr-013.cfm>, accessed on 17 December 2002.

References

Alper, D.K. 1997. Transboundary Environmental Relations in British Columbia and the Pacific Northwest. *American Review of Canadian Studies* 27(3): 359-83.
Bellevance, J.-D. 2001. Romanow Shuns Private Medicine. *National Post,* 5 April, A6.
Boyd, D.R. 2001. *Canada vs. the OECD: An Environmental Comparison.* Victoria: Eco-Chair of Environmental Law and Policy, University of Victoria. <http://www.environmentalindicators.com> (17 December 2002).
BusinessWeek. 2001. Global Warming: Look Who Disagrees with Bush. *BusinessWeek,* 30 April, 72.
Carlisle, T., and J. Bagole. 2001. Western Canada, a Rising Sense of Grievance. *Wall Street Journal* (Eastern edition), 20 March, A19.
Commission of Inquiry into the Deployment of Canadian Forces to Somalia. 1997. *Dishonoured Legacy: The Lessons of the Somalia Affair: Executive Summary.* Ottawa: Minister of Public Works and Government Services Canada.
Crowley, B.L., D. Zitner, and N. Faraday-Smith. 1999. *Operating in the Dark: The Gathering Crisis in Canada's Public HealthCare System, Research Report.* Halifax: Atlantic Institute for Market Studies.
Deimann, S. 1998. *R. v. Hydro-Québec:* Federal Environmental Regulation as Criminal Law. *McGill Law Journal* 43: 925-56.
Fafard, P. 1998. Green Harmonization: The Success and Failure of Recent Environmental Intergovernmental Relations. In *Canada: The State of the Federation 1997: Non-Constitutional Renewal,* edited by H. Lazar. Kingston, ON: Institute of Intergovernmental Relations, Queen's University.
Fialka, J.J., and J. Cummings. 2001. How the President Changed His Mind on Carbon Dioxide. *Wall Street Journal* (Eastern edition), 15 March, A20.
Fraser Institute. 1998. *Canada's Health Care System: Ideas for Reform.* Toronto: Fraser Institute.
Galbraith, J.K. 1967. *The New Industrial State.* Boston: Houghton Mifflin.
Grace, K.M. 2001. Alberta First. *Alberta Report,* 19 February, 10-15.
Gray, C. 2000. Health Canada Undergoes a Shakeup. *Canadian Medical Association Journal* 163(1): 80-81.
Gunton, T. 1998. Forestry Land Use Policy in British Columbia: The Dynamics of Change. *Environments* 25(2/3): 8-13.

Harrigan, M.-L. 2000. *Quest for Quality in Canadian Health Care: Continuous Quality Improvement*. 2nd ed. Ottawa: Health Canada.

Harris, K., and R. Brennan. 2002. Clean Water Charter Urged. *Toronto Star*, 24 May 2002, A1. Also available online, in the *Toronto Star* online archives: <http://www.torontostar.ca/NASApp/cs/ContentServer?pagename=thestar/Render&inifile=futuretense.ini&c=Page&cid=992945693891&pubid=968163964505#archive_text>.

Health Canada. 2000. *Canada Health Act Annual Report 1999-2000*. Ottawa: Minister of Public Works and Government Services Canada. <http://laws.justice.gc.ca/en/C-6/text.html> (17 December 2002).

Henderson, J.Y., M.L. Benson, and I.M. Findlay. 2000. *Aboriginal Tenure in the Constitution of Canada*. Scarborough, ON: Carswell.

Hoberg, G. 1993. Environmental Policy: Alternative Styles. In *Governing Canada: Institutions and Public Policy*, edited by M.M. Atkinson. Toronto: Harcourt Brace Jovanovich Canada.

–. 1997. Governing the Environment: Comparing Canada and the United States. In *Degrees of Freedom: Canada and the United States in a Changing World*, edited by K. Banting, G. Hoberg, and R. Simeon. Montreal and Kingston: McGill-Queen's University Press.

Kennedy, M., and J. Bryden. 2001. Romanow to Lead Inquiry into Health Care. *National Post*, 4 April, A4.

Kirton, J. 1997. The Commission for Environmental Cooperation and Canada-US Environmental Government in the NAFTA Era. *American Review of Canadian Studies* 27(3): 459-86.

Lucas, A.R., and C. Sharvit. 2000. Underlying Constraints on Intergovernmental Cooperation in Setting and Enforcing Environmental Standards. In *Managing the Environmental Union: Intergovernmental Relations and Environmental Policy in Canada*, edited by P.C. Fafard and K. Harrison. Kingston, ON: School of Policy Studies, Queen's University.

Mackie, R. 2002a. Red Tape Blamed for Water Lapses: Ontario Probes 19-Day Delay to Act on Tip. *Globe and Mail*, 14 June, A1.

–. 2002b. Walkerton Final Report Urges Fast Action to Safeguard Water. *Globe and Mail*, 24 May, A1.

Makuch, Z. 1994. The Environmental Implications of the NAFTA Environmental Side Agreement: A Canadian Perspective. In *Trade and the Environment: The Search for Balance*, vol. 1, edited by J. Cameron, P. Demarat, and D. Geradin. London: Cameron May.

National Energy Policy Development Group. 2001. *National Energy Policy: Report of the National Energy Policy Development Group*. Washington, DC: US Government Printing Office.

O'Connor, D.R. 2002a. *The Walkerton Inquiry: The Events of May 2000 and Related Issues*. Part 1. Toronto: Ministry of Attorney General. <http://www.walkertoninquiry.com/report1/index.html#full> (17 December 2002).

–. 2002b. *The Walkerton Inquiry: A Strategy for Safe Drinking Water*. Part 2. Toronto: Ministry of Attorney General. <http://www.walkertoninquiry.com/report2/index.html> (17 December 2002).

Paehlke, R. 2000. Environmentalism in One Country: Canadian Environmental Policy in an Era of Globalization. *Policy Studies Journal* 28(1): 160-75.

Panchak, Patricia. 2001. The Editor's Page: Foreign Policy Matters to Manufacturers. *Industry Week*, 16 April, 7.

Perkel, C. 2002. MOE Silent on Faulty Water Tests for 19 Days. *Toronto Star* online, 13 June 2002. <http://www.torontostar.ca/NASApp/cs/ContentServer?pagename=thestar/Layout/ArticlePrintFriendly&c=Article&cid=1022100082518> (17 June 2002).

Picard, A. 1996. Internal Bleeding: Even Voices within the Red Cross Are Now Urging It to Get Out of the Blood Business, if Only to Save Its Other Life-Saving Operations. *Saturday Night*, October, 31-37.

Prime Minister of Canada. 2001. *Address by Prime Minister Jean Chrétien to a Luncheon of the Canadian Association of Petroleum Producers*, 6 April. <http://pm.gc.ca/default.asp?Language=E&Page=newsroom&Sub=Speeches&Doc=cappcalgary.20010406_e.htm> (17 December 2002).

Rabe, B.G. 1999. Federalism and Entrepreneurship: Explaining American and Canadian Innovation in Pollution Prevention and Regulatory Integration. *Policy Studies Journal* 27(2): 288-306.

Revkin, A.C. 2001. After Rejecting Climate Treaty, Bush Calls in Tutors to Give Courses and Help Set One. *New York Times,* 28 April, A10.

Richardson, Susan. 1998. Sovereignty, Trade, and the Environment: The North American Agreement on Environmental Cooperation. *Canada–United States Law Journal* 24(177): 183-99.

Russell, Peter H. 1992. *Constitutional Odyssey: Can Canadians Become a Sovereign People?* Toronto: University of Toronto Press.

Savoie, Donald J. 1999. *Governing from the Centre: The Concentration of Power in Canadian Politics.* Toronto: University of Toronto Press.

Simeon, R. 2000. Recent Trends in Federalism and Intergovernmental Relations in Canada: Lessons for the UK? *Round Table* 354: 231-43.

Toronto Star online. 2002a. I'll Implement Walkerton Report: Eves, 24 May 2002. For the full text of the article, search thestar.com archives: <http://www.torontostar.ca/NASApp/cs/ContentServer?pagename=thestar/Render&inifile=futuretense.ini&c=Page&cid=992945693891&pubid=968163964505#archive_text> (18 January 2003).

–. 2002b. Eves Backs NDP's Safe Water Law, 27 May 2002. For the full text of the article, search thestar.com archives: <http://www.torontostar.ca/NASApp/cs/ContentServer?pagename=thestar/Render&inifile=futuretense.ini&c=Page&cid=992945693891&pubid=968163964505#archive_text> (18 January 2003).

Vogel, D., and A.M. Rugman. 1997. Environmentally Related Trade Disputes between the United States and Canada. *American Review of Canadian Studies* 27(2): 271-92.

Walker, M., C. Ramsey, and W. McArthur. 1999. *Healthy Incentives: Canadian Health Reform in an International Context.* Vancouver: Fraser Institute.

Notes on Contributors

Fikret Berkes is Professor and Canada Research Chair in Community-Based Resource Management, at the University of Manitoba, Winnipeg. He holds a PhD from McGill University. He works at the boundaries of social-ecological systems, on common-property theory, co-management, traditional ecological knowledge, and resilience. His publications include *Sacred Ecology, Managing Small-Scale Fisheries* (with R. Mahon, P. McConney, R.C. Pollnac, and R.S. Pomeroy), and *Navigating Social and Ecological Systems* (co-edited with J. Colding and C. Folke).

Steven Bernstein is Assistant Professor of International Relations at the University of Toronto. His research interests include global governance, global environmental politics, and internationalization of public policy. His book, *The Compromise of Liberal Environmentalism,* was named runner-up of the 2002 Sprout Award, given annually by the International Studies Association for the best book in international environmental studies. His other published work includes articles in *European Journal of International Relations, Canadian Journal of Political Science, ISUMA: Canadian Journal of Policy Research, Global Environmental Politics* and *Policy Sciences,* as well as a number of book chapters.

Richard Gilbert is a consultant in urban issues, specializing in transportation, waste management, energy systems, and urban governance. He serves as transport consultant to the Paris-based Organization for Economic Cooperation and Development (OECD) and as research director to the Toronto-based Centre for Sustainable Transportation. Earlier careers include psychology professor at universities in the UK and the US, research scientist with the Addiction Research Foundation of Ontario, and municipal councillor. He served as president of the Federation of Canadian Municipalities (1986-87), and as the first president of the Canadian Urban Institute (1990-93). He has a PhD in experimental psychology from the Queen's University of Belfast.

David Gurin is a city planning consultant and visiting professor, Ryerson University, School of Urban and Regional Planning. His past positions include Commissioner of Planning, Metropolitan Toronto; Deputy Commissioner of Transportation, City of New York. He has a Master of City Planning, Harvard University, and a BA from Cornell University.

Michael Howlett, Professor, taught at Queen's and at the University of Victoria before coming to Simon Fraser University. His research interests include public policy analysis, Canadian political economy, and Canadian resource and environmental policy. He is co-author of *In Search of Sustainability: British Columbia Forest Policy in the 1990s; Canadian Political Economy: An Introduction; Canadian Natural Resources and Environmental Policy: Political Economy and Public Policy;* and *Studying Public Policy: Policy Cycles and Policy Subsystems.* He is the editor of *Canadian Forest Policy: Adapting to Change* and co-editor of *The Provincial State in Canada: Politics in the Provinces and Territories; Innovation Systems in a Global Context: The North American Experience; The Puzzles of Power: Introductory Readings in Political Science;* and *Policy Studies in Canda: The State of the Art.* He has a BA from the University of Ottawa, an MA from the University of British Columbia, and a PhD from Queen's University.

Eugene Lee is Associate Professor at Sookmyung Women's University, Seoul. His main research interests are policies and politics in Japan and Canada. He has written on Canada's information highway policy and broadband strategy, on Japan's policy to privatize Nippon Telegraph and Telephone, and on Japan's nuclear policy. He has a BA from Yonsei University, Seoul, and an MA and a PhD from the University of Toronto. His earlier careers include Research Fellow, Korea Institute for National Unification, and councillor, Korean Overseas Information Service.

William Leiss is NSERC/SSHRC/Industry Research Chair in Risk Communication and Public Policy, Haskayne School of Business, University of Calgary; Professor, School of Policy Studies, Queen's University; and Executive-in-Residence, McLaughlin Centre for Risk Assessment, University of Ottawa. He is the author or co-author of eight books, including *The Domination of Nature* and *In the Chamber of Risks: Understanding Risk Controversies.* His website is <http://www.leiss.ca>.

Michael D. Mehta, PhD, is Associate Professor of Sociology and Director of the Sociology of Biotechnology Program, University of Saskatchewan. Before arriving in Saskatoon, he taught at Queen's University in the School of Policy Studies and the School of Environmental Studies. His research is in the area of risk perception and communication with a special interest in nuclear safety, biotechnology, and nanotechnology. He holds degrees in psychology, environmental studies and sociology. He also completed post-doctoral training in policy studies. His website is <http://www.policynut.com>.

Anthony Perl is Associate Professor of Political Science at the University of Calgary. He is co-editor of *The Politics of Improving Urban Air Quality* and author of *New Departures: Rethinking Rail Passenger Policy in the Twenty-First Century*. His research on environmental and transportation policy topics has appeared in *Governance*, the *Canadian Journal of Political Science, Transportation Research, Transportation Quarterly, World Transport Policy and Practice, Journal of Public Policy, Journal of Policy Analysis and Management, Canadian Public Policy*, and *Scientific American*, and was recognized through conference prizes at the World Conference for Transport Research in 1992 and the Canadian Transportation Research Forum in 2001. In 2003 he took leave from Calgary to launch the City University of New York's Aviation Institute. He received an AB in Government from Harvard, and an MA and a PhD in Political Science from the University of Toronto.

Index

McMillan, Tom, 86
methane, 99n8
Mexico, 100n12, *111*, 265-66
Miller, Doug, 39n3
minerals, 45, 49
mining
  British Columbia, 137
  mine reclamation, 59
  smelting, 46, 53
  uranium, 112-13, 115
MMT (gasoline additive), 29-30, 40n16
Molloy, John, 119
Molson Indy, 223, 229, 233, 236
Mulroney, Brian, 79-80, 86
multinational corporations, 112
municipal governments
  environmental responsibilities, 5, 11,
    169-71, 242, 249-50
  as policy community, 176, 178-79, 187-
    88, 250-51

NAFTA. *See* North American Free Trade
  Agreement
Nakusp, British Columbia
  area of study, 137, *138*
  history and description, 137-39
  humans, 138-39, 142, 154-56
  water, 151
  wildlife, 147-48
National Action Program on Climate
  Change, 88, 100n30
National Air Issues Co-ordinating
  Committee on Climate Change, 82
National Air Issues Steering Committee,
  82
National Implementation Strategy on
  Climate Change, 93
National Round Table on the Environment
  and Economy (NRTEE), 28, 80-81
National Trade Centre, Toronto
  building of, 229-30, 236-37
  future, 232-35
  management, 220
  transportation issues, 223, 229-30
  uses, 224, 230
national unity, 22
natural gas
  Canadian reserves, 106
  global reserves, 110, *111*
  widespread conversion to, 178
natural resource industries
  environmental disputes, 46
  political power, 21, 242, 244-45
  resistance to environmental regulations,
    7, 92

natural resources
  continued Canadian reliance on, 48-51,
    253
  depletion, 47, 160-61
  exploitation vs. preservation in policy
    making, 46-47, 244-45
  international trade in, 45-46, 50-51
  regional variations, 52-55
  as staples, 45
  and sustainable development, 135-36
  See also specific resource
Natural Resources Canada
  battles over CEPA, 29
  climate change policy, 30, 81, 88, 92-93
  political power, 243
Nelson, British Columbia, 142
neo-institutionalism, 7-16, 42-43
New Brunswick
  per capita incomes, *52*
  percent of Canadian production, 60n6
  primary sector components of GDP, *54*
New Brunswick Electric Power Commission, 112
New Democratic Party of Ontario, 173-76
New Denver, British Columbia, 142, 148
Newfoundland
  fishing industry, 46, 48, 245, 262
  per capita incomes, *52*, 53
  percent of Canadian production, 60n6
  primary sector components of GDP, *54*
  staples economy, 53
New Zealand, 57, 75, 87, 100n13
nitrogen oxides
  British Columbia, 182
  forming ozone, 206, 228
  Ontario, 171, 173, *207*
  policies to reduce, 99n8, 173
norms
  institutionalization of, 71
  of liberal environmentalism, 69, 71-73,
    85
  of sustainable development, 77-80, 85,
    89, 92
North America, oil reserves, *109*
North American Commission on
  Environmental Cooperation, 16, 266
North American Free Trade Agreement
  (NAFTA)
  automobile trade, 60n7
  effect on Canadian economy, 55
  effect on Canadian employment, 60n8
  pressures for harmonization with US
    policy, 15, 22, 74, 248, 265-66
Northwest Territories
  per capita incomes, *52*

Printed and bound in Canada by Friesens
Set in Stone by Artegraphica Design Co. Ltd.
Copy editor: Francis Chow
Proofreader: Jillian Shoichet
Indexer: Heather Ebbs